The Development of Human Resources

THE DEVELOPMENT
OF HUMAN RESOURCES

Education, Psychology, and Social Change

ROBERT R. CARKHUFF

*Center for Human Relations
and Community Affairs
American International College*

HOLT, RINEHART AND WINSTON, INC.

NEW YORK   CHICAGO   SAN FRANCISCO   ATLANTA
DALLAS   MONTREAL   TORONTO   LONDON   SYDNEY

The cover photograph and those in the text are used by permission of the photographer, Xenophon A. Beake.

To The Helper-Warriors
BERNARD G. BERENSON and ANDREW H. GRIFFIN

Foreword

This is a new age with new problems. Many of these problems are symbolized in the deterioration and decay of the urban community. Inadequate and inappropriate education is the core of this deterioration. Minority group deprivation is its effect.

Robert Carkhuff addresses himself to these problems and their effects. He is as important and as relevant in the 1970s as Freud was in the early 1900s and Dewey and later Rogers were in the 1930s and 1940s.

This book represents the highest level integration of the empirically based contributions of psychology and education to constructive social change. Its message is brilliant, its insights profound, its translations urgent.

The Development of Human Resources is written in vintage Carkhuff style —warmly responsive to desperate human needs and aggressively dedicated to acting upon these needs. In his own terms, there is no understanding without action and no action without understanding.

Carkhuff calls himself a "constructive activist." I prefer to call him a "militant humanist." He is neither a conservative nor an activist. He is simply a committed human being—a whole human being—who assumes full responsibility for making very fine discriminations and for acting upon them.

His commitment is to what he calls "operationalizing justice." For him this means both creating opportunities for the deprived and equipping them with the skills they need to take advantage of these opportunities.

of Paolo Freire

In this regard, Carkhuff is an "all-the-way" man. Whatever the price, there is no compromise with justice. And the price for this kind of courage is very high indeed in a world bent on its own destruction!

Carkhuff "calls 'em the way he sees 'em." Without mincing any words, he spells out what he calls the "sources of social failure." Appropriately, he holds

vii

us as educators responsible for perpetrating a system that systematically conditions inferiority into our minority group members.

As is his wont, he does not tear down without building up alternative responses. Nor does he close his eyes to the potential contributions of the past to the future. With his belief that in order to perpetuate itself a system must contain as much truth as myth, he has carefully developed the effective "ingredients of social emergence." He concludes that many of the same systematic procedures which have conditioned inferiority may be employed to actualize human resources. His chapters on the principles of human development and social action are classics in this regard.

In the major sections of the book, Carkhuff details the operations of helping, training, and selection and the extensive applications in social action for which they constitute the base. He is the first to operationalize "helping"—as significant a step forward for our time of personal and social change as was Weber's effort to measure human behavior for the nineteenth century.

While the chapters on "Human Service as a Preferred Motive" and "Internship as a Preferred Mode of Learning" are landmarks in social action, for me the most significant lessons are contained in the chapters on training—"Training as a Preferred Mode of Helping" and "Training as a Precondition for Teaching." The essential message is simply this: By and large, people learn what they are trained to learn. This is not a deterministic position! Rather it is one where freedom is predicated upon training in basic skills in the physical, emotional, and intellectual areas.

In the final section, the chapter on "Functionality and Effectiveness" puts Carkhuff's social action programs to the same tests of outcome to which he puts our social system. His chapter on "Planning for Constructive Change" is perhaps the most vital contribution to community and educational development that I have ever read.

Throughout the book, while the themes are developed in vigorously editorial language, they are carefully balanced by thoroughly researched demonstration projects.

What is significant is not so much the magnitude as the intensity of the author's accomplishments. In the pages of this volume Carkhuff has established models which constitute the basis for a truly effective social system dedicated to the development of the resources of each and every human within its reach.

What is most impressive is Carkhuff's perspective. His arena is the world—his family, human beings in this world.

It takes a large man to see beyond his own ego boundaries. It takes a great man to see beyond his immediate family. It takes a giant to make the world his family.

Perhaps the most significant meaning for me is the personal learning this book gave me. Beginning with his prologue, "Credo of a Conservative Activist," and concluding with his epilogue, "A Personal Note to Effective People," Carkhuff is constantly prodding, challenging us to deeper levels of awareness, making us responsible for our every action, leaving no room for the destructiveness of the unconsciousness.

In short, this is more than a book. While its pages record the thoughts of a giant's mind and the events of the environment in which he functions, it asks more of us than reading. Indeed, more than some of us can give. This book asks us to rise above our humanity to become our most constructive selves, for its author has.

Carkhuff has surmounted the barriers of class and race, time and distance to have vision among the sightless. Unfortunately, as he often reminds me, "In the land of the blind, the one-eyed man is not king and the two-eyed man is the enemy." This book provides us an opportunity to open at least one of our eyes.

His life is our conscience.

Time grows short.

David N. Aspy

Director of Research and
Professor of Educational Psychology
Northeastern Louisiana University

Preface

Social change is for many a noxious term. It has come to connote the now numerous, often loosely conceived, always loosely implemented, programs of social action. It has come to connote change for change's sake—without concern for effectiveness or delivery.

For others, and for the very same reasons, social change has positive connotations.

It is precisely because of this vacuum of creative and effective leadership that I have chosen this term for the subtitle of the book. We stand at the beginning of the great social service revolution. The first steps we take will have reverberations far beyond the problems which we search to resolve today.

It is the thesis of this volume that the same educational institutions which have been the sources of our technological advances can be the sources of constructive change and gain for the peoples they serve. The first steps of the social service revolution can be dictated by the vast educational resources available to us and by those who know how to utilize them. The first steps can be empirically based upon the best evidence available to man. The first steps can have their own direction yet be open to new directions based upon continuous feedback from their previous actions.

The sources of the social service projects described in this text are intensive and extensive studies of the effective ingredients involved in the development of human resources. The learnings from these efforts have been modified in numerous pilot investigations. What works is developed and extended. What doesn't work is extinguished. The applications of the social service projects to community and educational action programs represent a culmination of the learnings from all of our previous efforts in counseling and psychotherapy, education and human relations.

This book records an educational adventure into resolving some of the most critical problems of our time. It records the contribution that an agency of a small urban college can make to the development of the surrounding community. Specifically, it records the projects and the evidence for the effectiveness of the projects of the Center for Human Relations and Community Affairs, American International College.

The success of these projects, we believe, is a function of the direction of their authors. The direction is based upon years of pilot research in the social services—pilot research that was accomplished prior to making applications in social action projects. The projects themselves had to do with attempting to provide the community with the skills and resources necessary to shape, at least in part, its own destiny.

After working to get the internal and community relations of the college in order, programs in education, employment, family and community services, and racial relations were initiated. In all instances, these programs were based upon empirically validated methodologies. In most instances lay personnel indigenous to the population being serviced were trained as functional professionals to assume responsible social service positions within the program.

The social action programs recorded, then, have to do with human services in many respects. Foremost, they help the population being serviced to help themselves and in so doing prepare them for their own service occupations. Thus, a person may be the recipient of helping services which are conducive to his own personal development. At the same time, training in helping and human relations skills enables the trainee to relate most effectively to those who mean the most to him, his family and friends, and to provide them with the services that are conducive to their personal development. Finally, such training equips the trainees with the skills necessary for new careers in the human service areas.

The learning from these programs will lead, hopefully, to meeting national manpower needs for comprehensive preventive and treatment programs in the social and mental health services and social action spheres.

EFFECTIVE INGREDIENTS OF THIS BOOK

It is interesting how the efforts of my colleagues and myself ran parallel courses before converging in the present work. In the early 1960s, in the midst of the great civil rights struggle, community leaders like Professor Andrew H. Griffin were building with their own hands independent, grass-roots, educational, tutorial, and counseling agencies to service poverty areas. In the early 1960s, community leaders in Springfield, Massachusetts, were "moving mountains" to get reluctant concessions from business and industrial leaders for ten or fifteen vocational opportunities at the lowest economic level.

During the same years I was instigating pilot research that established the basis, years later, for the projects recorded in the pages of this volume.

In the early 1960s we were thrown out of a large state medical school for training subprofessionals (then a paltry few)—five hospital attendants—for helping roles in the mental health professions. We continued to study the essential ingredients for successful learning (or relearning), to operationalize those conditions so that they could be transmitted to any person with the necessary resources, professional or otherwise, and to implement programs incorporating the necessary selection and training methodologies. All of these projects were accomplished without the support—and often with the reticence and some-times in spite of the active resistance, not unlike that met by the community leaders—of the institutions involved. Dr. Bernard G. Berenson shared some of these experiences with me.

The unwritten parts of this story are the doubts, obstacles, indeed the traps, which were calculated to befuddle, confound, neutralize, and intimidate. And yet we owe their perpetrators a debt of gratitude, for in knowing the prob-lem makers we are spurred on to greater efforts in our search for solutions.

The heart of the Human Relations Center is people—strong people—black and white—side by side—committed to man and his emergence—back to back—standing against the destructive forces that enslave men's minds, feel-ings, and bodies.

To be sure, although a great deal has been accomplished, much more remains to be done. Indeed, compared to what remains to be done what has been accomplished is very small. Yet it is a beginning and, we believe, an important beginning, for if this can be done with the limited personnel and physical and economic resources of a Center of a small urban college, then how much more can be accomplished by the large educational, industrial, and political institutions? There is hope in this work—delivery of promises made, realization of American dreams—black and white—and beauty in a life un-folding where tomorrow does not have to be like today and where today has meaning in its own right.

But there is a warning too—a warning of danger to the powers that be in the community-at-large—a warning that, if unheeded, may portend disaster. For the workings of one small agency, if it does not become a model for the other agencies in the community, are not enough.

This book, then, focuses upon systematic extensions of learnings from research and practice to social action. The reader will find this volume well documented with evidence—although not, it must be emphasized, to the ex-clusion of editorial privilege—of one program of one small urban college. A sample of fifty-two different projects are employed to illustrate a rational-empirical approach to social change and the development of human resources.

The book is divided into seven parts as follows:

Part One, Prologue, "Credo of a Conservative Activist," provides an in-troduction in the form of a philosophical orientation to social action—a cos-mology blending the "truth" of empirical research and the "truth" of human experience. It is militant in its tone, for no one who stands for anything is not; yet it is conservative in its stance, for no one who is concerned can be so without considerations of delivery.

Part Two, "Ingredients of Social Failure," deals with some of the social failures of our time: the problems of the poor, the black, and the needy; the problems of the city. The attempt here is to discern the principles of social failure and intercept its repetitive cycle. In so doing the focus is upon the sources of social failure, particularly the educational institutions that systematically condition failure in one group of humans, and success in another. Finally, Part Two demonstrates how the professional programs which are calculated to ameliorate the difficulties are designed to fail just as the original programs have been designed to fail.

In the first part of Part Three, "Ingredients of Social Emergence," the sources of human development are considered, with special emphasis upon the helper as model and agent for the helpee's change or gain. In addition, the principles of social action that meet the problems of social need are delineated, with special attention given to the employment of functional as opposed to credentialed professionals. In the realm of human services, indigenous lay personnel can be selected and trained to do everything that credentialed professionals can do—and more!

The second part of Part Three develops the principles of personal effectiveness. An understanding of the effective person's phenomenology is the first step in operationalizing his effectiveness in a manner that it can be transmitted and learned. Personal effectiveness, we find, is a function of the quantity and quality of responses in an individual's physical, emotional, and intellectual repertoire.

Part Four, "Ingredients of Human Resource Development," attends to the effective ingredient of all social action programs: effective people, discussing how they function and how they may be developed. Helping, training, and selection procedures are operationalized and guides presented for their effective implementation. People constitute the heart of any program, and selection and training alone make the most effective people possible.

Part Five, "The Development of Human Resources," presents the core of most recent contributions to social action and the development of human resources. In each instance, process and outcome studies are presented as a vehicle to increasingly sharpened constructs and procedures. The different projects are, we believe, innovating and exciting and we hope that each in its own way may serve, as one reviewer has suggested, "as a model for the rest of the nation to emulate, a model for the 1970s."

Part Six, "Functionality and Change," strikes to the heart of our social ills in the development of criteria of functional utility which can serve to counteract the criteria of credentials and caste, dollars and domicile, power, politics, and pedigree. He who can do the job should do the job! The concept of functionality is developed with special emphasis upon the operationalization of goals, systematic development of means to achieve the goals, and systematic assessments of effects as a source of new and continuing learnings concerning the most effective approaches. In addition, the theme of planning for constructive change is developed, with the urban college proposed as center of a human and urban resource development system.

Finally, Part Seven, "A Personal Note to Effective People" on effecting constructive change, is presented in the epilogue of this book. It is a militant note.

This work builds upon a directionality developed and recorded in early writings, particularly the two volumes of *Helping and Human Relations,* and, in this order, *Beyond Counseling and Therapy, Sources of Gain in Counseling and Psychotherapy,* and *Toward Effective Counseling and Psychotherapy.* In a very real sense, this effort represents a culmination of these previous works, the recording of an "acid test" in real life of whether elaborate theories and sophisticated methodologies can make a difference in human lives.

This work would not have been possible without the efforts of Bernie Berenson, my courageous friend and colleague, who has also been my partner in some of the pathfinding pilot research which laid the base for our work, and Andy Griffin, my committed friend, colleague, and partner who, as a leader dedicated to the black community, has devoted his life's energies to the welfare of all our citizens, white as well as black. To these men I dedicate this book.

The learnings would not have been possible without the efforts of the community people who are sometimes my students, sometimes my teachers, sometimes both. I think in particular of our very intense experience with the first group of trainees, black and largely militant, who challenged me to new levels of functioning and whom I challenged to new levels of functioning. I trained for them and, in so doing, taught them to train themselves. I can vividly remember facing the ice-cold pool water on frostbitten New England November mornings and saying to myself: "If I can make the swim, I can handle those guys today." Many other experiences and many other personnel followed, but I will always remember the members of the first group, many of whom have gone to work with us and in the community in different capacities. They include Eddie Addison, Tom Akbar, Josephus Bass, Ron Carroll, Bill Clinton, June Glenn, Bill and Jay Griffin, the latter having joined our staff, Jim Hennesey, Bob Jackson, Ray Jordan, Bruce King, and Dorothy Savage. We "stuck" each other with each other. I dreamed black and they dreamed white. In this context, the first group of Human Relations Specialists for the Springfield School Department will always be close to me. Together we went through difficult periods—too numerous to mention. In addition to Addison and Carroll, this group includes Maurita Bledsoe, Terrell Burnett, Charles Culp, Iris Danforth, Richard Gladden, Donna Jordan, Mike Ireland, Elaine Irving, Edith Ray, and Carl Smith.

The entire effort would not have been possible without the cooperation of key members of the educational and black communities. AIC President, Harry Corniotes, helped make the implementation of the Center possible, and endorsed and is himself busy implementing, with modifications, my plan for the functional reorganization of the urban college (Chapter 16). Dr. Richard C. Sprinthall, chairman of the Department of Psychology and a leading educator and educational psychologist in his own right, helped us to get the Center off the ground.

For their part, we could not have received a higher level of receptivity, cooperation, and intelligent consultation than we did from members of the community such as Louis Frayser, past Director, Springfield Action Commission. In addition, Roger Williams, Director, Concentrated Employment Program, and Bruce Bowin, Supervisor, Department of Welfare, who gave support and impetus to a program of employment of functional professionals trained by functional professionals, deserve special mention. J. Walter Reardon, Second Vice-President of Corporate Relations, Massachusetts Mutual Life Insurance Company, was extremely cooperative on many counts and was a collaborator on a section of Chapter 16. Mrs. Martha Wilson, who is both administrative secretary at the Center and a community leader in her own right, is acknowledged for her contribution in holding the Center operation together administratively.

The contributions of all of the many persons who have shared in the evolution of research laying the foundation for these social projects are gratefully acknowledged. Dr. George Banks, who was a member of our staff at the Center and is now with the U.S. Defense Department, merits special recognition for his continuing research in the racial relations areas. In addition, I thank Dr. David Aspy, Dr. David Berenson, Dr. Ralph Bierman, Dr. James Drasgow, Dr. Ted Friel, Dr. Tom Hefele, Dr. Dan Kratochvil, Dr. William Pagell, Dr. Gerald Piaget, Dr. Richard Pierce, Dr. Charles Truax, and Dr. Raphael Vitalo.

Finally, beyond she who put him here, his mother, each contributor must have two women in his life: she who puts up with him, his secretary, and she who puts him in his place, his wife. To my wife, Bernice, who is both wife and secretary, my love!

R. R. C

Springfield, Mass.
March 1971

Contents

The Development of Human Resources

PART ONE
Prologue

CHAPTER 1

Credo of a Conservative Activist

I was privileged to be present recently at the Real People's Congress, conducted by the black community of Springfield, Massachusetts. This was more than the usual conference calculated to neutralize black attitudes rather than to change white behavior; I was impressed with a new black leadership assuming the initiative and responsibility for educating the whites on their joint problems. However, I was also dismayed and, indeed, appalled at the appearance of a new type of political conservative whose emergence parallels the development of the black leadership. He is not the old-line conservative who demanded a dollar's worth for a dollar's pay, delivery for promises made. He is a new type who is willing to acknowledge two key points: first, that all of our federal programs for the poor, the black, and the city are not working; second, that the programs are designed in such a way that they cannot work. He usually makes his point and leaves, feeling that he has made his contribution in his analysis. He is frightening!

I am frightened by business leaders who would allocate tax dollars and other monies with no expectation other than the assumption that things will not change. I am frightened by the paying of "guilt money" calculated to maintain rather than change the status quo. I am frightened by city fathers who protect images while the conditions of the city replicate point by point the preconditions of violence indicated in the Kerner Commission Report.

I am frightened, at the other extreme, by the new type of political radical who has emerged in reaction to the conservative. I am frightened by the rebellion of children who, in the face of directionless fathers, would overthrow everything and anything. I am frightened by children who, in their precrisis condition, dedicate their lives to eliciting reaction from their fathers—fathers who, however compromised, have at least met a personal crisis in their lives, something which the children try so hard to avoid. I am frightened by these strangers to work who in revulsion of an abstract autocrat are led by the warm, seductive abdicat, only to be abandoned at the first sign of strife by these men of peace, reconciliation, and compassion. I am frightened by these children, however apparently sophisticated, whose only substantive direction comes from the justice of another's cause, who feed off the blood of another's revolution. I am frightened by these "future leaders"—their intellects damaged by "trips" good and bad—who truly believe that in a brave, new world they will once again be elected Chiefs to govern the hapless Indians. How many Munichs make an Auschwitz?

These are the two extremes—with each now preparing to come down upon the other.

The course between this Scylla and Charybdis leads only to the tired soil of the Old World, where nothing lives and nothing dies, where nothing grows and nothing thrives. No, rather it is for the healthy conservatives who are mobilized to act only when the behavior of others impinges upon their spheres of functioning—for now is the hour of such impingement—to join hands; yes, minds; indeed, bodies—together with the healthy activists who are influenced to become concerned with the outcome of their programs only when the programs fail—for they have, to be sure, failed. It remains for healthy adults to act with constructive directionality where their unhealthy counterparts have not, and their children cannot. It is in this new union that we define an "extreme middle" position, not one built upon the twin principles of impotency—compromise and neutralize—but one built upon deep concern and effective action, imaginative and penetrating thrusts and the consolidation of gains accomplished by these thrusts.

The activist in me demands that I develop a course of action—and now! The conservative in me demands that whatever I do, I do my best. The point of convergence of the conservative and the activist is effectiveness. I relate the concern with effectiveness to the development of social action programs and extend it to the development of a sensible social order dedicated to the emergence of all of its constituents. While I write with particular relevance for the areas of human relations and human services—especially as they relate to the problems of the poor, the black and the city—I believe the message has broad implications for economic and political programs at all levels and in all areas.

SOME PRINCIPLES OF HELPING

The first and most basic principle of helping and human relations is the ability to see the world through the eyes of the other person. If we cannot see the world through the other's eyes, and communicate accurately to him what we see, then all advice, all directions, all reinforcements, rewards as well as punishments, are meaningless. If we cannot see the world through the other's eyes, then we must learn from him. Today, the black man says, "You cannot know what it is to be black!" With my own past experience in counseling and psychotherapy, this is not an easy precept to incorporate from any man. Yet, if we truly understand, we must know "where he is coming from." It is a fundamental assumption with which the black relates to the white. We must begin with this fundamental assumption—whatever our resources, whatever their resources. We must listen—and more important hear: The line between who is helper and who is helped is a fine one. *In order to help we must first be helped.*

A related proposition involves the question of whether the would-be helper —and, again, I use this term more broadly than to connote traditional helping relationships—has anything that the helpee wants. Put in the simplest terms: can the helper offer the helpee something that will enable the helpee to live more effectively in *his* world—not the helper's world? This is a most difficult concept for those of us who see the goals of the black revolution only in terms of "getting a piece of the [current] action" and not in terms of changes at the more deeply philosophical levels involving the issue of freedom for all men to grow to their fullest potential. Put in its most difficult terms: can the helpee look at the helper and make the determination, "He could have made it in my world," that is, "Given my circumstances, he could have made it more effectively than I"? We are so accustomed as would-be helpers to making judgments of the helpees that we forget that the helping process cannot take place unless the helpee has made judgments of us and ceded us the power and recognition as agents of his change. We are so accustomed to seeking permission from above that we seldom obtain permission from below. The first order of business, then, must be getting ourselves and our own houses in order before embarking upon projects that would help others.

Related to these propositions is the principle of competency; not just competency in knowing how to operationalize a helping process, but competency in definable skills. Helping and human relations are not, themselves, substantive skills. The helper can come to need a victim in order to be able to function. The skills only approach being substantive when they are translated into preventative action in teaching people how to avoid difficulties and, falling short of this, training them to help themselves and each other: for example, running their own social service agencies. If the helper does not have a demonstrable area of competency, an area of skills in which he can demonstrate a high level of expertise, he is not trustworthy, for the helpee knows that the helper must fall into one of two "bags": he needs the system as it is; or he thrives on the agony rather than the emergence of the oppressed. He will be threatened by the prospect of major change unless he can manipulate the situation so that he once again rises to the top on the basis of some criteria other than competency. Again, the fine line separating helper and helped may be found in answers to questions of who needs who more, social worker or client, policeman or criminal. Only those who have definable areas of competency can help, for they alone are free to make the giant strides—not the little steps that assure their positions—to free another to emerge, to go beyond them or to become their helpers. In this context, in my experience there are few "concerned" college students who have worked hard enough to acquire the skills and competencies necessary to make them trustworthy.

The helpees, then, are asking for the very best of the helpers. No longer are they satisfied with prospects for equality with their helpers. They seek the same freedom to pursue fulfillment that their helpers had, whether or not their helpers paid the price to find it. But whether or not their helpers have found fulfillment will determine whether they function by the cardinal rule of actualized men: "I will not accept you at less than you can be"; or by the cardinal rule of equalized men: "No one can have more than I can have." No longer, for example, are the blacks to be pacified with what is left over from the white world; the whites who know that while they're not competent enough to make it in the white world figure that they're good enough for the black. Now the blacks are setting up standards for those who would enter their worlds. Thus far they have done so implicitly, yet the prospect for operationalizing standards for functioning becomes clearer every day.

Not only are the helpees asking for the best of the helpers; they are also asking the helpers to train themselves out of *their* jobs. The Gordian knot of racial strife is cut by the creation of a potential internship or apprenticeship for every job. This is not to indicate that every position will necessarily be assumed by the intern. It is to indicate the creation of an opportunity to learn the skills necessary to demonstrate a level of competence in the area, with he who demonstrates the most effectiveness in terms of achieving the goals involved assuming the leadership position. Thus, in an educational system, those who service the children most effectively, whether credentialed or functional professionals, should have the authority that goes with the responsibility. At another level the helpees are saying, "If you're really committed, you'll start us off, provide us with the necessary skills, and serve as a resource person, but let us do the job." They're saying, "We want to know everything that you know that is relevant and meaningful for our purposes." In concrete terms, they're asking, as in a program which we recently conducted, "Do we go to welfare as recipients or casework aides?" The principle of internship also applies to many potential crisis areas, as, for example, community control of schools in which local citizens may be prepared for the enormous responsibilities.

SOME PRINCIPLES OF SENSIBLE ORDER

The point of convergence of the conservative and the activist, then, is effectiveness. It is ironical in this regard that the very question of effectiveness is first raised in loud voice on issues such as that of community control of schools that are not servicing minority groups. The first and foremost principle of sensible order involves the establishment of functional criteria of effectiveness. The criteria of functional utility must supersede the criteria of credentials. Credentials alone do not establish effectiveness, but they do serve to exclude the already forgotten people who do not have these credentials. We must provide the resources and the framework within which those persons who can function effectively in a given role can have the responsibilities and, indeed, the authority for functioning in that role. Criteria of effectiveness can be operationalized, and discriminations made concerning level of functioning in a given area.

A related proposition, then, involves the increased employment of lay or noncredentialed personnel in many capacities as functional professionals. This is not to say that unselected lay persons can discharge the responsibilities of properly selected and trained professionals, the latter being something which we cannot take for granted in many areas. It is to say that properly selected and trained lay personnel can discharge the responsibilities of properly selected and trained professionals. Rather than to continue to hide the keys to the chastity belt of professionalization, the closely guarded spheres of influence or control based upon credentials, it remains for the professional to recognize the privilege of its violation. Those who can do what professionals now do should spur the professionals on to a definition of professionalization based upon higher levels of creativity in bold, new frontiers. In our own efforts we have been guided by the principle of providing each organization with its own inservice training capacity. In one such project, functional professionals, systematically selected and trained, in turn trained large numbers of hard-core unemployed to function in social service capacities in nonprofit agencies. At a midpoint in training, the class leaders took over, as interns, the responsibilities of the functional professionals who had taken over our responsibilities, thus freeing the functional professionals, as we were freed by them, to seek new horizons of productivity. Obviously, this proposition does involve education that is relevant and meaningful for the functions that are being discharged. It dictates a reorganization of educational systems on functional bases that service responsible members of the community, student body, and, yes, the faculties of demonstrated competencies.

Not only does the "way out of the bag" involve the increased employment of lay personnel but it also involves, ironically enough, getting the real leaders that the system has bypassed into positions of responsibility in order to save— not the system, but what is of value in the system—and this not to the exclusion of a "new order." A system that does not provide the appropriate levels of authority to the natural leaders of its representative groups cannot survive. The essence of any revolution is bringing the representative leaders and groups to the fore where they can achieve the ends which they and their oppressed membership require. Such a revolution can be nonviolent—or it can be violent. It is the choice of the responsible persons in the system as to which it will be. The criteria of credentials do not allow the real leaders of an oppressed minority to emerge. The criteria of functionality facilitate the emergence of the real leaders.

The rewards and punishments of an effective social order, then, must be allocated differentially according to how the actors—not the critics—discharge their responsibilities. Those who function effectively are rewarded, independent of their credentials or lack of credentials. Those who do not function effectively are not rewarded, independent of their credentials or lack thereof. The power, then, does not lie inherently in the Establishment or in the Anti-Establishment. The power lies in the hands of those who can deliver, and it is the responsibility of those who can deliver in their areas to insist upon delivery in other areas. Thus, a second grade teacher in any school—urban, suburban, or rural—who elicits eighteen or twenty months' reading growth out of her class in the course of an academic year has more than met the criteria of effectiveness, whereas one who elicits eight or nine months' growth, as we have found, has not. As for the individual who does not meet the criteria of functional utility, there is the prospect of training and retraining in all of those skills necessary to discharge the responsbilities of the position to which he lays claim. However, no one has an inherent right to public service positions of any kind, and those who cannot be retrained and cannot deliver must be excluded from these responsible positions.

The effectiveness of the different programs must be demonstrated on the one hand, those in a position to influence the scene must contribute what they can to ensure the success of constructive programs on the other hand. In the development of a program of black human relations specialists who work with black and white children in integrated schools, for example, we find that we must have the support of the school administration. If the program is effective, it will serve to expose many ineffectuals who have helped to create the present crisis in education, that is, producing overwhelmingly disproportionate numbers of black suspendees, dropouts, and auxiliary class members. The program will require the support of an enlightened administration, for either the competent or the ineffectuals must ultimately go. Again, we must go to the criteria of functional utility. Are the youngsters for whom we claim to serve in fact being serviced? Criteria of effectiveness assessing the adjustment and emergence of the students can be operationalized. Criteria of effectiveness must, of necessity, involve assessments of the student's welfare—not assessments of how well the specialists relate to the school staff. And whoever—white or black—can meet these criteria must be given the responsibilities.

The construct of the criteria of functional utility is the key concept of a healthy society. Those who can discharge given functions effectively must have the responsibilities for doing so. It is not simply a question of the congruence of credentials and functioning. It is a matter of designating professional responsibilities to those personnel indigenous to the population being serviced who are capable of discharging these professional responsibilities—whether or not they are later formally credentialed for such responsibilities.

The criteria of functional utility enable us to operationalize constructive goals that can be achieved. They enable us to develop progressive steps for achieving these goals. They enable us to assess how effectively we have achieved these goals and, accordingly, to develop higher-level goals and more effective ways of attaining these goals.

A SUMMARY STATEMENT

It is clear that constructive change cannot be possible without the cooperation of both the conservatives and the activists. Peace in itself is not a goal. Effectiveness is. Where peace and effectiveness are mutually exclusive, we must choose the latter, for the former will most certainly lead to war. Where they are not mutually exclusive, the transformation may be a nonviolent one.

The credo of the healthy activist is based upon the basic principle that at the deepest level there is no understanding without action. To really understand someone is to understand his need to act upon his situation. The credo of the healthy conservative is based upon the basic principle that at the deepest level there is no action without understanding. To really act we must first understand the critical dimensions of the situation and then develop progressive step-by-step programs to achieve the goals desired.

This is not a call to arms for intellectual ineffectuals. Their day is past. They are going into hiding to await the restoration of "sanity" before they scramble to secure the positions whose power they abused in bringing about the present crisis. Rather, it is a declaration of war upon those who throw up the smoke-screens of "dialogue" to resolve communication problems only to hide their own basic incompetencies. The answer to their privilege is our power. Power not just in political and economic action but power to utilize our inherent resources and our created opportunities to the fullest.

This is a plea for the strong and the healthy of all factions—black and white, rich and poor, young and old—to join together, not simply to resolve the problems of the present, but to anticipate as mature adults the problems of the future in this and other lands.

This is a plea for those who are competent enough to entertain a lifetime of learning; for those for whom helping in its present form can at best be a transitional phase; for those who can die growing, secure in the understanding that the only meaning to life is growth, and that *no price is too high to pay for the opportunity to grow.*

PART TWO

*Ingredients
of Social Failure*

CHAPTER 2

Principles of Social Failure

The problems of the poor, the black, and the needy are not accidental or inadvertent. They did not occur by chance or fate.

Neither are they simply the necessary products of neglect of a crude and wasteful social system that must leave victims in its wake. For each system must assume the responsibility for the effects of its design.

Nor are they simply the product of man's unconscious feelings and prejudices toward other men. For the unconscious is simply man's excuse for avoiding the responsibility for his destructive impulses and actions.

No, the problems of the poor, the black, and the needy are a product of none of these things. They are a product of much worse—much more vicious—designs.

The problems of the poor, the black, and the needy are a culmination of systematic planning and systematic programming. Conceived in man's greed, nourished in his transgressions and acted out in the atrocities of man's inhumanities to man, the social problems of our time are a consequence of conspiring minds and methodical implementation.

The problems of the poor, the black, and the needy are the products of the systematic conditioning of one segment of society by another. With an economic motive clearly in view, minority groups have been systematically conditioned to internalize inferior attitudes and behaviors; and, conversely, and consequently, the remaining elements have been systematically conditioned to internalize superior attitudes and behaviors.

We can best understand the principles of conditioned inferiority and conditioned superiority by establishing a historical perspective of race relations in the United States.

13

A BRIEF HISTORICAL PERSPECTIVE OF RACIAL PROBLEMS

During the early days of the colonies, relations between Negroes and whites were harmonious. This is not to say that a perfect state existed either within or between races, for many of both races were held in bonds of servitude. Nevertheless, blacks and whites "seemed to be remarkably unconcerned about their visible differences. They toiled together in the fields, fraternized during leisure hours, and, in and out of wedlock, collaborated in siring a numerous progeny" (Stampp, 1956, in Bennett, 1966). In short, blacks and whites were treated and treated one another with equality and equanimity, accumulating land and servants—black and white—in the bargain. They shared the same hopes of freedom, of opportunity, of achievement. Indeed, blacks and whites died for one another.

Behind the Revolutionary rhetoric, behind the bombast, behind the living and dying and bleeding is the irony: black men toiled and fought so that white men could be free. This fact was not lost on the Revolutionary generation. It worried good men and women so much that they made Negro freedom an "inevitable corollary" of American freedom. James Otis and Tom Paine, the great propagandists of the Revolution, thundered against British tyranny *and* slaveholder tyranny. Abigail Adams told her husband John: "It always appeared a most iniquitous scheme to me to fight ourselves for what we are daily robbing and plundering from those who have as good a right to freedom as we have" (Bennett, 1966, p. 49).

At first, then, the situation and its concomitant alternatives or options, were, as Bennett suggests, quite fluid. However, for a variety of reasons, not the least of which were cotton and tobacco markets, and with a variety of rationales, not the least of which was an appeal to religious differences, Negroes were enslaved and forced to work on the plantations. However, by 1777 the Rights of Man movement once again activated the hopes of the black man.

Slavery died in the North as a direct result of forces set in motion by the Rights of Man movement. By legislative decrees and by court action, Negro slaves were declared free men. In some states, legislative emancipation was a gradual process extending over several years. The preamble of the Pennsylvania act for the gradual abolition of slavery accurately reflected the spirit of the age. The preamble said it was the duty of Pennsylvanians to give proof of their gratitude for deliverance from the oppression of Great Britain "by extending freedom to those of a different color by the work of the same Almighty hand."

It seemed for a time that slavery would die in the South, but the invention of the cotton gin and other mechanical devices cooled the Revolutionary ardor of Southern patriots (Bennett, 1966, p. 63).

From that point forward, the black has been an unwanted child in an otherwise vital, striving, but often discordant, family. From that point forward, the black has been systematically excluded from the opportunities that would enable him to actualize his resources, while his white counterparts have been, by and large, provided such opportunities. From that point forward the black has been systematically conditioned to expect less and less from himself while his white counterparts have been, by and large, taught to expect more and more for themselves. From that point forward, America was in revolt against itself, against the principles upon which it was founded, teaching men to neglect the intelligence which differentiates them from animals and, indeed, treating men like animals.

Formal emancipation following the Civil War did not change things. Rather, the original crime was repeated on a grander scale. Again, hope was offered and taken away. Again, a spirit that was not broken in over 100 years of slavery was frustrated. Again, *the black was the victim of a carefully constructed conspiracy against him.*

Where he had previously had no education, he now had a qualitatively different education. His new education was even more insidious in destroying his feelings of inner worth. Where he had had chains, he could define the enemy. Where he had books, he could not.

The books were the white man's books. The history was the white man's history. The ways were the white man's ways. The talents were the white man's talents.

In the face of his own education the black fell further behind the white man on all fronts. With his "separate but equal" education he found himself only catching up to where the white had been when the white man had moved on to new levels or new frontiers.

The effects of discrimination in servitude were obvious. The effects of discrimination in education were subtle, but nonetheless strangling.

Finally, in a mighty effort to break the chains upon his mind, many of the stronger blacks migrated or, for all intents and purposes, immigrated, for the South was indeed in many respects a foreign land, an alien island of sickness and perversion where men's bodies were beaten into submission, their minds shaped to deficiency, and their souls bewitched and possessed. Unfortunately, as we shall see in detail in our studies of northern cities, he again became victim of an organized plot.

It is important to maintain the perspective, that, in effect, when we talk about blacks we are talking about second-generation immigrants. It puts things into a perspective that can be understood by the Irish-American cop, the

Polish-American miner, the Italian-American peddler—and more important by their children, the teachers and engineers, now third- and fourth-generation Americans. In spite of the fact that the blacks are among the oldest Americans, having landed a year before the Mayflower, in spite of the fact that their blood and their sweat and their tears were as responsible for the building of this country as the blood, sweat, and tears of any other group—in spite of these things, it is as if the blacks only landed on these shores 30 or so years ago. For they have not shared in the American process; they have not shared in the American dream.

Indeed, *the black man's American experience was a handicap—no more!*

Any man who sets foot and walks on the American shore is advantaged over another who is buried six feet beneath its soil. It is as if the black man had been buried six feet under and only now has scratched his way close enough to see the surface. And when he emerges where he should have begun—at surface level—he will be nowhere—he will have nothing to show for 300 years of toil here and thousands of years of tradition before. *That is frustration!*

THE CYCLE OF SOCIAL FAILURE

The cycle of social failure begins, then, by conditioning one group to experience themselves as inferior in order to serve the interests, primarily economic, of other groups who are in the process, either implicitly and/or explicitly, shaped to experience themselves as superior. Again, the conditioning process was methodical. Discriminatory practices in all areas of existence taught the black that he was inferior, and his powerlessness to change this basic teaching reinforced the effects of the original teaching. Exploitation and privation in the areas of man's basic needs, the shelter he provides, the food he eats, the family

Figure 2–1
The cycle of social failure.

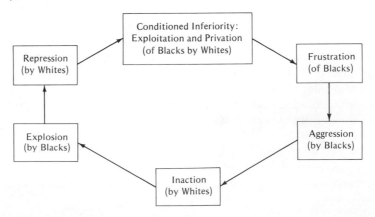

he protects, the freedom he has, the justice he receives, all converged to inten-sify the black's feelings of hopelessness and frustration (Clark, 1965) and, ac-cordingly, to initiate the second phase of the cycle of social failure.

What students of human behavior have long known is that aggressive be-havior is one of the alternative responses to frustration. The other modes of responding to frustration, such as submission, regression to simpler modes of coping, evading the situation, apathy and forgetfulness, have been as well demonstrated in experimental research (Berkowitz, 1962; Himmelweit, 1950; Scott, 1958) as in the history of the black man in America. Nevertheless, de-fining frustration as any condition that blocks attainment of a desired goal, researchers and theorists (Dollard, 1939) developed an hypothesis that aggres-sive behavior is to be anticipated as a logical and expected consequence of frustration and they found extensive evidence in a number of experimental situ-ations to support or confirm this hypothesis. Briefly, the model asserts that frustration produces aggression, defined as behavior whose purpose is to de-stroy or remove the frustrating block, which acts as a drive or motive.

Where the first two phases of the cycle of social failure involve the con-ditioned inferiority which leads to frustration, then, the third phase is the ag-gression that follows from this frustration.

The fourth phase, of course, depends upon the responses of the holders of political, economic, and police power. There are, as always, dangers in re-sponding to aggressive behavior. The basis of aggressive motivation, it must be emphasized, is in its instrumentality in meeting other needs. Responsiveness to the demands behind the behavior would be reinforcing. Aggressive behavior, if successful in eliminating the source of frustration, would become associated with the achievement of other needs. A pathogenic motivational system where aggression is employed as the only evident means to achieve the desired ends may result.

Faced with the probability that responding might operate to reinforce an aggressive life style, the powers that be choose what appears on the surface to be a "safer" course—they do not act. This course is apparently safer because it serves to avoid the responsibility for the consequences of action. In addition, and perhaps most important, it serves to diffuse responsibility.

Actors always assume personal responsibility. And they do not wait for an incident to precipitate their action. Reactors always dispense public responsi-bility. And in so doing they reinforce the aggressive behavior that led to their response. Inactors always diffuse responsibility. Rather then dealing with the source or even the symptoms of the difficulty, they, by their inaction, place the burden of responsibility upon the aggrieved.

The inactors are clever abdicators or "abdicats." However, the stance of the "abdicats" is only safe on the surface or in the apparency of things. In reality, their inaction is "shaping" the aggrieved to engage in more extreme behavior. Conscious or unconscious though their motives be, they cannot avoid the re-sponsibility for the consequences of their inaction. The knowledge of the early stages of the cycle, the conditioning that leads to frustration, only compounds their responsibility for the inequities that led to the aggressive behavior.

Where in the fourth stage of the cycle of social failure, responding to grievances runs the risk of reinforcing the aggressive behavior, the real danger lies in not responding at all. Inaction precipitates the fifth stage of explosion or explosive behavior on the part of the deprived and exploited. Unfortunately, at this point much of the behavior is aimless and no longer goal-directed. It is explosive because there are no other outlets available for its expression. It is no longer simply that "no one cares" but rather that "they care not to care." It is clear to the already endlessly frustrated that those who decide know what they are doing, that a lifetime of endless frustrations can only culminate in one ultimate frustration.

As conditioned "losers," they can no longer hope to become themselves "winners."

As conditioned "losers," the only kind of partial victory that they can see is to bring the conditioned "winners," the now obvious obstacle to their emergence, to their knees.

The alternatives are, of course, the thesis of this book. They involve independent determinations of opportunity and justice for all and the implementation of the necessary course that follows. They involve a winning process which involves bringing the loser up to the winner's level rather than the possibility of the fifth stage of the cycle of social failure, bringing the winner down to the loser's level.

The real danger of inaction, then, is that aggression can become an end in and of itself, with pointless striking out and destruction as its modality. It represents an explosive return in kind for the treatment which the aggrieved has experienced over a lifetime.

The sixth, and final, stage of the social failure cycle involves the same kinds of repressive activities that led originally to the privation and exploitation, the frustration and aggression. There is no way of avoiding the responsibility for entry into this phase. It is known in advance. It can be predicted. It is precipitated by inaction.

The real issue for the aggrieved, the frustrated, and the oppressed is when they want to die. It becomes clear to them that they are only the apparent aggressors. *The real aggression comes in the form of inaction when action is called for.* The real aggression comes in the form of the distorted female who understands the implications of her inaction and does not act: in her evil inactivity she only stimulates the potential victims to more extreme behavior, thus preparing them for the deathly rituals of the distorted male.

Put another way, the real issue is who is on whose schedule? From the point where the aggrieved become aggressive it seems that they have seized the initiative and that "the powers" are now on their schedule, fearing the loss of all the things they value. However, this is only apparently so; for when "the powers" do not respond, the aggrieved are once again on "the powers'" schedule, being shaped by inaction to more extreme and more violent behavior, behavior that will be dealt with by heightened repressive activities. No response to the source of frustration is as much of a response to aggressive behavior as a repressive response is to explosive behavior. Indeed, no response to aggression is a stimulus to explosion.

The repressive phase, then, represents both a culmination and an initiation of the ugliness of man, for it is one and the same with the conditioning phase which initiated the cycle of social failure in the first place. In a masturbatory ritual of perverted atrocities, man both ends and begins anew a cycle of now intellectual genocide, now emotional genocide, now physical genocide.

INGREDIENTS OF CIVIL DISORDER

The key phase of the cycle of social failure is the fourth phase, which is characterized by the inaction necessary to precipitate the extreme behavior necessary to elicit a repressive response. However ugly, the earlier phases of conditioning, privation, exploitation, frustration, and aggression are history. Their effects cannot be redeemed for any price. The rest is future. The key is whether or not the powers that be can, at this point, acknowledge their guilt, atone for their shame, reclaim their humanity. Or must they merely act out their role in a repetitious ritual of inhumanity?

The real issue, then, is whether or not the responsible powers can anticipate judicious ends and provide the necessary means so that the best of them do not have to be placed in the position of reacting or responding. The real issue is whether they, themselves, are free to see and hear and act upon what they see and hear.

Thus far, I have written loosely about the "powers that be." Who are these "powers"? "They" are you and me! "They" are the silent minorities that comprise the "silent majority." "They" are our representatives, our civil servants, those who are paid by us to fulfill their responsibilities to all of our peoples. "They" are those who did not ask us if we wanted to put a man on the moon but educated us first to its possibility, then its probability, inevitability, imminence, and finally its existence.

But most of all, "they" are the town fathers and the country fathers. "They" are those who have gained the most and who stand, in their minds, to lose the most without the edge of wealth and power which they and their offspring have over others, white and black. "They" are those who have stood by and said that while Detroit, Chicago, and New York were a mess, the Lexingtons and Concords and Springfields of this country were clean. "We" are dedicated to exploring this proposition.

In this context, citizens are always asking, "But what about my town?" What about your town? There is little evidence for overt manifestations of hostility and prejudice between the races. Or is there? "We" have examined "our" town, Springfield, Massachusetts, a metropolitan area of fewer than 200,000 inhabitants. The following white-black paper serves several purposes. First, it serves to educate the responsible citizenry of Springfield as to the social conditions on the national scene. In so doing it quotes extensively from the Report of the National Advisory Commission on Civil Disorders 1968. Second, it samples the social conditions on the Springfield scene for purposes of comparison with the social conditions on the national scene. It should serve the same purposes for the reader of this chapter, introducing him to Springfield and the conditions within which the projects related in *this* book took place. There are many Springfields around the country.

PROJECT 1

*Preconditions of Civil Disorder**

Nearly three years ago, following the riots of the summer of 1967, the National Advisory Commission on Civil Disorders, which has since become known as the Kerner Commission, was formed. Its members were men of substance, basically conservative in disposition. It included no radicals, no militants. Its prominent members included I. W. Abel, President of United Steelworkers of America; Edward Brooke, Republican Senator from Massachusetts; James Corman, Democratic Representative of California; Fred Harris, Democratic Senator from Oklahoma; Herbert Jenkins, Chief of Police in Atlanta, Georgia; Otto Kerner, then Democratic Governor of Illinois; John Lindsay, Republican Mayor of New York City; William McCulloch, Republican Representative of Ohio; Miss Katherine Peden, former Commissioner of Commerce of Kentucky; Charles B. Thornton, Chairman of Litton Industries, Inc.; Roy Wilkins, President of NAACP.

They studied the dimensions of the riots, analyzed their sources and made recommendations, upon the discharge of which they predicated the future welfare of the people of our otherwise great and growing nation.

Their conclusions, already well known to the black community, shocked and stupefied many quarters of the white citizenry. The only concept which the Commission could summon to account for the inability of normally responsible white citizens to act upon the deprivation and grievances of the blacks was white racism.

Let us consider some of the findings of the Kerner Commission and in

*Reprinted from a white-black paper written and published December 10, 1969, and distributed to leading business leaders, by Robert R. Carkhuff comparing the conditions in Springfield, Massachusetts, with the conditions in cities around the country that had experienced civil disturbance as reported by the National Advisory Commission on Civil Disorders. The quotes from this Kerner Commission Report are reprinted with permission from the New York Times Company and Bantam Books, Inc. [Statements prefixed by (*) are quotations from the Kerner Report; statements prefixed by (s) represent the present author's findings on conditions in Springfield.]

this context compare them with a sampling of the current conditions in the City of Springfield, more than two years after the publication of the Kerner Report. The issue of this report then is: Do the conditions in Springfield differ significantly from the conditions in riot-torn cities around the country?

Springfield, Massachusetts, is a city of approximately 178,000 persons, with a black population recently approximated at 25,000 persons and a Spanish-speaking Puerto Rican population of several thousand.

THE PRECONDITIONS OF CIVIL DISORDER

One of the major contributions of the Kerner Commission Report was to discern and delineate those conditions which constituted the essential ingredients of civil disturbance. Citing the complex and interacting factors, "varying from city to city and from year to year," the Kerner Commission felt, nevertheless, that certain fundamental matters were clear:

* Of these, the most fundamental is the racial attitude and behavior of white Americans toward black Americans.
* Race prejudice has shaped our history decisively; it now threatens to affect our future.
* White racism is essentially responsible for the explosive mixture which has been accumulating in our cities since the end of World War II.
* Among the ingredients of this mixture are:

    * *Pervasive discrimination and segregation* in employment, education and housing, which have resulted in the continuing exclusion of great numbers of Negroes from the benefits of economic progress.
    * *Black in-migration and white exodus,* which have produced the massive and growing concentrations of impoverished Negroes in our major cities, creating a growing crisis of deteriorating facilities and services and unmet human needs.
    * *The black ghettos* where segregation and poverty converge on the young to destroy opportunity and enforce failure. Crime, drug addiction, dependency on welfare, and bitterness and resentment against society in general and white society in particular are the result.
    * *Frustrated hopes* are the residue of the unfulfilled expectations aroused by the great judicial and legislative victories of the Civil Rights Movement and the dramatic struggle for equal rights in the South.
    * A *climate that tends toward approval and encouragement of violence* as a form of protest has been created by white terrorism directed against nonviolent protest; by the open defiance of law and federal authority by state and local officials resisting desegregation and by some protest groups engaging in civil disobedience who turn their backs on nonviolence, go beyond the constitutionally protected rights of petition and free assembly, and resort to violence to attempt to compel alteration of laws and policies with which they disagree.
    * *The frustrations of powerlessness* have led some Negroes to the convic-

tion that there is no effective alternative to violence as a means of achieving redress of grievances, and of "moving the system." These frustrations are reflected in alienation and hostility toward the institutions of law and government and the white society which controls them, and in the reach toward racial consciousness and solidarity reflected in the slogan "Black Power."

* *A new mood* has sprung up among Negroes, particularly among the young, in which self-esteem and enhanced racial pride are replacing apathy and submission to "the system."

* *The police are not merely a "spark" factor.* To some Negroes police have come to symbolize white power, white racism and white repression. And the fact is that many police do reflect and express these white attitudes. The atmosphere of hostility and cynicism is reinforced by a widespread belief among Negroes in the existence of police brutality and in a "double standard" of justice and protection—one for Negroes and one for whites.

These are powerful mixtures. Let us examine their dimensions insofar as they can be ascertained in the Springfield, Massachusetts, community.

In general, the Kerner Commission cites social, political, economic, and educational conditions as constituting "a clear pattern of severe disadvantage for Negroes compared with whites." Specifically, the Commission investigated the factors of all of the various levels of intensity. The recent eruptions in Springfield, Massachusetts, began at the educational level. Before examining the educational factors, let us examine the superstructure within which these factors operate.

Political Factors

One of the first factors pointed to by the Kerner Commission was the political structure including in particular the policing, justice, and grievance functions.

* The proportion of Negroes in local government was substantially smaller than the Negro proportion of population. Only three of 20 cities studied had more than one Negro legislator; none had ever had a Negro mayor or city manager. In only four cities did Negroes hold other important policy-making positions or serve as heads of municipal departments.

Let us examine Springfield in this regard.

s One of 9 city councilors is Negro, although under the present Plan A Strong Mayor form of government the black population is denied ward or precinct representation.

s Springfield has never had a Negro mayor.

s Negroes hold no important policy-making positions other than those federally funded programs calculated to alleviate the existing conditions, i.e., presently the Springfield Action Commission and formerly the Model Cities Program.

s One of over 30 heads of municipal government is black, and his province is specifically Intergroup Relations, i.e., dealing with relations between city government and the black community.[1]

With regard to police and grievance functions, the following national picture emerged in the Kerner findings:

* "Prior" incidents which increased tensions and ultimately led to violence were police actions in almost half the cases; police actions were "final" incidents before the outbreak of violence in 12 of the 24 surveyed disorders.
* Although almost all cities had some sort of formal grievance mechanism for handling citizen complaints, this typically was regarded by Negroes as ineffective and was generally ignored.

Let us examine Springfield with regard to the police, judicial, and grievance functions.

s There have been a number of recent instances of difficulties in police-community relations including the Octagon Lounge incident, the Court Square incident, the Winchester Square incident and the Lebanese-American Club incident.

s While the responses of older blacks are generally positive to police, the evidence from questionnaires indicates that the attitudes of blacks under 21 years of age are negative toward police, with many believing that they are a stimulus rather than a response to tension.

s While approximately 7 percent of the almost 300-man police force is black, one holds the responsibilities of a high-ranking officer.

s One of six police commissioners is black.

s The human relations commission, the only formal grievance mechanism, is generally regarded as ineffective by the black community and by its past directors and by many of its members.

s There is a generalized attitude among young blacks concerning different tracks of justice represented in recent cases: Whites kill whites and they receive suspended sentences; blacks kill blacks and receive a six-month sentence; blacks kill whites and receive life sentences.

s The differential administration of justice and protection is best illustrated by a contrast of two recent cases involving men with similar backgrounds.

In case A, a dozen police officers appeared to testify against a black man accused of assault and battery upon a policeman. However, with the services of a prominent lawyer and letters of recommendations from prominent citizens, the man, while convicted, was assessed a fine of $25.00.

In case B, a black man appeared alone, in his own defense, on a breach of peace charge involving refusing to move at the order of a police officer. He was convicted and sentenced to 6 months in the county jail.

[1] Since this report was released, the number of municipal government heads was increased to two when the Director of Intergroup Relations was appointed Director of Housing and his assistant assured directorship of Intergroup Relations.

Another major area of consideration is that involving economic dimensions, particularly employment and consumer factors.

Economic Factors

Economic factors laid the base for much of the frustration in the black community, as seen by the Kerner Commission.

* Negroes were twice as likely to be unemployed and averaged 70 per cent of the income earned by whites and were more than twice as likely to be living in poverty.
* Equally important is the undesirable nature of many jobs open to Negroes and other minorities. Negro men are more than three times as likely to be in low-paying, unskilled or service jobs. This concentration of male Negro employment at the lowest end of the occupational scale is the single most important cause of poverty among Negroes.
* The results of a three-city survey of various federal programs—manpower, education, housing, welfare and community action—indicate that, despite substantial expenditures, the number of persons assisted constituted only a fraction of those in need.
* Ghetto residents believe that they are "exploited" by local merchants, and evidence substantiates some of these beliefs. A study conducted in one city by the Federal Trade Commission showed that distinctly higher prices were charged for goods sold in ghetto stores than in other areas.

Let us examine the Springfield community with regard to economic factors.

s The unemployment rate for blacks of approximately 9 percent is nearly double the overall unemployment rate of approximately 5 percent for the Springfield community. [2]
s Several thousand black and Spanish-speaking families exist upon incomes of $3000 or less per year.
s The number of blacks in trade unions is so negligible as to be infinitesimal.
s The first black fireman was recently appointed and assigned duty at the Winchester Square firehouse.
s There are so few black-owned small businesses as to make the percentage of the total business population essentially infinitesimal.
s There are no black-owned large businesses.
s The jobs available to blacks continue to be those at the lower end of the continuum.
s Federal programs have serviced only a fraction of those in need.
s Concentrated Employment Program, one of the few potentially positive factors on the employment scene, will shortly have the control of its key components shifted from the community leadership to the Division of Employment Security, which was unable in the past to demonstrate effectiveness in helping the hard-core unemployed and underemployed.

[2] While these figures have changed substantially with the 1970 recession, the black-white unemployment ratio continues.

s Model Cities thus far has failed in terms of achieving its intended goals in the economic area. The few projects that have succeeded have been a function of the efforts of other, more effective agencies.

s While shopping prices at major food markets are not discriminatory in terms of prices, smaller local merchants charge significantly higher prices. The issue of the quality of products is yet to be investigated.

Another finding of the Kerner Commission concentrated on the problems of housing and population changes, including the related problems of health and recreation.

Housing and Population Factors

Housing and population factors contribute to the overall climate for civil disruption, as viewed by the Kerner Commission.

* Within the cities, Negroes have been excluded from white residential areas through discriminatory practices.
* Just as significant is the withdrawal of white families from, or their refusal to enter, neighborhoods where Negroes are moving or already moved into. About 20 per cent of the urban population of the United States changes residence every year. The refusal of whites to move into "changing" areas when vacancies occur means that most vacancies eventually are occupied by Negroes.
* The result, according to a recent study, is that in 1960 the average segregation index for 207 of the largest United States cities was 86.2. In other words, to create an unsegregated population distribution, an average of over 86 per cent of all Negroes would have to change their place of residence within the city.
* Between 2 and 2.5 million Negroes—16 to 20 per cent of the total Negro population of all central cities—live in squalor and deprivation in ghetto neighborhoods.
* Crime rates, consistently higher than in other areas, create a pronounced sense of insecurity in ghetto populations.
* Poor health and sanitation conditions in the ghetto result in higher mortality rates, a higher incidence of major diseases, and lower availability and utilization of medical services.
* Poor recreation facilities and programs is one of the most significant of the deeply held grievances.

Let us examine Springfield with regard to housing and population factors.

s Zoning and averaging techniques are employed by municipal authorities to obscure blatant differences in the living conditions of blacks and whites.

s Nearly one-half of the housing units in the Winchester Square neighborhood are rated substandard.

s Of the approximately 4000 units declared substandard in 1960 more than 50 percent were those housing black families.

s Whites are moving out of central city neighborhoods and blacks are migrating in.

s Blacks have limited opportunities to move into white residential areas.

s Health and sanitation conditions are significantly worse in the black community than in Springfield at large.

s Crime rates are significantly higher in the black community than in Springfield at large.

s The differential treatment of blacks and whites in health and recreation is best typified by the statistics of two of the community's key centers: the Dunbar Community Center, which services a population that is approximately 98 percent black, and the Springfield Boys Club, which now services a population that is approximately 97 percent white (having been moved from an area where it serviced a population that was approximately three-fourths black). The Dunbar Center services a population of approximately 9000 city residents or approximately 40 percent more than the Boys Club, which services a population of approximately 6600. Dunbar services an average of about 380 children a day, or approximately three times the number of children seen at the Boys Club daily. Boys Club has a budget of $215,-000 per year, or nearly four times the budget of Dunbar's $58,000 yearly. Dunbar's building and facilities are valued at approximately $25,000, including land, or less than one percent of the Boys Club facilities, excluding land, which were built at the cost of approximately $2,500,000 and include a year-round pool, full-length gym, and the services of many professional staff members, which Dunbar does not have.

Now let us turn to the educational situation, perhaps the most currently obvious scene of disruptive activities in Springfield.

Educational Factors

Education is a key ingredient in the consideration of the development of civil disorders, as seen by the Kerner Commission. In the light of the current difficulties it deserves most detailed consideration.

* For the community at large, the schools have discharged their responsibilities well. But for many minorities, and particularly for the children of the racial ghetto, the schools have failed to provide the educational experience which could help overcome the effects of discrimination and deprivation.

* The hostility of Negro parents and students toward the school system is generating increasing conflict and causing disruption within many city school districts.

* The most dramatic evidence of the relationship between educational practices and civil disorders lies in the high incidence of riot participation by ghetto youth who had not completed high school.

* Blacks are not represented proportionately at any levels within the educational systems.

* The black record of public education for ghetto children is growing worse. In the critical skills—verbal and reading ability—Negro students fall further behind whites with each year of school completed.

* Many more Negro than white students drop out of school.
* The vast majority of inner-city schools are rigidly segregated.
* Another strong influence on achievement derives from the tendency of school administrators, teachers, parents and the students themselves to regard ghetto schools as inferior.
* The schools attended by disadvantaged Negro children commonly are staffed by teachers with less experience and lower qualification than those attended by middle-class whites.
* Many teachers are unprepared for teaching in schools serving disadvantaged children.
* Teachers of the poor rarely live in the community where they work and sometimes have little sympathy for the life styles of their students.
* Attitudes of teachers toward their students have very powerful impacts upon educational attainment.
* Despite the overwhelming need, our society spends less money educating ghetto children than children of suburban families.

Let us turn to a consideration, again in some detail, of the conditions of education in Springfield.

s The percentage of black students in the Springfield school system is approximately 22 percent (Puerto Ricans are counted as white).
s The percentage of black teachers is approximately 5 percent (none is Puerto Rican).
s At Technical High School where 256 black students comprise 12 percent of the population, 1 of 106 teachers is black.
s At Commerce High School, where 406 black students comprise 22 percent of the population, 3 of 87 teachers are black.
s At Trade High School, where 261 black students comprise nearly 18 percent of the population, 4 of 102 teachers are black.
s At Classical High School, where 106 black students comprise over 7 percent of the population, no teachers are black.
s One principal out of 48 is black, and she will retire shortly from her grammar school.
s One assistant principal is black.
s One administrative officer (out of well over 30 administrative positions) is black and his responsibilities include directing the federally financed project for the inner-city child.
s The School-Community Relations expert under Racial Imbalance Law and federal funding is white.
s Blacks have no representation (voting or otherwise) on the School Committee.
s The percentage of blacks of total dropouts is approximately double the rate for the city.
s Five elementary schools range from 60 percent to over 90 percent black.
s Four of the five predominantly black schools have been considered substandard in physical facilities.
s The black students start slightly behind in achievement and grow progres-

sively worse. A sampling of predominantly black schools indicates that by grade 6 the children are already approximately a year behind in arithmetic and reading and even further behind national norms on the Iowa achievement tests.

s Black students comprise progressively larger percentages of auxiliary, or special, classes, ranging from nearly one-half at the junior high level to nearly three-fourths at the high school level.

s There is objective evidence to indicate that teachers and administrators and Pupil Personnel Service counselors, those formally charged with the responsibilities for individual guidance and counseling, are not functioning adequately on communication dimensions of understanding and initiative conducive to the constructive development and effective learning of students, black and white.

s The Superintendent of Springfield schools and Massachusetts Education Commissioner have acknowledged publicly that our educational system is not servicing minority groups, that teachers need to be reeducated, and that the black community must have a great deal more to say about the administration of their schools.

SUMMARY AND OVERVIEW

In the face of the increasing racial tensions in the educational settings and the inability of the persons responsible to act constructively to rectify the sources of these tensions, it was the intention of this report to sample the political, economic, housing and population, and educational conditions in Springfield and compare them to the conditions existing in communities around the country prior to civil disturbances. We have done that and we believe that a reasonable person would conclude that the conditions in Springfield do not differ significantly from those in riot-torn cities around the country.

It was not the intention of this report to make specific recommendations. That has been done elsewhere and many times. It can be done again in terms of developing concrete courses of action to ameliorate the difficulties and free the black community for emergence as a full political economic, social, and educational partner. It is the purpose of this report to recommend that the key responsible parties—the mayor and his staff, the superintendent of schools and his staff, and the directors of other key areas of community functions such as the chief of police—read the original Kerner Commission Report as part of their responsibilities. The 1968 Kerner Report has provided a number of useful guidelines for formulating constructive programs:

* Our recommendations embrace three basic principles:
    * To mount programs on a scale equal to the dimension of the problems;
    * To aim these programs for high impact in the immediate future in order to close the gap between promise and performance;

* To undertake new initiatives and experiments that can change the system of failure and frustration that now dominates the ghetto and weakens our society.

We cannot, in spite of the pleas of our city leaders, afford "a return to normalcy," for "normalcy" has not, as we have seen, been a happy circumstance for a large percentage of our fellow Springfield citizens. In this context, the Kerner Commission notes the following:

* A study of the aftermath of disorder leads to disturbing conclusions. We find that, despite the institution of some post-riot programs:
  * Little basic change in the conditions underlying the outbreak of disorder has taken place. Actions to ameliorate Negro grievances have been limited and sporadic; with but few exceptions, they have not significantly reduced tensions.
  * In several cities, the principal official response has been to train and equip the police with more sophisticated weapons.
  * In several cities, increasing polarization is evident, with continuing breakdown of inter-racial communication, and growth of white segregationist or black separatist groups.

Again, this report was written over two years ago. It is difficult to understand why so little has been accomplished in such a long time. The only concept that has been forwarded to account for our inability to act is elaborated upon in the Kerner Commission Report.

* What white Americans have never fully understood—but what the Negro can never forget—is that white society is deeply implicated in the ghetto. White institutions created it, white institutions maintain it, and white society condones it.
* The importance of this report is that it makes plain that the white, moderate, responsible American is where the trouble lies.
* The Commission itself reflected the inability of American society, dominantly white, to see and treat its Negro citizens fairly.
* It can only be a beginning because, patently, until the fact of white racism is admitted it cannot conceivably be expunged; and until it is far more nearly eliminated than this Commission—or any fair man—could find today, how can that great commitment of money and effort here recommended even be approached, much less made?

The choice is ours—here in Springfield as well as around the rest of the nation—whether to believe and pursue the American dream and with the black man's help try to make it viable for him—or dash it on the rocks of prejudice and poverty. The Kerner Commission reaches a similar conclusion:

* This is our basic conclusion: Our nation is moving toward two societies, one black, one white—separate and unequal.

The choice is ours: to release the *full* creative potential of the former repressor as well as the formerly repressed; or to continue in the ways in which we were conditioned—to continue on a collision course with the blacks, for they will no longer accept the ways in which they were conditioned. The Introduction to the Kerner Report is relevant here:

> * The rioters are the personification of the nation's greatest shame, of its deepest failure, of its greatest challenge. They will not go away. They can only be repressed or conceded their humanity, and the choice is not theirs to make. They can only force it upon the rest of us, and what this Report insists upon is that they are already doing it, and intend to keep on.

Finally, the conclusion of the Kerner Commission Report is a meaningful way to conclude the present report.

> * One of the first witnesses to be invited to appear before this Commission was Dr. Kenneth B. Clark, a distinguished and perceptive scholar. Referring to the reports of earlier riot commissions, he said:
>
> > I read that report . . . of the 1919 riot in Chicago, and it is as if I were reading the report of the investigating committee on the Harlem riot of '35, the report of the investigating committee on the Harlem riot of '43, the report of the McCone Commission on the Watts riot.
> >   I must again in candor say to you members of this Commission—it is a kind of Alice in Wonderland—with the same moving picture reshown over and over again, the same analysis, the same recommendations, and the same inaction.
>
> * These words come to our minds as we conclude this report.
> * We have provided an honest beginning. We have learned much. But we have uncovered no startling truths, no unique insights, no simple solutions. The destruction and the bitterness of racial disorder, the harsh polemics of black revolt and white repression have been seen and heard before in this country.
> * It is time now to end the destruction and the violence, not only in the streets of the ghetto but in the lives of people.

This might have been written in Springfield, Massachusetts, in 1969. This might have been written in hundreds of communities, large and small, around the country—before and after 1969 and 1970.

PRINCIPLES OF SOCIAL FAILURE

Put another way, the cycle of social failure may be summarized in principle form. The general principle of social failure is as follows: *If you want to initiate the cycle of social failure and create irreparable cleavage between humans, treat groups differentially in terms of the opportunity and justice provided them.* A number of specific principles may be summarized as follows:

The first principle of social failure: If you want one group of humans to take full advantage of another group, provide the dimensions which enable the former group to condition the latter to experience themselves and behave as if they were inferior.

The second principle of social failure: If you want to intensify the level of deprivation experienced by one group, provide the conditions for the other groups to intensify the level of exploitation of that group.

The third principle of social failure: If you want one group to experience a heightened and intensified level of frustration, provide the conditions for the other groups to periodically raise and dash that group's hopes and plans.

The fourth principle of social failure: If you want one group to engage in spontaneous eruptions of aggressive behavior, provide the conditions for the other groups to frustrate that group consistently over an extended period of time.

The fifth principle of social failure: If you want one group to explode in uncontained fury, provide the conditions which enable the other groups not to act upon the grievances of the first group.

The sixth principle of social failure: If you want to perpetuate the cycle of social failure, provide the conditions which enable the other groups to engage in repressive behavior toward the first group.

We Americans in 1971 are at the fourth stage of the cycle of social failure, the phase of inactivity, the phase of unresponsiveness to the grievances that constitute the sources of aggressive behavior. We are about to enter—again—the fifth phase of social failure, although many people have, in their minds, already skipped to the sixth and final phase.

By our inactivity and unresponsiveness we have given permission to the aggrieved group to engage in explosive behavior. Indeed, we have elicited this behavior knowingly. However, in order to do so we must have prepared ourselves for the final phase, the repressive phase which completes the cycle, initiating once again the necessary conditioning that accompanies repression.

Many persons in power, then, have bypassed the fifth and explosive phase, have already anticipated its terror, have already discounted its ravages. This is why in many communities, such as ours, the only organized and systematic plan of action which the political powers have involves how to employ repressive forces in the event of extreme violence and civil disorder:

They have no plan to prevent the crises.
They have no plan to anticipate the crises.
They have no plan to alleviate the crises.
They have only a plan to suppress the crisis.

They have no plan for opportunity.
They have no plan for equality.
They have no plan for justice.
They have only a plan for repression.

What the authorities, with all their intelligence, have failed to gauge is the intensity of the black man's fury, the depth of his hatred, the completeness of his commitment. What the authorities have failed to estimate is the intelligence of the black man in anticipating the failures of aimless destruction, in organizing for one common and final aim: the destruction of the obstacle to his emergence, to his wholeness, to his life. What the authorities have failed to realize is that there are many who have chosen to die quickly rather than slowly, for from the day they are born they are dying in America.

The price of unactualized resources and lost lives will be high, tragically so—all the more when we consider the real potentialities of man, black and white—all the more when we consider the real opportunities for man, black and white—in America in the 1970s.

There can be no victory.
This is a conflict which the black American cannot survive.
This is a conflict from which the white American cannot recover.

The real issue is whether the white man's own conditioned superiority is so deeply ingrained as to make him his own slave rather than his own master, for *only he* can break free of the vicious, inevitability of the cycle of social failure.

There is a history of man that supersedes the color of his skin. It has a tendency to repeat itself with unhealthy people.

If we turn to those restrictions that apply only to certain classes of society, we meet with a state of things which is flagrant and which has always been recognized. It is to be expected that these underprivileged classes will envy the favoured ones their privileges and will do all they can to free themselves from their own surplus of privation. Where this is not possible, a permanent measure of discontent will persist within the culture concerned and this can lead to dangerous revolts. If, however, a culture has not got beyond a point at which the satisfaction of one portion of its participants depends upon the suppression of another, and perhaps larger, portion—and this is the case in all present day cultures—it is understandable that the suppressed people should develop an intense hostility towards a culture whose existence they make possible by their work, but in whose wealth they have too small a share. In such conditions an internalization of the cultural prohibitions among the suppressed people is not to be expected. On the contrary, they are not prepared to acknowledge the prohibitions, they are intent on destroying the culture itself, and possibly even on doing away with the postulates on which it is based. . . . It goes without saying that a civilization which leaves so large a number of its participants unsatisfied and drives them into revolt neither has nor deserves the prospect of a lasting existence (Freud, 1964).

REFERENCES

Bennett, L., Jr. *Before the Mayflower: A history of the Negro in America.* Baltimore: Penguin, 1966.

Berkowitz, L. *Aggression: A social-psychological analysis.* New York: McGraw-Hill, 1962.

Clark, K. *Dark ghetto.* New York: Harper & Row, 1965.

Dollard, J. *Frustration and aggression.* New Haven: Yale University Press, 1939.

Freud, S. *The future of an illusion.* (Rev. ed.) Garden City, N.Y.: Anchor Books, 1964.

Himmelweit, H. Frustration and aggression: A review of recent experimental work. In T. H. Pear (Ed.), *Psychological factors of peace and war.* New York: Philosophical Library, 1950.

National Advisory Commission, *Report on civil disorders.* New York: Bantam Books, 1968.

Scott, J. P. *Aggression.* Chicago: University of Chicago Press, 1958.

Stampp, K. M. *The peculiar institution* (1956). Cited in L. Bennett, Jr. *Before the Mayflower: A history of the Negro in America.* Baltimore: Penguin, 1966.

CHAPTER 3

Sources of Social Failure

Social failures are educational failures. Just as our educational institutions, from the most basic grammar schools to the most extensive universities, private as well as public, take the major credit for the technological advances of our time, so must they also assume the major burden of responsibility for the social problems of our time. Discriminatory practices—whether in housing and employment, police and judicial practices, credit and shopping practices, government and political practices—have as their source discriminatory practices in education. The teachers, schools, and systems serve as models of discriminatory practices for other institutions to emulate.

BLACK AND WHITE IN EDUCATION

The crises in racial relations in every major northern city did not begin with recent outbreaks of violence. The crises in racial relations have deep roots in this country, beginning with the invention of the cotton gin, which put an end to previously harmonious relations between races. The economic revolution in cotton and other commodities gave birth to a new conditioning process. The new conditioning process took the form of education or lack of it: lack of it or poor quality of it for the blacks and poor whites, relatively superior education for most whites.

The educational systems of this country have constituted the core of this new conditioning process. They have systematically conditioned attitudes and behaviors of inferiority in blacks. They have systematically conditioned attitudes and behaviors of superiority in whites. The school system of any one community simply has its own version of this conditioning process.

This conditioning process which has gone under the guise of an educational program has cost the United States the rich talents, growth, and full potential of whites as well as blacks, but most assuredly blacks.

The conditioning process begins even before the child enters school. It begins with the deprivation that attends poverty. It begins with the poor health and inadequate diets of the parents. It continues with the poor health and inadequate diets of the children and later their children.

The brains and bodies of millions of black children are damaged by hunger and the lack of the proper kinds of food (Special Report, *Springfield Union,* 1970). The intellectual development of these children is further retarded by a lack of stimulation in the home—the absence of simple stimuli such as toys and books contribute to this retardation. When the lack of proper medical care and other disabilities are added to these crippling liabilities, the life prospects of the children are pathetic.

The report of a team of nutritionists and psychologists to the American Association for the Advancement of Science (1969) attests to these handicaps. An examination of several hundred unselected black infants in Mississippi indicated that their developmental IQs averaged 117 compared with a norm of 100 for white children in America. With the natural relationship of physical and mental functionality, the generations of breeding for physical functionality may, in fact, have produced a potentially superior person in the American black. However, by the time the children were of school age, their superior capacities had been stunted. Their IQs had dropped to 86, which meant that upon entering school they were already relatively inferior intellectually.

During the early years, so critical to a child's intellectual, social, emotional, motivational, and physical growth, the black child and the poor child are already undergoing a systematic conditioning process to develop their inferiority. Now, we can say that some of these conditions are out of our control. But they aren't! There is no excuse whatsoever for these conditions of deprivation and loss of lives—actualized and physical—in twentieth-century America.

But what of the schools over which we have control? What happens to the child when he enters school?

Let us look briefly at a sampling of the results of studies of the effects of education upon minority groups. It is abundantly clear from the data that our schools have done nothing to counteract these handicaps. Indeed, they have compounded the handicaps.

The schools have failed to effectively teach lower-class black students the basic skills which middle-class pupils learn readily. While the initial differences are small—in spite of all of the aforementioned liabilities—characteristically over the course of schooling the black students fall further and further behind normal achievement levels for their age groups. They may never learn to read effectively. They tend to achieve lower and lower intelligence quotients over the course of their schooling.

The effects of education in the urban North underscore these findings. For example, in the metropolitan Northeast black students on the average begin first grade with somewhat lower scores on standard achievement tests than white students, are about 1.6 grades behind by the sixth grade, and have fallen

3.3 grades behind white students by the twelfth grade (Coleman, 1966). The failure of the public schools to equip these students with basic verbal skills is reflected in their performance on the Selective Service Mental Test, where the failure rate for blacks is approximately two-thirds, whereas for whites it is about one-fifth (National Advisory Commission, 1968).

The result is that many more black than white students drop out of school. In the metropolitan North and West blacks are more than three times as likely as white students to drop out of school by age 16–17 (Coleman, 1966). As reflected by the high unemployment rate for graduates of ghetto schools and even higher proportions of employed workers who are in low-skilled, low-paid jobs, the National Advisory Commission Report suggests that many of the blacks who do graduate are not equipped to enter the normal job market, and have great difficulty securing employment.

Many sources of these effects, including the effects of segregation, the teachers themselves, overcrowding, poor facilities and inadequate curricula, the ghetto environment and poor community-school relations, have been cited and supported with evidence. All of these conditions are certainly contributory. Indeed, *they comprise significant sources of effect in the overall design for the systematic conditioning of black pupils.*

The assumption that blacks are innately not disposed toward utilizing even an effective educational experience (Jensen, 1969; Garrett, 1968) is strongly held in many quarters. As we have learned in our basic psychology courses, however, almost any argument that can be employed for the effects of heredity can be employed for the effects of environment and, to be sure, vice versa. "Racial discrimination clearly extends into the womb in the form of malnutrition and inadequate prenatal care; and no genetic mechanism is needed to account for systematic differences in cognitive capacity, since the differences in the way symbols are used in the homes of the very poor and of the middle-class are so great as to be perhaps ineradicable" (Friedenberg, 1969). Perhaps the most amazing thing in this regard, then, is that despite the conditions of deprivation and exploitation that disadvantage the black child the differences in aptitude and achievement are so small at the beginning of schooling.

Solely with regard to the argument of innate differences in the learning capacities of white and black children, which when extended to its logical conclusion argues against change of any kind, the perspective of history and geography would again be useful (Bennett, 1966). The fact is that the origin of the civilization which Europeans inherited began in black Africa, and this accounts in large part for the recent emphasis upon formal study of black history as a source of racial pride. Africans were in an advanced stage of civilization when many of our European ancestors were still living in stone huts.

In any event, what is perhaps most important is not whether there are innate differences but the fact that teachers as well as everybody else respond to black students as if they did not have the intellectual resources of white students. *The teachers and counselors respond to black students as if Jensen and Garrett were correct!*

In this regard the studies of Leacock (1968) and Rosenthal and Jacobson (1968) are distressing. Leacock found that lower-class black children in grammar school were treated consistently as unable to learn, groomed to accept their basic inferiority and their attendant status and level. *The level of intellectual achievement was lowest in those classes in which the teachers were kindest and most casual with the children.* "In the low-income Negro fifth grade those about whom the teacher felt positive or neutral had an average I.Q. score that was almost ten points lower than those toward whom she felt negative!" Rosenthal and Jacobson, in turn, reported on the effects of teacher expectations on pupil performance and noted: "The more the upper-track children of the experimental group gained in I.Q., the more favorably they were treated by their teachers. The more the lower-track children of the control group gained in I.Q., the more unfavorably they were viewed by their teachers." Thus, we consider the proposition that *teachers dislike the brighter black students who challenge their functionally autonomous perceptions and self-fulfilling prophesies.*

There are other variables that enter into the total picture and these revolve around the issue of teacher competency. It is our hypothesis throughout that helpees move toward the level of development of their helpers. That is, in school, the students move toward the level of functioning and knowledgeability of their teachers. In this regard, the recent research by Brenton (1969) is distressing. His work suggests that nearly two-thirds of our teachers score lower than the junior high school level on proficiency tests *in the teacher's specialty subject or area of assumed competency.* In effect, they could not pass their own exams! If nearly two-thirds do so poorly in general, how much larger a percentage do poorly in ghetto and predominantly black schools where it has been a long-standing tradition to assign the poorest teachers? In the context of the student's convergence upon the teacher's level of competency, it is understandable that many high school graduates do not achieve beyond the eighth or ninth grade level. We must hold our colleges of education responsible for producing people who are not only ignorant of the inner-city child but ignorant of the subject matter which they are getting paid to teach.

The burden of responsibility, then, is upon the level of functioning of the developers and implementers of the educational system: the administrators and supervisors as well as the teachers and counselors. In this context, Coleman's controversial finding that neither procedure, nor the class size, nor the quality of educational facilities is consistently associated with superior educational achievement is consistent with our belief that quality of learning is a function of quality of teaching; that is, the quality of the person and the level of understanding which he offers, not just his knowledgeability. The finding that those black students who were enrolled in well-integrated schools did significantly better than those in segregated schools, whatever the characteristics of the school, may be most meaningfully understood with the knowledge that the teachers of these well-integrated schools were superior to those of the segregated schools and, accordingly, expected and, indeed, demanded higher levels of performance.

Where, we ask, are the schools which have provided such a disservice to all of our populations? Why, they are no further away than the nearest neighborhood school.

The following white-black paper examines the effects of our neighborhood schools. Unfortunately, it followed a period of racial unrest and violence in the schools. Unheeded, it anticipates a period of greater racial unrest and violence in the schools and elsewhere.

PROJECT 2
Conditions of Educational Failure*

The school crisis in Springfield, Massachusetts, did not begin at Technical High School on November 5, 1969. The school crisis in Springfield began when each black child, and concomitantly the white child, entered formal schooling. Whatever his adjustment upon entering school, from that point forward the black child learned in a very systematic fashion that he was an inferior element in a white system. The process is subtle, so subtle in operation that its effects are hardly noticeable immediately. One Technical High School student described the process in this manner: "It is as if they have asked me to carry an additional feather upon my back for each day I attend school. I now feel that I am carrying a ton of feathers, and I don't know how to get rid of them. But they're not mine."

Let us study the effects of education in the Springfield school system.

THE NEGATIVE EFFECTS OF SCHOOLING UPON BLACK PUPILS

It is a difficult proposition to accept the validity of standardized achievement tests for black pupils. It is difficult for a variety of reasons including the following: the fact that many items on the tests are biased to favor whites; the fact that the norms of most of these tests are based upon white norm groups; the fact that white examiners in predominantly white school systems administered these tests; the bias due to cross-sectional sampling of different levels of maturity.

However, if we accept the validity of these tests for reflecting the academic achievement of black as well as white students, a more distressing picture emerges. The black students demonstrate progressively lower levels of achievement when compared to their white counterparts. Let us look more closely at these effects. In so doing, they may be portrayed diagramatically (see Figure 3-1.)

*Reprinted from a mimeographed white-black paper (December 26, 1969) on the school crisis in Springfield, Mass., by Robert R. Carkhuff and Bernard G. Berenson. Excerpts from this paper were printed in the *Springfield Union* newspaper in February 1970.

Figure 3–1
Illustration of progressively greater discrepancy in white and black pupil achievement with time in school.

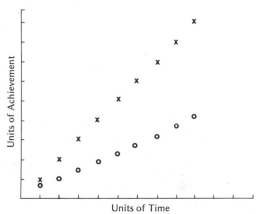

Key: x = White Students
        o = Black Students

As we can see in Figure 3–1 the black pupil enters school at levels of achievement that, while they may be slightly lower, are not *functionally* different from those of white pupils. However, with increased schooling the black students function at progressively lower levels of achievement until by the time they enter high school their achievement levels are a level or two behind those of white pupils.

Let us look in detail at one cross-sectional analysis of three predominantly black grammar schools in the Springfield school system. In schools ranging from 65 to 90 percent black the following picture emerges from the third to fifth grade level:

> On the arithmetic section of the Iowa achievement tests the children from these schools are already approximately one-half grade behind city-wide norms by grade 3; approximately three-fourths of a grade behind by grade 4; approximately one year behind by grade 5.
>
> On the reading section the findings are similar. The inner-city school children are approximately one-half year behind by grade 3; approximately six-tenths of a year behind by grade 4; approximately two-thirds of a year behind by grade 5.
>
> These differences are underscored by the fact that *the students of Springfield, Mass., both black and white, deviate negatively progressively from national norms so that by grade 5 the black pupils deviate more than a year from national norms on both arithmetic and reading.*[1]

---

[1] Since the black-white paper was published, further evidence concerning the educational scene in Springfield has been accumulated. According to data supplied by the superintendent of schools (*Springfield Daily News* and *Springfield Union*, July 1970), Springfield school chil-

> *The school system has differentially failed both the white and black students.*

This process continues systematically throughout all years of schooling. Its effects are telling in many ways.

First, the increasingly progressive deviation from the levels of achievement of the white students and, accordingly, from the means at the various grade levels, indicates that relative to their level groups the black pupils have relatively lower and lower standings. This same phenomenon also occurs in IQ testing.

Teacher expectancies for future pupil performance, based in part upon past performance, compound the original difficulties. Teachers expect more from pupils who have achieved the most in the past and expect less from pupils who have achieved the least in the past. In this regard, there is extensive evidence from other quarters to relate teacher expectancies to pupil performance.

---

dren perform at the following grade levels on the Iowa achievement test taken at the end of the school year: children in grade 3 perform at 3 years and 8 months, in grade 5 at 5 years and 4 months, in grade 6 at 6 years and 2½ months, and in grade 8 at 7 years and 9½ months. These results indicate a standing that deteriorates with each year of schooling. Thus, on national norms Springfield public school students drop progressively from the 52nd percentile in third grade to the 27th percentile in eighth grade. Against northeastern norms, the Springfield public school children drop progressively from 52nd percentile in the third grade to the 11th percentile by the eighth grade. Even against the norms of the other large cities (ranging in size from 100,000 to several million), the Springfield public school children drop progressively from the 70th percentile in third grade to the 36th percentile by eighth grade. In the eighth grade, the white school children who constitute 70 percent of the students are functioning at approximately 8 years and 3 months. The nonwhite school children (30 percent, up from 24 percent in 1966, with students of Spanish background constituting less than 2 percent of the total number of school children) are functioning at approximately 7 years and 0 months—more than a year behind white children. To attain the 50th percentile at end of year testing, national norms require a performance at 8 years and 6 months and northeastern norms at 8 years and 8 months. This means that by the eighth grade white school children in Springfield are functioning at approximately the 37th percentile (national norms) and the 19th percentile (northeastern norms), while black school children are functioning at the 9th percentile and 1st percentile respectively. Thus, children who begin school at levels higher than more than half of the school children in the country or in the region are functioning by eighth grade at levels lower than the great majority of school children around the country and in the region. Projected scores for the deterioration effect from first to twelfth grade suggest a still more intensified deterioration effect. In addition, the scores represent a drop from testing five years earlier, where the third grade scores for all school children placed in the 70th percentile on both national and northeastern norms and in the 80th percentile on large-city norms. In summary this suggests that the Springfield educational system has served neither black nor white school children. It demonstrates a progressively increasing achievement deficit with each year of school for all of its school children when compared to all norm groups. In addition, while its white school children fall further behind all norms with each year of schooling, the black school children fall even further behind the white. Finally, while there is a deterioration with each year of school relative to other communities around the country (including larger urban communities), there has also been a progressive decline in standing over the last five years.

The progressive deterioration in achievement of black pupils relative to white pupils is reflected in other areas such as percentage of membership in auxiliary, or special, classes.

> At the junior high level, black pupils comprise nearly one-half of the students in these special classes. By high school, black students comprise approximately three-fourths of the auxiliary class members. Thus, since 1029 black high school students comprise 15 percent of 6778 total high school students, by high school, three-fourths of the auxiliary class is drawn from 15 percent of the population.
>
> This occurs in spite of a dropout rate approximately double that of the white students, a dropout rate which eliminates many of the lowest-ranking black students from eligibility for auxiliary classes.

The dropout and the auxiliary class are the logical outcome of a sequence of failing experiences for many black students.

These progressively deteriorating performances of black students are due to a variety of sources.

THE SOURCES OF NEGATIVE EFFECTS

The sources of the burdens for the black student are many and varied, but for each there is extensive evidence in the research literature.

First, the slightly lower but not functionally different initial performances of black pupils when compared to those of white pupils may, in addition to the testing factors already noted, be accounted for by a number of additional conditions. Perhaps most important, culturally different environments activate different aspects of the neural learning centers of the child. The results of early differences in experience, then, are early differences in the physiological makeup of the child.

In addition, psychological factors interact with the physiological factors. Upon entry into the school system the black child becomes aware that some of his unique cultural learnings are not valued in a white-dominated system. This experience is increasingly intensified over the course of schooling when the initial learning dispositions of the white pupil are reinforced and the initial learning dispositions of the black pupil are not reinforced.

Most blatant here are the differences between responsive and initiative behavior. With the white pupil and the teacher fully tuned to each other's needs, the white pupil can be immediately responsive to the teacher's wishes, whereas the black child may not. In this context, then, the behavior initiated by the white child will be understood clearly by himself and the teacher. The behavior initiated by the black child, in turn, may not be understood by the teacher and, accordingly, will not be rewarded, thus driving a deeper wedge into the child, splitting his, so to speak, "cultural self" from his, so to speak, "educational self."

If these initial but functionally insignificant differentials are not attended, they compound themselves with other factors to contribute to the total differential over the course of schooling. In other words, even under equal treatment in school, the average black student may over time demonstrate a continuing discrepancy in performance due to different cultural experiences during the preschool period when compared to the average white student. However, there is no systematic evidence to indicate that this discrepancy would be functionally significant.

All of these factors account in part for the increasing discrepancy between the performances of black and white students and interact with teacher and helper level of interpersonal functioning and communication, attitudes and behavior, expectancies and competencies.

There are a number of other sources of negative effects which may be summarized under the effects of the race of the helper.

First of all, almost all of the data which we have on black children are contaminated by the fact that white examiners have obtained the information or elicited the responses from the children. There is evidence to indicate that black children respond differentially to white and black examiners, in general tending to achieve higher scores on achievement and IQ tests with black examiners than with white examiners.

Second, the results of the educational process or classroom teaching, only partially based upon the data obtained from testing, are contaminated by the fact that white teachers who cannot communicate fully with the black children conduct the classes. There is evidence to indicate that black children respond differently to white and black teachers, with those black children deviating upwardly from the teachers' expectations for scholastic performance being viewed unfavorably and treated negatively, while those black children who met the teachers' expectations were viewed favorably and treated positively.

Finally, the results of the various guidance and counseling procedures designed to ameliorate the difficulties produced by the school system are further contaminated by the fact that white counselors who cannot communicate effectively with the black students conduct the counseling. There is evidence to indicate that black children respond differently to white and black counselors, with black students being retarded or deteriorating in their emotional and intellectual growth when treated by white counselors who did not understand them.

Together, these sources of differential effects summate to produce negative effects upon black students. In this regard, it should be emphasized that *all black helpers are not automatically effective. They are not. In addition, this is not to say that white helpers cannot be effective. Some are and others can be trained to be so.*

Deteriorative effects upon black students are largely a function of the low level of understanding and communication of this understanding by the helpers, whether they are white or black. It is simply that many of the white helpers who dominate the school system have great difficulty in "tuning in" on the black students. If they cannot "tune in," they cannot develop courses of action to ameliorate the difficulties involved.

The key to effective teaching and helping is systematic selection and systematic training based upon an operationalization of the pupil benefits which we are trying to achieve. In this regard, it is clear that the colleges which sponsor and certify the teachers and counselors are most responsible for the prevailing level of ineptitude on the part of credentialed professionals.

SUMMARY AND CONCLUSIONS

Let us review these findings. The black pupil in Springfield, Massachusetts, enters school with a slightly lower developmental IQ, although he is not functionally different from his white counterpart, with the slight difference due perhaps to the disadvantages of poverty. With time and "education" the black pupil falls further and further behind. He achieves less in critical academic skills than white students. He tends to drop out of school more than white students. The greatest part of special sections for slow learners are drawn from the ranks of black students.

Thus far, we have dealt primarily with the intellectual scars upon the black child. The emotional scars, and now the physical scars, are just as great. Emotionally, we have scarred the black student by conditioning him to experience himself as inferior to the white on critical task performances. Now we have scarred the black student physically, by bringing him to form mobs for purposes of physical violence and by making him the victim of other mobs formed for purposes of physical violence.

In addition, we might add emphatically, in designing and implementing a system that provides advantages for the white student we have scarred him. We have scarred the white student intellectually in that we have not asked him for optimum performance and actualization of his intellect. We have scarred the white student emotionally by conditioning him to experience himself as superior to persons of different races and colors. And, now, we have scarred the white student physcially by causing him to form mobs for the purpose of physical violence and by making him the victim of other mobs formed for purposes of physical violence.

By the time he gets to high school, then, the black student, already two or more years behind on the average, is seized with a sense of frustration and powerlessness. He feels the weight of the "feathers" which he has accumulated. He knows fully now that the educational family is not his family. At the outbreak of violence at Technical High School, while black students constituted 15 percent of the overall total of high school students, only 8 of 363 teachers or 2 percent were black, and several of these acknowledged little or no disposition to or communication with the black students. The black student has few, if any, constructive black models available to him.

Indeed, he has never been a member of the educational family. As with any family, the child who is told that he is a member but is not treated as such rebels. He rebels against things that have held him back—often things which he himself does not fully understand—but he rebels. He strikes out at the family that has lied to him. He strikes out at its parents. He strikes out at its members.

When he strikes out he finds out just how much of an outsider he is to this educational family. The teacher-parents are threatened by the unrest. True to form, they are hostile, fearful, anxious, and view the black students' demands as a defiance of authority. They respond with suspension and tightened discipline to avoid the exposure of the fact that there never was any love for these members of this family. Predictably, they blame outside agitators, overcrowdedness, the need for more money, and now drugs. They advocate security guards, the employment of which serves only to heighten school tensions and increases the polarizations already in effect. *These adults "shape up" the children, black and white, to violence in order to avoid the exposure of their own incompetence.* Battle lines are drawn and more conflict ensues. The effects of the battle serve only to reinforce the frustration of the black students. Force is employed primarily against them. Arrests are made primarily from their ranks. Hatred becomes a fire smoldering beneath the surface, exploding periodically in greater and greater intensity.

We can only assume that the adults responsible for the conduct of the city and its educational system are aware of these outcomes. They cannot placate the students by simply assigning as counselors at the high school level five black teachers who were neither systematically selected nor trained for effectiveness. They cannot ease racial tensions by simply creating a third lunch session, for that is clearly treating symptoms rather than sources. They cannot eliminate frustration by increasing it with increased discipline and law and order platforms. They must know this and, accordingly, accept the full responsibilities for the consequences of their efforts.

A law and order response is only justified in a system which has been deeply sensitive and responsive to the needs of young growing people of all races. It is only justified in a system dedicated to competence, and intolerant of ineffectuals.

It has not been the purpose of this report, then, to make specific recommendations; although a number of recommendations, including in general the systematic selection and training of white and black helpers and including in particular a massive infusion of black helpers into the system and a redefinition and reorganization of the teacher and counselor preparation programs of our colleges, are apparent. Other recommendations have been made on numerous occasions in the past.

It is the purpose of this report to point up the need to rectify the sources of the current difficulties.

We can only conclude that the school crisis did not begin at Technical High School on Wednesday, November 5, 1969. It began when each child, black and white, but particularly black, entered the school system. It began in discriminatory practices in housing, police, and judicial practices, credit and shopping practices, and government and political practices as well.

At best, we conclude that the black student is not serviced by our current educational system.

At worst, we must view the educational programs as part of a systematic program to condition black students to achieve less and less relative to white students.

BLACK AND WHITE IN HELPING

The most obvious dimensions of the conditioning process are the racial differences of the conditioner, the white teacher, and the conditioned, the black student.

The differential effects of helper race and other characteristics upon helpee performance in different helping situations are vivid. Not only in teaching but in guidance, counseling and psychotherapeutic activities, testing, interviewing and information gathering, and even experimental situations the negative effects of white helpers upon black helpees is demonstrable.

The constant thread woven through all of these studies is the conditioned defensiveness of the black in a relationship with whites. Due to years of destructive experiences with whites, it is hypothesized, the black enters the situation with a set of attitudes and behaviors, which if not attended, have a deleterious effect upon both process and outcome. In actuality, we believe this theme represents an overemphasis upon the descriptions of the feelings of the black and an evasion of assessments of the efficacy of helper training and practice in dealing with the relevant variables for black people (Banks, 1971).

Let us look at the evidence in the projects assessing these effects. In experimental task performance situations, black experimenters were generally more effective than white experimenters with black children, although physiological responsiveness was found to be affected more by the subjects' racial attitudes than by the experimenters' race (Sattler, 1969). Nevertheless, the differential effects hold.

In interviewing and information gathering, the great majority of studies indicate that the interviewers' race affects the respondents' replies (Banks, 1971; Sattler, 1969). Respondents emit responses that conform to existing racial stereotypes to an interviewer of the opposite race in order to avoid generating threat or hostility. In the solicitation of attitude and preference variables similar findings emerge with experimenter race affecting a number of subtle attitudes and preferences such as the preference for same-race figures with same-race rather than with opposite-race questioners. In general, the social class status of black and white respondents is related to their replies, with lower-class respondents more sensitive to the interviewers' race than middle- and upper-class respondents. Williams' (1964) conclusion from the social class data is also appropriate for the ethnic group data: "The greater the disparities among status characteristics between interviewer and respondent, the greater is the pressure felt by the respondent to bias his response."

In the areas of testing so critical to education and the development of human resources both personality and intelligence effects are noted. In general, black examinees express more test anxiety and less hostility to white than to black examiners (Baratz, 1967; Katz, Robinson, Epps, and Wally, 1964). Perhaps black examinees avoid expression of their feelings to white examiners because of the threat involved and, accordingly, feel it is more socially acceptable to express anxiety than to express hostility.

A number of investigators have emphasized that racial differences are critical to intelligence testing, indicating that they lead to examinee fear, suspicion, verbal constriction, strained and unnatural reactions, and defensively poor performances. What is most clear is that the black, when working with a white examiner, is concerned about other things: he cannot see the testing as a means to an end and is more concerned with how to work around or even against the examiner than he is with how to work for himself. Pettigrew (1964) emphasizes not only the relationship differences but also the blacks' perception of the testing situation: blacks perceive the test situation as a means for a white person to get ahead in society, but not as a means for their own advantage. In addition, much of the anxiety and unproductive behavior of black examinees may be due to thoughts about invidious comparisons of their performance with that of white students (Katz, Epps, and Axelson, 1963).

In counseling and psychotherapeutic relationships, the most intense and intimate of all interpersonal processes, the results are consistent. Clearly, as a consequence of racial and cultural differences between counselor and counselee, different interpretations of different situations may be made. Unfortunately, the recommendations that the counselors study more closely the cultural background of minority group counselees comes largely from theoretical literature.

The naturalistic work of Phillips (1960), who studied white counselors who had failed and black counselors who had succeeded with black counselees, is an exception. He concluded that black students may be submissive, suspicious, or even hostile while working with white counselors while being free of these feelings with black counselors. Heine's (1950) interpretation of the difficulty for white therapists working with blacks is that the blacks act out the black stereotype created by "the man" in an attempt to cope with the attendant anxiety.

From the other side of the desk, the therapists' difficulty in coping with their own attitudes toward blacks is apparent (Adams, 1950; Bernard, V. W., 1953). Yamamoto, James, Bloombaum, and Hatten (1967), in another naturalistic study, note that low-prejudiced white therapists have longer therapeutic contacts with blacks than high-prejudiced white therapists. Thus, the attention which the counselee receives is a function of the therapist's prejudicial attitudes.

These same themes of the negative effects of race on outcome have been reported in clinical diagnosis (Chess, Clark, and Thomas, 1958) and in dealing with the parents of children diagnosed as emotionally disturbed (Kahn, Buckmueller, and Gildea, 1951). Unfortunately, the evidence is again largely anecdotal.

Indeed, the preponderance of theoretical and anecdotal literature pointing in the direction of the effects of helper race upon helpee process and outcome sets the stage for the only two legitimately experimental studies of helping that meet both the criteria of meaning and rigor.

In almost all of the literature on helping, the effects of social class (Bernard, H. W., 1963; Hollingshead and Redlich, 1958; Jessor, 1956; Moore, Benedek, and Wallace, 1963) have been confounded with the effects of race, particularly in the common instance of the white helper working with the black helpee. Thus, the effects of either of these characteristics, race and social class, may be accounted for by the other. The following study was designed to partition out the effects of helper race and social class upon helpee therapeutic process movement.

PROJECT 3
Effects of Helper Race and Social Class*

The effect of the social class of the counselor or therapist upon the therapeutic movement and outcome of the patient in therapy has been recognized in the psychological literature. It has been suggested that lower-class patients are not amenable to treatment by therapists who, by the usual criteria of education and vocation, are members of higher socioeconomic classes. The assumption is that the social class differences present a communication barrier which does not allow facilitative interpersonal processes to take place.

Similarly, racial effects upon outcome have been hypothesized in the areas of therapy, test examination, and education. Typically, the inhibiting effects of white counselors upon the responses of Negroes are noted.

The effects upon patient process movement of each of these therapist characteristics may be accounted for by the other characteristic. Thus, the effects of social class may account for what have been presumed to be racial

*Reprinted in part with permission from the *Journal of Consulting Psychology,* 1967, 31, 632–634, where it first appeared as "Differential Effects of Therapist Race and Social Class upon Patient Depth of Self-exploration in the Initial Clinical Interview," by Robert R. Carkhuff and Richard Pierce.

effects, and racial effects may, in some instances, have contributed to studies establishing social class as a significant source of effect. The example of the white upper-class therapist offering treatment to the lower-class Negro is a situation frequently replicated in our outpatient and inpatient services.

The present study was designed to ferret out the differential effects of (a) the race and (b) the social class of the therapist upon patient depth of self-exploration, a critical index of patient therapeutic process involvement and a significant correlate of positive therapeutic outcome.

METHOD

Four lay counselors, who had completed a mental health training program, were functioning at high levels of empathy, positive regard, and genuineness. With group therapy patients, these counselors had elicited a therapeutic change significantly greater than that demonstrated by a control group of patients. The counselors were: (a) an upper-class white, (b) an upper-class Negro, (c) a lower-class white, and (d) a lower-class Negro. Thus, all lay counselors had (a) similar training, (b) similar kinds of therapeutic experience, and (c) had demonstrated no significant differences in their levels of counselor-offered conditions as measured by rating scales of empathy, positive regard, genuineness, and the depth of self-exploration elicited in patients in clinical interviews. A two-factor index of social class involving the educational and vocational (professional or nonprofessional) level of the counselors and their spouses was employed for the counselors, while only educational level was considered for the inpatients. Study beyond the high school level was operationally defined as upper class for both counselors and patients. The upper-class white counselor was 35 years of age and had completed 3 years of graduate study in education. While she was a volunteer worker at the time of this study, she had previously been employed as a teacher. The upper-class Negro counselor was 38 years of age, had completed 2 years of undergraduate college, and was employed as a physical therapist. The lower-class white counselor was 45 years of age, had completed high school, and was employed as a hospital attendant. The lower-class Negro counselor was 50 years old, had completed high school, and was employed as a hospital attendant. All were female. The husbands of the upper-class counselors were employed in professional capacities, while the husbands of the lower-class counselors were employed in semiskilled occupations.

A Latin-square design was replicated across four different groups of four hospitalized mental patients: (a) four upper-class white patients, (b) four upper-class Negro patients, (c) four lower-class white patients, and (d) four lower-class Negro patients. All 16 patients were female with diagnoses of schizophrenia. The upper-class white patients averaged 14.5 years of schooling; the upper-class Negroes 14 years; lower-class whites 9.75

years; and lower-class Negroes, 9.5 years. Overall, the patients averaged 42 years of age and 4 years of institutionalization with no significant differences between any of the four groups. All therapists and all patients were Southerners.

Each counselor saw each patient in a design counterbalanced to control for the effects of order. In order to control for counselor fatigue factors, each group of four patients was seen 1 week apart. The patients rotated to the counselors' rooms, and each 1-hour interview was recorded. All counselors began each session encouraging the patient in an open-ended fashion to discuss "whatever is important" to the patient "at this moment in time."

Six 4-minute excerpts were randomly selected from each of the 64 recorded clinical interviews and rated on the scale "depth of self-exploration in interpersonal processes" by two experienced raters trained in rating patient self-exploration. Pearson correlations yielded intrarater reliabilities over 1 week of .80 and .88 and an interrater reliability of .78. The five-point scale ranged from the lowest level, Level 1, where "the second person does not discuss personally relevant material, either because he has had no opportunity to do so, or because he is actively evading the discussion even when it is introduced by the first person," to Level 5, where "the second person actively and spontaneously engages in an inward probing to newly discover feelings or experiences about himself and his world."

RESULTS

Race and social class of both patient and therapist were significant sources of effect, and the interaction between the patient and therapist variables was significant. Thus, both racial and class variables have an effect upon patient depth of self-exploration, and the effect of the patient variables is contingent upon the therapist variables.

In general, the ratings of patient self-exploration ranged from Level 1 to Level 3, with an average of slightly under Level 2. Also, in general, the patients most similar to the race and social class of the counselor involved tended to explore themselves most, while patients most dissimilar tended to explore themselves least.

There were no significant effects of the order in which the patients were seen, and the effects of race were not dependent upon the level of social class in both patient and therapist.

DISCUSSION

Both race and social class of both patient and counselor appear to be significant sources of effect upon the depth of self-exploration of patients in initial clinical interviews. As patient depth of self-exploration during early clinical interviews has been highly correlated with outcome indexes of constructive patient change the results have implications for counseling and psychotherapy. For example, increasingly larger numbers of lower-class Negroes are represented in inpatient and outpatient treatment populations, but are very poorly represented on the treatment staffs offering the services. If, indeed, the white upper-class counselors and therapists who are readily available have an inhibiting effect upon the self-exploration of their lower-class Negro patients, then the whole process of rehabilitation and improvement for lower-class Negroes is limited.

The significant finding, for our purposes, was that both race and social class were significant sources of the helpee's ability to involve himself in the helping process. Helpees tended to explore themselves most and to experience themselves most fully when they were interacting with helpers of similar race and social class. The effects of neither race nor social class were accounted for by the other.

Race and social class are characteristics which we cannot do anything about. Training and experience leading to how a person functions in helping are things which we can do a great deal about. Unlike the first study, where helper training and experience were held constant, a second study investigated the differential effects of race and training and background.

PROJECT 4
*Effects of Helper Race and Training**

The retarding effects of counselor race upon the responses of Negroes have been hypothesized in the areas of counseling and psychotherapy, test-examination and education. This study attempted to determine the effects upon eight Negroes in initial clinical interviews of an inexperienced Negro counselor and three white counselors of varying degrees of experience and types of training.

METHOD

Four counselors were involved: Counselor A, an inexperienced 20-year-old Negro senior undergraduate student who had taken only an undergraduate course in "Counseling Theory and Practice" oriented toward counseling as a communication process between two parties to a relationship; Counselor B, a relatively inexperienced 25-year-old white second-year graduate student who had previously seen several clients in a coun-

*Reprinted in part with permission from the *Journal of Clinical Psychology,* 1967, 23, 70–72, where it first appeared as "The Effects of Counselor Race and Training upon Counseling Process with Negro Clients in Initial Interviews," by George Banks, Bernard G. Berenson, and Robert R. Carkhuff.

seling psychology program oriented in the same manner; Counselor C, a relatively experienced, 25-year-old white third-year graduate student in a separate guidance counselor education program of a differing orientation who had had a year of experience in guidance activities but who also had taken the same undergraduate course as the Negro counselor; and Counselor D, a 32-year-old white Ph.D. with eight years' experience from a nationally prominent program with a traditional trait-and-factor counseling system not oriented toward counselor-client differences. The three white counselors were selected by two experienced clinicians to match the personal attractiveness, intelligence, politeness, quietness, and apparent sincerity of the Negro counselor. The Negro counselees included four male and four female undergraduate students at the University of Massachusetts.

In a counterbalanced design, during consecutive weeks, each counselee saw each counselor for an initial clinical interview. Each counselee was given the following instructions: "All of us, in the present or during the past year or so, have had a number of experiences or problems which have been difficult for us. If you feel that the person you will be seeing is helpful, please feel free to discuss these experiences." Most of the problems discussed involved the difficulties in making an adjustment in the educational setting. The counselors were instructed to be as helpful as they could with the counselees. The interviews were recorded, and following each interview the counselees filled out inventories on each counselor and following all interviews answered questions concerning all of the counselors.

Random excerpts were taken from the tapes and rated by trained raters on five 5-point scales assessing the following dimensions of interpersonal functioning which have been related to constructive client changes in counseling and psychotherapy: Counselor empathy *(E)*; counselor respect *(R)*; counselor genuineness *(G)*; counselor concreteness or specificity of expression *(C)*; client depth of self-exploration *(Ex)*. *E* ranges from level 1, where the counselor is unaware or ignorant of even the most conspicuous surface feelings of the counselee to level 5, where the counselor communicates an accurate empathic understanding of the counselee's deepest feelings. *R* ranges from the counselor's clear demonstration of negative regard to his communication of a deep caring for the counselee. *G* varies from the communication of a wide discrepancy between the counselor's experiencing and his verbalizations to his being freely and deeply himself in a nonexploitative relationship. *C* ranges from vague and abstract discussions to direct discussion of specific feelings and experiences. *Ex* ranges from the lowest level, where the counselee does not explore himself at all, to the highest level, where he is searching to discover new feelings concerning himself and his world. The Pearson *r* rate-rerate reliabilities for the two raters involved were as follows: *E*, .99, .96; *R*, .94, .99; *G*, .96, .93; *C*, .93, .99; *Ex*, .79, .99. The intercorrelations between the raters were as follows: *E*, .83; *R*, .95; *G*, .89; *C*, .72; *Ex*, .74.

In addition, a 50-item relationship inventory assessing the counselor's level of functioning and incorporating ten items, half negatively phrased, on each of these dimensions involved was administered to the counselees. Each item had a 6-point scale ranging from "(1) Yes, I feel that it is true" to "(6) No, I feel strongly that it is not true." Finally, following all interviews, the counselees were asked the following questions: (1) Concerning each individual counselor, would you be willing to see him again in counseling? (2) In what order of counseling effectiveness would you rank the counselors involved?

RESULTS

Tape-Ratings of Conditions

There were no significant differences between the levels of the individual facilitative conditions offered by the three counselors with varying degrees of relationship-oriented training (counselors A, B and C). However, all relationship-trained counselors provided significantly higher levels of all facilitative conditions than the traditionally trained counselor (counselor D). Only the differences between counselor C and counselor D on C and Ex did not attain statistical significance at the .05 level. Summarizing the conditions, the counselors ranked in the following manner and with the following overall average: (1) counselor B, 2.28; (2) A, 2.08; (3) C, 1.95; (4) D. 1.61.

Counselee Inventory Assessments of Conditions

Again, on the counselor conditions summed overall, counselors A and B did not differ significantly from each other, and neither differed from counselor C. However, counselors A and C were assessed as functioning at significantly higher levels than counselor D, while counselor B barely missed significant differences when compared to counselor D. The following rank-ordering and average inventory assessments of counselors prevailed: (1) A, 4.35; (2) C, 4.32; (3) B, 4.21; (4) D, 3.95.

Counselee Return

All eight Negro counselees indicated that they would return to see the Negro counselor (A) again. Five counselees said that they would return to see counselor B and three indicated they would return to see counselor C. None of the eight would return to see counselor D.

Counselee Rank-Ordering of Counselors

The counselees' average rank-ordering of the counselors is as follows: (1) B, 1.37; (2) A, 1.88; (3) C, 2.63; (4) D, 4.00.

DISCUSSION

Overall, the following trends are noteworthy. At one extreme, the relatively inexperienced Negro (A) and the relatively inexperienced counselor (B) with training in a program oriented toward attending to differences between counselor and counselees functioned at the highest levels. At the other extreme, the experienced and traditionally trained counselor (D) functioned at the lowest level. The relatively experienced counselor (C) fell in between. The evidence thus suggests that counselor experience *per se* may be independent of counseling effectiveness with Negro counselees. In fact, the most experienced counselor, a respected member of his profession, whose training and orientation did not emphasize attending to important differences between counselor and client in counseling, proved the least effective. Race and type of orientation and training appear more relevant variables.

It is significant that the Negro counselee inventory trends were not as pronounced as the objective tape ratings. Follow-up questioning indicated that the counselees uniformly gave the benefit of the doubt to the "white man." In other words, under the conditions of the research, there was a regression of counselee assessments toward a more socially acceptable mean, a finding which has implications for testing Negroes in studies of Negro-white interactions.

Perhaps most important, all Negro counselees indicated that they would return to see the Negro counselor, while none indicated that they would see the traditional counselor. Further, if the data on the Negro counselor were not considered, 16 of 24, or *two-thirds of the counselees, would not return to see a white counselor for a second session.* In addition, even the most facilitative white counselor was rejected by three counselees, thus suggesting a possible "hard core" of Negroes who would reject all white counselors.

It is noteworthy that the counselees all ranked the traditionally trained and experienced counselor (D) last. However, five of the Negro counselees ranked the relationship-trained counselor (B) first. All of the three Negro counselees who indicated that they would not return to see counselor (B) ranked him second overall, or first among the white counselors. Thus, if the Negroes would be willing to see a white counselor, they would see the counselor with the most training in attending to the conditions of the relationship.

Along with the effects of race, the effects of training in the form of teaching helpers to attend to the relevant variables in helping are demonstrated. That is, although the stated preference of black helpees for black helpers is significant, it is clear that the helpers who were trained to attend to the helpee's frame of reference and other relevant helpee variables were most effective. Later studies (Carkhuff and Banks, 1970) have supported the hypothesis that white helpers who are functioning at high enough levels and who are fully responsive to the black helpees can be as effective or perhaps even more effective, according to the level at which each is functioning, than black helpers.[1] Unfortunately, as we shall see shortly, most professional helpers are not functioning at levels high enough to be effective.

The implications for education are profound. The results of experimentation upon which hypothesized differences in task performance and physiological responsiveness are based is a function of black-white experimenter-experimentee differences. The results of polls and surveys upon which hypothesized differences in opinions, attitudes, preferences, and other information are based are a function of black-white interviewer-interviewee differences. The results of testing upon which hypothesized differences in intelligence and personality are based is a function of black-white examiner-examinee differences. The results of helping upon which hypothesized differences in constructive change or gain are based are a function of black-white helper-helpee differences.

The black-white differences upon which our educational programs are premised are suspect.

It is only a short step to conclude that the results of education upon which hypothesized differences in achievement and other indexes of intellective functioning are based are a function in large part of black-white teacher-student differences.

Again, we are not talking solely to primary and secondary school experiences. We are talking to the colleges and universities which prepare the teachers who perpetuate the traditions, which prepare the administrators who perpetuate the traditions, which prepare the citizens who perpetuate the traditions.

Our educational institutions have simply not serviced minority groups. Indeed, they have not only *not* enabled minorities to free themselves but they have imposed the chains which bind them.

DESIGNS FOR FAILURE

The programs that are calculated to ameliorate the problems of the poor, the black, and the needy are part of the same picture that produced the difficulties in the first place. They have been designed to fail just as the original programs were designed to fail, because they have built in defeat just as the original programs did. Indeed, they have done so in such a manner as to raise the question of whether their promulgators believe in the possibility of success.

A repetition of failures in education is no accident, and the repetition of failures in these helping programs did not occur by chance.

The sources of failure as well as the sources of success are a function primarily of personnel and programs. If the personnel are inadequate, the programs

---

[1]This study, "Training as a Preferred Mode of Facilitating Relations between Races and Generations," will be elaborated upon in Chapter 12 of this volume.

which they administer cannot achieve the intended success; if the programs are inadequate, the personnel who administer them cannot achieve the intended success. If both personnel and programs are inadequate, they converge upon each other in random designs for failure.

The abundance of designs of failure leads us to suggest that the real question is not whether the promulgators of these designs believe in the possibility of success but whether they feel that they can afford success. Their professional lives, we shall see, are predicated not upon the success that would obviate their positions but upon the failure necessary to insure these positions.

Again, the real question is not whether the promulgators of these designs believe in the possibility of success but *whether they feel that they can afford success.*

The designs for failure abound in all realms of life, seeking, it seems, to perpetuate the original social disasters. For want of another outlet, attempts to cope with social problems have fallen into the province of professional rehabilitators and into the professional rehabilitation programs of psychology, psychiatry, social welfare, and education. Unfortunately, many of these programs have been unable to develop and maintain their own constructive directionality.

Ineffectual teachers and trainers combine with ineffectual programs to produce their contribution to the desperate needs of mankind—ineffectual helpers.

A sampling of the results of studies of the professional helping programs is shocking (Carkhuff, 1966); it is clear that these programs have simply not established their efficacy in terms of helpee benefits. Indeed, the dominant programs are universally resistant to the idea of assessing the outcomes of their programs. The few carefully controlled studies present a distressing composite picture.

The professionally trained helper's ability to judge the personality characteristics of others bears an inverse relationship to the actual measured characteristics (Taft, 1955). With increasing training and increasing expressions of confidence in clinical judgments, there are decreasing validities (Kelly and Fiske, 1950) and reliabilities (Arnhoff, 1954) for these judgments. Further, persons with the same amount of graduate training (physical scientists) irrelevant to the understanding and judgment of behavior, judge personality characteristics with a high degree of accuracy (Taft, 1955) and are better predictors of behavior, with increasing information and personal encounters (Weiss, 1963).

Other studies have assessed the effects of professional training upon the level of functioning on those dimensions related to constructive helpee change or gain. Bergin and Soloman (1963) found the level of empathic understanding of final year, postinternship graduate students in a long-standing program of some repute to be positively correlated with therapeutic competence, another finding in a long and growing list of studies relating dimensions such as empathy to a variety of helpee outcome criteria. However, the authors found their ratings of empathic understanding to be slightly negatively correlated with both the students' grade point averages—and most important—the students' practicum averages.

The studies raise the question of the efficacy of the professional helper. Yet, from what we know about the entering professional trainee, he is bright, verbal, articulate, and relatively resourceful at every level of functioning when compared to other persons (Carkhuff, 1968). Indeed, on the average he communicates higher levels of empathic understanding and other related dimensions at the beginning of professional training than does his nonprofessional counterpart.

Unfortunately, as we have found in our studies of several graduate training programs, the average trainee does not grow over the course of several years of training, and in many instances he actually deteriorates in his level of functioning on dimensions critical to his helping others. In a cross-section study, it was found that graduate students in a clinical psychology program approved by the American Psychological Association began graduate training at communication levels significantly higher than nonclinical students. However, by the fourth year of training the clinical students had deteriorated so much in communication skills that the differences between them and the nonclinical students (who had not improved in communication skills) were insignificant (Carkhuff, Kratochvil, and Friel, 1968). Ratings of the clinical psychology professors at the school indicated that they were functioning at communication levels lower than those of entering graduate students. This suggested that over the course of training the students moved in the direction of their professors' level of functioning. Interestingly enough, the students did improve in their ability to discriminate (although not significantly more than nonclinical students), again moving in the direction of their accurately discriminating faculty.

In a longitudinal study at another approved graduate training program, it was found that the clinical trainees who remained in the program functioned at lower levels during their second year than they had in the first (Carkhuff, Kratochvil, and Friel, 1968). In addition, the trainees who remained in the program functioned at lower levels during the first year than those who dropped out of the program, a finding since replicated at other schools.

The results of these studies in conjunction with those of a number of other studies (Carkhuff, 1969) reinforce questions concerning the efficacy of professional training. At best, the professional-trainee product is himself a victim of a deteriorative learning process. At worst, he has pledged himself to an explicit mutual nonexposure pact with his ineffectual mentors. Whether he is a sophisticated victim or a willing conspirator, he cannot help the innocent victims of the programs of social failure.

The results of these studies, then, raise questions of the efficacy of the professional helper, independent of his entry into the realm of social action. The professional helpers have been unable or unwilling to rectify their own inadequacies. We compound our original errors when we call upon them to resolve the problems of society at large. If the credentialed professional has been unable or unwilling to resolve the life and death conflicts in his own personal life, we compound our earlier death wish when we call upon him to resolve the life and death conflicts in someone else's life.

If the helper is not functioning at high levels or has not himself changed constructively—indeed if his training experience has not demanded that he change constructively nor provided him with the programs necessary for such change—then how can he enable another person to change constructively? If the helper cannot "get himself together," how can he enable another to "get himself together"? In short, he cannot!

Thus far, we have looked at the calibre of the personnel. Let us now turn to the programs which these personnel have offered as the panacea in the areas of social disorder.

For someone who has not experienced and does not believe in the possibility of real change, it is the only—and easy—step to formulate games that have the appearance of effecting change. If his own life amounts to no more than a cheap game, he can do no more for others than to formulate and implement similarly cheap games for others.

The basic ingredient in this gamesmanship is that the process *look as if* it is accomplishing the changes which are for others so desperately needed. As long as the process looks as if it is relevant to the necessary changes, it can pass for the "real thing."

The first step, then, is to develop a process that appears relevant and to label it as such. The example of "sensitivity training" is a relevant one and the usurpation of the term "sensitivity," is a major coup d'etat. In the instance of "sensitivity training," it would appear that the group experiences involved were relevant to effecting changes in the sensitivity to self- and other-awareness. To be sure, depending upon how it is done, it is relevant for people to share their feelings and experiences of each other with each other. Unfortunately, the "sensitivity training" does not go far enough in building in success from the very beginning of the process and in developing the necessary follow-through at the end (Banks and Carkhuff, 1971; Carkhuff, 1971). In short, it fails to achieve any relevant goals associated with increased sensitivity.

But, as some of my distant colleagues tell me, "It is a lot of fun!" It is precisely this response that gives the game away.

The missing ingredient is work—good, hard work—for real change is hard work.

PROJECT 5

The Sensitivity Game*

On Wednesday, November 5, 1969, violence broke out between black and white students at a technical high school of 1100 some odd students in one of the larger urban communities in New England. While racial tensions had existed for some time, this was the first overt manifestation of violence

*Reprinted from a mimeographed paper written and published in April 1970, as "The Schools and Sensitivity Training: Requiem or Reveille?" by Robert R. Carkhuff.

in a town that prided itself as being somehow "different" from its north-eastern neighbors.

In spite of repeated recommendations to utilize a special team of 13 black human relations specialists, lay personnel systematically selected and trained, the school department placed the matter immediately in the hands of its director of School-Community Relations, a white man, who quickly established a basis for optimism. Asserting on Thursday, November 6, 1969, that he was "white and proud" just as the black students were "black and proud," the community relations director indicated that dialogue between black and white students had been established.

On Friday, November 6, 1969, the lid blew off and racial violence erupted on a grander scale.

Over the next two weeks, the community became just another scene in a cycle of failure oft-repeated around the country. The teachers felt that they should have an opportunity to resolve the crisis. The guidance counselors and pupil personnel services were looked to for their "expertise." The principals and administrators met regularly. Central Office personnel released statements reporting with the same optimism as their community relations director that things were getting under control and that a basis for a "return to normalcy" was being established.

Meantime, fights between black and white students accelerated. Mobs of black students and mobs of white students roamed in and out of school, threatening each other. In a number of instances, the mobs searched for particular students or teachers. In one lunch-room scene reminiscent of lynch mobs in the deep South, the white students chanted the names of black student leaders. Students, black and white, were being injured. Students, black and white, were being arrested.

In related developments, then, the police were brought into the school, the principal of the school dropped out of the picture due to "nervous exhaustion," and the mayor took a "long overdue" vacation to one of the islands in the Caribbean.

The town was a mess! There were no new ingredients!

Finally, after two weeks of failure on the part of all credentialed professionals, the over $30,000-a-year superintendent of schools called in two $5,000-a-year human relations specialists. Within hours, the crisis was "turned around." The students, black and white, responded. The students, black and white, were communicating due to the efforts of the specialists.

The new ingredients worked!

Quickly, things "returned to normal." However, in spite of recommendations to the contrary, the specialists were returned to their "home" junior high schools within three days and, in their stead, policemen patrolled the school doors and corridors.

What were these new ingredients? What makes these specialists effective? How were they selected and trained? How does their training *differ* from currently popular "sensitivity training" programs being implemented by school departments around the country with questionable success? First, let us look at the different "sensitivity training" programs.

"SENSITIVITY TRAINING"

While it is always folly to attempt to capture in words the essence of a movement which is essentially anti-intellectual in character, the "sensitivity training" groups are based upon some fundamental assumptions concerning fear and trust. Growth, the sensitivity training people tell me, is a process of breaking free of fears and the social roles which bind people. The group process of openness, honesty, and awareness is calculated to reduce fears and increase trust.

Typically, "sensitivity training" programs move in and out of a community in a weekend—seldom more than a week—at most two. In this time they claim to effect changes in the personal and social structure of key members of the community.

The focus of the "T" or training group has usually been upon the "here and now" experience, the immediate and common experiences of the group. "T" groups come in two forms which are distinguished more by the degree of previous relationships of the participants than by the uniqueness of their procedures and techniques. Standard "T" groups involve persons who do not work and live together. Organization development groups, a term very appealing to business and industry and education, simply involve persons who work together in private or public institutions.

Usually there is no structure or organization to the group. The group leader does not direct discussion. The task of the participants, then, is to fill the vacuum left by the absence of a dominant leader and of an assigned topic for discussion.

The participants are often encouraged to respond to each other with what many have termed "brutal candor." Through analysis of their behavior by the rest of the group, participants are supposed to gain a deeper understanding of themselves and others.

The "T" group, then, is designed on the surface to sharpen the participants' perceptions of themselves and others and of group dynamics. National Training Laboratories, the "T" group's place of origin, has the longest history of conducting training programs for industry, the military, and industrial institutions.

The encounter groups are less concerned with group dynamics. They have instead tended to focus upon the individual and on getting each group participant to talk about and express and act out his feelings as fully and spontaneously as possible. Although group members talk mainly about the present, they sometimes try to work out past, personal problems within the group.

The techniques of encounter are supposedly calculated to enable each participant not only to see himself through the other group members' eyes but also to be able to demonstrate how he feels about them, to relate to them and be real with them. The work of Esalen, the encounter group's place of origin, is of recent, albeit pervasive, vintage.

Recently, the encounter and "T" groups have evolved into "touch and feel" groups calculated to encourage trust and intimacy through physical techniques of touching and feeling. In this regard, I was surprised to find at a Symposium on Groups at a southeastern university to which a self-acknowledged proselytizer of the "T," a self-acknowledged guru of Esalen and myself were invited, that both of the other participants emphasized variations of "touch and feel." On the first day, after inviting the audience to partake of other more pharmacological means to similar benefits, the one employed many physical techniques beginning with touching and feeling another's face and ending with various forms of intimacy, largely male-female relationships. On the second day, the other built upon this base of relationship, encouraging the participants to higher levels of trust and intimacy, the success of which was demonstrated under the stairwells and on the elevators of the Education Center. Finally, I presented. After this conference and a similar experience last year at another university with "sensitivity" advocates, I am beginning to think that I am the straight man in a bizarre tragic comedy of life, being directed to evoke guilt and bring educators back to the reality of their responsibilities!

MOUNTING CRITICISMS

Criticisms have been mounted against "sensitivity training" on several fronts. First, there is little or no hard evidence to demonstrate the effectiveness of these experiences.

Encounter groups have not been vigorously or rigorously assessed. The limited investigations of "T" groups have produced evidence relating only to apparent attitude change and these findings are suspect on several counts.

Indeed, the main claim to effectiveness of both the "T" and encounter groups is customer satisfaction, i.e. in some instances the group leaders are invited back.

There is no tangible evidence for any translation to behavior change. There is no tangible evidence for a lasting translation to human benefits.

Beymer in his recent article entitled "Confrontation groups: Hula hoops?" in *Counselor Education and Supervision* (1970), a journal of the American Personnel and Guidance Association, levels several additional criticisms against "sensitivity training." First, he is critical of the overt disregard for the necessity for careful training and supervised practice. In that context, he is critical of the fact that "sensitivity" group leaders are unusually reluctant to accept reasonable responsibility for the consequence of their actions and inactions. Beymer relates two incidents known personally to him. "During a summer institute at a midwestern university, one participant was precipitated into psychosis by involvement in a confrontation group where the leader was skilled in removing defenses but either unable or unwilling to deal with what was exposed by this process. He rejected any personal responsibility for this tragedy. The second case involves a group leader who has lost three of his group participants to suicide during the last year or so. He is reported to have replied in answer to an inquiry that, 'People do what they have to do.'"

Criticisms of the anti-intellectual nature of "sensitivity training" have led reviewers like Thomas to entitle his article in the *Phi Delta Kappa* (1968) "The white-collar hippie movement," a movement in which feeling —rather than thought—reigns supreme. In this same vein, Dreyfus, a prominent psychiatrist, suggests in the journal *Adolescence* (1967) that young people outwardly express a need for closeness, contact, and relatedness, but also fear such intimacy should the possibility exist.

Dreyfus comments that "manifestations of this search and conflict can be seen in the various movements which adolescents engage in: free sex, occultism, Zen, pot parties, and LSD seances. . . . The extent of this feeling . . . is further reflected in the large numbers of students who participate in 'sensitivity training' and other group therapeutic experiences where they are searching for meaning, dialogue and a sense of community and fellowship." Unfortunately, he adds, "flight into intimacy . . . an overwhelming urgency . . . leads to premature, hence, superficial familiarity."

Beymer is also critical of the fact that while "sensitivity" trainers label what they do as group dynamics, they make conscious and deliberate attempts to move the groups they work with in the direction of group therapy. In this context, our own work has by now established well the fact that "sensitivity training," as any psychological experience, can cause the participants to become better or worse adjusted, depending upon the level of physical, emotional-interpersonal, and intellectual functioning of their leaders.

Perhaps one of the most telling criticisms involves the risk in trying to transfer the learnings from the group atmosphere to real life, for there are no built-in safeguards to insure such a generalization effect. Calame in his article entitled "The truth hurts: Some companies see more harm than good in sensitivity training" in the *Wall Street Journal* (1969), notes that many businessmen returning from "sensitivity training" have experienced great difficulty in transferring their new found personal value systems to the old profit structure systems.

At best, then, "sensitivity training" experiences may press a release mechanism for honestly searching but naive and inhibited people who have an opportunity to relax their defenses and reveal their doubts, confronting each other with their positive as well as negative experiences. At worst, "sensitivity training" experiences are a perversion of the worst sort of a directionless middle class, aimlessly indoctrinating the naive and the vulnerable, but spasmodically spewing debris in their wake.

ENCOUNTERS IN BLACK AND WHITE

With regard to the racial relations area specifically, the ostensible purpose of the black-white encounter groups is to sensitize whites to the blacks' problems, and a series of techniques have been developed accordingly. For example, in some "touch" groups whites and blacks learn to touch and "trust" one another at a physical level. Sometimes they may hold and roll around with each other, supposedly in order to change the attitudes of each to the other. Aside from the fact that this physical contact appears much more of a middle-class white than a lower-class black problem—and, indeed, in the service of the black the program might deemphasize the black's need for any form of contact with whites—the program is calculated to achieve exactly the opposite effect it is represented to effect.

Recently, the perpetrators of these programs have developed for distribution and, most assuredly profit, sales kits involving, among other things, white masks for blacks and black masks for whites. Again, the purpose is to give each the "feel" for the other's role and experiences. In some instances, remarkably, white groups supposedly achieve effective "encounters" with blacks in the absence of black participants in the groups by simply donning black masks. *We can now get a feel for the black man's world without even involving him physically!* Does he strike so much fear? It would be more highly creative and meaningful to have the whites wear white masks and the blacks wear black masks for each, to be sure, has been taught to hide behind the color of his skin.

Whereas the real goal of any "sensitivity" groups in the black-white area should be a *change in white behavior* which causes the discriminatory practices *outside of the group,* with the belief that concomitant changes in attitudes would serve to integrate and strengthen the behavior, in practice these groups are calculated more to neutralize black attitudes than to change white behavior. That is, they provide an outlet for the rage which the black man has accumulated in his frustration with a system that passed him by. This outlet is calculated to attenuate, at least temporarily, the possibility of his translating this rage into violent aggression.

Perhaps the greatest danger of these groups in the racial relations area is in allowing the white participants to leave thinking that they have made "their little contribution for the year." The greatest tragedy is that the effects will be quite the reverse of those claimed, with the increasing discordance between self-reports and overt behavior concealing the fact that already well-established prejudices are reinforced and the effort to change them minimized.

In addition, it has become increasingly apparent to both sophisticated and unsophisticated blacks that there is no encounter group without aggressive confrontation of whites by blacks. In a truly historical reversal of roles, the groups are predicated upon the black turning outward to attack his environment and the white turning inward in his guilty acceptance of the black's verbal explosion. There is an anecdote that is tragically humorous in this regard.

When I first came to one community, I found that the blacks had been "T-grouped to death." Many of them had been through several "sensitivity" group experiences and none were any better for them and some were, indeed, worse. After having been introduced to systematic training programs in helping and human relations skills, several of the men who had been through the systematic training experience with me and some of whom were now employed in various social service capacities as functional professionals were invited to a black-white encounter group conducted by the department of education at a nearby state university in the summer of 1969. They had participated before and had always been frustrated with the lack of progress made after these groups. That is, there were no changes in white behavior. On their own, the blacks decided not to confront, choosing instead to reflect the feelings of the white participants. The white participants' expectations for confrontation built up. Increasingly, they addressed themselves to the blacks with statements such as, "You've been nice to us so far," and "I guess we'll get the worst tomorrow." Needless to say, the blacks did not confront the whites and the encounter groups were a failure. Only the whites were left frustrated this time and that is appropriate for therein lies the source of discriminatory practices.

A not unrelated point, also deeply conditioned in many whites and some blacks, is the ability to make a living off another's misery. White and black "sensitivity" group leaders are very expensive. They make a very exhorbitant living off the black man's affect, off his precious feelings. It is as if they are saying, "Be honest with me while I make a living off your affect."

It is ironic that these so-called "sensitivity" groups are labeled laboratory groups. For the black man they are indeed laboratory groups — again, *the black man has been the laboratory for the white man's experimentation and benefit!*

A STUDY IN CONTRASTS

While some of the "sensitivity" techniques may be stimulating and may be employed by effective people as levers into important personal development, they remain techniques. As techniques, they do not facilitate *a full and intense exposure to a full and intense person, the only real modality for constructive or reconstructive behavior change.*

Although effective people try to develop effective programs in ways that they can be transmitted, they are not attracted to these gimmicky techniques.

Effective persons need no props, for they know that they themselves are their most important resource for effecting change.

In the few instances where "sensitivity" programs may be effective, they are effective because of the qualities of personal effectiveness of the trainers. However, *"sensitivity" programs are not often effective—simply because effective people or people striving for effectiveness—trainers as well as trainees—are not attracted to such gimmicky maneuvers.*

In this vein, Melchiskey and Wittmer's research on the "Personality characteristics of counselor candidates accepting and rejecting sensitivity training" appearing in *Counselor Education and Supervision* (1970) is relevant. They found that persons who have a need to do their best and to accomplish something important with their lives—that is, to achieve and be independent (high need achievement)—reject "sensitivity training," while those whose greatest need is to receive sympathy (high need nurturance) embrace it.

remarkable

A world dominated or conducted by "victims" is a doomed world!

In this regard, the experience in this community may be contrasted with the experiences in other communities. For example, at another northeastern high school of essentially the same number of students in a town of essentially the same number of people, the same conditions of racial tensions prevailed last fall. In this instance local leaders prevailed upon the school authorities to allow school time for "sensitivity training" of teachers, parents, and students. Group leaders "trained" by the "touch and feel" method conducted eight such heterogeneous groups with near disastrous results. Teacher turned on teacher, community against teacher and vice versa, children against adults and vice versa. The effects are still being felt. Nervous breakdowns of participants were in evidence. Some of the potentially best people quit, refusing to participate.

Things are now not only no better at this second school, they are worse! The original black-white tensions have been buried beneath the debris of the "sensitivity conflicts." If the conflicts created by "sensitivity training" are ever dealt with successfully, the concerned citizenry of this town may once again deal with the black-white conflicts. The "sensitivity training" only served to compound the original problems. The "sensitivity training" only served to sensitize rather than make sensitive each to the other.

This, and similar distressing consequences, have led Harvard psychiatrist Farnsworth to comment as follows in Rakstis' article (1970) on "Sensitivity training: Fad, fraud, or new frontier?": "Compassion without competence becomes quackery."

And competence without compassion becomes sterile learning.

Despite the first town's inability to fully utilize and expand its human relations specialist program, a potential source of real help lies in systematically selected and systematically trained persons indigenous to the community being serviced. With the dominant concern of professionalization for spheres of influence rather than effectiveness, the natural reluctance to utilizing the specialists was clear. White, credentialed professionals were resistant to calling upon black, functional professionals to "bail them out." Indeed, aside from supporting and facilitating the efforts of the specialists, the professionals' main concern should have been to acquire the helping and human relations skills for themselves.

In this context, the term "systematic human relations training" derives from the systematic application to selection and training of those ingredients or conditions found to be effective in all helping and human relationships. Basically, the model indicates that all human relationships, including in particular teaching and counseling as well as their supervision, may have constructive or retarding or even deteriorative consequences. There are certain dimensions of the human relationship which may be rated to account for effectiveness or ineffectiveness. These dimensions include responsive conditions (responding to another person's experience) such as empathic understanding, respect, and specificity of expression; and initiative dimensions (initiating from one's own experiences) such as genuineness, confrontation, and interpretations of immediacy. Direct translations are made to selection and training of the scales utilized to measure these conditions in helping and human relationships.

In systematic human relations training a trainee is taken, one step at a time, from the simplest form of responsiveness to the most complex communications involving both responsive and initiative behavior. The basic principles involve systematically exposing the trainee to alternate modes of behaving. The process is goal directed and action oriented. It provides a work-oriented structure within which creative and spontaneous human processes can take place. Perhaps most important, it emphasizes practice in the behavior which we wish to effect, thus leaving the trainee-helpee with tangible and usable skills which are retained following training. Finally, it offers a built-in means for assessing the effectiveness of the program. All of these concepts are alien to "sensitivity training."

With regard to the assessment of selection, training, and practice, *the evidence for the efficacy of these programs in effecting constructive changes in human behavior is now voluminous* (Carkhuff, 1969).

A FINAL NOTE

As the school crises around the nation accelerate with increasing frequency, a number of stages in a repetitious cycle can be predicted. First, school authorities will say that the misbehavior of "a small minority of students does not represent a generally positive school atmosphere." Next, as the crises intensify, the authorities will blame, in order, outside agitators, locally available "scapegoats," and a lack of funds. Then, they will hit upon commonsense solutions, what I call the "lunch-room remedies." In the first town it was creating a third lunch period to alleviate overcrowding. In the second town it was getting the children to bus their own trays so that the administrators did not have the responsibility. Finally, after the failure of each of these disguises, and before the initiation of "sensitivity training," they will adopt a "law 'n order" platform.

"Sensitivity training," as we have known it, is just another stage in the cycle of social failure. After failing in industry and the military, it is now to be given an opportunity to fail in education. Indeed, failure is by now an integral part of educational philosophy in some quarters. As one school superintendant has stated recently in a speech termed a "social prophesy," "[Education] should be given the opportunity to fail and to try again."

As long as the problem solvers are asked to frame their solutions in terms that the problem makers can endorse, there can be no solution at all. *The solution must be as extreme as the crisis.* It is absurd to believe that the same people who helped to create the crisis can help to resolve it. There must be new ingredients!

There is no basis for immediate optimism. Things may have to hit bottom before there is real basis for hope. There are too many people in responsible positions who would prefer anything—certainly turmoil—even death—to exposure as incompetents and ineffectuals.

The choice is ours. Whether we join the ranks of unfettered spirits on their never-ending "marathons" to oblivion or engage in the hard work and creative problem-solving activities of productive humans will determine whether our efforts signal requiem or reveille for our world and the world of our children.

In our attempt to understand the sources of social failure we have been made aware that the so-called rehabilitators and the so-called rehabilitation programs are designed not to ameliorate, eliminate, or prevent the social problems. Rather, they are designed in such a manner that they can do only one thing—perpetuate the original disaster. Send an ineffectual product of an ineffectual social work program into the inner-city and things will get worse (Teuber and Powers, 1953). They will get worse not because the alleged helpers have opened the helpees up to a whole new world. No! They will get worse because they throw the inner-city resident into an even more intensified conflict. They—the would-be helpers—are living examples of people who have nothing to offer yet are endorsed by a system for reasons other than their functionality. Worse still, representing the system, they would make a living off "helping" those whom the system has bypassed.

That designs for failure are abundant and flourishing has been the conclusion of our investigation. That these designs for failure are replicable in a progressively intensified social deterioration process is also quite clear. The essential ingredients for perpetuating and intensifying social crises until they culminate in major disasters are the combinations of inadequate people and inadequate programs. The advantage of these designs for failure is that the apparency of progress veils the redundancy of destruction. People can delude themselves all the way to the funeral pyre.

The alternatives to social failure are the thesis of this book. However, they are not fun. They are not easy. They are not dramatic. They are hard work! But, in turn, they work.

Most important, the alternatives to social failure build block by block upon what we know. They involve refining and defining those practices that are effective and repeatable. They involve researching the efficacy of our efforts and modifying our programs in accordance with the results of our research, reinforcing those people and those programs which make a constructive difference, extinguishing those which do not, and eliminating those which make a destructive difference.

We cannot experiment with the lives of others. We can no longer afford to fail. *We must afford success!* Too many more lives will be wasted—theirs and ours.

REFERENCES

Adams, W. A. The Negro patient in psychiatric treatment. *American Journal of Orthopsychiatry,* 1950, **20,** 305–310.

American Association for the Advancement of Science. Symposium on developmental intelligence of Negroes. Boston, December, 1969.

Arnhoff, F. N. Some factors influencing the unreliability of clinical judgments. *Journal of Clinical Psychology,* 1954, **10,** 272–275.

Banks, G. Black confronts white: The issue of rapport in the interview situation. *Social Service Review,* 1971, in press.

Banks, G., Berenson, B. G., & Carkhuff, R. R. The effects of counselor race and training upon counseling process with Negro clients in initial interviews. *Journal of Clinical Psychology,* 1967, **23,** 70–72.

Banks, G., and Carkhuff, R. R. Sensitivity training: A bibliography and review. *Professional Psychology,* 1971, **3,** in press.

Baratz, S. S. Effect of race of experimenter, instructions, and comparison population upon level of reported anxiety in Negro subjects. *Journal of Personality and Social Psychology,* 1967, **7,** 194–196.

Bennett, L. Jr. *Before the Mayflower: A history of the Negro in America.* Baltimore, Md.: Penguin, 1966.

Bergin, A., & Soloman, S. Personality and performance correlates of empathic understanding. *American Psychologist,* 1963, **18,** 33.

Bernard, H. W. Socioeconomic class and the school counselor. *Theory into Practice,* 1963, **2,** 17–23.

Bernard, V. W. Psychoanalysis and members of minority groups. *Journal of the American Psychoanalytical Association,* 1953, **1,** 256–267.

Beymer, L. Confrontation groups: Hula hoops? *Counselor Education and Supervision,* 1970, **9,** 75–86.

Brenton, M. *What's happened to our teachers?* New York: Coward-McCann, 1969.

Calame, B. E. The truth hurts: Some companies see more harm than good in sensitivity training. *Wall Street Journal,* July 14, 1969, p. 1.

Carkhuff, R. R. Training in counseling and psychotherapeutic processes: Requiem or reveille? *Journal of Counseling Psychology,* 1966, **13,** 360–367.

Carkhuff, R. R. The differential functioning of lay and professional helpers. *Journal of Counseling Psychology,* 1968, **15,** 117–126.

Carkhuff, R. R. *Helping and human relations: A primer for lay and professional helpers. Vol. II. Practice and research.* New York: Holt, Rinehart and Winston, 1969.

Carkhuff, R. R. Editorial: The sensitivity fraud. *Journal of Clinical Psychology,* 1971, **26,** 158–159.

Carkhuff, R. R., & Banks, G. Training as a preferred mode of facilitating relations between race and generations. *Journal of Counseling Psychology,* 1970, **17,** 413–418.

Carkhuff, R. R., Kratochvil, D., & Friel, T. Effects of professional training: Communication and discrimination of facilitative conditions. *Journal of Counseling Psychology,* 1968, **15,** 68–74.

Carkhuff, R. R., & Pierce, R. Differential effects of therapist race and social class upon patient depth of self-exploration in the initial clinical interview. *Journal of Consulting Psychology,* 1967, **31,** 632–634.

Chess, S., Clark, K. B., & Thomas, A. The importance of cultural evaluation in psychiatric diagnosis and treatment. *Psychiatric Quarterly,* 1958, **27,** 102–113.

Coleman, J. S. *Equality of educational opportunity.* Washington, D.C.: U.S. Government Printing Office, 1966.

Dreyfus, E. A. The search for intimacy. *Adolescence,* 1967, **2,** 25–40.

Friedenberg, E. Z. What are our schools trying to do? *Special Education Supplement, New York Times Book Review,* September 14, 1969.

Garrett, H. E. *Children: Black and white.* Kilmarnock, Va.: Patrick Henry Press, 1968.

Heine, R. W. The Negro patient in psychotherapy. *Journal of Clinical Psychology,* 1950, **6,** 373–376.

Hollingshead, A. B., & Redlich, F. C. *Social class and mental illness.* New York: Wiley, 1958.

Jensen, R. *Environment, heredity and intelligence.* Cambridge, Mass.: Harvard Educational Review, 1969.

Jessor, R. Social values and psychotherapy. *Journal of Consulting Psychology,* 1956, **20,** 264–266.

Kahn, J., Buckmueller, A. D., & Gildea, Margaret. Group therapy for parents of behavior problem children in public schools: Failure of this method in a Negro school. *American Journal of Psychiatry,* 1951, **108,** 351–357.

Katz, I., Epps, E., & Axelson, L. Effect on Negro digit symbol performance of anticipated comparisons with whites and other Negroes. *Journal of Abnormal and Social Psychology,* 1963, **66,** 562–567.

Katz, I., Robinson, J. M., Epps, E. C., & Wally, P. Effects of race of experimenter and test vs. neutral instructions on expression of hostility in Negro boys. *Journal of Social Issues,* 1964, **20,** 54–60.

Kelly, E. L., & Fiske, D. W. The prediction of success in the VA training program in clinical psychology. *American Psychologist,* 1950, **5,** 395–406.

Leacock, E. B. *Teaching and learning in city schools.* New York: Basic Books, 1968.

Melchiskey, S., & Wittmer, J. Personality characteristics of counselor candidates accepting and rejecting sensitivity training. *Counselor Education and Supervision,* 1970, **9,** 132–134.

Moore, R. A., Benedek, E. C., & Wallace, J. G. Social class, schizophrenia and the psychiatrist. *American Journal of Psychiatry,* 1963, **120,** 149–154.

National Advisory Commission. *Report on civil disorders.* New York: Bantam Books, 1968.

Pettigrew, T. F. Negro American intelligence: A new look at an old controversy. *Journal of Negro Education,* 1964, **33,** 6–25.

Phillips, W. B. Counseling Negro pupils: An educational dilemma. *Journal of Negro Education,* 1960, **24,** 504–507.

Rakstis, I. J. Sensitivity training: Fad, fraud, or new frontier? *Today's Health, American Medical Association,* January, 1970.

Rosenthal, R., & Jacobson, L. *Pygmalion in the classroom: Teacher expectation and pupils' intellectual development.* New York: Holt, Rinehart and Winston, 1968.

Sattler, J. M. Ethnic experimenter effects in experimentation, testing, interviewing and psychotherapy. Mimeographed manuscript, San Diego State College, 1969.

Springfield Union (Springfield, Mass.). Special report, Hunger, poverty doom 6 million U.S. children from birth. January 3, 1970.

Taft, R. The ability to judge people. *Psychological Bulletin,* 1955, **52,** 1–23.

Teuber, H. L., & Powers, E. Evaluating therapy in a delinquency prevention program. *Proceedings of the Association for Research on Nervous and Mental Disorders.* Baltimore: Williams & Wilkins, 1953, 138–147.

Thomas, D. T. T-Grouping: The white-collar hippie movement, *Phi Delta Kappa,* 1968, **49,** 458–460.

Weiss, J. H. The effect of professional training and amount and accuracy of information on behavioral prediction. *Journal of Consulting Psychology,* 1963, **27,** 257–262.

Williams, J. A., Jr. Interviewer-respondent interaction: A study of bias in the information interview. *Sociometry,* 1964, **27,** 338–352.

Yamamoto, J., James, Q. C., Bloombaum, M., & Hatten, J. Racial factors in patient selection. *American Journal of Psychiatry,* 1967, **124,** 630–636.

PART THREE

*Ingredients
of Social Emergence*

CHAPTER 4
Sources
of Human Development

The black revolution puts this consideration squarely before us: for now and for all time the most basic issue facing man is whether or not he can design and develop a social system that will provide the opportunity for the fulfillment of each and every one of its members.

The inability of our educational and social institutions to contribute to the optimum development of all human resources leads readily to a consideration of the sources of such development. We must, then, understand in depth the variables that make possible the development of the healthy and fully functioning person. Where that is not possible we must understand in depth the variables that make possible change and growth in unhealthy and less than fully functioning persons. Where gain is not possible, change must be effected.

Where parents have not been sources of nourishment for their children, they must be equipped to be so. Where they cannot, parental surrogates who can must be introduced, for a human life must not be subject to the same chance factors as its origin.

Where teachers have not been facilitative of the efforts of their students, they must be equipped to be so. Where they cannot, specialists who can must be introduced, for a human being cannot, in truth, flunk a year of growth.

Where counselors have not been therapeutic in the rehabilitation of their clients, they must be equipped to be so. Where they cannot, rehabilitative agents who can must be introduced, for the only meaning to human life is growth, and the opportunity for each man to grow to his fullest is the medium to man's fulfillment of his humanity.

Let us consider the sources of man's growth and development. In doing so, I will focus upon those sources for which the evidence is most extensive (Brayfield, 1968) and, in that context, consider the implications for current social problems.

MODELING AND IMITATION

Perhaps the most significant source of human development is modeling, or imitation. Most of a child's learning is imitative of the adults and older children in his environment. These significant figures are automatically important influences on the child's behavior because they provide services which he needs and have abilities which he desires. For example, in a healthy household the adults are protective and nourishing on the one hand, and yet have the freedom to assert their own authority and develop their own direction on the other. In this context we say that these adult figures are constructive models to be emulated and imitated: behavior on the part of the child which more closely approximates that of the adult is reinforcing; behavior which deviates is not reinforcing.

However, in many helping relationships the conditions which establish the helper as a model for the helpee's development are not built in as in the early parent-child relationship. In order to establish himself as a potent reinforcer, the helper must first establish that he has something that the helpee wants and in order to accomplish this he must establish that he understands "where the helpee is coming from," the way the helpee sees the world, his needs, his hopes, his frame of reference. If the helper can communicate to the helpee his ability to facilitate the helpee's development toward achieving the helpee's ends, then the helper has set himself up as a potent reinforcer for the helpee and a model for the helpee's behavior. Thus the helper becomes not only a source of insights but also a source of reinforcement and, perhaps most important, a direct source of behavioral repertoires (Bandura, 1965). The focus of interest, then, is upon the helper's intentional or unintentional performance of complex behavioral patterns that may be imitated and adapted by the helpee.

Modeling approaches have been employed in the development and rehabilitation of human resources. In more naturalistic studies, Persons and Pepinsky (1966) have found an identification of successfully treated delinquents with their helper's vocational interest patterns and self-presentation, including phrases and gestures. Modeling effects have also been reported in studies of psychotherapy by Welkowitz, Cohen, and Ortmeyer (1967) where they found the convergence of therapist-client values over the course of therapy to be significantly related to judgments of client improvement. Of course, the different therapists studied did not share a homogeneous value system, so that while the "improved" client is moving closer to his own therapist's values, he may be moving, simultaneously, away from other therapists' values. Unfortunately, in these studies we do not have the necessary objective evidence for the helper's level of functioning and the success of the client's treatment. What is perhaps most clear, however, is that, at a minimum, the client has found a value system that has functioned effectively as an alternative to his own ineffective system.

Specific human development programs have systematically employed the helper as model. Training programs in interpersonal skills have utilized modeling as a source of learning in training lay as well as professional trainers and in the employment of training as a preferred mode of treating patients (Carkhuff, 1969a, 1969b): where the trainer-helper is functioning at high levels the trainee-helpees demonstrate progressive increments in movement toward the trainer-helper's level of functioning. In other studies, Bandura (1965) has demonstrated that as a consequence of children's observation of models' moral responses, the frequency of the children's moral responses increased significantly. Krum-boltz and Thoreson (1964), in turn, have successfully employed modeling techniques in groups in the modification of the information-seeking behavior of students. Sarason (1968) has demonstrated that delinquent boys who participated in a variety of modeling sessions showed more change in the direction of desirable behavior and attitudes than boys in a comparison group who did not participate.

However, again, these studies do not provide us with the necessary measurements concerning the helper's level of functioning in a given area or, in other words, the degree of his potency as a model. Nevertheless, the implications for the systematic development and utilization of helper-models as both the means and ends of helping are profound. People can be trained to function at the highest levels of all relevant dimensions. In turn, they can be trained in the skills necessary to erect themselves as potent and reinforcing models and, accordingly, be utilized to elicit gain or change on the part of the helpees in the direction of their functioning. Healthy people can be utilized to develop healthy people!

In the educational and social action areas the implications become particularly critical. Thus, for example, in our social, educational, political, and industrial institutions constructive models selected on the basis of critical characteristics such as color that facilitate the helpee's identification with emergence and achievement must be employed. Thus, healthy black people can be utilized to develop healthy black people. Healthy Spanish people can be utilized to develop healthy Spanish people. If there are no blacks or Spanish or Mexicans in the helping role, it is difficult for the helpee to identify himself in that role. If the helpee cannot identify himself in that role, it is difficult to motivate him to develop himself fully under the helper's guidance. The presence of models representing the critical human dimensions of color and other cultural dimensions cut the knot of discord, of racial strife and human folly.

For their helpees, helper-models from the same background represent what can be, what they can be. For their helpees, helper-models from the same background represent hope.

INSIGHT AND ACTION

Obviously, modeling alone is not enough to effect gain or change in the development of human resources. Other important sources of development include the didactic or teaching function emphasizing the imparting of new concepts. In this context, recent research is exploring the relationship of ideas and behavior, discrimination and communication, insight and action. The basic assumption is that once an insight has been developed, it can serve as a discriminative stimulus and, thus, increase the probability that related behaviors will occur. However, the subject or helpee's ability to commit himself to action is contingent upon the same kind of training that enables him to make the necessary discrimination. Nothing can be taken for granted. Action does not necessarily follow insight. But action can follow insight. What is required is systematic training in following through on the insights. Thus, the helpee can be provided with the opportunity to acquire experience in developing a relevant course of action and in trying out new behaviors in implementing that course of action.

McClelland (1961) and his associates have developed in their subjects the idea of achievement through discussion of the nature and measurement of achievement motivation. In a follow-through phase they have placed their subjects in a variety of simulated life situations where they could experiment with new ways of behaving. Thus, the development of insights is followed with the opportunity for the development of behaviors that flow from the insights. They have presented evidence relating the development of achievement motivation to the strengthening of achievement behavior for mostly students and businessmen. In one such program Kolb (1965) found achievement scores in simulated situations to be related to changes in grades among underachieving high school boys enrolled in the achievement motivation training program.

However, in many programs the translations from insight to action have not been made. We have lived long, for example, with patient populations which have "understood" but have been unable to act upon their insights into their problems. Some studies of professional counselors suggest the sources of these discrepancies. While professional clinical-psychology trainees improve significantly over the course of training in their ability to discriminate effective helper responses, they tend to deteriorate in their ability to make these responses (Carkhuff, Kratochvil, and Friel, 1968). Thus, there is a discrepancy between discrimination and communication or, in other words, insight and action. Further, experienced therapists' ratings of their own effectiveness are not related to either objective ratings of their actual effectiveness or to client ratings of their effectiveness (Carkhuff and Burstein, 1970). Indeed, those therapists who were rated the highest by objective ratings tended to be most congruent in their self ratings with the objective ratings, while those rated lowest objectively tended to rate themselves highest. These findings take on further significant meaning when we realize that it is communication—and not discrimination—action—and not insight—that are related to dimensions of self-actualization (Foulds, 1969).

In any event, the implications for training in the systematic development of effective courses of action to follow upon training in the development of the insight are important. The implications for training in the communication skills to complement the training in the discrimination skills are profound. Without systematic communication training, the most efficient and effective use of modeling and the shaping of new responses cannot occur.

In the educational and social action areas, the systematic development of programs of insight and action become particularly critical. The would-be helpers must fully understand the problems of racial injustice before they can act on them. They must then be given the opportunity to try out new behaviors and practice in the systematic development of effective courses of action. Again, the problem is the training in follow-through action. In some instances, the behavior change may more effectively precede the insight than vice versa (Hobbs, 1962). Thus, once an individual is engaged in new behavior, for example, integrated education (Clark, 1950), his insights into the behavior are more keen and they act to consolidate the behavior.

REINFORCEMENT AND CONSTRUCTIVE GAIN

With regard to the translation of insight to action in general and the shaping of new behaviors specifically, perhaps the most powerful tool available to man is the selective or differential reinforcement of responses. Much of human behavior is produced and maintained by the contingencies of reinforcement existing in everyday life. For the layman the concept of differential reinforcement may translate simply into a system of rewards and punishments in which constructive or goal-directed behavior is rewarded, neutral behavior is not rewarded or extinguished, and destructive behavior is punished. The reinforcement systems are, to be sure, in practice more complex (Carkhuff and Berenson, 1967). As a preferred mode of therapeutic treatment, for example, behavior modification approaches offer the following sample of modification principles derived from (a) instrumental conditioning: (1) shaping of the successive reinforcement of small segments of desired behavior; (2) direct manipulation of the sociophysical environment; (3) punishment; and (4) omission learning; from (b) classical conditioning: (1) counterconditioning; (2) direct conditioning; (3) reciprocal inhibition; (4) extinction. Nevertheless, the basic principles involving the rewarding of desirable behavior and the nonrewarding or punishment of undesirable behavior hold for most purposes. These principles have been systematically applied in a variety of different settings and with a variety of different populations, with a pronounced degree of success (Krasner and Ullmann, 1965; Krumboltz, 1965). Desirable changes have been effected in the classroom behavior of normal children as well as in the behavior of emotionally disturbed, delinquent, and retarded populations. Treatment procedures have been varied and creative, dictated by the view of behavior which the helper holds. Thus, for example, in rehabilitation we find Lovaas (1964) successfully treating autistic children by "shaping" patient behavior so that appropriate responses were made to food employed as a secondary reinforcer, and Ayllon and Haughton (1962) treating a fastidious female patient by spilling food on the patient whenever she did not eat.

Perhaps most important are the applications of these principles of differential reinforcement that are made in daily living, in child-rearing, in education, in other potential growth relationships. Factors in the home and school which mitigate against learning can be reduced and factors which facilitate learning can be increased according to the application of these principles. In addition, training programs that further facilitate the development of human resources may be made more efficient and effective by applying these principles. Thus, in addition to the systematic programs in desensitization to anxiety-eliciting stimuli and training in self-assertion, systematic training programs in communications skills have been developed and refined based upon these principles of differential reinforcement (Carkhuff, 1969a, 1969b). Accordingly, the very communication skills which enable a helper to become a potent reinforcer of a helpee's behavior are themselves a product of programs based upon the principles of differential reinforcement.

The implications for all programs of human development are clear. Individuals—parents as well as children, teachers as well as students, counselors as well as clients—each can be encouraged to his most effective level of functioning by the positive reinforcement of his most effective behaviors, the extinction of his more neutral behaviors, and the negative reinforcement of his least effective behaviors.

In educational and social action programs where effective action must be mobilized with immediacy within groups the implications are especially clear. In order that the programs can elicit optimum changes in their helpees, within groups the parents, the teachers, and the counselors must be encouraged to their most effective levels of functioning by positive reinforcement of their most effective members, nonreinforcement of their more neutral members, and negative reinforcement of their least effective members.

There are no *effective* programs in any area—business, industry, civil service, military service, as well as education and social service—that do not operate by principles of differential reinforcement.

EXPECTATIONS AND GROWTH

Increasingly, expectancies or expectations have come to be recognized as one of the most important shapers of behavior. Expectancies on the part of significant authority figures lead to individual behavior that is congruent with the expectancies. Thus, helpers whose expectations for a given helpee or group of helpees are high elicit constructive gain or change, whereas helpers whose expectations for the helpees are low have retarding effects upon the behavior of the helpees.

Naturally, helpees, whether children, students, or clients, come to expect of themselves what their helpers expect of them (Carkhuff, 1969a). In turn, the helpers' expectancies are based upon their past experiences. Those who have been successful tend to have high expectations; those who have not been successful do not.

It is important to note that the effects of the expectancies hold independent of the assumptions concerning the resources of the individual helpee. That is, expectations based upon erroneous information concerning the individual's ability to achieve, nevertheless have effect upon that individual's ability to achieve. The explanation indicates that expectations may involve a very subtle process in which the helpers elicit and reinforce a changed self-image on the part of the helpee.

But there may also be gross manipulations by the helper to effect conditions which bring the helpee to conform to the expectations of the helper. Most of the significant work in this area has been accomplished by Rosenthal and his colleagues (Rosenthal and Jacobson, 1968). Let us explore these different hypotheses for a moment.

If we take a group of unselected rats and assign them randomly to one of two groups and tell the experimenters arbitrarily that one group is bright and the other dumb, the rats will perform according to the expectancies of the experimenters. It is not sufficient to say that we have induced a change in the self-expectancies of the subjects. We must instead assign further responsibility to the behavior of the experimenter, for in some way, whether consciously or unconsciously, he manipulated the situation to conform to his expectations.

Studies in the human realm show similar results. If we take a group of unselected children and randomly designate some of them as demonstrating unusual scholastic promise, the teachers will come to expect high levels of achievement from these pupils. Where the pupils do not in fact differ at the beginning of a school year and where the differences between pupils exist entirely in the minds of the teachers, the children from whom teachers expected intellectual excellence will actually demonstrate gains significantly greater than their undesignated counterparts. In addition, the designated pupils will be described by their teachers at the end of the year as having a better chance of being happier, more curious, more interesting and as having the best opportunity to be successful in later life, which indeed they do.

The implications for our social and educational problems are profound!

We must learn to utilize such a powerful tool systematically. For example, the expectations for the achievement of black students are low and the achievement of black students is low (Clark, 1965). We can modify these expectations with education and information. We can expect that a program of study in black history informing the teacher of an advanced stage of civilization in Africa long before European civilization was possible would place the current black-white scene in historical perspective. A realization that before the invention of the cotton gin and the need for cheap labor, black-white relations in the American colony were exemplary would enable the teacher to understand the years of conditioning that enter the phenomenology of the student before him.

At a minimum, these programs of study should be required of all teachers functioning in inner-city schools.

An understanding and constructive utilization of expectations and the phenomena which accompany such expectations could be a foundation stone of an equitable system in which each individual has the opportunity to live up to his capacity rather than the conditioned expectations of others.

PARTICIPATION AND MOTIVATION

A final source of human development is the participation in problem-solving or decision-making processes. That is, whether student or teacher, child or parent, black or white, benefits accrue to the participant in the development of a program.

In the individual instance we may think of a variety of helping relationships. If the outcome of helping is to be effective, we must have the "input" of the helpee. The helper must first understand "where the helpee is coming from" before he can be helpful to the helpee. Participation by the helpee means that at least his frame of reference was taken into consideration in the development of the program calculated to benefit him. In this respect, while the helper is expert in guiding the development of courses of action and preferred ways of functioning, he is always helpee-centered in the sense that he serves for the benefit of the helpee and aids in the development of goals that are desirable for the helpee.

In the same sense, in group instances we may think of a variety of educational and social action programs. If the outcome of these programs is to be effective we must have the "input" of those concerned with the operation of the programs and particularly of those whom the programs are to benefit.

At a minimum, participation increases motivation and personal satisfaction. At a maximum, increased motivation may lead to increased performance and, accordingly, a high-quality outcome of the program. However, again the need for systematic attention to the follow-through stage is evident

Participation in the development of solutions and the motivation and satisfaction which they encourage are, by themselves, not enough. They are, though, the necessary ingredients of working and effective programs, whether for individuals or groups.

Studies of food habit changes conducted by Lewin (1951) during World War II are classics in this respect. He found that participation in decision-making, when accompanied by public commitment, strengthens the behavior consequent to the decision. Thus, in programs having social consequences we may define the formula for success as follows:

participation + public commitment + follow-through training = success.

Even where the outcome of a particular program is not successful, there may be intrinsic benefits to the participants involved. As Brayfield (1968) suggests, increases in satisfaction and morale, worthy goals in themselves, are the means to feelings of self worth and the ally of responsible behavior.

In this context, many of our educational and social action programs fail because they do not allow for the full participation of the interested parties in their formulation. If not paternalistic, they are authoritarian, and although there is a place for paternalism and authoritarianism in some aspects of child-rearing and some instances of education there is no place for them in programs calculated to elicit and reinforce constructive adult behavior. If adults cannot participate in the development of the solution to adult problems, then they cannot function as adults in the implementation of the solution.

THE HELPER AS MODEL AND AGENT

We have viewed several sources of human development and seen how they influence both individual and group effectiveness. The helper or the program director, then, must himself be the model for the helpee's development. He is the living representative of a person who is himself living effectively. As such, he represents the means and the ends of the helping process.

But the helper is not simply a model for effective living. He is also the agent for the helpee's gain or change. Thus, he is able to facilitate the development of insights into the helpee's behavior and aid in the systematic development of effective courses of action based upon these insights. But he does so only with the full input of the helpee and the helpee's full participation in the development of the course of action. The helper is further able to implement the course of action with differential reinforcement programs, rewarding the most effective behaviors and eliminating the least effective behaviors. Finally, in this context the effective helper also employs his expectations explicitly to influence and shape the helpee's behavior to the highest level possible.

Let us look at the effects of the helper as model and agent in a straightforward study of individual counseling. In this study the primary focus was on the convergence of the helpee's level of interpersonal functioning with that of the helper. Thus, the effects of modeling are most directly studied.

PROJECT 6
*Helping and Interpersonal Functioning**

There is extensive evidence indicating that the levels of the facilitative dimensions of empathy, respect, genuineness, and concreteness or specificity of expression offered by the counselor or therapist are related to client

* Reprinted in part with permission from the *Journal of Clinical Psychology*, 1967, **23**, 510–512, where it first appeared as "The Predicted Differential Effects of the Level of Counselor Functioning upon the Level of Functioning of Outpatients," by William A. Pagell, Robert R. Carkhuff, and Bernard G. Berenson.

process involvement and movement toward constructive change or gain. A model has been developed within which both counselor and clients are measured on the same facilitative dimensions and by which differential predictions concerning gains in interpersonal functioning by the client may be generated according to the discrepancies in the initial level of functioning of both counselor and client. This study attempts to validate this model in a study of therapeutic outcome.

METHODOLOGY

Four male veterans (Springfield, Massachusetts, Outpatient V.A.) and four male college students (University of Massachusetts Counseling Center) were randomly assigned to eight different male counselors. Both prior to their initial sessions and following six months of treatment, each patient was cast as a counselor in the helping role for one session with standard clients or interviewees in order to obtain random rating assessments of the patient's maximum potential level of interpersonal functioning. In addition, inventory ratings of the patient's (a) level of interpersonal functioning, and (b) level of gross behavioral functioning were made by each of the four following sources: (1) "outside experts" (a psychiatrist at the V.A. and the Dean of Students at the Counseling Center) who conducted an interview with the patient; (2) the standard clients or interviewees who were seen by the patients cast in the helping role; (3) the patients themselves; and (4) the therapists who, following their initial therapy sessions with the patients, rated their patients.

The interpersonal dimensions assessed by both the tape ratings and the rating scales inventories were as follows:

Empathy (E) is a five-point scale ranging from the lowest level, level 1, where the counselor does not respond or if he responds, he responds in such a way as to subtract significantly from the response made by the client, to the highest level, level 5, where the counselor's responses add significantly to the communications of the client in such a way as to enable the client to move to deeper levels of self-understanding and experiencing. Respect (R) ranges from level 1, where the counselor is communicating clear negative regard, to level 5, where the counselor communicates a very deep respect for the client's potential. Genuineness (G) varies from level 1, where the counselor's verbalizations are clearly unrelated to his other behavioral communications, to level 5, where the counselor is clearly being himself and employing his own genuine responses constructively. Concreteness (C) ranges from level 1, where the counselor allows all discussions to deal only with vague and anonymous generalities to level 5, where the counselor leads the client into specific discussions of feelings and experiences. Facilitative self-disclosure (SD) varies from level 1, where the counselor discloses nothing about his own feelings or personality, to level 5, where the counselor volunteers very intimate material about himself, appropriate to the needs of the client. The gross behavior scales assessed the client on his degree of psychological disturbance, self-care and social participation and, on the post measure, the degree to which the client had improved.

The Pearson coefficients for rate-rerate reliabilities of the two tape raters were as follows: E, .92, .95; R, .90, .93; G, .89, .92; C, .87, .89; SD, .93, .82. The inter-rater reliabilities were as follows: E, .98; R, .99; G, .83; C, .91; SD, .91.

Predictions were made from the level of the counselor's functioning in his initial session with the client. Although originally the study was designed to generate differential predictions of patient gain or no gain or deterioration according to (1) those counselors who were functioning overall (an average of all conditions) above level 3 (minimally facilitative by definition) and those who were not, and (2) those counselors who were functioning overall one level above the level of client's overall functioning when he was cast in the helping role and those counselors who were not, the same two of the eight counselors alone met both criteria, and thus predictions of improvement were generated only for their clients. None of the remaining six counselors were either functioning above level 3 overall or a level above their client's level of functioning. It should be noted that prior to the study, representative tapes from ongoing therapy were collected from the participating counselors. The Spearman Rho correlation between the ratings of the tapes prior to the study and the ratings of the tapes in the study was .81, significant beyond the .05 level.

RESULTS

The data were in the predicted direction for all dimensions of all indices from all sources. In general, the patients of the two facilitative counselors demonstrated the greatest amount of constructive change on all dimensions of all indices, while only one of the remaining six patients exhibited constructive change on some of the dimensions and the remaining five patients demonstrated no change or deterioration on almost all of the dimensions. Specifically, the hypotheses were tested by the Fisher Exact Probability Test, with the following results: (1) In general, the expert ratings were the most effective discriminators of the predictions on all dimensions, yielding significant results at the .05 level on all but one dimension *(C)*, and followed in order by the ratings of (a) the therapists, (b) the tape ratings, (c) the ratings of the standard interviewees, and (d) the patients, themselves; (2) On the dimensions of interpersonal functioning, E most frequently yielded significant differences, followed by R and G, with the fewest changes discerned on C and SD; (3) On the dimensions of gross behavioral functioning, differences were discerned in order on sociability, self-care and improvement but not on degree of psychological disturbance.

DISCUSSION

Perhaps the most important finding is that casting and assessing patients in the helping role can, in conjunction with assessments of the therapist's level of functioning, be an effective means of generating differential predictions of client change in interpersonal functioning. Mental health practitioners and researchers have reasoned for some time that the patient should generalize from his therapy relationship to other interpersonal experiences. Placing the patient in a situation where he is asked to help another person both prior to and following therapy should give an important index of his level of functioning.

It is noteworthy that the outside experts were the most effective discriminators in terms of outcome predictions, perhaps reflecting their greater objectivity in making assessments. In turn, the dimension of empathy discriminated those clients gaining and those not gaining most successfully, a finding consistent with those of Blackman, Smith, Brockman and Stern (1958) who established that the patient's degree of empathic understanding is the main determinant of his progress in functioning.

The presence of two of eight counselors functioning at minimally facilitative levels is considerably greater than the base rate data would indicate for the possibility of a chance occurrence. It is noteworthy that one of the patients (a patient of one of the two high level functioning counselors) was functioning above level 3 following therapy as assessed by the tape ratings. Thus, of the 16 persons involved in the study (eight counselors and eight patients), three were functioning above level 3 — two counselors and one patient. The potential impact of a high level functioning counselor may be great.

SUMMARY

Eight outpatients, four from the V.A. and four from a University counseling center, were seen by eight different counselors in the two different settings. Predictions for patient gain in interpersonal functioning were generated by the differential between tape rating assessments of the counselor's level of functioning (empathy, respect, genuineness, concreteness, self-disclosure) in his initial session with the client and tape assessments of patients cast as counselors in the helping role with standard clients. In general, the inventory ratings were in the predicted direction for all dimensions for all indices of interpersonal and gross behavioral functioning by all of the following sources: experts; therapists; patients; standard interviewee; objective tape ratings.

The results of the study suggest the direct effects of modeling. Helpers and helpees can be assessed on the same dimensions, and predictions concerning a convergence of the helpee's level of functioning with that of the helper can be made. In this context, perhaps the most significant finding is that one of the helpees gained so considerably in interpersonal skills that at the termination of counseling he was functioning at levels higher than six of the professional helpers.

Of course, the helper was not simply the model for effective functioning. He was also the agent, although in this instance he did not set up an explicit and systematic program to effect such changes. In the following study the helper is more explicitly the helpee's agent in a sphere of functioning other than the interpersonal. In a path-finding extension of the earlier work, the following project evaluates the teacher's role as an agent of gain in studying the effects of the teacher's level of interpersonal functioning upon students' intellectual achievement.

PROJECT 7
Helping and Intellectual Functioning*

There is extensive evidence to suggest that all interpersonal learning or relearning processes share the same core of conditions offered by the "more knowing" person to the "less knowing" person. In particular, the conditions of empathy, positive regard and genuineness have been related to constructive client change or gain in guidance, counseling and therapy. Indirect evidence has been presented for the effect of these conditions both in child-rearing and in teaching. Unfortunately, none of the studies of the effectiveness of teaching have systematically explored the relationship of the conditions of empathy, positive regard and genuineness to teaching effectiveness. It is the purpose of this study, then, to (a) assess the levels of these facilitative conditions that teachers are communicating, and (b) determine the differential effects of these conditions upon the cognitive growth of students as assessed by achievement tests.

METHODOLOGY

Teachers

Six third grade teachers tape recorded their interaction with reading groups during one week in March and one week in May of the same academic year. The recordings were done as randomly as possible to account for such influences as time of day and day of week.

*Reprinted in part with permission from the *Florida Journal of Educational Research*, 1969, 11, 39–48, where it first appeared as "The Effect of Teacher-Offered Conditions of Empathy, Positive Regard and Congruence upon Student Achievement," by David Aspy.

Subjects

The subjects were selected from the teachers' classes and included (a) the five boys with the highest IQ's, (b) the five boys with the lowest IQ's, (c) the five girls with the highest IQ's, and (d) the five girls with the lowest IQ's. Thus, twenty students were selected from each teacher's class. The differences between the mean IQ's for each of the low groups were non-significant, and the same was true for the high groups. That is, all the high IQ groups and all the low IQ groups were statistically equated since their differences were non-significant. Of course, there were significant differences between the high and low groups. The selection process controlled for sex and IQ.

The students were administered five subtests of the Stanford Achievement Test during September and again during May of the same academic year. The differences between the subjects' scores were used as the measure of the students' academic gain. The subtests were (a) Word Meaning, (b) Paragraph Meaning, (c) Spelling, (d) Word Study Skills, and (e) Language, all of which relate to verbal quantities. This seemed appropriate since the teachers were recording their reading groups which are verbal situations.

Ratings

The teachers had recorded two hours of classroom interaction, and eight four-minute segments were selected randomly from each teacher's performance. These segments were assigned numbers randomly, so the raters identified them only by their numbers.

Three trained raters, experienced at evaluating recordings of counseling and psychotherapy, assessed the levels of empathy, positive regard, and congruence provided by the teachers on each of the segments. Each rater evaluated the segments independently. The ratings for each teacher were summed and a composite or mean rating for each teacher was obtained.

The rating scales were designed to allow trained but otherwise naive raters to evaluate the levels of (a) empathy, (b) positive regard and (c) congruence provided by a therapist. The raters formulated their opinions by listening to randomly selected samples from psychotherapeutic interviews.

Accurate Empathy (AE) is assessed according to a 9-point scale with a rating of 1 representing the lowest levels of empathy and 9 the highest. At Stage 1 the therapist seems completely unaware of even the most conspicuous of the client's feelings. His responses are not appropriate to the mood and content of the client's statement and there is no determinable quality of empathy. At Stage 3, the therapist often responds accurately to the client's more exposed feelings. He also displays concern for the deeper, more hidden feelings, which he seems to sense must be present though he doesn't understand their nature. At Stage 5, the therapist accurately responds to all of the client's more readily discernible feelings. He shows awareness of many of the feelings and experiences which are not so evident, too; but in these he tends to be somewhat inaccurate in his understanding. At Stage 7, the therapist shows awareness of the precise intensity of the underlying emotions. However, his responses move only slightly beyond the area of the client's own awareness, so that feelings may be present which are not recognized by the client or therapist. At Stage 9 the therapist unerringly responds to the client's full range of feelings in their exact intensity. He expands the client's hint into a full-blown but tentative elaboration of feeling or experience with unerring sensitivity.

The *Positive Regard (PR)* Scale is a 5-point scale attempting to define stages along a continuum of the therapist's levels of functioning. At Stage 1, the therapist may be telling the patient what would be best for him, or may be in other ways actively either approving or disapproving of his behavior. At Stage 2, the therapist responds mechanically to the client and thus indicates little positive regard. At Stage 4, the therapist clearly communicates a very deep interest and concern for the welfare of the patient. At Stage 5, the therapist communicates positive regard without restriction. At this stage the patient is free to be himself even if it means that he is regressing, being defensive, or even disliking or rejecting the therapist himself. The only channeling by the therapist may be the demand that the patient communicate personally relevant material.

The scale for *Congruence (C)* is a 5-point scale attempting to specify stages along a continuum of therapist genuineness or self-congruence. At Stage 1, the therapist is clearly defensive in the interaction and there is explicit evidence of a very considerable discrepancy between his experiencing and his current verbalization. At Stage 2, the therapist responds appropriately but in a professional, rather than in a personal manner. At Stage 4, there is neither implicit nor explicit evidence of defensiveness or the presence of a facade. At Stage 5, the therapist is freely and deeply himself in the relationship. There is openness to experiences and feelings by the therapist without traces of defensiveness or retreat into professionalism.

RESULTS

The mean rating for each of the six teachers on each of the three conditions is summarized in Table 4–1. The composite ratings indicate the same rank ordering for each teacher for each of the three characteristics. Therefore, it was possible to compare one analysis of variance for all of the conditions. The term "facilitating conditions" was implemented in the discussion of the analysis of data and includes empathy, positive regard and congruence in its meaning.

Since teachers 1, 2 and 3 received higher ratings than teachers 4, 5 and 6 for each of the characteristics, the following categories were used in the analysis of the data: high condition teachers (1, 2 and 3), and low condition teachers (4, 5 and 6).

Table 4–1
Mean Ratings for Accurate Empathy (AE), Positive Regard (PR), and Congruence (C) for Teachers

TEACHER	AE (9-pt scale)	PR (5-pt scale)	C (5-pt scale)
1	4.7	3.9	4.0
2	3.9	3.8	3.8
3	3.5	3.7	3.8
4	3.0	3.0	3.0
5	2.9	2.9	3.0
6	2.3	2.1	2.6

The achievement test results are summarized in Tables 4–2 through 4–7.

As can be observed, in Paragraph Meaning, Language, Word Meaning, and Word Study Skills the average amount gained by the students of the high level functioning teachers was substantially more than the students of those teachers offering low levels of conditions, while on Spelling the differences are negative but minimal. Overall, on the total gain, the students of the high level teachers demonstrated greater gain than those of low level teachers. An analysis of variance for each of the subtests yielded the results summarized in Table 4–8.

Table 4–2
Mean Score for Paragraph Meaning for Each Group

Teacher	MALE		FEMALE		Average by Teachers	Level of Conditions
	High IQ	Low IQ	High IQ	Low IQ		
1	1.68	.66	.76	.40	.88	High
2	1.22	.32	1.44	1.32	1.08	High
3	1.12	.44	1.44	1.00	1.00	High
4	1.10	.74	.80	.68	.83	Low
5	.58	.22	.40	.28	.37	Low
6	1.02	.74	.76	.64	.79	Low
Average for IQ Groups	1.12	.52	.93	.72	Average for Entire Group	0.82

NOTE: The test norms indicate that the gain by the average third grade student is 1.0 years.

Table 4–3
Mean Score for Language for Each Group

	MALE		FEMALE			
Teacher	High IQ	Low IQ	High IQ	Low IQ	Average by Teachers	Level of Conditions
1	2.04	.78	1.16	.44	1.11	High
2	2.30	.90	2.88	1.78	1.97	High
3	1.70	1.24	1.26	1.12	1.33	High
4	.70	.58	1.18	.92	.85	Low
5	1.04	.42	.84	.18	.62	Low
6	.00	.40	1.36	.74	.62	Low
Average for IQ Groups	1.30	.72	1.45	.86	Average for Entire Group	1.08

NOTE: The test norms indicate that the gain by the average third grade student is 1.0 years.

Table 4–4
Mean Score for Word Meaning for Each Group

	MALE		FEMALE			
Teacher	High IQ	Low IQ	High IQ	Low IQ	Average by Teachers	Level of Conditions
1	1.44	.98	.76	.82	1.00	High
2	1.44	.82	.86	1.32	1.11	High
3	1.30	.56	.66	.60	.79	High
4	1.28	.30	.90	.70	.80	Low
5	1.28	.20	.76	.72	.74	Low
6	.62	.70	1.06	.60	.75	Low
Average for IQ Groups	1.23	.60	.83	.79	Average for Entire Group	.86

NOTE: The test norms indicate that the gain by the average third grade student is 1.0 years.

Table 4–5
Mean Score for Word Study Skills for Each Group

| | MALE | | FEMALE | | | |
Teacher	High IQ	Low IQ	High IQ	Low IQ	Average by Teachers	Levels of Conditions
1	1.78	1.74	1.94	.74	1.55	High
2	2.00	.08	2.24	2.44	1.69	High
3	.16	.82	.98	.18	.46	High
4	.88	1.02	.78	.76	.86	Low
5	1.36	.80	.44	.12	.62	Low
6	1.50	.08	.72	.96	.82	Low
Average for IQ Groups	1.23	.76	1.18	.83	Average for Entire Group	1.00

NOTE: The test norms indicate that the gain by the average third grade student is 1.0 years.

Table 4–6
Mean Score for Spelling for Each Group

| | MALE | | FEMALE | | | |
Teacher	High IQ	Low IQ	High IQ	Low IQ	Average by Teachers	Levels of Conditions
1	1.00	.92	1.08	.50	.87	High
2	1.42	.18	1.22	1.68	1.12	High
3	.52	1.30	.78	.74	.83	High
4	.94	1.14	1.80	1.26	1.28	Low
5	1.38	.66	1.24	.58	.96	Low
6	.92	.88	1.22	1.22	1.06	Low
Average for IQ Groups	1.03	.84	1.22	.99	Average for Entire Group	1.02

NOTE: The test norms indicate that the gain by the average third grade student is 1.0 years.

Table 4–7
Mean Score for Total for Each Group

	MALE		FEMALE			
Teacher	High IQ	Low IQ	High IQ	Low IQ	Average by Teachers	Levels of Conditions
1	8.54	5.22	5.76	2.96	5.62	High
2	8.38	2.50	8.64	8.54	7.01	High
3	4.48	4.34	5.20	3.50	4.38	High
4	4.50	3.78	5.46	4.32	4.51	Low
5	5.94	2.74	3.68	1.68	3.51	Low
6	3.96	2.88	5.12	4.16	4.03	Low
Average for IQ Groups	5.96	2.57	5.64	4.19	Average for Entire Group	4.84

NOTE: The test norms indicate that the total gain for five subtests by the average third grade student is 5.0 years.

SUMMARY AND CONCLUSIONS

The levels of empathy, positive regard and congruence provided by teachers in their actual classroom procedure related positively to the cognitive growth of their students. This positive relationship was found for four subtests of the Stanford Achievement Test and the total gain. These relationships were statistically significant at or above the .05 level of confidence. For the Spelling subtest the teacher conditions were related negatively to the test score gains, but the relationship was not statistically significant at the .05 level of confidence.

This study supports the general hypothesis that there is a positive relationship between the levels of teacher-offered empathy, positive regard and congruence and the cognitive growth of the students. It extends the generalization of the effect of the core conditions to all instances of interpersonal learning processes. In particular, it points up the need for assessing teachers on other than intellective indices. However, while assessments were made independent of teacher knowledgeability, it is also quite pos-

Table 4–8
A Summary of the Statistical Significance of the Sources of Variance

Source	Total Gain	Paragraph Meaning	Language	Word Meaning	Word Study Skills	Spelling
1. IQ	.01	.01	.01	.01	.01	N.S.
2. Level of facilitating conditions	.01	.01	.001	.05	.01	N.S.
3. Sex	N.S.	N.S.	N.S.	N.S.	N.S.	N.S.
4. IQ and facilitating conditions	N.S.	N.S.	N.S.	N.S.	N.S.	N.S.
5. IQ and sex	N.S.	N.S.	N.S.	.01	N.S.	N.S.
6. Facilitating conditions and sex	N.S.	N.S.	N.S.	N.S.	N.S.	N.S.
7. IQ, Facilitating conditions and sex	N.S.	N.S.	N.S.	N.S.	N.S.	N.S.
8. Teachers within levels of facilitating conditions	.01	N.S.	N.S.	N.S.	.01	N.S.
9. Teachers and sex within levels of facilitating conditions	.01	N.S.	N.S.	N.S.	N.S.	N.S.
10. Teachers and IQ within levels of facilitating conditions	N.S.	N.S.	N.S.	N.S.	N.S.	N.S.
11. Teachers, sex, and IQ within levels of facilitating conditions	N.S.	N.S.	N.S.	N.S.	N.S.	N.S.

N.S. = Nonsignificant.

sible that those offering the highest levels of conditions were most knowl-
edgeable, and future studies should incorporate such necessary controls.
In addition, there are further questions which must be asked. Are, for example, the levels of facilitative conditions offered by the teacher more
critical during the early grammar school years than in later phases of education? In any event, this project can serve as a model for further research
into the effectiveness of teaching, and if replicated, the results of this study
have potentially profound implications for teaching and teacher-training
programs.

The important finding is that helpers who communicate at high levels of interpersonal dimensions such as empathic understanding are able to become significant sources of learning in academic areas for their students. All this is not to say, for example, that teacher knowledgeability of subject matter is not a relevant variable. It is to say, however, that we can relate the conditions of one area of helper functioning, the emotional-interpersonal, to another area of helpee functioning, the intellectual. Other studies such as that of Stoffer (1970) replicate these findings and establish a relationship not only between interpersonal functioning and student achievement but also between interpersonal functioning and classroom behavior.

In extensions of earlier works, Kratochvil, Carkhuff, and Berenson (1969) sought to study the cumulative effects of parent and teacher level of interpersonal functioning upon the physical as well as the emotional-interpersonal and intellectual functioning of fifth grade pupils. Unfortunately, while the one teacher judged to be functioning at the highest interpersonal levels elicited the greatest achievement gains in her students, there were not enough high level functioning teachers to assess the cumulative effects adequately. While this in itself is an indictment of the educational system involved, the more important learnings pointed up the complexities of assessing human development in general and the lack of indexes of helper physical and intellectual functioning specifically.

Perhaps the most interesting finding was the significant interrelationship of the physical, emotional, and intellectual functioning of students. Pupils who are functioning at relatively high levels physically tend to function at relatively high levels intellectually and interpersonally, and vice versa for all of these spheres.

However, the potential implications for the production of helpees who are at the highest levels in all spheres of functioning are even more critical. With the presence of helpers who are at the highest levels, the helpers will make most effective use of both the modeling and agent sources in effecting the development of the helpees to the highest level in all of these spheres.

The effective helper is, however, not simply one who is himself functioning at high levels of interpersonal and other dimensions. He is not fully the helpee's agent until he has, in the context of his offering high levels of interpersonal dimensions, developed effective programs for the helpee's benefit.

In path-finding research on the differential effects of people and programs, Vitalo (1970) found that both the helper's level of functioning on interpersonal dimensions and the systematic program were significant sources of effect in verbal conditioning of personal pronoun emissions by the helpee. Examination of the interaction effects revealed that the presence of conditioning was dependent upon the level of the experimenter's level of functioning. Only the high-functioning experimenters elicited learning rates from the experimental group that were different from those produced by a control group.

While verbal conditioning does not appear immediately relevant to helping programs it extends directly into systematic programs that translate to human benefits. Thus, for example, the following study investigated the effects of verbal reinforcement counseling as a preferred method for increasing high school students' acquisition of information relevant to their educational and/or vocational goals and found that high level functioning helpers produced a significantly greater amount of helpee information-seeking behavior than low level functioning helpers. For our purposes perhaps the most significant result was the finding that while the verbal reinforcement program was effective at the beginning of the session for the helpees of the low-functioning helpers, as the session went on these nonfacilitative helpers had "turned off" their helpee's information-seeking behavior.

PROJECT 8
Helping and Systematic Programs*

The thrust of much of the current research on counseling outcome has revolved around the utilization of behavioral techniques to effect behavior change. Often neglected by such researchers has been the impact of the behavioral counselor and the conditions of living, i.e. empathy, warmth, and genuineness he offers his clients. Although there is recognition of the fact that the behavioral therapist must become in some way a potent reinforcer, it is believed that he need not offer high levels of the core dimensions.

The development of the concept of facilitative conditions suggests that client movement is, to a large extent, a function of the therapist. Given particular interaction patterns of relevant variables, a variety of counseling approaches may be employed to produce favorable results. Borrowing from existing bodies of knowledge, the therapist selects the preferred mode of treatment. When the treatment is offered in the context of high facilitative conditions, the probability of successful counseling is enhanced.

Almost any approach may be considered a potential preferred mode in an individual case. The critical questions for any preferred mode are its unique contributions and under what circumstances it is applicable.

Behavioral counseling is a potential preferred mode in dealing with observable patterns of behavior, i.e. behavior whose origins may be readily observable. The behavioral counselor views client problems as problems in learning, and the counselor needs to view his function as assisting clients to learn more effective ways of solving his own problems.

The operant learning paradigm postulated by B. F. Skinner provides the framework for a behavioral counselor. The major tenet within the operant model is that behavior, or rate of emitted rather than elicited re-

---

* Reprinted in part with permission from D. J. Mickelson, "The Differential Effects of Facilitative and Non-Facilitative Counselors upon Student Information-Seeking Behavior." Doctoral dissertation, State University of New York at Buffalo, 1970.

sponse, is controlled by its consequences. These consequences, whether positive or negative, are in turn contingent upon the occurrence of the response. The strength or rate of a behavior, therefore, is a function of the consequences of that behavior. On the basis of these principles, behavior may be shaped, advertently or inadvertently, in a predetermined direction.

Krumboltz (1966) suggests that the effectiveness of counseling can be increased through the application of behavioral techniques. Several research studies have demonstrated the feasibility of applying such techniques to problems such as career development, decision-making, the acquisition of information, and the reduction of feelings of alienation. These studies have provided support for the proponents of behavioral counseling.

The behavioral techniques employed by the counselors in the above studies were verbal reinforcement and model reinforcement. While the research indicated the effectiveness of reinforcement techniques, differential response rates have been found when differing types of examiners were used.

The purpose of this investigation was to test the effectiveness of verbal reinforcement counseling as a preferred mode of treatment by facilitative and non-facilitative counselors. Client information-seeking behavior was selected as the primary criterion variable. Not only has previous research indicated its susceptibility to reinforcement counseling, but the importance of information to the decision-making process is crucial. The decision-making process has been equated with the application of the scientific method where the student learns to collect data, make predictions, assess probabilities, and conduct evaluations of self-potential. An effective way to learn how to make sound decisions within the high school setting is to engage in such behavior, i.e. to acquire additional information about one's own vocational and educational plans.

METHODOLOGY

Information-Seeking Behavior

Information-seeking behavior within the counseling session was the primary criterion variable for this investigation. Such behavior was defined as a discrete unit of a client's verbal statement which specified the client's past seeking, present consideration of seeking, active-seeking, or future intention to seek information relevant to his educational and/or vocational goals. Also, the client's behavior was categorized as non-information seeking responses. Thus, each client's response was classified into one of two categories: verbal information-seeking behavior (VISB) and verbal non-information-seeking behavior (VNISB).

Selection of Counselors

A tape recording of nine client stimuli originally used by Kratochvil, Carkhuff and Berenson (1969) was the primary instrument used to select the counselors for this study. The instrument is a modification and extension of standard stimuli involving adult problems for which extensive normative and validity data are available (Carkhuff, 1969a). The stimuli contained information relative to students in the age group 11–14.

The sample of counselors used in this investigation was taken from the general population of graduate students enrolled in the introductory counseling courses in the Department of Counselor Education, State University of New York at Buffalo. Counselors were selected according to two criteria: (1) no previous counseling experience and (2) responses to the client stimuli achieving a mean rating of 2.5 or greater or 1.5 or less. Thus, two groups of counselors were established: facilitative and non-facilitative. Truax and Carkhuff (1967) offer predictive validity for such a technique of identifying facilitative and non-facilitative counselors. Each counselor received training in the application of verbal reinforcement techniques.

Selection of Clients

A total of 12 high schools in the western New York area participated in the investigation. Each regular school counselor in the participating schools was contacted to prepare a list of eleventh grade students, by sex, who were undecided about their educational and/or vocational goals and who had expressed an interest in acquiring additional information. The students whom the counselor determined were interested and willing to participate in the study were personally contacted and invited to speak with the participating counselors. Those students who expressed an interest in acquiring additional information were included in a numbered list of males and females. Three clients were randomly selected to speak with each participating counselor. This procedure was followed by all of the participating schools. A total of 48 eleventh grade students participated in the study, 24 males and 24 females.

Nature of the Treatment

Two treatment groups were established. The first group contained counselors who had been identified as being facilitative. The second group contained counselors who had been identified as being non-facilitative. Each treatment group contained eight counselors and 24 clients. The total number of participants in this investigation was 64, 16 counselors and 48 clients.

The two treatment groups followed a pre-arranged schedule. Each counselor was scheduled to meet three different clients over a three-week period. A counseling session of 30 minutes was suggested. However, the length of the interview was determined by the needs of the client, i.e. when the client's interests were satiated, the session was terminated.

Verbal reinforcement procedures were employed in both groups. All clients were selected on the basis of their need and interest in acquiring additional educational and/or occupation information. During the counseling session, the counselor initiated the discussions. Once the discussions were under way, the counselor employed cue statements to keep the session focused upon the acquisition of relevant information. The purpose of such counselor direction was to increase the client's awareness of differing sources of information and to encourage his using them.

In addition to the cue statements of the counselor, the counselor used positive verbal reinforcement when the client indicated consideration, intent, or active-seeking of relevant information. The goal of such counseling was to get the client to increase the frequency of his information-seeking behavior and thereby have a generalized effect upon his behavior in his decision-making. Non-information-seeking behavior would decrease through the process of non-reinforcement.

Measurement of Information-Seeking Behavior

The criterion measure for this investigation was the frequency of verbal information-seeking behavior (VISB) within the counseling session. The tapes of each counselor were evaluated to determine the frequency of such client verbal behavior. Each tape was randomly assigned to one of four raters for the analysis. The raters were not connected with the study. To establish the comparability of raters to frequency, the proportion of agreement technique was employed to demonstrate the coincidence of independent observation. The proportion of agreement among raters was from .88 to .96.

Each rater categorized the client's verbal remarks into one of two categories: VISB and VNISB. Also, the sex of the counselor and the sex of the client were noted. The length of the counseling session was timed and recorded. For the selected 15-minute segment, the frequency of counselor verbal reinforcing stimuli was recorded.

The major research hypotheses of this investigation were as follows:

1. There will be more VISB exhibited by those clients being reinforced by facilitative counselors as opposed to those clients being reinforced by non-facilitative counselors.
2. There will be no differences in the frequency of VNISB by those clients being reinforced by facilitative counselors as opposed to those clients being reinforced by non-facilitative counselors.
3. There will be no differences in the length of the counseling session of facilitative and non-facilitative counselors.
4. There will be no differences in the frequency of reinforcing stimuli between facilitative and non-facilitative counselors.

Hypotheses one, two, and three were tested for significance by using a 2 × 2 mixed model, nested design, analysis of variance. The three factors in the model were type of counselor, sex of counselor, and client. Type of counselor contained two levels, facilitative and non-facilitative, sex of counselor contained two levels, male and female, and client contained two levels, male and female. Type of counselor and sex of counselor were treated as fixed effects while the third factor, client, was treated as a random effect. In the model, a nested design was employed as sex of counselor was nested within counselor type. VISB, VNISB, and length of the session were the dependent variables.

Hypothesis four was tested for significance by using a 1 × 2 mixed model for the analysis of variance. The two factors were (1) client, and (2) type of counselor. The second factor contained two levels, facilitative and non-facilitative.

In all of the hypothesis testing, the .01 level of probability was utilized.

RESULTS

The means and standard deviations for each of the four groups were computed and are presented in Table 4–9. VISB was the dependent variable. An analysis of variance was then performed to determine whether any significant differences existed among the means of these groups. Among the variance group means, only the effects of the facilitative counselors were significant. The F ratio of 20.17 was significant at the .01 level.

Similar analyses were conducted with VNISB and length of the interview as dependent variables. The group cell means and standard deviations are presented in Tables 4–10 and 4–11. Inspection of the data indicated that the only significant F ratios were found when VNISB was the dependent variable.

The sex of client effect produced an F ratio of 22.21. Also, there was an interaction effect of type of counselor × sex of client. The resulting F ratio of 9.49 was also significant at the .01 level.

The means and standard deviations for the two groups of counselors offering reinforcement are presented in Table 4–12. Frequency of reinforcement was the dependent variable. The analysis of variance yielded nothing between group differences.

DISCUSSION

The results of the analysis of data demonstrated that facilitative counselors were able to engage their clients in a significantly greater amount of verbal information-seeking behavior than non-facilitative counselors. This finding suggests that facilitative counselors are more effective in assisting high school students in their acquisition of information.

Table 4–9
  Observed Cell Means and Standard Deviations of Verbal Information-Seeking
  Behavior Elicited by Facilitative and Non-Facilitative Counselors

		FACILITATIVE COUNSELORS		NON-FACILITATIVE COUNSELORS	
		Male	Female	Male	Female
CLIENTS	Male	33.20	46.25	15.75	23.86
		14.96	12.11	2.21	9.02
	Female	34.50	35.00	20.40	20.13
		12.07	6.76	5.21	5.06

Table 4–10
  Observed Cell Means and Standard Deviations of Verbal Non-Information-Seeking
  Behavior Elicited by Facilitative and Non-Facilitative Counselors

		FACILITATIVE COUNSELORS		NON-FACILITATIVE COUNSELORS	
		Male	Female	Male	Female
CLIENTS	Male	10.40	14.25	13.00	11.00
		5.94	6.94	6.98	3.46
	Female	6.25	8.14	10.60	10.63
		5.18	1.95	5.73	5.15

Table 4–11
  Observed Cell Means and Standard Deviations of Length of the Interview for
  Facilitative and Non-Facilitative Counselors

		FACILITATIVE COUNSELORS		NON-FACILITATIVE COUNSELORS	
		Male	Female	Male	Female
CLIENTS	Male	18.00	17.88	16.75	22.71
		2.45	4.26	5.74	6.25
	Female	15.50	15.58	14.40	19.75
		1.73	3.20	4.45	7.98

Table 4–12
  Observed Cell Means and Standard Deviations of Reinforcing Stimuli for Facilitative
  and Non-Facilitative Counselors

		Facilitative Counselors	Non-Facilitative Counselors
CLIENTS	Means	28.75	22.63
	SD	4.20	5.95

The crucial variable affecting the response pattern of the clients would seem to be the quality of the relationship created by the facilitative counselor. The lack of between group differences in the frequency with which the counselors made rewarding phrases or statements emphasizes this point. Verbal reinforcement, by itself, was not an effective technique in engaging the client in information-seeking behavior. The reinforcing value of the relationship significantly affected the acceptance by the client of the reinforcing stimuli. The facilitative counselor emerged as a more potent reinforcer.

The study also suggests that facilitative counselors, with an equivalent amount of training as non-facilitative counselors, are able to make more effective use of such training. Short term training programs on in-service courses would be able to maximize their impact by careful screening of applicants. Maximum utilization of facilities would thus be insured.

A subjective rating of the tapes indicated that the operant paradigm may have been inappropriate as the counseling theory for reinforcement procedures. The behavioral counselor may serve as a stimulator by "setting-up" the client and then rewarding him for the desired response. When necessary, he may offer support. Functional definitions of these two roles would result in support of the concept of the counselor being a man and a woman.

The thrust of this investigation has been directed at the process of client change in behavioral counseling. Strong evidence is offered to suggest that an important ingredient in such counseling is the type of counselor who employs behavioral techniques. In working with high school youth, counselors can no longer assume that their offerings of reinforcement will be accepted. Critical self-evaluation must be continually undertaken to insure counselor effectiveness. For too long, the emphasis of behavioral counseling has been upon the techniques of the counselor. Effort needs to be redirected to examining the characteristics of the behavioral counselor. Behavioral counseling is necessary but not sufficient.

The linear relationship between helpee verbal information-seeking behavior and the length of the interview for high level functioning helpers emphasizes dramatically the role of personnel and programs in effecting constructive helpee change or gain. The longer the high level helper and his helpee interacted in the information-seeking program the more the helpee engaged in the appropriate information-seeking behavior.

We may hypothesize, then, that designs for success are a function of the highest level personnel offering the highest level programs. Only helping personnel functioning at the highest levels of interpersonal and other relevant dimensions are able to effect constructive change or gain in the helpee's life. Only the most directionful and systematic helping programs offered in the context of helping personnel functioning at the highest levels can effect maximum constructive change or gain in the helpee.

The equation for delivery in designs for success is as follows:

$$\text{Effective personnel} + \text{Effective programs} = \text{Effective outcome.}$$

The effective personnel, it must be underscored, are themselves historically a product of effective personnel in conjunction with effective programs. In turn, effective personnel do not become most fully both model and agent for the helpee's change or gain until they have developed fully and systematically programs incorporating all of the effective sources of human resource development.

REFERENCES

Aspy, D. , The effect of teacher-offered conditions of empathy, positive regard and congruence upon student achievement. *Florida Journal of Research,* 1969, **11,** 39–48.

Ayllon, T., & Haughton, E. Control of the behavior of schizophrenic patients by food. *Journal of Experimental Analysis of Behavior,* 1962, **5,** 343–352.

Bandura, A. Behavioral modification through modeling procedures. In L. Krasner and L. P. Ullmann (Eds.), *Research in behavior modification. New developments and implications.* New York: Holt, Rinehart and Winston, 1965.

Blackman, N., Smith, K., Brockman, R. J., & Stern, J. A. The development of empathy in male schizophrenics. *Psychiatric Quarterly,* 1958, **32,** 546–553.

Brayfield, A. Human resources development. *American Psychologist,* 1968, **23,** 479–482.

Carkhuff, R. R. *Helping and human relations: A primer for lay and professional helpers.* Vol. I. *Selection and training.* New York: Holt, Rinehart and Winston, 1969. (a)

Carkhuff, R. R. *Helping and human relations: A primer for lay and professional helpers.* Vol. II. *Practice and research.* New York: Holt, Rinehart and Winston, 1969. (b)

Carkhuff, R. R., & Berenson, B. G. *Beyond counseling and therapy.* New York: Holt, Rinehart and Winston, 1967.

Carkhuff, R. R., & Burstein, J. Objective therapist and client ratings of therapist-offered conditions of moderate to low functioning therapists. *Journal of Clinical Psychology,* 1970, **26,** 394–395.

Carkhuff, R. R., Kratochvil, D., & Friel, T. The effects of professional training: Communication and discrimination of facilitative dimensions. *Journal of Counseling Psychology,* 1968, **15,** 68–74.

Clark, K. The effects of prejudice and discrimination on personality development. *Proceedings Mid-Century White House Conference,* 1950.

Clark, K. *Dark ghetto.* New York: Harper & Row, 1965.

Foulds, M. Self-actualization and the communication of facilitative conditions during counseling. *Journal of Counseling Psychology,* 1969, **16,** 132–136.

Hobbs, N. Sources of gain in counseling and psychotherapy. *American Psychologist,* 1962, **17,** 18–34.

Kolb, D. A. Achievement motivation training for underachieving high school boys. *Journal of Personality and Social Psychology,* 1965, **2,** 783–729.

Krasner, L., & Ullmann, L. *Research in behavior modification.* New York: Holt, Rinehart and Winston, 1965.

Kratochvil, D., Carkhuff, R. R., & Berenson, B. G. The cumulative effects of parent and teacher-offered levels of facilitative conditions upon indexes of student physical, emotional and intellectual functioning. *Journal of Educational Research,* 1969, **63,** 161–164.

Krumboltz, J. D. (Ed.) *Revolution in counseling: Implications of behavioral science.* Boston: Houghton Mifflin, 1966.

Krumboltz, J. D. Behavioral counseling: Rationale and research. *Personnel and Guidance Journal,* 1965, **44,** 383–387.

Krumboltz, J. D., & Thoreson, C. E. The effect of behavioral counseling in group and individual settings on information-seeking behavior. *Journal of Counseling Psychology,* 1964, **11,** 324–333.

Lewin, K. *Field theory in social science.* New York: Harper & Row, 1951.

Lovaas, O. Clinical implications of relationships between verbal and nonverbal operant behavior. In H. J. Eysenck (Ed.), *Experiments in behavior therapy.* New York: Macmillan, 1964.

McClelland, D. C. *The achieving society.* Princeton, N.J.: Van Nostrand, 1961.

Mickelson, D. J. The differential effects of facilitative and non-facilitative behavioral counselors upon student verbal information-seeking behavior. Doctoral dissertation, State University of New York at Buffalo, 1970.

Pagell, W., Carkhuff, R. R., & Berenson, B. G. The predicted differential effects of the level of counselor functioning upon the level of functioning of outpatients. *Journal of Clinical Psychology,* 1967, **23,** 510–512.

Persons, R. W., & Pepinsky, H. B. Convergence in psychotherapy with delinquent boys. *Journal of Counseling Psychology,* 1966, **13,** 329–334.

Rosenthal, R., & Jacobson, L. *Pygmalion in the classroom: Teacher expectation and pupils' intellectual development.* New York: Holt, Rinehart and Winston, 1968.

Sarason, I. G. Verbal learning, modeling and juvenile delinquency. *American Psychologist,* 1968, **23,** 254–266.

Stoffer, D. L. Investigation of positive behavior change as a function of genuineness, warmth and empathic understanding. *Journal of Educational Research,* 1970, **63,** 225–228.

Truax, C. B., & Carkhuff, R. R. *Toward effective counseling and psychotherapy.* Chicago: Aldine, 1967.

Vitalo, R. L. Effects of facilitative interpersonal functioning in a conditioning paradigm. *Journal of Counseling Psychology,* 1970, **17,** 141–144.

Welkowitz, Joan, Cohen, J., & Ortmeyer, D. Value system similarity: Investigation of patient-therapist dyads. *Journal of Consulting Psychology,* 1967, **31,** 48–55.

CHAPTER 5
Principles of Social Action

We are on the verge of the greatest revolution the world has ever known. We, the greatest, wealthiest nation in the history of mankind, while literally reaching for the stars, may literally get knocked on our collective rump. The problems of the poor, the black, and the city bring us back to the earth we hasten to leave.

It is an earth where man has violated the beauty and polluted and wasted the resources—not just the physical beauty and resources, and this is man's most grievous sin to God—but the beauty and resources of his fellow man, and this is man's worst sin, his most unforgivable sin: the sin of man's inhumanity to man. It is, nevertheless, our earth. Until the day we leave, it is our home. Indeed, good or bad, it is a home we may never leave. Depending upon which revolution we engage in, this earth continues to have the potential for a good home, a very good home.

We are on the verge of two revolutions, then. Either the most extraordinary social and human service revolution that the world has ever known—for once in history the resources are there to meet the needs—or the most catastrophic revolution the world has ever known—for once in history we are so close to yet so far from the elimination of survival conditions, from the actualization of growth.

Survival or growth. That is our choice. Survival—where one man believes winning involves keeping another on his knees and where the second believes winning would be to bring the first to his knees. Both are losers.

Growth—where one man believes winning involves going as far as he can go and where the other believes winning involves going as far as the first can go—or further—and where, as part of going as far as he can go, the first helps make it possible for the second. Both are winners.

"To pursue our present course will involve the continuing polarization of the American community and, ultimately, the destruction of basic democratic values.

"The alternative is not blind repression or capitulation to lawlessness. It is the realization of common opportunities for all within a single society.

"This alternative will require a commitment to national action—compassionate, massive and sustained, backed by the resources of the most powerful and the richest nation on this earth. From every American it will require new attitudes, new understanding and, above all, new will" (National Advisory Commission, 1968, pp. 1–2).

PRINCIPLES OF PERSONAL ACTION

Until the survival of all human beings is assured, the right to growth of any one human being is questionable. The major issue facing the United States of America and the world today is that of *creating a world which enables each and every person in it to utilize to his fullest his natural physical, emotional, and intellectual resources*. In the cause of justice, opportunity, and growth for all, let us enunciate some basic principles of effective social action.

Before proceeding further, however, it is critical that we spell out a personal stance or disposition toward social action programs and the development of human resources in general. First and most basic, those of us who would help others must first get our own houses in order. This alone will leave us free and clean in working with others. This alone will enable us to avoid the distortions born of frustrations in our own lives. If we do not have ourselves, our families, and our communities in order, we have no business entering the lives, the families, and the communities of others. Indeed, if we do not have our own homes in order, those we would help do not welcome us into their homes, for we do not have anything that they want and could not, given their circumstances, handle problems they have been unable to solve.

Second and related, those of us who would help must learn to listen and —more important—to hear those whom we would help. A broad and deep basis of understanding will point to workable and effective courses of action. A broad and deep basis of understanding will enable us to do for others what, given the same circumstances, we would want done for ourselves or our children. However, while there is no real and constructive action without understanding, so also there is no real and constructive understanding without action.

Those who would help must hear keenly enough to understand the distressed person's need for something to be done about his problem. We must, therefore, learn how and when to develop and implement effective courses of action. We must develop basic competencies which enable us to make tangible contributions to the welfare of others. In this regard, we must know where we are going and how to get there. And we must be willing to move into crisis areas where these questions are not immediately answerable, relying upon our basic directionality and developed methodologies and, most of all, upon creativity in modifying our programs to meet the unique needs of the crisis situation.

PRINCIPLES OF SOCIAL ACTION

The first and most basic goal of social action, then, is that the program translate itself into tangible human benefits. The programs of social action must produce demonstrable gain or change in the welfare of the population being serviced. Each participant must be able to point to skills or means which he has, which he did not have before or at least not to the degree produced by the program. Written and verbal changes are not enough. A program can demonstrate its effectiveness only when it has produced change or gain in the physical, emotional, or intellectual behavior of the individual involved.

In order to produce such change, social action programs must deal with the total person in the total environment. They must produce physical, emotional, and intellectual gains, not only in the individual, but also in the environment which supports the individual and makes possible the sustenance of the gains the individual has achieved.

In order to achieve the goal of tangible human benefits, the programs must be systematically developed to this end. The programs must be empirically based. They must be based upon the best evidence available to man, and where such evidence is not available, they must be piloted in short-term analogues of the conditions involved. Mass experimentation is not only not fruitful, but can be disastrous without the benefit of such evidence. It is better never to have entered some social problem areas than to promise and fail, to raise hopes and dash them, to bypass frustrations and then aggravate them.

In this context, the social action programs must be based upon principles learned in research in psychology, sociology, and other related disciplines; in education, guidance, counseling, therapy and other learning and rehabilitation applications. What works, works. And in an application of one of the most basic principles of learning, that people by and large learn what they are trained to learn, the people involved must be systematically taught the skills necessary to enable them to achieve physical, emotional, and intellectual gains. They must be taught the necessary skills in step-by-step reinforcement experiences ensuring the highest probability of their successfully incorporating and integrating them in an effective life style.

Man's real freedom of choice is based in large part upon his ability to respond differentially to different situations and, accordingly, his ability to discriminate these different situations. We can increase both abilities through appropriate training.

In conducting the training, the promulgators must integrate all of the sources of learning, the experiential, modeling, and didactic approaches. Perhaps most important, the person being helped must have the experience that in some significant way we are offering him the opportunity for a more effective and better way of life. In this context, it is the helper who is both model and agent for a more effective way of living. Finally, we must share with the helpee and, indeed, if necessary "shape" him up to be able to utilize all that we ourselves have found to be effective in our learnings. In this vein, we must influence the self-fulfilling expectancies of both helper and helpee, for people, like the rats discussed in Chapter 4, come to respond as we expect them to respond and come to expect of themselves what is expected of them.

A related principle of social action, then, involves the necessity for training people to develop their own programs for their own benefits. In this regard, we must allow for the participation in program-planning, problem-solving, and decision-making. Indeed, all of these phases are an essential part of an effective training program. Participation at all levels not only increases the participant's personal satisfaction but develops in him a high level of responsibility. This is not to advocate an abdication of responsibility by the directors of a program. Rather, it is part of his direction to develop his position in interaction with the participants in the program. He must take all aspects of a problem into consideration before implementing a given course of action, for he serves as a model for future directors in the program. We have lived too long with the artificial dichotomy between autocrat and abdicat.

In this context, the people involved must be trained to service themselves. The only effective social action programs are those where the trainers are constantly training themselves out of their jobs. In order to accomplish this, natural leaders with natural abilities must be sought out and developed in their areas of expertise. Everyone involved must be trained in the skills necessary to hold positions commensurate with his abilities. Concomitant educational experiences, including remedial skills, must be initiated, and education provided to all those who demonstrate some interest and ability regardless of academic background and credentials.

A first order of business, then, in developing social action programs is to employ program slots as a basis for job opportunities for the people being serviced. The internship principle, "An internship for every job," where an individual with the relevant ability can serve an apprenticeship, is critical here. A program that does not have a potential internship for every job cannot function at its maximum capacity. An agency involved in social action programs should not receive federal, state, or local aid if it does not create internships for personnel indigenous to the community being serviced. The role of the functional professional is relevant, and is elaborated upon below.

Finally, the social action programs must prepare the community-at-large for the changes they have helped to bring about. The human and physical environment can have facilitative or retarding effects upon a given program. In this regard, we can analyze the sources of positive and negative effect in the environment and modify the environment to modify man's behavior.

FUNCTIONAL PROFESSIONALS AS HELPERS

Social action programs culminate in the development and employment of functional professionals, that is, persons with the natural abilities in a given area who are trained to a high level of expertise in that area. Although they do not have the formal or educational credentials, they can function effectively as professionals.

There is a growing recognition of the potential work contribution, particularly to their own causes, of indigenous personnel. The role of the so-called nonprofessional, subprofessional, paraprofessional, or lay helpers has been developed and expanded. It has come to connote an assistantship to the professional in a variety of areas: performing clerical details, doing legwork, and, in general, freeing the professional for his professional functions.

However, the very evolution of the nonprofessional is a function of the professional's inability to discharge his responsibilities adequately in a given area, whether for inability or lack of personnel and other resources. That is, for many programs, it has been found not only that the subprofessional can complement or supplement the activities of the professional, but also that he can do the job as well or better than the professionals. For a variety of reasons he had an edge over the professional in certain areas of functioning.

Thus, persons indigenous to the populations being serviced appear to have a greater ability (1) to enter the milieu of the distressed; (2) to establish peerlike relationships with persons needing help; (3) to take an active part in the distressed person's total life situation; (4) to empathize more effectively with the distressed person's life style; (5) to teach the distressed person, from within his frame of reference, more effective actions; (6) to provide the distressed person with an effective transition to higher levels of functioning within the social system (Carkhuff, 1969). In short, the lay helper when appropriately employed can be the human link between society and the person in need of help—a necessary link that professionals are not now adequately providing.

For these reasons I find the term *functional professional* much more preferable to the other terms. The functional professional can do everything that the professional can do in working with the service population—and more.

All this is not to say that some credentialed professionals cannot also be functional professionals. Some are and others can be. It is to say that the role of the capable professional can be elevated to truly professional responsibilities as consultant to the social action programs and personnel. That is, the professional can consult on setting up, selecting, training, conducting, and evaluating the programs.

Nor is all of this to say that functional professionals cannot become credentialed professionals. Part of the training of the functional professional involves an initiation and follow-through on educational programs.

Areas that offer an important opportunity for the development of functional professionals are the social or human service areas themselves—the service areas that are dedicated to the welfare of populations in trouble. These areas offer not only the prospect for service but the prospect for the development and expansion of vocational opportunities. The human services, then, become both means and ends, albeit transitional, for the troubled population. They provide training in the skills necessary to effect personal change as well as the skills necessary to effect change in others, family as well as community members, while at the same time they provide "up and out" job-type opportunities.

A number of systematic attempts to train functional professionals have been accomplished. In the first of a series of studies, Carkhuff and Truax (1965a) demonstrated that, in a relatively short period of time, lay hospital personnel as well as graduate students in clinical psychology could achieve high levels of interpersonal functioning and involve their patients in psychotherapeutic process movement commensurate with the levels of prominent and experienced therapists such as Ellis, Gendlin, May, Rogers, Seeman, and Whitaker.

However, the success of the training required a further refinement of training methods. In addition, the original project did not incorporate a number of necessary methodological controls. First, we did not have the necessary pre-training assessments of functioning on the relevant indexes. Second, while Martin and Carkhuff (1968) employed a control group of students meeting for the exact time period to study a related content area of psychology, we did not have training control groups which met for the same number of sessions and participated in all of the activities except those critical to the training program proper. Finally, we did not incorporate indexes of functioning beyond the objective tape ratings. Accordingly, a classical research design incorporating all of these controls was implemented to train dormitory counselors as effective helpers.

The results were conclusive. Not only did systematic training effect objective changes greater than training control and time control groups but it also effected changes on indexes of the standard interviewee's experience, inventory reports of significant others, and inventory self reports (Berenson, Carkhuff and Myrus, 1966). Other studies demonstrated that such training can bring functional professionals as well as credentialed professionals to function at effective levels. Thus, nurses (Kratochvil, 1969), community volunteers (Pierce, Carkhuff, and Berenson, 1967), and prison guards (Megathlin and Porter, 1969) were added to the growing list of successful programs. However, even this is not enough to conclude the effectiveness of the functional professionals. The effects of functional professional helpers upon helpees must be studied. In the next study, systematically trained hospital attendants were assigned groups of patients, and their effectiveness with these patients was assessed.

PROJECT 9
Effects of Functional Professionals*

Since the introduction of effective tranquilizers and other psychomimetic compounds, a very large percentage of the nation's hospitalized mental patients have become susceptible to psychotherapeutic intervention.

*Reprinted in part with permission from the *Journal of Consulting Psychology*, 1965, **29**, 426–431, where it first appeared as "Lay Mental Health Counseling: The Effects of Lay Group Counseling," by Robert R. Carkhuff and Charles B. Truax.

Further, psychotherapeutic approaches to facilitating constructive personality change are being widely used in the treatment of neurotic and emotionally disturbed persons. Essentially psychotherapeutic approaches are used in present-day counseling programs in schools, industries, and rehabilitation programs throughout the nation. It has become strikingly clear, however, that available and projected manpower at the disciplines currently practicing psychotherapy fall severely short of the available and projected demand.

Further, recent research identifying certain specifiable elements of effective psychotherapy has opened new avenues for the specific training of therapists. It has been suggested that the research measuring instruments which have successfully discriminated between specific behaviors of effective therapy and noneffective or psychonoxious therapy could be applied directly to training programs. Thus, tape-recorded samples of psychotherapy rated very high in the known elements of effective psychotherapy could be selected to provide concrete examples for the beginning therapists. More specifically, the measuring scales such as the accurate empathy scale could be used to rate samples drawn from a trainee's own early therapeutic interviews and thus give the trainee immediate and concrete informational feedback about his own performance. Such an approach would mark a very radical departure from current training practices which heavily emphasize intellectual learning, too often perhaps at the expense of learning the art of operationalizing the concepts involved in effective psychotherapy.

Also, since the training of a therapist in a clear sense involves the personality change of the trainee, it might be expected that variables in effective psychotherapy should logically be applied to the training of the therapists. This implies, for example, that the teacher-supervisor should provide the conditions of accurate empathy, unconditional positive regard, and self-congruence or genuineness for the trainee during supervisory sessions. The continuing use of such therapeutic conditions in a supervisory trainee program not only would be expected to contribute to the trainee's personality change directly, but also to provide the trainee with a clear and observable model of a therapist to be imitated. A training program dealing in this fashion with recent research evidence identifying some of the effective elements in psychotherapy has been described. The program involves both concrete didactic and more molar experiential aspects including a quasi group-therapy experience for the trainees. This training program has been implemented both with lay hospital personnel and with postgraduate clinical psychology students. An analysis of the findings indicated that after a training program involving less than 100 hours, both lay personnel and clinical psychology trainees did not differ markedly from a group of highly experienced psychotherapists in the process measures of the psychotherapeutic interviews they produced. On at least one dimension from the only study which was available for purposes of comparison, empathic understanding, the lay personnel performed at levels significantly higher than postinternship graduate students. The present study is an attempt to evaluate the effectiveness of the lay personnel involved in the program by comparing the improvements observed in groups of hospitalized mental patients seen by them in group psychotherapy with equivalent control groups not receiving lay group counseling.

Recent reported evidence suggests the potential therapeutic effectiveness of minimally trained nonprofessional personnel. Thus, Appleby (1963) demonstrated significant improvement in chronic schizophrenics who were treated by hospital aides functioning in effect as lay therapists. Mendel and Rapport (1963) have also shown the value of lay personnel over a 51-month period of observation in helping chronic patients remain outside of the hospital with only periodic supportive interviews.

The present program differs quite markedly from the training program reported by Rioch and associates (1963), who clearly demonstrated that specially selected, bright, sophisticated, and educated housewives could learn from very intensive and long-term training (similar to that involved in graduate schools with good practicum programs) and could be as well regarded by their supervisors as those training in regular graduate schools. The program described by Rioch, while important as a demonstration, would be extremely difficult to replicate elsewhere and in general would be as expensive to duplicate as it would be to pay for graduate school (which of course has the advantage of professional status).

By contrast, the counseling or psychotherapy training program described here, since it involves less than 100 hours of training (and less than 65 hours of supervisor time), is not more expensive to implement than a great many hospital aide training programs. Further, since it relies heavily upon research instruments and training tapes it is more readily replicable.

The present training program is also of theoretical significance. A number of studies have now amassed evidence suggesting that three therapist-offered conditions and one critical dimension of patient behavior are significantly associated with constructive personality change in a variety of hospitalized and nonhospitalized patients: (a) therapist accurate empathic understanding, (b) therapist communication of warmth or unconditioned positive regard, (c) therapist genuineness or self-congruence, and (d) patient depth of self-exploration. These studies have been conducted with trained and relatively experienced therapists so that the variables studied operated in the context of a thorough knowledge of patient psychopathology and dynamics. It could very well be that these four elements of effective psychotherapy are in fact effective only in the context of a thorough knowledge of psychopathology and dynamics. Since the training program with the lay personnel involved no training in psychopathology and personality dynamics, an evaluation of their effectiveness would throw some light upon the necessity or value of training in psychopathology and personality of dynamics.

METHODOLOGY

Five volunteer but otherwise unselected hospital personnel from Eastern State Hospital, Lexington, Kentucky, were involved in the training program. These volunteers consisted of three aides, a volunteer worker, and an industrial therapist. Only the industrial therapist had a college education. The hospital personnel ranged in age from 32 to 50 (Mean, 41.40; SD, 7.42).

Briefly, the training involved the supervisor didactically teaching the trainees about effective therapeutic dimensions in the context of a relationship providing the trainees the experiential base of these dimensions. Research scales which had successfully measured the levels of therapeutic conditions of tape-recorded therapy in research predictive of therapy outcome were employed in teaching the trainees to discriminate levels of the four conditions involved. The trainees then received empathy training in which they listened to patient statements and then were asked to formulate their responses in terms of the feeling and content of the communication. The trainees role-played and finally had initial clinical interviews with hospitalized patients. All phases of training were recorded for purposes of rating within the class so as to give the trainees immediate and concrete informational feedback on how well they were learning to operationalize the concepts involved.

Three of the lay personnel were assigned to two groups each of 10 patients in each group. Due to limitations in the population available, the two remaining counselors were assigned only one group each of 10 patients. With the exception that 10 less patients were represented in the control groups, the patients were divided into groups according to the years institutionalized and randomly assigned to treatment groups. In total, then, 150 Eastern State Hospital patients were involved, with 80 in the treatment groups and 70 in control groups. Three of the treatment groups were females ($N = 30$), and 24 members of the control groups were females.

Criteria for patient selection included the following: patients who were not expected to be discharged within a 3-month period, patients who were not currently being seen in any form of psychotherapeutic treatment, and patients who were not diagnosed to be mentally retarded or to have organicity. The patient population involved the typical multiplicity of diagnostic categories not only among various patients but also within the clinical histories of the individual patients. The variety of current diagnosis included manic-depressive reactions of the manic and depressive types, psychotic-depressive reactions and schizophrenic reactions, simple catatonic and schizo-affective types, with the great majority of all patients diagnosed as hebephrenic, paranoid, or chronic undifferentiated types. One patient fell into each of the following categories: psychoneurotic anxiety reaction, sociopathic personality disturbance, passive-aggressive personality trait disturbance, and transient adult situational personality disturbance.

The treatment group ranged in age from 24 to 64 with a mean of 50.03 years (*SD*, 11.14). These patients had had an average of 7.44 (*SD*, 3.65) years of education, with some patients having had no schooling and some having college degrees. The number of hospital admissions, including their present stay, ran from the first admission to the fourth and averaged 1.96 (*SD*, .92), and the length of stay during the present hospitalization ranged from 1 to 36 years with a mean of 13.62 (*SD*, 11.23).

The control group members varied in age from 20 to 66 (Mean, 46.96; *SD*, 11.47) and schooling from 0 to 16 grades or college (Mean, 7.51; *SD*, 3.36). The average number of hospital admissions was 2.09 (*SD*, 1.04) range again from 1 to 4, while the years of the present hospitalization varied from 1 to 34 with a mean of 10.03 (*SD*, 8.19).

In summary, the population was essentially an older chronic one with an average of two admissions. While the sample was a severely disabled one, it represented the great bulk of the hospital population which is usually not serviced by the professional staff and thus provided a testing ground for the usefulness of lay treatment.

The patients were seen twice a week for a total of 24 sessions over a period of approximately 3 months in time-limited group counseling. There was no problem-oriented or personnel-oriented basis for group assignment. Patients were simply randomly assigned to the individual treatment and the control groups. The sessions were recorded for the purposes of supervision and any subsequent analyses. The lay counselors continued to meet as a group for purposes of being supervised twice a week for an hour each time.

In the treatment process, the lay counselors were oriented only toward providing high levels of therapeutic conditions. They had no cognitive map of where they were going except to attempt to elicit a degree of self-exploration relating to the problems and concerns which the patients brought to the session. The therapist's role was to communicate a warm and genuine concern and depth of understanding. There was no special focus for discussion; no topics were forbidden; and in general as the sessions evolved they included discussions of the usual range of emotion-laden or intellectualized topics from sexual material to concerns regarding autonomy and more immediate and pragmatic concerns like the method for "getting out" of the hospital, or even "staying in."

Outcome criteria to be assessed included hospital discharge rates and pre- and posttreatment ratings of ward behavior by the nurses and ward attendants of the particular wards from which the patients came. In all, seven wards were involved, so the nurses and ward attendants of these seven wards were involved in the rating. An attempt was made to give pre- and posttesting using a battery of psychological tests including the MMPI, the *Q* sort for Self and Ideal Self, and an Anxiety scale. Unfortunately, because of the degree of chronicity and pathology as well as the general low level of educational attainment, less than 30% of both groups or 18 members of the treatment group and 16 members of the control group proved testable, so that the evaluation of patient change was based upon changes in ward behavior.

RESULTS

Of the 80 patients who were seen in counseling, 6 dropped out, all within the first six sessions. Eleven of the remaining 74 patients who continued with some great degree of regularity were discharged after 2 or more months of therapeutic treatment. Of the 70 control patients, 6 were discharged within the 3-month period of time. While the direction and absolute values are meaningful, the tests did not yield statistically significant differences.

All of the patients were rated before and after treatment on the short-form "Gross Ratings of Patient Behavior," a series of four nine-point scales where 9 represents the highest value in the positive direction and 1 represents the lowest value in the negative direction. The scales assessed four critical areas: (a) "degree of psychological disturbance"; (b) "degree of constructive interpersonal concern"; (c) "degree of constructive intrapersonal concern," and perhaps most important, (d) the "degree of overall improvement over the past 3 months," for which only postratings were obtained. The posttreatment ratings were available for all treatment and control group members. Twenty of the preratings necessary to assess the first three indexes of ward behavior of the control group were, however, lost or misplaced. Analysis of the posttreatment "overall improvement" ratings indicates that the 20 patients whose preratings were misplaced tended to be rated slightly worse than the control group in general, thus suggesting that the differences between treatment and control groups on the three other scales are conservative. Five of the 20 were rated improved; 5, deteriorated; and 10, no change. As can be seen from Table 5–1, all scale differences between treatment and control groups were statistically significant by chi-square. It is notable that only one of the treatment group patients was rated as deteriorated in his overall behavior over the previous 3 months, while 38 were judged improved. Twelve of the control-group members were rated behaviorally deteriorated overall, while 19 were rated improved. Furthermore, it is clear from the other scale values that control group members tended to remain unchanged, while there was a greater variability in the treatment group ratings.

DISCUSSION AND IMPLICATIONS

The evidence points to uniformly significant improvement in the patients treated by lay group counseling when compared to control patients. The suggestion is that a specific but relatively brief training program, de-

Table 5-1
Direction of Changes of Gross Ratings of Patient Behavior by Ward Personnel

	PATIENT GROUPS	
	Treatment	Control
Overall improvement (Postratings only)	(N = 74)	(N = 70)
Improved	38	19
Deteriorated	1	12
Unchanged	35	39
Psychological disturbance (Pre- and postratings)	(N = 74)	(N = 50)
Improved	28	8
Deteriorated	19	5
Unchanged	27	37
Interpersonal concerns (Pre- and postratings)	(N = 74)	(N = 50)
Improved	33	16
Deteriorated	14	2
Unchanged	27	32
Intrapersonal concerns (Pre- and postratings)	(N = 74)	(N = 50)
Improved	28	15
Deteriorated	16	4
Unchanged	30	31

void of specific training in psychopathology, personality dynamics, or psychotherapy theory, can produce relatively effective lay mental health counselors. It is significant that three of the five lay counselors in the present study had only a high-school education or less, two had attended college, and only one had completed college. In view of the relatively brief training, it would seem feasible to train a large percentage of currently existing hospital aide staff, *at no extra cost,* and thus provide regular lay group counseling to almost all hospitalized patients.

It is of significance that the patient population used in the present evaluation was an unselected one, by and large involving a preponderance of chronic hospitalized patients. A recent study by Spitzer, Lee, Carnahan, and Fleiss (1964) has indicated that the Kentucky Hospital population is significantly more pathological and less communicative, perhaps due to a lower socioeducational status, than patient populations in similar institutions in northern and more urbanized states. Thus, lay group counseling produced significant improvement in patients who on the average had spent an average of 13½ years in their current hospitalization, had had one previous hospitalization, had a seventh-grade education, and who were already 50 years of age.

Since pre- and postratings of ward behavior were used as the basic measure of change, biased reports from the ward staff should be considered. We have long been somewhat suspicious of reported improvements when the ward doctor treated patients and asked the ward staff to evaluate his effectiveness. The lay counselors had no direct connection with any of the wards involved. It should be noted also that in the present case the ward staff and the hospital personnel in general were initially resistant to the idea that hospital attendants should even be allowed to conduct group counseling. The lay therapist did not initially enjoy high status. The admitted and outspoken bias of the ward personnel involved in the behavioral ratings was against rather than for lay group counseling: the expectation of the ward personnel initially was that the lay group counseling would upset the patients and that therapy with nonprofessional therapists would be harmful rather than helpful.

The "attention factor" in relation to the patients themselves should, however, be considered. Most of the patients had received no special treatment, especially no psychotherapeutic treatment during their many years of hospitalization. There was in fact great difficulty initially in getting patients to attend the group sessions, although most attended regularly after the first few weeks, many looking forward to this special form of attention which they were receiving. Although present resources did not allow for such a control, future replication should incorporate a second control group of patients attending "sessions" conducted by untrained lay personnel.

The evidence that the treatment group produced greater variability in outcome compared to the control group parallels equivalent findings in psychotherapy. It is perhaps of some significance that only one treated patient was judged deteriorated in overall behavior. This compared most favorably with reported effects of professional group psychotherapy with even less chronic hospitalized patients.

In addition, the absolute number of treatment group members getting out, while not statistically significant due to the patient N involved, and, while always qualified by what goes into the process of patient discharge, nearly doubled those of the control group.

In summary, the present research has demonstrated the effectiveness of time-limited lay group counseling, evolving from a short-term integrated didactic and experiential approach to training. It is felt that the results indicate great promise for the possibly critical role which lay personnel might play in coping with our ever-growing mental health concerns. The results point to the need for further and continued search and research into the potentially vast and untapped resource.

As can be seen, the lay helpers were effective in altering the ward behavior of the patients. In addition, although the differences were not statistically significant, the absolute numbers of those discharged in the treatment and control groups are meaningful. All this was not accomplished without great difficulty, including, in particular, active resistance from many of the hospital staff members, who later acknowledged the success of the program. A humorous anecdote illustrating the severity of the disturbance of the patients and the enormity of the attendants' therapeutic task occurred when, after several unsuccessful group sessions, one of the attendants made the comment that for the first time she noticed that several of the patients had zipped their flies. I can remember saying, "I think we have made it."

Again, most important throughout each of these research and demonstration programs was the generalization of results from lay population to lay population. Professionals in mental and medical institutions are not alone capable of doing the helping job that is required of them. Hospital attendants, nurses, and patients can help! Professionals in penal institutions cannot alone do the helping job that is required of them. Guards and prisoners can help! Professionals in schools and colleges cannot alone do the helping job that is required of them. Students can help! Professionals in the community cannot alone do the helping job that is required of them. Community volunteers can help!

Most critical, professionals in social action programs cannot alone do the helping job that is required of them. Functional professionals who are indigenous to the population being serviced can help!

PRINCIPLES OF COMMUNITY ORGANIZATION

While the effective ingredient of social action involves the utilization of functional professionals, its objectives cannot, of course, be accomplished without other ingredients. Effective community organization for creating and implementing programs is a necessary ingredient of social change. Even the conscientiously accomplished Kerner Report with all of its dire predictions concerning the world which we are leaving to our children has been unable to get many cities moving to save themselves.

The literature is obviously filled with statements to support action by a concerned populace to bring about constructive change in the cities. Why has the change not occurred? Is there no working plan for organizing communities into well-planned and sustained action groups to head off disaster by initiating, leading, and directing programs encompassing benefits for all of the people?

If there is not such a plan, how does a city become an effective, organized community? What steps must it go through, what strategy must it employ? How does it realistically analyze its problems? In other terms, how do we systematically develop guidance for what must occur to become an effective community —how do we change direction in the course of the cities?

In Springfield, almost all of the meaningful social action programs have been introduced by black leadership in the community—not the mayor, or members of the school board—not the city council or the rest of the people who are paid to govern, but by the black leadership. The paid officials have seen their roles as the evaluators rather than the promulgators, critics rather than doers. The list of programs initiated and developed by black leaders include the following: model inner city learning center; human relations specialist program; school for suspendees; special educational program for pregnant girls; youth bus monitors; family educational workshop; cultural center; family camp programs; special community educational programs at local colleges; special tutorial program (Northern Educational Services); police camera corps for citizen protection; police community relations committee. These are only a few of the programs instigated by the leadership of the black community. Another 57 specific recommendations were made by the Real Citizen's Congress conducted by the black community for the education of the white community.

The following guide illustrates the principles which have directed the efforts of the black leadership in one community. It is broadly based and progressive, suggesting that ideally reorganization of the community should be made within the Establishment's frame of references. Failing this, the guide suggests that attempts be made to organize community action from without in order to bring pressure upon the system to change. In this context, then, the guide is one for effective organization for any group, not simply for community organization.

PROJECT 10
*Guide for Effective Community Organization**

I. How to Organize the Community—Principles

    A. *Principle: The man at the top (the mayor, in most cases) must assess his personal self, then make up for his weaknesses by surrounding himself with proven successful leaders from the total community to head his departments.* He must operate on the same principle of Big Business by actively recruiting top flight personnel to head his cabinet posts, i.e. if weak in race relations, he must be sure he has a man next to him who has proven success in the field of race relations, or if weak in business concepts, he must find a top man in that field to serve as advisor. In other words the mayor must be surrounded by effective, functional people, *not* appointed

* Reprinted in part from a master's thesis in human relations and community affairs, American International College, entitled "Principles of Community Organization" prepared in February 1970 by Andrew H. Griffin.

for reasons of political patronage, to insure a successful community.

1. Ideally, community organization begins from within the organization set up to conduct community affairs.
2. This principle is the one that should be employed by the President in assessing himself, then building his cabinet from the most able men who also share his ideology and total commitment to the welfare of all citizens.
3. Once the man in charge shows he believes that political reorganization is the key and starts to act to prove he believes it, it will take place. He must reinforce all positive behavior and extinguish or negatively reinforce all that isn't, but he must start by working on himself.
4. Mayor must be honest and know himself well enough to surround himself with competent people who are willing to take risks, "to stand up and be counted." This should happen in all areas of community endeavor. The Mayor cannot surround himself with "yes" men but men he has faith in to do the job allowing them to grow and create to their fullest.

B. *Principle: Assessment and evaluation of all city departments and agencies must take place at the outset.* All personnel must be assessed for effectiveness (including the amount of time spent on the job in order to achieve it).

1. The evaluator must utilize as criteria the functional productivity of the worker, *not* the criteria for qualification; i.e. if the man can do the job, we must not insist that he have certain credentials. The community must not fall into the trap of asking for irrelevant proof of competence in non-related fields.
2. Evaluation should be comparable to time-motion studies in business. Also, are personnel suited to the job performed?
3. City departments should be evaluated according to their stated goals and duties and their ability to get those accomplished.

C. *Principle: Reorganization within is based on making effective whatever is ineffective by shifting personnel, reassigning duties and, if necessary, the creation of a new department to coordinate and consult on the activities of all departments in order to make them more effective in relating to the community's needs.* As communities have grown larger and government has become more centralized, the citizen has lost interest, doesn't attend meetings, vote, or otherwise take an interest, feeling that his participation won't matter anyway. A reorganization of the community government and departments must reverse this trend, so that the ordinary citizen has faith that the city is working for him.

1. One probable outcome of reorganization will be decentralization of all city departments (as recommended for education in Education Bill #2485, Massachusetts Legislature, which proposes sub-district governing boards for neighborhood schools). This will eliminate red tape and break down language barriers, giving all an opportunity to participate in the destiny of their children. State legislation should not be necessary, as a mayor can instigate decentralized programs by simply choosing his heads of departments carefully and wisely.

2. In a reorganization of the existing structure, it is possible for minority groups to feel new hope through the opening of new doors and channels.

D. *Principle: Orientation and training of all personnel in the fields of Civics, Characteristics and Sociology of the City, and Human Relations must be a feature of all strata of city government—elected and paid officials and everyone on all staffs.*

1. Initial orientation to become familiar with the city and how it operates, how responsibilities are meted out, what its resources are, etc. will familiarize public servants with their "working partner"—the city, the people in it, the problems, and their own role.

2. In-service training must be continual so that all new approaches and ideas can be utilized in creating new solutions to today's new problems.

3. Social awareness or appreciation of what it means to be Black or Puerto Rican, how to approach minority problems, the pathology of the ghetto, the fears of the white man and need for change, should be ingredients of any training programs, as well as a continual training in human relations which includes a constant evaluation of the self and an improved ability to work with others.

E. *Principle: Utilization of the resources which already exist within the community must be a principal concern to all members of the government structure of the city.* This includes a knowledge of the availability of expertise in any given field, as found in local colleges, business and individuals and should also include the personnel and programs of the state federal systems.

1. From such a pool of talent and expertise should be drawn an Advisory Cabinet for the mayor's top-level advisors, on the order of a brain trust, à la FDR and JFK.
2. The utilization of such people also reinforces those that are functioning at high levels and doing their job, demonstrating concretely a clear stand of what the city is all about and providing the rest of the community a concrete model, which they can attempt to emulate.
3. It also keeps the "gamesmen," cons and other ineffectuals away because they know that they have to produce not sell.

II. Organization of Small Groups

In the event that the community does not reorganize from within —the ideal situation—due to an inept man in any key position, it may be necessary to organize small pressure groups within the smaller sections, geographical, racial, or ideological, or the larger community. If this happens, the small groups need principles, just as the city departments do, to guide them to effective action. These principles may be stated, or more accurately asked, in a very different way.

A. *Principle: What's your problem?*

1. Very often we read about problems in the news media, or more correctly, we read about the symptom of the problem. That is, when we see a story of Black students beating up a white teacher, we are reading about someone's attempt to bring a problem to our attention, or his frustration that we never saw it on our own. This is an overt demonstration that there is a problem.
2. We may find out about a problem in a dozen different ways—government reports, word-of-mouth, or seeing poorly kept streets and parks in a certain section of town.
3. *Research the subject as well as possible.* If your child brings home a report that a teacher made a degrading comment about a minority group, you must do a lot of searching to find out the true conditions in your child's school. You must know who is in charge of hiring the teacher, what requirements a teacher must have, what type of training the teacher received prior to her coming to school, analyze her school and its curriculum, whether there are any minority group teachers, whether there is special training for city teachers, where in the curriculum the subject of minority group cultures

appears, whom you depend on to vote for your interests on the School Committee.

4. These steps are true of problems in Housing, Police-Community Relations, Employment, Welfare, etc.

5. How have problems in this area been handled in the past—what precedent was established?

6. Know the community in which the problem lies.

7. Know how the problem relates to the rest of the municipality.

B. *Principle: Who might help you work on a solution?*

1. If you know any individual who has experienced a similar situation or expressed that he is disturbed by the problem, he would be a potential ally.

2. If any group was formerly recorded as having had an interest in the area of your concern, include them.

3. If there are agencies, or arms of the city government, you will want to know how they fit in.

4. You will want to know all the background for the problem. If there is federal money being poured into the schools, find out if the money is being used for the purpose it was acquired.

5. Is there a legal precedent you can use to support your stand?

6. Do not rule out any potential allies until you map a strategy—sometimes you can use an unlikely partnership to achieve your goal like bringing militant whites and blacks, police and blacks, together as we did.

7. Never make statements to the news media until your plan is formulated; then use them fully if they prove their trustworthiness.

8. Remember, all action plans to be truly effective must include a change of policy by big business and city government—always watch for possible tie-ins.

9. Evaluate existing material on the subject, such as pamphlets, and guides for community organization so you will know what you are up against if you suggest a new approach.

C. *Principle: What is your plan?*

1. Strategy

   a. Will I start soft and gradually build or come on hard?

   b. Will I make demands or agree to dialogue meetings; if the latter, how many and with whom?

   c. Do I want to court the friendship of the elected officials or would that neutralize my position?

      d. What are my expectations of the news media? When do I want them involved?

      e. How can I communicate my problem to others in order to win their support for the cause?

      f. How long am I going to be content to wait for results before bringing into play a more overt demonstration of my displeasure?

      g. Will I speak the Establishment's language or my own?

  2. Executing my plan

      a. Call a meeting of concerned people—discussion.

      b. Timetable and action flow from group meeting.

      c. Organization of group.

      d. Training of group—find person of oppressed group with status and expertise or select and train new leaders to represent community.

      e. Establish the goals of the group.

      f. Whom do we include and contact to achieve goal (must include representatives of group being victimized)?

      g. What threats do I make, to whom and in what form?

      h. What are the risks? How do I minimize them?

  3. Constant Assessment: During the crisis period, meetings are held often with minutes taken of all that happens, which will include discussions of latest activity and evaluation.

 D. The group continues meeting after immediate problem dealt with: Community organization, to be seen as an instrument of peaceful change of society, must be continuous and not erupt and die abruptly as crises flare up and subside.

III. Conclusion

The principles of organizing small groups can apply just as well to large powerful groups. The power structure should know their resources and have researched the same problems we have mentioned. If they did, and would, however, there would be little dissatisfaction on the part of those served by the various arms of the power structure. The principle here is the one usually seen in the company which is moving toward being more effective and functional and in which the ranks will be a part of the existing pattern of change. It was when companies got fat and excluded workers from sharing the wealth that unions were formed. This can apply to cities too—if they don't reorganize within (Plan A), the larger the city the greater the need for decentralization, for example. The biggest single factor hindering this kind of self-improvement is the fear the established groups feel toward someone who could do a potentially better job than they could. The result of effective community organization could be to develop the best answer to the question of the lag between the urgent civic problems and the application of initiative and will by those in power to correct those problems. What we are seeking is effective ways to make new, vital institutions out of the sagging, ineffective old ones.

The models for progressive programs in human resource development dictated from within an organization by mandate—although not without consultation—of the "man at the top" include the programs of President Harry S. Truman and Branch Rickey. In integrating and attempting to equalize opportunity in the armed forces and professional athletics, these men took the initiative, built in success by the personnel and the programs which they employed, and ensured success by employing the power of their office within their respective organizations.

In this context, the principles of community organization are not substantive but methodological. They serve rather to complement or supplement the more basic principles and are employed only in lieu of the active introduction and implementation of human resource development programs by progressive representatives of government. Organizations of any kind can only rationalize their existence by relating effective personnel to effective programs in a manner that maximizes the contribution of each.

Principles such as those of reinforcement are always operative. They are operative within the community organization, with the actively constructive receiving leadership roles and other positive reinforcements and the others relegated to other schedules of reinforcement in order to shape up their behavior so that they may assume more actively constructive roles. The principles of reinforcement are operative in relation to other agencies. An agency that is resistant to constructive change in a given instant may be negatively reinforced with negative statements; an agency that attempts something that is not "real" may be ignored, that is, no recognition is given to its supposedly attempted contribution; an agency that really does something meaningful may be positively reinforced with positive statements.

For example, and this is common to any community, the newspapers and television stations are frequently not favorably disposed to reporting news from the frame of reference of the black community. Indeed, what little is reported, on School Committee meetings and the like, is frequently distorted by reporters trying to curry the favor of the empowered committeemen who were resistant to the innovating programs. These distortions, in turn, are met by a refusal of community leaders to give interviews to those who only distorted them. The sources of change are also the sources of news and when they refuse to give stories there is no news of note. Gradually, some of the news media will come around to reporting more accurate stories and providing wider coverage. The community leadership will not reinforce them for this, for they were only doing what they were supposed to be doing in the first place: presenting the picture of things as they were. For example, when one television station freed itself to take the initiative in presenting progressive programs in relation to community needs, it was invited to important meetings, while another was not. When one newspaper assigned progressive reporters to cover the stories, the paper was deluged with letters—and more important—increased subscriptions. These activities culminated in November of 1969 when, following a series of disruptions in the school system, the *Springfield Union* printed a series of lead articles and editorials—since submitted for prizes—putting the focus once again on the city officials and school administrators who, in the childish fashion of politicians, had been attempting to shift the burden of responsibility for the crisis to the school children—white as well as black.

TOWARD DESIGNS FOR SUCCESS

In the previous section, "Ingredients of Social Failure," we concluded with a final chapter, "Designs for Failure," treating sensitivity and encounter groups as an illustration of supposedly ameliorative programs which perpetuate the original failures. In the next several sections we are going to deal with the alternatives.

With regard to an orientation toward principles of effective social action and the development of functional professionals the alternatives are clear. Let us look again at the educational system which is not servicing minority groups, particularly black and Spanish-speaking groups.

The alternatives involve setting up helping and human relations training programs that help all of its participants, white as well as black, professional as well as lay, to develop tangible, usable, translatable skills that they can employ not only in helping themselves but in helping others in their family, school, and community. Thus, one immediate gain will be the reorientation and re-education of all teaching and professional staff members.

Perhaps even more important, with the introduction of the role of the functional professional, the educational program can open up to the contribution of community helpers. A massive infusion of young, black, and effective models can certainly make a difference in the lives of the young, black, and the troubled.

In this context, functional professionals can be developed in many capacities in school, in the community, in their families. Communities can be systematically prepared to influence dramatically, if not control, their own schools and, thus, their educational destinies. Criteria of effectiveness can be designed to meet the needs of the students, not the professionals or even the parents, to maximize their abilities to use their talents to the fullest, wherever these talents lie. Functional professionals can do the job that professionals are not now able to do.

We are in a period of great crisis. We must choose between serving a system that does not serve all men or modifying and developing a system which serves all men. We must choose between serving a system or having the system serve us.

As I know so well from my own life and the lives of people in whom I have involved myself, crises may have constructive as well as destructive consequences, depending upon how they are handled.

Crises in the lives of individuals, great and small, may be "for better or for worse."

Crises in the lives of nations, great and small, may be "for better or for worse."

I welcome these crises in our nation if it means that we are still alive, still free to choose a course of action that may be "for better" for all involved.

It all depends upon how we deal with these crises.

REFERENCES

Appleby, L. Evaluation of treatment methods for chronic schizophrenia. *Archives of General Psychiatry,* 1963, **8,** 8–21.

Berenson, B. G., Carkhuff, R. R., & Myrus, Pamela. The interpersonal functioning and training of college students. *Journal of Counseling Psychology,* 1966, **13,** 441–446.

Carkhuff, R. R. *Helping and human relations: A primer for lay and professional helpers.* Vol. I. *Selection and training.* New York: Holt, Rinehart and Winston, 1969.

Carkhuff, R. R., & Truax, C. B. Training in counseling and psychotherapy: An evaluation of an integrated didactic and experiential approach. *Journal of Consulting Psychology,* 1965, **29,** 333–336. (a)

Carkhuff, R. R., & Truax, C. B. Lay mental health counseling: The effects of lay group counseling. *Journal of Consulting Psychology,* 1965, **29,** 426–431. (b)

Kratochvil, D. Changes in values and interpersonal functioning of nurses-in-training. *Counselor Education and Supervision,* 1969, **8,** 104–107.

Martin, J. C., & Carkhuff, R. R. Changes in personality and interpersonal functioning of counselors-in-training. *Journal of Clinical Psychology,* 1968, **24,** 109–110.

Megathlin, W. L., & Porter, T. *The effects of facilitation training provided correctional officers stationed at the Atlanta Federal Penitentiary.* Washington, D.C.: U.S. Justice Department, 1969.

Mendel, W. M., & Rapport, S. Outpatient treatment for chronic schizophrenic patients: Therapeutic consequences of an existential view. *Archives of General Psychiatry,* 1963, **8,** 190–196.

National Advisory Commission, *Report on civil disorders.* New York: Bantam Books, 1968.

Pierce, R., Carkuff, R. R., & Berenson, B. G. The differential effects of high and low functioning counselors upon counselors-in-training. *Journal of Clinical Psychology,* 1967, **23,** 212–215.

Rioch, Margaret J., Elkes, E., Flint, A. A., Usdansky, B. S., Newman, B. G., & Silber, E. NIMH pilot study in training mental health counselors. *Journal of Orthopsychiatry,* 1963, **33,** 678–689.

Spitzer, R., Lee, Joan, Carnahan, W., & Fleiss, J. A comparison of rural and urban schizophrenics in differing state institutions. Paper presented at American Psychiatric Association, Los Angeles, California, May 1964.

CHAPTER 6
Principles of Personal Effectiveness

The heart of any program is people. It is the caliber of the people that make the program go or not. This most basic precept is particularly critical in the educational and social action spheres where many high beginnings have met with low endings, where constructive change has been promised but not delivered, where hopes have been wakened and wakened and wakened. We have seen, for example, New Careers programs in which less than 15 percent of the previously unemployed or underemployed trainees have more or less completed some form of haphazard training which is reflected directly in the trainees' tenuous vocational adjustments. We have seen, by contrast, programs in which more than 75 percent of trainees "off the streets" have successfully completed very systematic and demonstrably effective training programs and where the trainee-products have gone on to hold responsible human service positions successfully. The difference? The difference is the level of functioning of the program's promulgators and this is reflected directly in the program.

A good program and a good director cannot be separated. A good administration and a good staff cannot be separated.

The essence of any program dealing with people, then, is the level at which it deals with people. Social action programs with definitive goals come into being only when existing programs do not deal effectively with and for the people they are calculated to serve. Any program, traditional or otherwise, may constitute a social action program. A traditional education program that truly "hooks" a child, black or white, rich or poor, in a lifelong learning process is an agent of social change or gain for all concerned. A business community that provides outlets for the skills learned is an agent of social change or gain for all concerned. Some few—very few—good institutions meet these criteria. These institutions cannot be separated from the people who run them, translate them, and implement them.

128

A good class and a good teacher cannot be separated. A good session and a good counselor cannot be separated.

Conversely, a social action program that cannot reach the people it was meant to benefit is not an agent of social change or gain. The direct relationship between numbers of social workers and social work programs in an area and the social tragedies of the area bears a sad and silent witness to this. Indeed, it is better that the programs were never created, for they validate many times over in hopes dashed the experience they were meant to modify.

The social action programs, then, must offer something more than that which they replace. They must offer the personnel who can reach the poor and motivate them. They must offer the personnel who can reach the apathetic and electrify them. They must offer the personnel who can reach the ignorant and teach them.

PHENOMENOLOGY OF THE EFFECTIVE PERSON

All effective programs, then, begin with effective people. Some literature has been written about the phenomenology of the effective person (Carkhuff, 1969b, Chapter 16; Carkhuff and Berenson, 1967, Chapter 13). Perhaps most important, he is himself and is in the process of becoming more and more fully himself. In short, he is in the process of growing and is committed first and foremost to his own personal growth. He has chosen his own mountain to climb and is in no way threatened by another's choice of mountains. Indeed, he does everything in his power to enable another to actualize his own resources.

The unavoidable beginning point of all effective social action in all areas of human endeavor is with the person designated "more knowing" by the system in which the parties function. This person's life, and thus his relationships with significant others, are in the process of either deepening or deteriorating. Although open and searching, the effective person is defined and directionful, holding forcefully his integrated learnings until confronted with the new learnings discriminated by his fine sensitivities. He is as he lives—an hypothesis to be tested and modified in everyday life. The people he comes to influence can enjoy the same intense rewards of full emergence and full life.

The effective person knows that his own personal phenomenology is more basic than any system that is available to him. That is, his own experience of the world is most basic. The systems that man chooses to employ simply reflect and describe his ways of perceiving himself and others in his world. The effective person is not "hung up" in any "free" versus "determined" conflict. He believes that some people see themselves and their worlds as being "determined": they *are* "determined" and they seek to populate the world with "determined" people. He believes that others see themselves as "free": they *are* "free" and they seek to populate the world with "free" people. The effective person seeks simply to make enlightened and systematic inquiries into his efforts

impact

to know what is knowable by deterministic means and to prepare himself for what is and what may remain unknowable.

In this context, the effective person is not bound by any one system and is free to choose from any system in developing his own personal system. While he develops his own personal cosmology he is guided yet not dominated by it. His system is as effective as it is able to incorporate and integrate the continuing flow of experiences to which he expresses himself. His system is as effective as it is able to generate meaningful and valid expectations and conclusions. His system is as effective as it is open to the contributions of any and all systems as they become, at a given point in time, necessary to effect translations to human benefits.

In developing his system, the effective person does not lose sight of his deep-rooted belief that no system enables man to avoid the responsibility for making individual discriminations and acting upon them. No system, personal and integrated at the highest level or otherwise, allows man to avoid making his own individual discriminations. Indeed, man seeks systems, procedures, and techniques precisely for the purpose of avoiding the responsibility for making fine discriminations in the individual case; he would put the system "on the line" rather than himself. Whatever it has in common with past experience, each new experience has its unique aspects, which, if left unattended diminish the potential effectiveness of the relationship and yield no new learnings to either party in the relationship. There is no effective discrimination without action based upon that discrimination. Fine and sensitive discriminations demand action, whether implicitly or explicitly. To discriminate yet not to act upon the discrimination is to reduce the effectiveness of the validating process and, thus, the potential validity of the next discrimination. Actions may be channeled through systems, but they are not, in the individual instance, bound to be channeled through these systems. Feelings for others which are not acted upon are simply not feelings for others. Again, as with discrimination, the individual—not the system—has responsibility for his action.

Perhaps most significant, the effective person knows that he is both the means and the ends in an effective helping program. He presents both a structural model for the effects of a sustained relationship as well as an integrated means for attaining such effects. In his disposition and demeanor he is confident yet open, directionful yet flexible, integrated yet changing; he offers high levels of what he teaches; he teaches about what he offers. He is about what he is about, and all of his behavior reflects this. He is who he represents himself to be, yet is not bound by who he is. These dimensions constitute both the means and the ends of effective helping programs.

In this regard, the effective person is fully aware that he is capable of hurting as well as helping. He is cognizant of the necessity that to help some people is to hurt others. The emergence of the forces of life, both within and between persons, involves the destruction of the forces of death. He is also aware that some persons, impotent and destructive, can employ his understanding and energies only to become potent and destructive, and in this respect destroy the life around them, life that they now only in their impotence tolerate. The effective person may choose a variety of courses, including those leading directly to the elimination of these destructive forces. In this context, the effective person may engage, based upon his fine discriminations, unavailable to others, in activities that may for the moment, or for all time, *appear* destructive to others. He does so with full responsibilities for his actions, whether or not the actions are a function of a motivation to help.

The effective person knows, then, that he must implement a potent course of action based upon his own fine discriminations. Having integrated the dimensions of the healthy male and female in an effective life (Carkhuff, 1969a, 1969b), he remains unmoved by the agitated mutual reactions of either the distorted male or female (death). Neither the distorted female, who in daily living sues for peace at any price, nor the distorted male, who commits only holocaust, has a pull upon him as he proceeds in his own direction, often an "extreme" or strong middle position when seen through the eyes of others. He can accomplish appropriately both the confrontation which leads to love and the love that leads to confrontation. He is guided by the discriminations yielded by his wholeness and is fully aware that the deepest level of understanding often involves filling in what is missing rather than reflecting, however deeply, what is present.

The effective person knows, therefore, that he must employ all of his vast resources in all of his significant experiences. Both in relation to himself and to others who so motivate him, the effective person is committed to bringing to bear all of his physical, emotional, and intellectual resources in order to achieve higher and higher levels of self-actualization. He lives fully and honestly in the present, discharging all of his energies in developing further competencies in the work of his choosing, believing that a constructive future is possible only with work in the present. He lives in this moment as if it were his last, doing only those things he would if this moment were his last. His life has meaning simply because his life is meaning. The lives of others will have similar meaning because they come to share similar commitments.

Finally, the effective person knows that the only worthwhile society is a helper society. With full recognition that a man who is looking forward is not looking back, the effective person recognizes that the only meaningful society is one in which helpees are transformed into helpers. Yet, he knows that only those who, in a very real sense, break free of society can return to contribute to it, and accordingly, he reserves a special freedom for those who are not necessarily best served by any society.

To achieve both these means and ends, the effective person knows that he will involve himself only on his terms. Knowing who he is and at what stage of development he is, he makes extremely fine discriminations concerning the levels at which others are functioning—in large part knowing others in their reactions to his actions. To be sure, if motivated to help another, he takes the other's experience into full consideration. However, he knows too well that dysfunctioning is largely a function of life on the terms of the weak and the unhealthy. Placing the highest premium on his own continuing health and competence, he does not subject his energies to the waste and abuse of others. His capability for deferring, on his terms, to persons functioning at still higher levels is simply a function of his recognition that *helping, as life, must be on the terms of the healthier person.*

In a word, the effective person recognizes that he is as creative as he is honest. Any semblance of compromising responsible honesty results in attenuated creativity. The *real* risk for the whole person is involved in honesty *not* being a way of life, in all his actions, with and including all physical implications.

PROGRAM EFFECTIVENESS

The most important single variable in the effectiveness of a program, then, is the level of functioning of its implementers. While the system of a program has its own distinctive contributions to make, the success of the program stands or falls primarily on the effectiveness of the individuals who are conducting it. As we have already seen, the helper functioning at high levels serves as both model and agent for the helpee: helpees functioning at low levels move in the direction of their high-level helpers over the course of the helping process. The following series of projects assesses the differential effectiveness within programs of high and low functioning helpers upon the functioning of their helpees. That is, individual helpers implementing the same or different programs have differential effects upon their helpees according to their individual levels of functioning.

In the earlier study of the effects of helper level of functioning upon helpee level of functioning (Pagell, Carkhuff, and Berenson, 1967), we found that the helper's absolute level of functioning was a critical determinant of helpee gain or change. However, while pre- and post-assessments of the helpee's functioning are taken of necessity, most often only the initial level of the helper's functioning is taken. The implicit assumption would seem to be that the helper's level of functioning does not change. In practice we know that it does. The hypothesis that the helper who is himself engaged in a growth process is the most effective model and agent for the helpee's growth was supported in research by Kratochvil, Aspy, and Carkhuff (1967).

The most significant finding for our purposes is that direction of helper development may under some circumstances be a more critical variable than absolute level of functioning. Helpers as helpees may grow or deteriorate. Helpers who are growing, even if they begin initially from relatively low levels of functioning, may have a constructive effect upon the helpee: it is a stimulating experience simply to be with a person who is growing—for whom life unfolds each day in a different manner. And a person for whom life unfolds anew each day is best equipped to serve as both model and agent for his helpee's growth.

We may make generalizations of the effects of helper level of functioning to other instances of interpersonal learning experiences. Just as we study the differential effects of the level of functioning within helping programs, so may we also study the differential effects of the trainer's level of functioning within particular training programs.

In this regard, a study was conducted to assess the effects of trainer level of functioning where the type of human relations training program was held constant, that is, where the trainers involved implemented the same systematic training programs (Pierce, Carkhuff, and Berenson, 1967). Employing high and moderately low level functioning counselor-trainers, it was found that the trainees of the high-functioning trainer continued in training and gained significantly in their interpersonal skills while over half of the trainees of the moderately low level functioning trainer terminated and did not gain significantly over the course of training. Indeed, while the trainees of the high-level trainer moved in the direction of his functioning, they did not achieve his level of functioning over time-limited training. Similarly, the trainees of the moderately low-functioning trainer moved in the direction of his level of functioning, with those who were functioning initially at relatively higher levels gaining very little and those who were functioning initially lower than the trainer gaining slightly more. Over and above the effects of the systematic training program, then, the gains are a function of the trainer.

A follow-up study at another university investigated the differential effects of graduate supervisor level of functioning without holding the nature of counseling supervision constant. It was found that the supervisees of the high-level supervisory group improved significantly over time in their interpersonal functioning and were functioning at levels significantly higher than the supervisees of the low-level supervisory group (Pierce and Schauble, 1970). The trainees in the low supervisor group were not significantly different from their supervisors to begin with and, while they deteriorated slightly as a group, they showed no significant change over time. Again, those few supervisees who entered the supervisory situation with low-level supervisors at or near minimally facilitative levels dropped precipitously during the course of the year. Thus, the generalizations concerning the differential effects of the helper's individual level of functioning hold within programs of teaching and training as well as within programs of counseling and psychotherapy.

Just as we assess the differential effects within programs of the helper's individual level of functioning upon helpee level of functioning, so we can also assess the differential effects between programs of the combined levels of functioning of personnel of these different programs. The effectiveness of a given program is a function in large part of the personnel who comprise the program. Thus, just as individuals can be rated and ranked according to their effectiveness, so also can programs be rated and ranked according to their effectiveness. Wall Street does it all of the time with business and industry—and pays them accordingly. It would not be a bad idea at all for programs of education and social action to do likewise.

The following project assessed 16 training and treatment programs ranging from the highest level Ph.D. programs through intermediate level professional programs to subprofessional programs and finally treatment or helpee programs (Carkhuff, 1969c). The results are startling on many counts!

PROJECT 11
Leader Level of Functioning*

important study

From the vast amount of literature on the training of counselors and psychotherapists, three factors, alone and in their various interactions, emerge as critical variables: (a) the trainer's level of functioning on interpersonal dimensions related to constructive helpee change; (b) the trainee's level of functioning on the relevant dimensions; (c) the type of training programs operationalized.

LEVEL OF TRAINER FUNCTIONING

Perhaps the most critical variable in effective counselor training is the level at which the counselor-trainer is functioning on those dimensions related to constructive helpee change. In relation to helpee change, research has led to the discernment of what is termed both facilitative and action-oriented interpersonal dimensions (empathy, respect, concreteness, genuineness, self-disclosure, confrontation, immediacy) as the critical ingredients of effective interpersonal processes. Hopefully, the trainer is not only functioning at high levels of these dimensions but also attempting to impart learnings concerning these dimensions in a systematic manner, for only then will he integrate the critical sources of learning, the didactic, the experiential, and the modeling. In this regard, it simply makes good sense that, whatever the task, whether it be research or counseling, science or art, the implementer of any training program should fulfill at least the following key conditions: (a) he should have demonstrated a level of expertise or excellence in the relevant area; (b) he should be experienced in the relevant area.

A number of research projects assessing the effects of training have addressed themselves directly to these questions. While there are many more such projects, they do not provide for systematic assessments which can be employed for comparative purposes. Table 6–1 summarizes the levels of overall functioning of trainers at the beginning and trainees at the beginning and the end of training when cast in the helping role with adults,

*Reprinted in part with permission from the *Journal of Counseling Psychology,* 1969, **16,** 238–245, where it first appeared as "Critical Variables in Effective Counselor Training," by Robert R. Carkhuff.

Table 6-1

Mean Levels of Overall Functioning of Beginning and Advanced Trainees and Their Trainers

LEVELS OF PROFESSIONALIZATION OF PROGRAM

LEVELS OF FUNCTIONING	PROFESSIONAL					INTERMEDIATE		
	I–Clin. (PhD)	II–Clin. (PhD)	III–Clin. (PhD)	IV–Couns. (PhD)	V–Rehab. (MA)	VI–Guid. (MA)	VII–Teacher-counselor (MA)	VIII–Beginning psych. (MA)
Beginning of training	2.1 (N = 8)	2.1 (N = 14)		2.1 (N = 10)	1.4 (N = 8)	1.9 (N = 14)	1.7 (N = 8)	1.8 (N = 10)
Advanced state (noted)	2.0 (N = 8) 4th yr.	1.8 (N = 8) 2nd yr.	3.0 (N = 12) 100 hr.	3.0 (N = 10) 3rd yr.	1.8 (N = 8) 2nd yr.	2.8 (N = 14) 50 hr.	2.6 (N = 8) 50 hr.	2.3 (N = 10) 30 hr.
Trainer level	1.9 (N = 9)	1.7 (N = 3)	3.3 (N = 2)	3.6 (N = 3)	1.6 (N = 7)	3.5 (N = 1)	4.0 (N = 1)	3.0 (N = 2)
Trainees' net change	−.1	−.3		.9	.4	.9	.9	.5

LEVELS OF FUNCTIONING	SUBPROFESSIONAL					HELPEE		
	IX–Nurs. (nondegree)	X–Dorm counsel (nondegree)	XI–Commun. volunteer (nondegree) A / B	XII–Hosp. attend. (nondegree)	XIII–Parent-teacher (racial relations)	XIV–Child psychiatric parents (treatment)	XV–Inpatients (treatment)	XVI–Inpatients (treatment)
Beginning of Training	1.7 (N = 10)	1.8 (N = 12)	1.6 / 1.5 (N = 9, 8)		1.4 (N = 25)	1.5 (N = 10)	1.2 (N = 7)	1.2 (N = 12)
Advanced state (noted)	2.3 (N = 10) 20 hr.	2.7 (N = 12) 20 hr.	2.4 / 1.9 (N = 9, 8) 20 hr.	2.8 (N = 5) 100 hr.	2.6 (N = 25) 20 hr.	2.9 (N = 10) 25 hr.	2.4 (N = 7) 25 hr.	2.6 (N = 12) 30 hr.
Trainer level	3.0 (N = 1)	3.0 (N = 1)	3.1 / 2.0 (N = 1, 1)	3.3 (N = 2)	4.0 (N = 2)	4.5 (N = 1)	3.5 (N = 2)	3.8 (N = 1)
Trainees' net change	.6	.9	.8 / .4		1.2	1.4	1.2	1.4

NOTE: All scores reflect communication level between adults only. Studies from which data were taken are: I: Carkhuff, Kratochvil, and Friel, 1968; II: Carkhuff, Kratochvil, and Friel, 1968; III: Carkhuff and Truax, 1965; IV: Carkhuff and Berenson, 1967b; V: Anthony and Carkhuff, 1970; VI: Martin and Carkhuff, 1968; VII: Carkhuff, 1969e; VIII: Carkhuff, Kratochvil, and Friel, 1970; IX: Berenson, Carkhuff, and Myrus, 1966; XI: Pierce, Carkhuff, and Berenson 1967; XII: Carkhuff and Truax, 1965; XIII: Carkhuff and Banks, 1970; XIV: Carkhuff and Bierman, 1970; XV: Pierce and Drasgow, 1969; XVI: Vitalo 1970. Studies III and XII include transformed scores for empathy, regard, and genuineness only.

and thus establishes the overall effect of training. It should be emphasized that, independent of duration of training, only those programs or those aspects of programs that have made full discharge of all relevant aspects of training as seen by their promulgators are included for consideration. In addition, while changes in trainee level of functioning are noted, only the initial level of trainer functioning is available and similar differentials are not recorded for the trainer. Indeed, it is quite likely that just as in counseling, the direction of change in trainer functioning may be just as critical or more critical than absolute level of functioning.

As can be seen, in all cases where the data are available the trainees move in the direction of their trainers. In one instance, it may be noted, the trainees beginning at an extraordinary low level progress over the course of training to the point where they are even functioning at a level slightly (although not significantly) above their relatively low-functioning trainers (Program V). As can also be seen, in general, the higher functioning trainers tend to invest themselves in the more innovating, shorter term, "lower level" training programs while the lower functioning trainers become involved in longer-term, professional graduate programs. Overall, subprofessional and helpee-trainees tend to gain more in their level of functioning over the course of brief training than professional trainees do over years of training. However, this again is not unqualified. For example, while two of the professional programs assessed demonstrate low final levels of trainee functioning (Programs I and II), within the professional programs trainees of high-level trainers demonstrate highly positive results (Programs III and IV).

The contrasting findings of studies of intermediate, subprofessional and helpee programs demonstrating significantly positive changes with high level functioning counselor-trainers may be summarized as follows: In general, those trainees whose trainers are functioning (a) above minimally facilitative levels (Level 3) and (b) approximately one level above the trainees demonstrate the most positive changes. In this regard, the fact that the trainers in many of these projects were functioning well above the norms of their membership groups is relevant. In addition to the results of the rehabilitation counselor program (Program V), the fact that one of the trainers in Program XI who was functioning above his trainees but not at minimally facilitative levels elicited some constructive change from his trainees suggests that a trainer who approaches meeting one of these conditions may make a contribution, albeit a limited one, to the growth of his trainees. On the other hand, those trainers who are functioning neither at minimally facilitative levels nor significantly above their trainees have nothing to offer their trainees while those who are functioning at levels lower than their trainees can only promise their trainees no change or deteriorative change.

Overall, the results can be summarized in tabular form in terms of the

Table 6–2

Mean Level of Trainer Functioning and Mean
Level of Trainee Gain

Program	Mean Level of Trainer Functioning	Mean Level of Net Trainee Gain
XIV	4.5	1.4
VII	4.0	.9
XIII	4.0	1.2
XVI	3.8	1.4
X	3.7	.9
IV	3.6	.9
XV	3.5	1.2
VI	3.5	.9
XII	3.3	1.0[a]
III	3.3	.9[a]
XI A	3.1	.8
VIII	3.0	.7
IX	3.0	.6
XI B	2.0	.4
I	1.9	—.1
II	1.7	—.3
V	1 6	.4

[a] Estimated from Table 6–1.

trainers' levels of functioning, independent of all other considerations, that is, number of trainers or trainees, level of trainees, type and duration of program, etc. As can be seen in Table 6–2, whether or not the estimates for Programs IV and XII derived from Table 6–1 are employed, there is a very high relationship between trainer's level of functioning and the mean gain in level of functioning of the trainee. Thus, the level of the counselor-trainer's functioning would appear to be the single most critical aspect of effective training.

Some insights into the dynamics of interpersonal functioning may be obtained by viewing the data on the discrimination of counselor functioning by trainers and trainees. Whereas, initially, trainees enter training deviating approximately one level or more from the ratings of experts, just as with communication, the trainees demonstrate movement in the direction of their trainers' levels of discrimination over the course of training. Indeed, a high or accurate level of discrimination (approximately one-half level deviation from experts) by the trainers in the rehabilitation counselor-training program may account in part for the fact that the trainees were able to go beyond their trainers in level of interpersonal functioning, that is, the trainers can make accurate discriminations concerning the trainees even if they cannot establish an accurate experimental and modeling base for training. Obviously, what is most puzzling is that the trainers function at fairly high levels of discrimination and low levels of communication, a finding that is consistent with those results establishing the independence of discrimination and communication among low-level communicators. It appears that many people see but do not act upon what they see with perhaps a socially conditioned dynamic base in not believing what they see or being afraid to act upon what they see. Since the problem is not unlike the insight-action conflict of therapeutic processes the relevant questions might be whether systematic training or psychotherapy or both are the answers for these trainers. At a minimum it must be concluded that those persons functioning at the highest levels behaviorally are not conducting the professional training programs.

LEVEL OF TRAINEE FUNCTIONING

The level of trainer functioning cannot be considered independently of level of trainee functioning. The results of Table 6–1 which are consistent with base-rate data in the field, indicate that, in general, trainees functioning relatively at the highest levels are selected by themselves or the professional programs, whether inadvertently or not. The intermediate level program trainees are essentially unselected from those persons in the general public with interests in helping, with at least one program (V) apparently receiving those trainees who are functioning at unusually low levels, perhaps reflecting a "leftover" nature of this sample, that is, those applicants who are unable to get into the doctoral clinical and counseling programs.

Unfortunately, the results also indicate that, in general, those trainees functioning relatively at the highest levels initially tend to deteriorate over the course of training. With the professional-subprofessional dimension confounded with trainer level of functioning, it can also be seen that the highest level trainees are most often interacting with the lowest level trainers; thus a deterioration effect is to be anticipated. The follow-up studies of Programs I and II provide relevant data. In the longitudinal study of Program I, there were 6 dropouts by the second year from among the 14 original first-year students. The two highest level functioning students and four of the six functioning above Level 2 terminated or were terminated. Overall, the initial level of functioning of those who ultimately dropped out was approximately 2.2 to approximately 2.0 for those who were to continue in the programs. Further, a tentative hypothesis that the best and the worst trainees might be eliminated from traditional programs received no additional support from the results of a follow-up of Program I. From the eight first-year clinical and eight first-year nonclinical trainees, five had dropped out voluntarily by the first semester of the second year: the five dropouts were five of the six trainees who were functioning above Level 2; overall, their comparative mean levels of functioning were approximately

1.9 for those who remained. Another interesting follow-up process study revealed that, in addition to level of facilitative functioning, those dropping out tended to be functioning in the more action-oriented direction (masculine), that is, they were trying to do something about their clients' problems, while those who remained functioned in a more passively acceptant manner (feminine), a finding consistent with interpretations of Patterson's review of selection literature. Thus, it appears that the only consistent finding is that the trainees functioning at the highest levels of both facilitative and action-oriented dimensions will be eliminated from traditional programs.

another irony!

Needless to elaborate, Programs III and IV in which relatively high-level trainees interact with high-level trainers provide a vivid contrast to the results of the other programs. In addition, those trainees in the intermediate, subprofessional, and helpee programs who were functioning initially at low levels tend to demonstrate positive gains over the course of training. Again, in general, these trainees have had the benefit of interacting with high-level trainers. The positive results of the one program (Program V) with trainers functioning at low levels can be accounted for in part by the extraordinarily low initial trainee level of functioning. In effect, these trainees stood to gain by getting back to the average level of functioning of the population at large.

While at first glance, then, initial level of trainee functioning bears no relationship with trainee gain; when it is considered in interaction with trainer level of functioning, a number of critical trends emerge. Perhaps the most significant of these is the intensity of the discrepancy between trainer and trainee level of functioning. In general, where the differential is greatest between trainer and trainee level of functioning the greatest positive or negative change can be expected. A gross summary of a prediction equation for change indicates that, independent of all other variables (including, in particular, duration of training) over the course of training, the amount of trainee change is approximately one-half of the discrepancy between initial trainer and trainee level of functioning. This may be checked by calculations from Table 6–1.

These findings, of course, have implications for selection. That is, knowing the level of trainer functioning, differential predictions according to level of trainee functioning can be generated. In predictive validity studies an index of communication has been found to be the best predictor of future functioning in the helping role: In interaction with a high level functioning trainer, trainees functioning initially at relatively high beginning levels (in general around Level 2) (a) functioned at the highest final levels and (b) gained the most, while those functioning initially at relatively low levels functioned at lower final levels and gained the least. In regard to discrimination there was no relationship between discrimination indexes and functioning in the helping role. Again, in general, trainees move in the direction of their trainers on discrimination. In those instances where the trainers are discriminating at relatively high levels and communicating at low levels, then, this means that the trainees improve in discrimination while not improving in communication.

TYPE OF TRAINING PROGRAM

Trainer and trainee levels of functioning, in turn, cannot be considered independently of the type of program implemented. Again, the apparent effects of type and duration of program are confounded by the level of functioning of the trainers promulgating these programs. Thus, the professional programs conducted by low level functioning counselors are also characterized by the curious blend of psychoanalytic and behavioristic approaches that dominate many academic training centers today. Similarly, Program V, the rehabilitation counselor training program, is dominated by another curious blend of nondirective and trait-and-factor orientations. In each instance it may be said that the programs involved focus upon what might be called secondary dimensions or potential preferred modes of treatment rather than systematically upon those core dimensions for which the greatest support has been received. Similarly, these programs tend to focus exclusively upon the didactic source of learning, even in the case of the client-centered training where, interestingly enough, the emphasis appears to be upon teaching and "shaping" rather than the experiential base of the trainee. All too often these experiences leave the trainees in a "double-blind" situation where, for example, the effects of modeling counteract those of the trainer's teaching. Finally, concerning the duration of the program, while the negative relationship with trainee change is confounded, the best that can be said is that these programs are wasteful in the time allotted to effect trainee functioning in the helping role.

By contrast, the remaining programs for which there is positive evidence may be considered eclectic programs focusing (a) upon core conditions shared by all interview-oriented processes for which there is research support complemented by a consideration of the unique contributions of the various potential preferred modes of treatment and (b) integrating the different critical sources of learning. The model that has been employed means that the counselor-trainer not only offers high levels of facilitative and action-oriented dimensions (thus providing the trainee with the same experiential base as the helpee is to be offered) but also establishes himself as a model for a person who can sensitively share experiences with another as well as act upon these experiences, both within and without the pertinent interpersonal process. In addition, the training process is that much more effective when the trainer is also systematically focusing in his didactic teaching and "shaping" upon the conditions which he is employing in interaction with the trainees. These programs have produced changes on not only the objective measures assessing level of functioning in the helping role but also on expert and self-ratings, the ratings of clients and significant others, and on indexes of the constructive personality change of the trainee. These programs have produced changes significantly greater than training control groups of traditional programs as well as the usual control groups.

Concerning what is taught, there is evidence to indicate that concentration upon the didactic teaching of discrimination results in changes in discrimination only. The direct implication that people functioning at low levels by and large learn only what they are taught, making no generalizations, is further buttressed by the differential findings of Anthony and Carkhuff (1970) where they found changes in attitudes toward the physically handicapped in a program emphasizing such changes, and Kratochvil (1969), who did not find changes in values in a program placing no stress upon such. The fact that discrimination does not translate itself readily into functioning in the helping role in conjunction with the fact that there is no evidence to relate discrimination to client or patient benefits in any way has implications for a behavioristic approach to training.

While there is empirical as well as experiential evidence to indicate that high level functioning people can generalize from one learning experience to another (as, e.g., from discrimination to communication), the inability of low-level persons to do likewise has implications for training both high- as well as low-functioning persons to do what one wants them to do. If one wants trainees to function effectively in the helping role then they must be given plenty of practice in the helping role. If one wants the trainees to learn to communicate effectively they must be given practice in communication. In particular, in relation to the low-functioning trainees, if one does not do so, they will be functioning at levels commensurate with the clients and patients whom they are treating and thus will have nothing to offer. Those behaviors which are in fact helpful and those which are not must be reinforced differentially. One must explicitly and systematically teach that which one wishes for them to learn. Again, particularly in relation to the low-functioning trainee, nothing must be left implicit and no indirect effects must be expected in other spheres of the trainee's life or upon other individuals in the trainee's life. Gradations of practice must be worked up in "shaping" effective behavior. Upon conclusion of training, those changes which have been effected must be further supported. Again, in relation to the low-level trainee, generalization to other behaviors, and other situations cannot be expected. The environment and the systems of reinforcements within the environment to which they return must be controlled in order to maintain lasting effects. In particular, for the low level functioning trainee the immediate effects of one learning experience will be neutralized by the effects of succeeding experiences. Simply stated, while the hope for low level functioning trainees is to enable them to function at higher levels, in general, they function in a given role in a manner in which they are trained to function via all of the sources of learning under the control of the trainer. They change only if they are trained to change. Obviously, it is an advantage to begin with higher level functioning trainees but even they can benefit from explicit and systematic programs offered in the context of a facilitative atmosphere.

One alternative, then, is to select relatively high level functioning trainees. However, the necessity for high level functioning trainers in these instances is imperative. Indeed, under the present professional system and trainers which dominate, trainee losses would be minimized by selecting low-level trainees. Concerning selection, the evidence indicates that the best index of a future criterion is a previous index of that criterion. Thus, in order to predict future functioning in the helping role, one must obtain an index of present functioning in the helping role. In this regard, again, there is no evidence to indicate that discrimination gives an index of anything other than discrimination and unless persons are being trained to discriminate at high levels, as for example, research raters, there is no value to such extended efforts. Even here, however, there is clear-cut evidence to indicate that those persons who are (a) functioning at the highest levels interpersonally and (b) are most experienced in the relevant interpersonal relations, as for example, counseling and psychotherapy, are the most accurate discriminators or raters.

In summary, it is apparent that dependent upon the level of functioning of (a) trainers and (b) trainees and (c) the types of programs implemented in training, the effects may run the gamut from severe loss in trainee functioning over years of training to significant gains within months. In this regard, in addition to assessment of facilitative and action-oriented dimensions, means are necessary for assessing the effectiveness with which helpers implement the techniques of potential preferred modes of treatment, as for example, assessments of how effectively a helper implements a counterconditioning process or employs and interprets a Strong Vocational Interest Blank. Accordingly, programs of both high and low level functioning trainers may focus explicitly upon relevant or extraneous learnings. For example, many, if not most, programs emphasize trainee "statements of positive attitudes toward patients," and indeed eliminate those candidates who do not conform to meeting this expectation, yet the dimension emphasized remains unrelated to indexes of client change or gain. In the same vein, many of the trainees' learnings, whether from high or low level functioning trainers, have been inadvertent. That is, for example, a high level functioning trainer may effect constructive trainee changes on dimensions related to helpee change even while emphasizing extraneous learnings; similarly, a low-level trainer may effect deteriorative trainee change while focusing upon very relevant dimensions. The direct implication, then, is that those programs in which high level functioning trainers focus explicitly upon dimensions relevant to helpee gains and make systematic employment of all significant sources of learning, including, in particular, modeling, are most effective.

The results have implications not only for the selection of trainers and trainees and the conduct of their training programs but also for treatment. One may, for example, be able to employ the same relevant indexes for assessing the level of functioning of clients. In addition, within treatment the same behavioristic principles that apply to low level functioning trainees will apply to low level functioning clients. In this regard, explicit teaching and systematic "shaping" and programming through differential reinforcement schedules and control of the environment at least to the point where one can anticipate and similarly program otherwise difficult conditions, particularly those involving people in the environment to which the helpee returns, may constitute a preferred mode of treatment.

Again, for our present purposes, the critical variable is the level of the helper's functioning. While there is an interaction between helper and helpee level of functioning, what is most critical is that the helpees of high-level helpers demonstrate constructive gains, whereas the trainees of low-level trainers do not. Although the type of program is important, what is most critical is that even in the absence of an effective program the high-level trainer can effect significant positive gains.

We study the effective person so that we may understand the source of his effectiveness. We attempt to understand his phenomenology so that we may understand "where he is coming from" and where we must go to. We attempt to operationalize his effectiveness so that we may bridge the gap from where we are to where he is.

If the heart of educational and social action programs is personally effective persons, then it is because these persons, and these persons alone, can make personal effectiveness possible for other persons. They alone have the means. They alone live effectively. They alone know the secrets to effectiveness and are willing to pay the price of hard work, discipline, and training for life. But even this is not enough, for they must also transmit their understanding to those for whom they are concerned.

The effective person transmits his understanding through responsiveness and initiative in helping. He transmits his understanding through system and reinforcement in teaching and training. He transmits his understanding through standards and conditionality in selection.

The effective person transmits his understanding through love and action in life.

OPERATIONALIZATION OF PERSONAL EFFECTIVENESS

It is not enough to describe the phenomenology of the effective person or even to realize the effects of the leaders' level of functioning upon the persons for whom they are responsible. We must study and understand the sources of personal effectiveness in a manner in which it can be achieved. Most important, we must operationalize personal effectiveness in a manner in which it can be achieved. That is, we must analyze the dimensions of effectiveness in terms that are attainable.

With regard to understanding the sources of effectiveness, we must attempt to understand the processes by which positive and negative changes are achieved. Thus, for example, while high level functioning persons effect positive gains and low level functioning persons effect no gains or negative change, we must understand how these changes come about. In the emotional-interpersonal realm there is evidence to indicate the processes that lead to constructive or deteriorative outcomes.

One means of assessing the interpersonal helping process has been that involving the introduction and analysis of crises. These crises may occur within and without the helping process, for helper as well as helpee. In the final analysis, there is no growth without crisis and the confrontation of self and others which the crisis precipitates. The effective helper, as well as helpee, grows at the crisis point. While he may not be systematically prepared for the particular crisis involved, the crisis makes the helper tap his own resources and push out his own boundaries. Within the crisis, the helper is fully committed to the struggle enabling the helpee to develop directionality.

In this context, a number of research projects are relevant. In order to study the processes by which the helper affected the helpee, experimental "crises" were operationalized and introduced. During the first third of a helping hour, the helper offered his usual level of helping conditions; during the second third, the conditions were lowered when the helper selectively withheld the best possible responses that he might otherwise have made. Finally, during the last period, the helper again offered helping conditions at his usual level. In effect, the helpee experienced a crisis in the sense that he was trying to communicate with a helper who was not communicating. The findings were striking.

The depth of self-exploration engaged in by both psychotic inpatients (Truax and Carkhuff, 1965) and students who were functioning at low emotional-interpersonal levels (Holder, Carkhuff, and Berenson, 1967) was found to be a direct function of the level of conditions offered by the helper: when the helper employed his entire range of responses and his most highly creative responses, the low functioning helpees explored themselves at relatively high levels; when the helper was restrictive in the quality of his responses, the helpee explored himself at low levels; finally, when the helper was again fully responsive, the helpees again explored themselves at relatively high levels. Thus, the helper's effectiveness in facilitating the helpee's growth was found to be a function of the helper's responsiveness.

The helpee did indeed experience a crisis when the helper was restrictive in his responses. When the crisis involving low levels of communication is precipitated by low level functioning helpees, the communication process breaks down completely; the helpee can no longer function effectively. The range and the level of the helper's responses are critical to the helping interaction and, accordingly, the helpee's welfare.

On the other hand, when high level functioning helpees are seen by the same high level functioning helpers the results are quite different. With high-level helpers, high-level helpees continue to explore themselves independently of the helper's lowering of conditions during the experimental period (Holder, Carkhuff, and Berenson, 1967). Within the range and level of responses immediately available to the helpee, the communication process is not totally dependent upon the helper. It appears that once the high-level helpee has made the discrimination that the helper is high level he continues to function on his own during the experimental period. Indeed the higher the level of helpee functioning, the greater his likelihood to function independently of the high-level helpers.

In an extension of the earlier work, moderately low as well as high level functioning helpers experimentally manipulated the level of interpersonal conditions which they offered with high and low level functioning helpees (Piaget, Berenson, and Carkhuff, 1967). It was found that both the high- and low-functioning helpees demonstrated progressively lower depths of self-exploration with the low-functioning helper. On the other hand, both the high- and low-functioning helpees demonstrated progressively higher depths of self-exploration with the high-functioning helper. The implications for helping over time are profound. With time and with crises, the helpees of low-functioning helpers will deteriorate while those of high-functioning helpers will improve. The outcome, positive or negative, represents the culmination of a process of progressive increments or decrements to that outcome.

Just as we study the effects of helper responsiveness upon the helpee so also can we study the effects of helpee expressiveness upon the helper. In effect, another kind of crisis may be introduced by the helpee. In a prototypical experimental study, unknown to the helper involved, a helpee was given a mental set to explore herself deeply during the first third of an interview, to talk only about irrelevant and impersonal details during the middle third, and to explore herself deeply again during the final third of the interview (Carkhuff and Alexik, 1967). Thus, the helpee experimentally introduced a "crisis" for the helper; after the helpee was exploring herself deeply and meaningfully, she suddenly regressed to the inconsequential and offered no responses to the helper's attempts to reestablish communication. However, whatever the helper did, he was unable to reestablish contact. The communication process, for which he was largely responsible, had broken down.

The results were telling. Helpers functioning at low levels dropped to precipitously low levels of functioning when the crisis was introduced, with those at the lowest levels tending not to recover. Helpers functioning at high levels did not drop in functioning, with those functioning at the highest levels tending to increase their levels of functioning. These process patterns may be extended with repeated contacts and repeated crises. The low-functioning helpers demonstrate a progressively declining pattern over time while the high-functioning helpers present a progressively rising pattern over time (Carkhuff, 1969a; Carkhuff and Berenson, 1967a). For the low helpers it would appear that following the exercising of the initial repertoire of responses during early contacts, with the helpee's continuing presentation of crises, the low-functioning helpers deteriorate. Indeed, their limited and stereotyped response repertoire would seem to work to preclude their even acknowledging the existence of a crisis. The responsiveness of the high-level helper, in turn, would appear to be of high quality and improving with contacts — in the helpee's eyes the helper's response repertoire is inexhaustible.

QUANTITY AND QUALITY OF RESPONSES

Effectiveness, then, is a function of the individual's (or group of individuals') ability to attain goals in any particular or general area. This ability to attain goals, in turn, is defined by the quantity and quality of the responses which an individual has in each and all spheres of functioning. Again, the quantity and quality of responses of an individual in any one sphere of functioning will be reflected in the achievement of desirable effects in a particular area; the quantity and quality of responses of an individual in all spheres of functioning will be reflected in the achievement of desirable ends in general. Therefore, effectiveness in each of these spheres of functioning is operationalized; effectiveness in all of these spheres is operationalized.

In other words, effectiveness is a function of the number and level of responses which an individual has. Only with a large number of high-level responses is the person able to integrate the responses in new combinations to make applications unique to a given stimulus. To be sure, an individual may be limited by his own personal resources in his ability to make these new combinations. However, he cannot make these combinations if he does not have the relevant responses in his repertoire.

Creativity, then, as well as adjustment is a function of the quality and quantity of responses available to a given individual. An individual is as creative as the number of high-level responses he has in his repertoire. The quantity and quality of responses in the different spheres of functioning are interrelated, with the quality of responses not only building upon the quantity of responses but also the quantity of responses building upon the quality of responses. The sources of these responses deserve brief attention here.

By and large people learn what they are trained to learn. This is not to negate the critical nature of innate dispositions or inherited characteristics. Rather, it is to concede the interaction of the inherent and acquired characteristics. However, it is necessary to emphasize the critical nature of learning with regard to the development of responses.

The learner is trained via the critical sources of learning, the experiential, the modeling, and the didactic. The learner, whether child or student or helpee, is first exposed to a wide variety of responses from a person or multiple persons with a large repertoire of responses. The learner's experience of the effectiveness of some of the responses to which he is exposed is a key source of his motivation to acquire the responses (the experiential source of learning). The effectiveness of the response in the helpee's experience serves to erect the teacher as a model to imitate and emulate (the modeling source of learning). Finally, the teacher helps to guide the learning process and to facilitate the learner's comprehension of it by his pedagogic teaching concerning the experience (the didactic source of learning).

Each source alone is not enough. Schools of learning and counseling have emphasized the experiential source. "Just water the tree and it will grow in its own way," they say, ignoring the modeling and didactic sources of learning. And yet we see example after example of the duplication of the voice, tone, and words of the learners of child-centered, student-centered, and client-centered teachers. The experiential source of learning alone is not enough to account for these circumstances.

Schools of learning and counseling have emphasized the didactic or "shaping" process of learning. The behaviorists and the directivists indicate that the learner is simply the sum total of his responses which they have conditioned. And yet they cannot account for the creative evolution and emergence of the harbingers of change. The didactic source of learning alone is not enough to account for these circumstances.

Schools of learning and counseling have emphasized the modeling source of learning. They have indicated that the imitation of the teacher by the learner is the key source of all learning. And yet they cannot account for the critical differences between the child and the parent, the student and the teacher, the client and the counselor. The modeling source of learning alone is not enough to account for these circumstances.

Integrated at once in an effective person, however, these sources of learning yield potent results. Having been exposed to a wide variety of responses, the learner has the opportunity to experience and experiment with responses that have the potential for working for him. He tends to repeat and retain those which work most effectively for the present and at a later age, for his future purposes. He tends to identify and to identify with those persons who have something to offer him in terms of still different and even more effective responses. He makes these responses his by fully comprehending their dimensions and their dynamics in the development of his own personal working cosmology.

The effective teacher engages in a similar process, for the effective teacher is an effective learner.

Only as an effective learner can the teacher become a potent reinforcer and effectively lay the experiential, modeling, and didactic bases of learning. Only as a potent reinforcer can the teacher contribute to the response development of the learner. The more effective these potent reinforcers are, *that is, the more high-level responses which they have in their response repertoire, the more effective will the individual become,* that is, *the more high-level responses he will acquire for his repertoire.*

In some environments one sphere of functioning is emphasized over another. Thus, the ghetto youngster learns early to move to his left and to his right in basketball and to make a lay-up off either foot while at the same time the middle-class child is singing and reciting, reading, and writing his alphabet. At a later point in time the ghetto child will be creative in his application in a ball game, moving from right to left as his guard moves, shifting the ball from his right hand to his left as his guard seeks to block his first shot. At the same time the middle-class child will be using the alphabet in different combinations to form different words, and the words in different combinations to form different phrases.

The implications for education are obvious. The frustrations and retardation of the ghetto youngster in school as a function of a limited intellectual response repertoire are just as obvious as the frustration and deterioration of the hospitalized psychiatric patient as a function of a limited emotional or interpersonal response repertoire. Suffice it to say that it is silly to argue, as many psychologists and educators do, about the differences in responses of white and black and Spanish children, for it is precisely the quantity and quality of responses which they have trained into the children that they are arguing about.

Effectiveness, then, is a function of the level and number of responses which an individual has in his repertoire. Again, the repertoires operate for each sphere of functioning individually and for all spheres in general. Again, they also relate to goal attainment in individual and general spheres.

We know that we can measure physical functioning in terms of the attainment of physical goals. Thus, employing comparative age norms, we can assess both an individual's relative as well as absolute functioning in the physical sphere. For example, we can assess the time it takes the individual to cover a long distance (at least a mile) either running or walking and compare the results to norms for the individual's age group. In addition, we can assess the number of consecutive sit-ups which the individual can do and compare them to age norms. Each of these physical indexes, in turn, relates to different kinds of physical goal attainment. Also, and most important, each of these indexes correlates highly, almost perfectly, with an individual's cardiovascular processes, the best medical index of overall physical functioning: that is, those persons who demonstrate the greatest ability to function on physical tasks are physically the healthiest individuals.

Let us remain in the physical sphere for a moment, for there is much to learn in physical analogies. Athletic analogies are abundant. For example, in basketball the effectiveness of an individual will be a function of the quality and quantity of his "moves," that is, the level and number of responses in his repertoire. The individual will score more points, "feed" more effectively, defend more effectively, rebound more effectively, and in general serve his team most effectively according to the number and level of responses he has in each and all areas.

In baseball a pitcher will be effective according to the quantity and quality of the pitches he throws. The more pitches he throws and the better each pitch is, the more effective he will be in maintaining a low earned run average and in winning ball games. There are many other examples too numerous to mention.

Of course, there are many qualifications. For example, where the quality is high enough the quantity need not be great. Thus, if a Feller or a Koufax or a Gibson can throw the ball 100 miles per hour, he need not develop many more pitches. Or if a West or a Baylor can throw the ball in the hoop from 30 feet, he may not need many more moves. However, even here there is a likelihood of each of these athletes developing new responses as they are required. As Feller, Koufax, and Gibson matured and the fastball slowed down, they developed unusual breaking pitches. Similarly, as the defenses are varied and intensified, a West or a Baylor must develop new moves to meet the new strategies. With the development of these new physical responses, we find emotional and intellectual components coming into play.

Thus, the physical, emotional, and intellectual responses are interrelated in an effective physical act. However, we also see that not only are these different spheres of functioning interrelated but also the quality and quantity of the responses are related. Thus, the number and caliber of moves or pitches will be related, with each building upon the other, quality upon quantity and vice-versa in a highly interactional process.

In a similar manner we can measure intellectual spheres of functioning with indexes of the quality and quantity of intellectual responses such as different problem-solving tasks, and the emotional-interpersonal sphere of functioning with indexes of the quality and quantity of emotional responsiveness to different stimuli. These indexes, in turn, correlate highly with real-life indexes of functioning. That is, those persons who demonstrate the largest repertoire of the highest level responses are those who are most capable of discovering and successfully implementing the most effective solutions in the relevant areas.

Let us look in some detail at one research project which assessed both emotional and intellectual responsiveness. In the following article, helper responses are studied as a function of helpee stimulus expressions. The stimulus expressions involve both differing emotional and differing content areas (Carkhuff, 1969d). Accordingly, the helper's responses are seen as having potentially both emotional and intellectual components. Responses to personal feeling and meaning will be discussed and operationalized more fully in later chapters.

PROJECT 12
*Level of Functioning and Response Repertoire**

It was the purpose of this research to survey and analyze prospective helpers' discrimination and communication response patterns as a function of differing helpee affective expressions and content areas.

*Reprinted in part with permission from the *Journal of Counseling Psychology*, 1969, **16**, 126–131, where it first appeared as "Helper Communication as a Function of Helpee Affect and Content," by Robert R. Carkhuff.

METHOD

Materials

Communication. A tape involving 16 2-minute helpee expressions (thus of a playing time of approximately ½ hour) was prepared to present as stimuli to elicit prospective helper responses. The helpee stimulus expressions were role played and taped. They were based upon real counseling experiences recorded in previous pilot research in assessing communication. The stimulus expressions crossed three dominant affect areas with five dominant content areas. The affect areas included the following: (a) depression-distress, (b) anger-hostility, and (c) elation-excitement. The content areas included the following: (a) social-interpersonal, (b) educational-vocational, (c) child rearing, (d) sexual-marital, (e) confrontations of counselor. Thus, the excerpts were arranged in such a way as to match each affect area with each content area. In addition, a silence was included as a stimulus for eliciting helper responses. Overall communication levels of *S*s were determined by the ratings of two experienced counselors who had demonstrated highly reliable levels of communication and discrimination.

Discrimination.   A second tape involving four helper responses to each of the 16 helpee stimulus expressions was prepared to present to *S*s to elicit their ratings of responses. The helper responses, representing helper statements from live counseling and based upon previous research in discrimination were designed to cross level of helper-offered facilitative conditions with level of helper action orientation and activity. Thus, in a random order the following combinations of helper responses were offered for rating: high facilitation–high action orientation; high facilitation–low action; low facilitation–high action; and low facilitation–low action. Discrimination scores were established in levels by determining the absolute deviation (independent of direction) of *S*s' ratings from the consensus ratings of two experts (different from the raters of communication) who had demonstrated predictive ability in previous outcome studies.

Procedure

Prospective helpers and counselors of varying degrees of experience were employed as *S*s. They were first presented with the 16 helpee stimulus expressions with instructions to formulate and record in a written form meaningful responses to these expressions:

> The following includes 16 helpee stimulus expressions; that is, expressions by a helpee of feeling and content in different problem areas. In this particular case, the same helpee is involved in all instances.
> You may conceive of this helpee, not necessarily as a formal client, but

simply a person who has come to you in a time of need. The helpee, for example, may be a student from one of your classes. We would like for you to
respond as you would if someone came to you seeking assistance in a time
of distress or need for them.

In formulating your responses keep in mind responses that the helpee can
use effectively in her own life.

Following the elicitation of helping responses the S-helper was asked
to rate the 64 helper responses (discrimination test) employing the following
gross ratings of interpersonal functioning:

The facilitator is a person who is living effectively himself and who discloses
himself in a genuine and constructive fashion in response to others. He communicates an accurate empathic understanding and a respect for all of the
feelings of other persons and guides discussions with those persons into
specific feelings and experiences. He communicates confidence in what he is
doing and is spontaneous and intense. In addition, while he is open and flexible in his relationships with others, in his commitment to the welfare of the
other person he is quite capable of active, assertive, and even confronting
behavior when it is appropriate.

You will hear a number of excerpts taken from therapy sessions. Rate
each excerpt 1.0, 1.5, 2.0, 2.5, 3.0, 3.5, 4.0, 4.5, or 5.0 using the continuum
below.

The ratings of the S-helper's level of communication were obtained by
two experienced raters who also employed the gross ratings form. Their
rate-rerate reliabilities employing the gross rating form were .95, .93 and
their interrater reliability was .89.

In addition to obtaining communication and discrimination scores, the
communication responses were content analyzed by still another group of
raters to determine the following alternative characteristics of Ss' responses:
(a) response is to content, affect, both, other; (b) response is to past, present,
future, other; (c) response is to helpee, self (helper), interaction, other;
(d) response is experiential, didactic, other; (e) response is directive, nondirective, other.

The S-helpers at seven different levels of experience were surveyed:
(a) unselected beginning undergraduates ($N = 330$); (b) volunteer but
otherwise unselected undergraduates in a mental patients companion program ($N = 30$); (c) psychology students in a senior seminar on counseling
($N = 30$); (d) unselected teachers ($N = 10$); (e) beginning psychology
graduate students ($N = 10$); (f) experienced counselors and therapists who
had not been systematically trained in any way in relation to counselor-
offered conditions ($N = 20$); (g) experienced counselors and therapists
who had been systematically trained ($N = 10$).

In addition, in the five of these groups most intimately involved with
helping, S-helpers were given a set to respond as many times as they could
and the helpee stimulus expressions were played until S-helpers acknowl-

edged that they had exhausted their response repertoires. Thus, the groups at the last five levels were involved in the response repertoire study: senior psychology students, teachers, beginning graduate students, experienced but not systematically trained counselors, experienced and systematically trained counselors. Response repertoires were assessed by simple frequency tabulations of helper responses to helpee stimulus expressions.

RESULTS

The overall results appear in Table 6–3. As can be seen, progressively graduating increments in level of communication accompany increasing levels of experience and/or training. Communication level progresses from midway between Levels 1 and 2 to Level 3. While response repertoire for the five levels of experience examined ranged from 1.9 to 3.7, the increase in frequency was substantial only with systematically trained, experienced counselors. Discrimination level, in turn, followed a pattern similar to communication. Represented in absolute deviations from expert ratings, the discrimination scores move from 1.2 to .4 with the ratings of the most experienced and/or trained most closely approximating the ratings of the experts.

Communication level was found to be a function of affect and content.

Table 6–3

Mean Levels of Communication, Discrimination and Response Frequency of Prospective Helpers of Varied Levels of Experience

Levels	N	Level of communication (ratings of helper responses on 5-point scales)		Level of discrimination (absolute deviations of helper ratings from experts)		Repertoire of responses (response frequency upon repeated administration)	
		M	SD	M	SD	M	SD
1. Unselected undergraduates	330	1.6	.5	1.1	.2		
2. Undergraduate "companions"	30	1.5	.2	1.2	.3		
3. Senior psychology students	30	1.6	.5	1.1	.3	2.1	.4
4. Unselected teachers	10	1.8	.6	1.0	.3	1.9	.8
5. Beginning psychology graduate students	10	1.9	.5	.8	.2	2.5	1.2
6. Experienced counselors (not systematically trained)	20	2.2	.5	.6	.2	2.3	1.1
7. Experienced counselors (systematically trained)	10	3.0	.4	.4	.1	3.7	1.7

However, while statistically significant, the mean differences across groups were so small (no greater than one-tenth of a level) as to question their functional utility. In terms of clinical meaningfulness, both level and repertoire of responses appeared characteristic of the individual respondent.

All relevant variables were also found to be significant sources of effect for discrimination. Thus, helpee affect and content, along with levels of group experience and helper facilitation and action response level, reject the hypothesis of equality of means. The independence of the helpee affect-helper response level suggests that how one rates items involving different affects is independent of how one discriminates level of facilitative and action-oriented conditions. In all other cases, the interaction is significant, indicating that all scores are dependent upon all levels of the variables involved.

In casting further illumination upon the communication results, it is noteworthy that with the exception of the experienced groups, the mean levels of communication of all groups grew systematically lower on repeated administrations of the helpee stimulus expressions. That is, on successive administrations the respondents communicated at lower levels. Thus, the groups involved dropped accordingly over four administrations: senior psychology students dropped from 1.6 to 1.3; teachers from 1.8 to 1.5; beginning graduate trainees from 1.9 to 1.5. This is qualified, of course, by the fact that the number of respondents also decreased systematically on successive administrations. The results contrast with those of the experienced (whether systematically trained or not) groups which maintained a high level of consistency (between 2.9 and 3.0 for the trained and between 2.0 and 2.2 for the untrained experienced) across administrations.

The content analyses yield interesting findings. Inexperienced and/or low-functioning respondents (on both communication and discrimination) tend to respond to content almost exclusively while experienced and/or moderate-functioning respondents tend to respond to affect about as frequently as content. Experienced and trained and/or high-functioning respondents tend to respond to both affect and content. Both experienced and inexperienced as well as high- and low-functioning respondents demonstrate strong tendencies to respond to the present rather than the past or future. Similarly, all groups tend to respond to the helpee rather than themselves (the helpers) with the experienced and trained and/or high-functioning respondents demonstrating an increasing tendency to respond to the interaction between helpee and helper. The experienced and high-functioning respondents tend to respond experientially although not to the exclusion of didactic responses, while the inexperienced and low-functioning respondents emphasize didactic responses but not to the exclusion of experiential and other responses. The directive-nondirective discriminations are more complex with experienced, low-functioning practitioners tending to be either directive or to ask questions (often irrelevant, if not stupid), while experienced, high-functioning practitioners demonstrate a more even balance between directiveness and nondirectiveness. On the other hand, however, among the inexperienced respondents, the high-functioning respondents tend to be more directive and the low-functioning more nondirective.

DISCUSSION

In general, the results indicate increasingly higher communication levels, response repertoires, and finer discrimination levels with experience and/or training. However, the differences are greatest for systematically trained helpers. There is a great jump in communication level and response frequency from experienced counselors who are not systematically trained to those who are, all of which suggests the necessity for training programs built systematically around the kinds of conditions assessed in this study. Indeed, the level of communication of experienced, nonsystematically trained counselors, while higher than all other groups assessed, is significantly less than minimally facilitative. In this regard, it is noteworthy that the levels of communication established here are essentially replications of previous data obtained in standard interviews. Thus, the data not only establish the construct validity of the instruments employed but also the stability of the findings.

It is noteworthy that all groups consistently had the fewest responses available for elation-affect and confrontation-content, with each perhaps suggesting social-psychological phenomena related to the aspects of interpersonal functioning which are most difficult for helpers. However, in relation to the latter finding, although the helper's response repertoire is related to the helpee's problem area, nevertheless the helpee will tend to receive the highest levels of discrimination and communication and the largest repertoire of responses from those helpers who are most experienced and/or systematically trained. To be sure, a central occurrence in effective counseling may involve a helper functioning at relatively high levels of communication and discrimination increasing the levels of both communication and discrimination of a helpee functioning initially at relatively low levels and concurrently enabling the helpee to increase his response repertoire and thus his degrees of freedom in different problem areas.

The major methodological problem involves the employment of written helper communications in response to the taped helpee stimulus expressions. Research currently being assessed suggests that while there is variability among prospective helpers functioning at low levels of communication in interviews with standard helpees, the helpers function at low levels of both written and verbal response indexes: low-functioning helpers may vary according to whether they are responding to live helpees or into a tape recorder or in writing but they remain low on all indexes. On the other hand, helpers functioning at high levels of communication in a standard interview not only function at high levels on all indexes but also maintain essentially the same rank ordering within the high group between indexes. The main effect of the written response form appears to be to limit the upper levels of communication of high level functioning counselors. That is, the low helpers remain low while the high do not achieve as high levels as they do in interaction with live helpees. An additional question concerns the potential effects of the respondents' set for or insight into the task. The critical consideration here, it must be underscored, involves whether or not the effective responses are in the repertoire of the respondent; that is, available to him when they are appropriate, not whether or not the respondent believes he might prefer to make one response or the other.

Perhaps the major clinical problem confronting the helping profession involves the communication/discrimination differential. Relative to inexperienced helpers, the experienced helpers do not communicate nearly as well as they discriminate. One can only conjecture concerning the underlying dynamics of why people cannot translate discrimination into communication, a problem not unrelated to the insight/action discrepancy in client treatment. It simply cannot be assumed that a high level of discrimination translates itself into communication. Perhaps more behavioristic means must be employed to successfully achieve the desired training goal of high-level communication.

Finally, the overall drop in response repertoire from beginning graduate students to experienced counselors in conjunction with a rise in level of communications suggests that not only has the experienced counselor learned more effective responses but also that less effective responses in the repertoire may have been extinguished with experience. This conjecture is supported by (a) the consistency of communication level across repeated administrations in conjunction with (b) the relatively limited response repertoire that is exhibited. In contrast, however, the systematically trained counselors demonstrate not only higher response frequencies but also higher communication levels across repeated administrations. Indeed, judging from the trends over administrations, there is no reason, other than the reasonableness of the task, to assume that these persons could not continue almost indefinitely to emit high-level responses, perhaps building upon the additional and more subtle messages which they hear each succeeding time. The main inferences from the content analyses are consistent. In general, with increasing experience and/or training and/or high levels of communication and discrimination, the respondents tend to demonstrate more flexibility and integration in their responses. With feedback from the helpee, the helper may demonstrate an increasingly richer repertoire of responses and these dimensions may become even more apparent.

In summary, the taped helpee stimulus expressions in conjunction with helper responses offer a useful and efficient way of assessing the level of communication and discrimination as well as the response repertoire of prospective helpers. Outcome studies are currently being assessed with tentative evidence indicating that these procedures may be employed as standard and valid selection indexes in determining who can benefit from different kinds of training experiences.

The most important point for our present purposes is the relationship between level of communication and effectiveness in the helping role as measured by constructive change or gain in helpee outcome indexes (Carkhuff, 1969a, 1969b), a point to be elaborated upon in the next few chapters. Not only do the highest level functioning helpers, then, have the largest repertoire of responses but also on repeated administrations the high-functioning helpers maintain their level of functioning while the lower functioning helpers drop in level of functioning, that is, the more administrations the lower the level of response if there is any at all. By contrast, the highest functioning·helpers appear to have an inexhaustible number of responses and actually exhibit a tendency to raise their level of responses upon repeated administrations, that is, the larger the repertoire of responses the higher level the responses. Again, the highest level helpers appear to put the responses together in new and creative combinations upon repeated administrations. Finally, in addition to the relationship between response repertoire and number of responses there is also a relationship between both of these indexes and discrimination. Thus, the effective person is equipped with the fine discriminations necessary to know where and when to employ the appropriate response.

The increase in the quality and quantity of responses is usually what teachers and supervisors attempt to accomplish, usually in a nonsystematic way, and coaches, like Lombardi, sometimes in a very systematic way. We will see in later chapters that in some spheres of functioning this may be accomplished in a very systematic manner. For example, in the development of emotional-interpersonal responsiveness, not only does the trainee have the benefit of concrete informational feedback in the form of ratings for his own responses in the helper's role but he is also exposed to the responses formulated by every member of the training group as well as those formulated by the trainer. In addition, the trainee in the helpee's role, who has presented real-life problems, is allowed to respond to the different responses formulated. In this manner each trainee is systematically exposed to a wide range of responses and, therefore, has the opportunity to incorporate and practice those found most effective.

We have discovered, then, that program effectiveness is in large part a function of the personal effectiveness of its promulgators, although not, to be sure, to the exclusion of the development of an effective working program, as we shall see in Part Four. Personal effectiveness, in turn, we have found, is a function of the quantity and quality of the responses available to the individual in all spheres of functioning: physical, emotional-interpersonal, and intellectual.

In general, effectiveness can be assessed in terms of the achievement of definable goals. These goals may appear to be predominantly in one realm or the other—the physical, the emotional-interpersonal, or the intellectual. Nevertheless, successful achievement of these goals is a function of effective performance in all spheres of functioning.

Thus, we find that intellectual achievement is at least in part a function of physical and emotional-interpersonal as well as intellectual resources. Similarly, success in the emotional-interpersonal realms such as psychotherapeutic improvement or marital relations or even relations between races is in part a function of physical and intellectual factors. Finally, high levels of physical attainment such as athletic accomplishments are in part a function of intellectual and emotional-interpersonal as well as physical resources.

In each of these spheres of functioning the quantity and quality of the response repertoire enable us to operationalize the ingredients of personal effectiveness. The quantity and quality of the responses available to an individual enable us to generate predictions concerning his effectiveness in given situations. The concepts of effectiveness enable us to select those persons best equipped either to discharge responsibilities in educational and social action programs or to utilize a training experience equipping them to discharge such responsibilities. The training programs, in turn, can systematically equip the person with the necessary responses. Finally, programs can be developed to guide the helper in the discharge of his responsibilities.

The quantity and quality of the response repertoire enable us to operationalize all of the positive and salutory things that can be said about an individual's personal effectiveness.

In short, *the level of functioning and the response repertoire of an individual in the physical, emotional-interpersonal, and intellectual spheres determine his health, his creativity, his wholeness—indeed his life.*

REFERENCES

Anthony, W., & Carkhuff, R. R. The effects of rehabilitation counselor training upon discrimination, communication and helping attitudes. *Rehabilitation Counseling Bulletin,* 1970, **13,** 333–342.

Berenson, B. G., Carkhuff, R. R., & Myrus, P. The interpersonal functioning and training of college students. *Journal of Counseling Psychology,* 1966, **13,** 441–446.

Carkhuff, R. R. *Helping and human relations: A primer for lay and professional helpers.* Vol. I. *Selection and training.* New York: Holt, Rinehart and Winston, 1969. (a)

Carkhuff, R. R. *Helping and human relations: A primer for lay and professional helpers.* Vol. II. *Practice and research.* New York: Holt, Rinehart and Winston, 1969. (b)

Carkhuff, R. R. Critical variables in effective counselor training. *Journal of Counseling Psychology,* 1969, **16,** 238–245. (c)

Carkhuff, R. R. Helper communication as a function of helpee affect and content. *Journal of Counseling Psychology,* 1969, **16,** 126–131. (d)

Carkhuff, R. R. The prediction of the effects of teacher-counselor training: The development of communication and discrimination selection indexes. *Counselor Education and Supervision,* 1969, **8,** 265–272. (e)

Carkhuff, R. R., & Alexik, M. Effects of client depth of self-exploration upon high- and low-functioning counselors. *Journal of Counseling Psychology,* 1967, **14,** 350–355.

Carkhuff, R. R., & Banks, G. Training as a preferred mode of facilitating relations between races and generations. *Journal of Counseling Psychology,* 1970, **17,** 413–418.

Carkhuff, R. R., & Berenson, B. G. *Beyond counseling and therapy.* New York: Holt, Rinehart and Winston, 1967. (a)

Carkhuff, R. R., & Berenson, B. G. Effects of systematic training. Unpublished research, State University of New York at Buffalo, 1967. (b)

Carkhuff, R. R., & Bierman, R. Training as a preferred mode of treatment of parents of emotionally disturbed children. *Journal of Counseling Psychology,* 1970, **17,** 157–161.

Carkhuff, R. R., Kratochvil, D., & Friel, T. The effects of professional training: The communication and discrimination of facilitative conditions. *Journal of Counseling Psychology,* 1968, **15,** 68–74.

Carkhuff, R. R., & Truax, C. B. Training in counseling and psychotherapy: An evaluation of an integrated didactic and experiential approach. *Journal of Consulting Psychology,* 1965, **29,** 333–336.

Holder, B. T., Carkhuff, R. R., & Berenson, B. G. The differential effects of the manipulation of therapeutic conditions upon high- and low-functioning clients. *Journal of Counseling Psychology,* 1967, **14,** 63–66.

Kratochvil, D. Changes in values and interpersonal functioning of nurses in training. *Counselor Education and Supervision,* 1969, **8,** 104–107.

Kratochvil, D., Aspy, D., & Carkhuff, R. R. The differential effects of absolute level and direction of growth in counselor functioning upon client level of functioning. *Journal of Clinical Psychology,* 1967, **23,** 216–217.

Martin, J., & Carkhuff, R. R. The effects of training upon changes in trainee personality and behavior. *Journal of Clinical Psychology,* 1968, **24,** 109–110.

Pagell, W., Carkhuff, R. R., & Berenson, B. G. The predicted differential effects of the level of counselor functioning upon the level of functioning of outpatients. *Journal of Clinical Psychology,* 1967, **23,** 510–512.

Piaget, G. W., Berenson, B. G., & Carkhuff, R. R. The differential effects of the manipulation of therapeutic conditions by high- and moderate-functioning therapists upon high- and low-functioning clients. *Journal of Consulting Psychology,* 1967, **31,** 481–486.

Pierce, R., Carkhuff, R. R., & Berenson, B. G. The differential effects of high- and low-functioning counselors upon counselors-in-training. *Journal of Clinical Psychology,* 1967, **23,** 212–215.

Pierce, R., & Drasgow, J. Teaching facilitative interpersonal functioning to psychiatric inpatients. *Journal of Counseling Psychology,* 1969, **16,** 295–299.

Pierce, R., & Schuable, P. Graduate training of facilitative counselors: The effects of individual supervision. *Journal of Counseling Psychology,* 1970, **17,** 210–215.

Truax, C. B., & Carkhuff, R. R. The experimental manipulation of therapeutic conditions. *Journal of Consulting Psychology,* 1965, **29,** 119–124.

Vitalo, R. Teaching improved interpersonal functioning as a preferred mode of treatment. Doctoral dissertation, University of Massachusetts, 1970.

PART FOUR

Ingredients of Human Resource Development

CHAPTER 7
Principles of Helping

The effective person is a product of effective human relations. Just as effective programs are a function of effective people, so also are effective people a function, in a very real sense, of effective programs. That is, the question of the sources of the effective person is answered by the kinds of experiences and people to which he is exposed. To be sure, the effectiveness of the experiences are again in large part a function of the effectiveness of the persons offering them. But they are also in part a function of the kind of process or program being offered the learner.

The learner's or helpee's personal experience is the source of the discrimination of which of the experiences to which he is exposed are helpful and which are not. He will attempt to incorporate those experiences that are helpful and discard those that are not. Indeed, if nonhelpful or harmful kinds of experiences are imposed upon him, he may react, sometimes violently, often by displaying the opposite behavior.

The effective learning process is an interactional one where the teacher or helper offers the most effective responses which he has gleaned from his experience and the helpee has the opportunity to check them through his experience, choosing to incorporate those which work for him.

Social action programs, then, must offer effective programs to go with effective people as well as effective people to go with effective programs. The programs must be based in experimentation as well as experience. They must have the truth of research tests, for the real people will no longer be prostelytized. They must have the truth of human experience, for the real people will no longer be deluded.

AN EMPIRICAL BASE FOR HELPING

Perhaps the most distinctive contribution which education has to offer is its rationale and research tools for discovering an understanding of all effective human relationships in which one individual helps another to higher levels of functioning. Great strides have been made in the discovery of the effective ingredients of these helping and human relationships. From all spheres of life these learnings come.

They relate to what makes a parent-child relationship work. They relate to what makes a teacher-student relationship work. They relate to what makes a counselor-counselee relationship work.

Briefly, the findings are this. The relationship between the helper and the helpee constitutes the core of all effective learning or relearning experiences. The relationship conditions enable the helper to understand the helpee, and the helper to establish himself as an important influencer or potent reinforcer of the helpee's behavior. In this context, the relationship conditions enable the helper to discover, develop, and implement courses of action or programs that are effective for the helpee.

This relationship between helper and helpee can be operationalized in terms of the level of communication of certain conditions between helper and helpee (Carkhuff, 1969a, 1969b). These conditions are termed responsive or facilitative dimensions and initiative or action-oriented dimensions. The responsive dimensions center around the helpee's experience and facilitate the helpee's development. The initiative dimensions center around the helper's experience and direct the helpee toward developing an orientation toward acting.

The responsive dimensions include dimensions such as empathic understanding, respect, and specificity or concreteness. The degree to which the helper offers high levels of these facilitative dimensions will be related directly to the degree to which the helpee can understand, respect, and be specific with himself and, ultimately, others.

The initiative dimensions include dimensions such as genuineness, confrontation, and immediacy. The degree to which the helper offers high levels of these action-oriented dimensions will be related directly to the degree to which the helpee can confront, be genuine and immediate with himself and, ultimately, others.

Together, these responsive and initiative dimensions involve the helpee in a process leading to constructive change or gain (Berenson and Carkhuff, 1967; Carkhuff, 1969a, 1969b; Carkhuff and Berenson, 1967; Truax and Carkhuff, 1967). Moderate levels of responsive dimensions serve to elicit a depth of helpee self-exploration and immediacy of experiencing with regard to a wide range of problems. High levels of responsive dimensions in conjunction with moderate levels of initiative dimensions make possible a depth of understanding on the part of the helpee. High levels of both responsive and initiative dimensions enable the helpee to act upon his more accurate self-understanding.

The cycle of helpee exploration, understanding, and action continues with each serving to sharpen the constructiveness of the other. The feedback from action stimulates new areas of exploration and increasingly accurate understanding which, in turn, help to define more effective action.

The evidence is strong. *In child-rearing, teaching, and counseling, the helpees of those helpers who offer high levels of these responsive and initiative dimensions are healthier physically, emotionally, and intellectually than the helpees of those helpers who offer low levels of these dimensions* (Carkhuff, 1969a, 1969b).

The contribution of education, then, is an important one. In its empirical base, it provides us with a direction that is all too often absent in our gropings for answers. In its research methodologies, it operationalizes approaches, to be modified in experience, with which we can approach the problems of our day and, perhaps, any future day. It is this modification in experience that we will next consider.

Human experience has a contribution to make.

AN EXPERIENTIAL BASE FOR HELPING

The further removed that any program comes to be from the "truth" which each of us knows in human experience the greater its likelihood of ultimate extinction. This is particularly true in helping and human relationships. The further removed that any mode of practice becomes from the "feeling-knowledge" of what is effective the less likely the lasting significance of its contribution.

Thus, a given approach must have experiential meaning as well as empirical validity.

The experiential base within which any program takes place, then, is crucial. With high level functioning helpers, high levels of communication enable the helpee to experience a sensitive understanding of his communications; that is, the helpee has the experience of having his own expressions understood in depth with a fineness of discrimination that extends his communications and allows him to understand himself at deeper and deeper levels. When the helpee actively and spontaneously engages in an inward probing to newly discover feelings or experiences about himself and his world, then he has the opportunity to reorganize and reassess these previously distorted perceptions about himself and his world. When the helpee focuses upon his here and now relationships, particularly that between himself and his helper, then he has an opportunity to work through and comprehend his feelings and experiences regarding himself and others in a direct and constructive manner.

In a program with an effective experiential base, the helpee has the experience not only of being responded to, but also of having someone else share his experience with the helpee. The communications, then, are not only sensitive and warm but also directionful and forceful. They provide not only the helpee's experience of action-oriented dimensions but also a model for a helper who initiates behavior based upon his own personal experience. Thus, a sound experiential base enables the helpee to experiment himself with different modes of functioning in the hope of finding those that in interaction with particular situations are most appropriate and functional for him.

Both in terms of the helper's direct influence upon the direction and content of helping as well as in terms of the "homework" assigned the helpee, the helpee learns initially that it is possible to act for himself and upon his world. Ultimately, the helpee must be able to act under his own direction and control. Here, again, the helpee's experience of the helper's large repertoire of behavioral responses serves to increase the helpee's number of responses and, accordingly, his degree of flexibility and independent action.

The court of last appeal, then, is the visceral response of the helpee—the "gut" reaction that tells him this is "good" and that is "bad." To be sure, the helpee cannot always tell initially what is "good" or "bad" for him. Depending upon his level of development and functioning, he may discriminate facilitators or retarders with great ease or great difficulty. Indeed, there is some reason to believe that the effects of facilitative as well as retarding relationships are cumulative. Thus, the individual who has had a succession of facilitative experiences will be more open to facilitative experiences and more closed to retarding ones. The person who has had a succession of retarding experiences will have great difficulty discriminating a facilitative one and will, accordingly, be more vulnerable to the retarding experiences. However, with time and effort on the part of the helper to overcome such potential handicaps, the helpee will know ultimately that he is growing stronger or weaker, healthier or sicker.

It is in the helper's strength and health that the helpee comes to know his own strength and health. It is in the helpee's own strength and health that he comes to know the "truth" of human experience.

HELPING AND HUMAN RELATIONS

In this context, let us consider a program for helping and human relations that is grounded in both the empirical and experiential bases for helping. The program is an attempt to make meaningful to the would-be helper what the evidence has indicated to be the effective ingredients and process of constructive relationships between human beings. In utilizing the evidence to appeal to his experience, the program attempts to take the prospective helper from "where he is." Specifically, this guide was developed for orienting lay personnel for their training as "functional professionals." The guide and its implications for helping are self-explanatory.

PROJECT 13

A Brief Guide for Helping for Functional Professionals*

This guide is meant for the person who wants to help but who has had no formal training or experience in helping. Maybe people have come to you to seek your help but you are not always sure you have been most helpful to them. Many times people have come to you to share their problems and they have made you their helper whether or not you wanted to be. Maybe your job has brought you into contact with people and calls for you to be helpful. Maybe you simply want to understand more effective ways of helping yourself and your relations with those most close to you: your husband or wife, your children, your friends and neighbors, your co-workers. This guide will provide you with a structure that will help you to understand how you can help most effectively. The guide is set up in a series of statements that outlines what you need to know about helping and how to help.

WHAT YOU NEED TO KNOW ABOUT HELPING

1. Helping may be for better or worse.

The very first thing that you should know is that what you may or may not do with someone else may be harmful as well as helpful. It just makes good sense that if you can help someone, you can also hurt him. The fact is that the things that you do with him may make a difference in his life. So if the person means something to you, you want to do those things that are most helpful. We call the person whom you are trying to help in a helping relationship, the helpee.

2. The helper is most helpful when he understands and acts upon his understanding.

Those helpers whose helpees improve are persons who understand themselves and can act upon this understanding in their own lives. The helpees seek their help because the helpees are unable to understand themselves or unable to act upon this understanding. The helper understands the helpee and communicates this understanding to the helpee. The helper also understands the helpee's need to do something about his problem and he helps the helpee to do something about it. Understanding and action are the key ingredients of effective helping.

3. Lay people can learn to help as effectively as professional helpers.

By lay people we simply mean those of you who have not been trained

---

*Originally organized and written in November 1968 by Robert R. Carkhuff for the Activities of the Human Relations Center, American International College.

to help but are interested in being helpful. For most purposes and most problems, these lay people can learn to help as effectively and often more effectively than professional helpers, that is, teachers, guidance counselors, psychologists, psychiatrists, and social workers. For one thing, professional helpers do not have a monopoly on understanding and action. Lay persons can learn to understand others as well as or better than professionals and they can learn to act upon this understanding as well as or better than professionals.

4. Helpers from within the community involved will be more effective than helpers from outside.

The people in the community are closer to the problems involved, whether these problems are individual problems or community-wide problems. The people in the community can see the problems more easily through the eyes of the helpee. The people in the community can communicate this understanding more easily to the helpees because they speak their language. The people in the community know what actions are available to the helpee because they know the community from the inside. Black people can help black people more effectively than whites can. Spanish people can help Spanish people more effectively than others can. Poor people can help poor people more effectively than others can.

WHAT YOU NEED TO KNOW TO HELP

It isn't enough to be a lay person or to be a member of the same community as the person seeking help. Not everyone can help. For one thing, we have to have ourselves in order before we can help someone else to get himself together. For another thing, there are certain things that we must learn in order to be as helpful as possible with those who mean something to us. There are some guidelines that will help us to understand our goals in helping.

1. The first goal of helping is to get the helpee to explore his problem.

We cannot help a person unless we first understand his problem. How often when we are attempting to be helpers we give advice before we fully understand the problem. Since the advice is not based upon the necessary understanding, it will be "hit or miss" advice. Sometimes the helpee comes to us and presents us with a problem that is not the real problem. It is as if he is testing us to see how good we are. If we cannot sense the real problem then he will not share it with us. And this sharing of the real problem as seen by him is the necessary first goal of helping. When the helpee explores himself he helps the helper to understand his problem better.

2. The second goal of helping is to get the helpee to understand himself.

The fact that the helpee explores his problem does not necessarily mean that he understands it as well as he should. Sometimes he doesn't understand it at all and only shares it in bits and pieces. It is the helper's job to put these bits and pieces together in such a way that he can help the helpee to understand the problem more fully.

3. *The final goal of helping is to get the helpee to act upon his understanding.*

As the helpee understands his problem more fully he will see more clearly the different courses of action that are available to him. Together helper and helpee can consider the short-term and long-term advantages of each course of action. They can choose the best course of action and develop programs or ways of accomplishing that course of action. If he acts successfully he comes closer to dealing with the problem or problems that brought him to look for help in the first place.

4. *The different goals of helping are related to each other.*

The goals of exploration, understanding, and action are related to each other. After the helpee has acted upon his understanding of the problem, he finds out the consequences of his action. That is, he learns new things. He comes to explore and understand more of himself and his problem. As he understands more of himself, he prepares to act once again in a way somewhat different from the way he acted before. Again, there is new learning that comes from his action. Often the cycle of exploration, understanding, and action is repeated over and over again. Each time, the helpee learns to understand his problem more accurately and, therefore, to act more constructively for himself and others.

HOW TO HELP

Now that we know what it is we are trying to accomplish let us consider the ways that we can accomplish these goals. Clearly, helper understanding is the best means to helpee understanding, and helper action is the best means to helpee action. The helper provides the helpee with the experience of being understood and the experience of being with someone who acts upon his understanding. The helper also provides the helpee with a model to imitate just as the child imitates his parents: the helper is someone who understands and acts upon his understanding.

So far we have focused upon the helper characteristics of understanding and action. When an individual understands another individual he gives his full attention to that individual. The talk centers around the feelings and experiences of the second person. We say that the first person (helper) *responds* to the second person (helpee).

When an individual acts in relation to another individual he acts on the basis of his experience. The action centers around the feelings and experiences of the first person. We say that the first person (helper) *initiates* action in relation to the second person (helpee).

1. The helper will be most effective during the early phases of helping when he responds to the helpee.

The helper will be most effective if he gives his full attention to the helpee, doing all that he can to listen and to hear the helpee and to let the helpee know that he understands what the helpee is really saying. When the helper responds to the helpee, the helpee becomes involved in a process of self-exploration leading to self-understanding. There are a number of things that the helper can do in order to respond effectively. We call these the *conditions* that *facilitate* the helpee's effort to explore and understand himself. These *facilitative conditions* may be described as follows:

A. *Empathy, or understanding:* Understanding, or *empathy,* is the ability to see the world through the other person's eyes. In helping, it is as if the helper "crawls" inside of the helpee's skin and feels the things the helpee feels, and experiences the world the way the helpee experiences it. The helper not only sees things the way the helpee sees things, but lets the helpee know what he sees, that is, he communicates what he sees to the helpee.

B. *Respect, or caring for someone:* Respect is the ability to respond to the other person in such a way as to let him know that you care for him and that you believe in his ability to do something about his problem and his life. At the very beginning of helping, the helper may not know enough about the helpee to communicate this specifically. As helping continues, the helper will come to know the helpee in specific ways so that he can communicate this respect for the helpee directly and specifically.

C. *Concreteness, or being specific:* Concreteness is simply the ability to enable the other person to be specific about the feelings and experience he is talking about. The helper helps the helpee to be specific about the helpee's own experiences and not the experiences of other people. This is particularly critical during the early stages of helping when concreteness helps to develop empathy. At later points the helper may attempt to be concrete in developing the stages of problem-solving.

2. The helper will be most effective during later phases of helping when he initiates action.

The helper will be most effective if he uses what he learned by responding to the helpee as a basis for initiating his own expressions. That is, on the basis of what the helper learned from the helpee's exploration of his problem, the helper tries to put the picture together. The helper gives the process direction, attempting to get the helpee to understand himself at a deeper level and finally to act upon this understanding. Those conditions initiated by the helper we call *action* or *action-oriented* dimensions because they involve some action on the helper's part and because they lead the helpee to initiate his own ideas of what's going on and to act upon these ideas. These *action conditions* may be described as follows:

A. *Genuineness, or being real:* Genuineness is simply the ability to be real in a relationship with another person. At first the emphasis is more on not being phony. Later the emphasis is upon the helper being as real as he can be. That is, he is free to be himself. He is really himself. The only important thing to remember here is that you're still trying to help the other person. So, if you have had feelings about him, it will be more helpful to ask about where these feelings came from rather than to dump them on him. Helping is for the helpee.

B. _Confrontation, or telling it like it is:_ Part of being real is to tell the other person just like it is. Confrontation is just telling the other person what you've been hearing as you've been listening to him. For example, you see him doing things different from the way he is talking and you put it to him. Or you confront him with the reality of a situation that is quite different from the way he's been picturing it. Or you just tell him that you see things a lot different from the way that he does. Once you confront you need to follow through and work out the differences between you.

C. _Immediacy, or what's really going on between the two of you:_ Immediacy is your ability to understand different feelings and experiences that are going on between you and another person. The helpee may be telling the helper something about how he feels about the helper without even knowing it. Often he can't tell the helper directly how he feels about him. The helper must be tuned in on these things so that he can understand the helpee. The helper must tell the helpee what is going on so that the helpee can understand himself. The helper must know where the helpee is coming from.

3. _The responsive and initiative conditions must be related to each other._

The helper must first respond to the helpee's feelings and experiences. He must then put things together and initiate action on the basis of what he has learned by responding to the helpee. It is almost like a mother preparing a child for a father. The mother _responds_ to the child and _facilitates_ his efforts. The father _initiates_ his own direction and _acts_ upon his understanding. Even when the helper confronts, if he does so effectively, he will follow his confrontation with empathy for the feelings of the helpee. In other terms, if the helper tells it like it is, he must follow-up by understanding where the helpee is at. On the other hand, sometimes the helper must initiate action dimensions on his terms before he can get the helping process going. But, again, this is a last resort measure that he uses only if the helpee can't get started on the helpee's own terms. In effective helping as in effective child-rearing an understanding mother prepares the child for an action-oriented father. The mother gives the father the necessary recognition that he must have in order to be an important source of strength for the child to imitate. Whether you have a year or an hour to help, the order of helping is to respond first and initiate action later. Even if you have just 15 minutes to help, you must use five minutes or so responding to the helpee in order to find out for sure where the helpee is at before starting to put the picture together and acting upon that picture. The effective helper must be both mother and father—sometimes one, sometimes the other, sometimes both at the same time.

4. The helper will be most effective in the end when he helps the helpee develop a course of action for handling his problem.

It isn't enough for the helpee to be both mother and father. Based upon the helper's understanding of the helpee's need to do something about his problem, the helper must help the helpee develop a better way of doing things. A *course of action* is just a way of doing things in a way that is better than you did them before. When you consider a course of action, you have to choose that way of doing things that gives you the best chance of being successful. You have to weigh short-term success with long-term success. Sometimes things that will do well in the short run won't make it in the long run. If you have the time, you will help the helpee set up a way of doing things that doesn't just work for the problem that he has now but also for the problems that he will have over a lifetime. If you don't have the time, you must help the helpee to deal with his present problem and hope that if he can handle this problem he'll have a better chance of handling other problems in his future.

HOW TO TRAIN TO HELP: ILLUSTRATIONS

Discrimination

Discrimination is simply learning to understand the different levels of the different conditions involved. The key to learning to understand the conditions (level 3, see Table 7–1a) is to set up some kind of a mid-point which, if people reach it, means that they are doing enough to help. Above this point (levels 4 and 5) they will be doing as much as they can do. Below this point (levels 1 and 2) they are doing less than they should do to help. With empathic understanding, for example, the goal at this mid-point would be to give the helpee back at least as much as he gave to you in terms of the feeling and the personal meaning that what he was expressing had for him. The real question in rating is: Could the helper have said what the helpee said and the helpee have said what the helper said? That is, could the helper have been the helpee and the helpee have been the helper? If so, then we call the responses *interchangeable*. Above the mid-point, the helper is *adding* to the helpee's understanding and below the mid-point the helper is *subtracting* or taking away from the helpee's understanding of the problem. Above and below the mid-point, the judgments are a little more difficult. That is, if responses are not interchangeable we must decide whether they are good for the helpee or bad for him. Either they help the helpee or hurt him in some way like taking away from what he said. We rate the helper's responses in just that way—in terms of their effects on the helpee:

Table 7-1a
Guide to Understanding Levels of Helper Conditions

LEVELS	HELPER CONDITIONS					
	IN RESPONSE TO HELPEE				INITIATED BY THE HELPER	
General	Empathy (E) (Understanding)	Respect (R) (Caring)	Concreteness (C) (Being specific)	Genuineness (G) (Being real)	Confrontation (Cf) (Telling it like it is)	Immediacy (I) (What goes on between us)
5 + +	Really understanding (adding a lot)	Really caring (positive regard)	Really being specific	Really being real	Really telling it like it is	Really saying what's going on between us
4 +	Understanding (adding)	Caring (positive regard)	Being specific	Being real	Telling it like it is	Saying what's going on between us
3 Openness to + (↑)	Interchangeable expressions	Open to caring	Open to being specific; not caring	Open to being real; not being abstract	Open to telling it like it is	Open to saying what's going on between us
Absence of − (↓)						
2 −	Not understanding (subtracting)	Not caring (negative regard)	Not being specific (being abstract)	Not being real (being phony)	Not telling it like it is	Not saying what is going on between us
1 − −	Really not understanding (subtracting a lot)	Don't give a damn (really being completely negative)	Really not being specific (really being completely abstract)	Really not being real (really being completely phony)	Really not telling it like it is	Really not saying what's going on between us

173

Table 7–1b

Guide to Understanding Levels of Helpee Conditions

HELPEE CONDITIONS	
Self-Exploration (looking at the problem)	*All other conditions* *E R C G Cf I*
Really looking at and feeling the problem on own	5 Presence of positive ($+$ $+$)
Looking at and feeling the problem on own	4 Presence of positive ($+$)
Open to looking at and feeling on own	3 Openness to positive ($+$)
	Absence of negative ($-$)
Not looking on own	2 Presence of negative ($-$)
Not looking at all	1 Presence of negative ($-$ $-$)

Did the helper's responses help the helpee to go on to explore and/or understand himself better than he had before? If so, we give the helper a higher rating (above 3). If not, if the helper's responses held the helpee back in some way, we give the helper a lower rating (below 3).

It's the same way with the other conditions. At the mid-point of respect the helper communicates that he is open and ready to respect the helpee; above that he actively communicates positive regard or positive feelings for the helpee and below that he communicates negative regard or negative feelings for the helpee. At the mid-point of concreteness, the helper communicates that he is open and ready to deal with specific feelings and experiences; above that he is actively specific and below that he is not specific. It's also the same way for the conditions initiated by the helper. At the mid-point of genuineness the helper is open and ready to be genuine or real while above that he is actively genuine and below that he is phony. At the mid-point of confrontation the helper is open and ready to confront while above that he confronts and below that he avoids confronting. At the mid-point of immediacy the helper is open and ready to say what's really going on between helper and helpee while above that he actively does so and below that he does not. With this understanding of the different levels of the conditions involved, let us turn to how we can train people to communicate at high levels of these conditions.

Communication (Interchangeable)

Again, the key to the helping process is having and communicating understanding, or empathy, to the helpee. Communicating is just letting the helpee know what you know. The first goal in training will be establishing an interchangeable base of communication with the helpee; that is, giving back to the helpee at least as much as the helpee gave to you in terms of the personal feeling and the personal meaning that he was expressing. The communication of empathy can be practiced at different stages: (1) in response to taped helpee expressions; (2) in role-playing interactions; and (3) in live helper-helpee interactions that are recorded and later supervised.

Let us consider the role-playing interaction, for this is the one employed most of the time in training. One of the trainees will be cast in the role of helper and one will be cast in the role of helpee. The helper may be given the following instructions: (1) he must listen to the helpee for at least 30 seconds; (2) he must respond to the helpee in a sentence beginning with "you feel . . ."; (3) he must offer a response to the helpee that is interchangeable in terms of the feeling and the meaning of what the helpee is expressing. The helpee's instructions are simply to talk about material that has personal meaning for him. At first the helpee will prefer to talk about problems involving someone else and this is o.k. because the helper's responses will be brief. But later as the role-playing process becomes longer, the helper has to keep the helpee talking about material that involves the helpee's personal feelings or feelings about himself. At first, then, the helper may make very brief responses to the helpee's situation indicating that he understands the helpee's feelings. He may say "You feel very sad," reflecting how low a helpee might feel. The helper may then work toward putting together statements involving both the feeling and the meaning of the helpee. He may say, "You feel very sad because she has left you, and she meant everything in the world to you." The helper may, then, work toward putting these sentences together in paragraphs that will have meaning for the helpee. It is the same for the other dimensions in the first stage of helping. The helper will learn first to communicate an openness and readiness and then will offer respect and deal with specific feelings and experiences. At all times, the other trainees, in addition to the trainer, will provide the helper with ratings of how well they thought that he did. The ratings give the helper feedback as to what levels of empathy, respect, and concreteness he offered the helpee. In addition, the same persons can rate the helpee on his self-exploration: Did he explore himself at the mid-point (level 3, see Appendix B, in Carkhuff, 1969b) and if he did, did he do it with feeling (above level 3) or did he avoid exploring himself or explore himself only when the helper directed him to do it (below level 3)? Again, the focus is on what the helper did. What levels of conditions did he offer the helpee? How much did he involve the helpee in self-exploration? In this regard the helpee will also rate the helper as to how well he felt the helper did.

As the helpee comes to share more fully his problems and the helper continues to understand them we may say that we have initiated a communication process. We have set up an interchangeable base of communication in which the helper has responded to the helpee. In this sense, the communication process is a one-sided one at the beginning of helping.

Communication (Higher Levels)

The real purpose of setting up an interchangeable base of communication is to enable both helper and helpee to move to higher levels of understanding of the helpee (levels 4 and 5). The higher levels of understanding will enable the helper and helpee to develop courses of action that will help to deal with the problem that the helpee brought in the first place. There are several ways that higher levels of understanding and communication may be approached. In training we may set up different rules at different stages. For example, we may insist that the helper make six or more interchangeable (level 3) responses before he attempts to initiate higher level (4 and 5) types of responses. If the helper has successfully made these interchangeable responses, and if the helpee has used these responses in exploring himself (in both of these instances we can depend upon rating feedback from the group), then the helper is allowed the privilege of attempting to put things together for the helpee at a deeper level. The helper may, for example, formulate things in the following manner: "What I really hear you saying is this" or "What this all adds up to for me is this." The helper attempts not only to put together the meaning of the picture that the helpee is expressing but also the music behind that picture, that is, how he really feels about things.

Higher levels of empathic understanding often lead right into conditions initiated by the helper. In order to be additive in empathic understanding, the helper must filter the helpee's expressions through the helper's experience. In doing so he introduces initiative dimensions. In addition, when the helper presents the picture that he sees emerging, the helpee might accept it but he also might accept it too quickly, modify it, or reject it. It is the helper's job to reflect his understanding of the helpee wherever the helpee is. So, if the helpee rejects the picture the helper developed, the helper might say, "You really don't feel that's the way it is." Or, if the helpee accepts part of the picture but changes it somewhat the helper might say, "That's part of the way it is for you, but there are things about it you really don't understand." After considering the helpee's way of looking at it, the helper could come back to his original or a similar picture. At this point he might confront the helpee with the differences in the way they see things or with differences in the helpee's behavior: "On the one hand you say that's not the picture but on the other hand you keep acting like it is."

There are a lot of *cues* that the helper can be trained to look for in practice. The first involves helpee exploration of his problems. The helper offers an interchangeable base of communication to the helpee in order to get the helpee to explore his problem fully. The cue for the helper to attempt to move toward higher levels of communication is the helpee's ability to explore himself with feeling *on his own* (level 3 or above). When the helpee can introduce his own material and he no longer needs the helper to help him to do so, then he is asking the helper to help him to understand what he has been exploring, to put the picture together. A second cue tells us when the helpee is asking for even higher levels of communication by establishing that he can offer himself his own interchangeable or additive levels of communication. That is, when the helpee can respond to himself with the same level of understanding that the helper had previously offered following something that he said, then he is signaling the helper to try to put things together at higher levels. Finally, when the helpee responds to the helper in such a way as to get the helper to explore himself in that area, then we know that the helpee understands this area well enough to be able to respond to another person and it signals his readiness to move into the next area. The same thing happens with the other conditions and the same cues may be used to tell where the helpee is on the different conditions as are used to tell where the helper is. (See Appendix B, in Carkhuff, 1969b.)

In summary, this second phase of helping involving movement to higher levels of communication between helper and helpee, involves the helper initiating communication as well as responding to the helpee. Where in the first phase the helper spent almost all of his energies attempting to respond to the helpee, now he initiates communication. He also responds to the helpee's response to what he initiated. If it was worth initiating, it is worth responding to the helpee's response.

Developing Course of Action

The whole purpose of the helping process is to help someone to do things differently from how he did them before, since the way he did them before didn't work out well for him. So we set up the interchangeable base of communication so that we can be accurate in moving to higher levels of communication or understanding in order to do something about the real problems involved. There are several stages that we go through in developing courses of action. The first involves describing the problem area fully. The second involves describing goals that will help to handle the problem. The third involves breaking down the goals into their most important parts. The fourth involves considering the different courses of action available to reaching the important parts of the goals (here we must consider the advantages and disadvantages, long-term as well as short-term). Finally, the helper must help the helpee to develop a program that will give the helpee the best chance of succeeding in his course of action. Here, the program can be physical, emotional, and intellectual and the programs must begin very gradually and move step by step.

Examples of physical programs might be diet, rest, and exercise. Examples of emotional programs involving other people might involve training people to respond to other people and to initiate communication with other people, just as we have done in this helping program. Examples of intellectual programs might involve study and training, reading and developing ideas in a systematic way. These programs will be related to each other. Each will affect the other. The physical program will affect the emotional and the intellectual and vice versa. Most important, we must begin in small steps. We must learn to walk before we learn to run. We bite off only those pieces that we can chew if we want to make a difference in the helpee's life.

Now let us reverse the order in effective helping. We take the first step of the program so that we have the best chance of accomplishing the entire program. The program gives us the best chance of accomplishing the course of action which gave us the best chance of accomplishing our goal. Our goal involved dealing with the difficulty that brought the helpee to seek help in the first place.

PUTTING IT ALL TOGETHER IN HELPING

Let's put all of these considerations together. The helpee comes to seek help because he can't help himself and because the people around him can't help him. The helper offers him understanding that is interchangeable in terms of the feeling and meaning that the helpee is expressing so that the helpee will explore his problem more fully. As the helpee explores his problem more fully the helper offers higher levels of understanding. As the helper offers higher levels of understanding the helpee comes to understand his problem more fully. As the helpee comes to understand his problem more fully the helper senses the helpee's need to do something about it. Together they develop courses of action that give the helpee the best chance of dealing with his problem.

Let us put it another way as is indicated in Table 7–2. The helper offers minimally effective or level 3 of the responsive (R) or facilitative dimensions in order to enable the helpee to explore (Ex) himself in the relevant problem areas. The helpee's self-explorations enable the helpee to move toward levels 4 and 5 of the R dimensions while at the same time introducing the initiative (I) or action-oriented dimensions at minimally effective levels (level 3). Together, the responsive dimensions (levels 4 and 5) and the initiative dimensions (level 3) make it possible for the helpee to move toward self-understanding (U) or responsiveness (R) to self at higher levels (3 and above). The higher self-understanding provides the cue for the helper to offer high levels (4 and 5) of both initiative as well as responsive dimensions which, in turn, make it possible for the helpee to move toward action (A) or self-initiative (I) dimensions at higher levels (3 and above). Finally, then, helper and helpee together develop a constructive course of action leading to more effective functioning on the part of the helpee.

Helping does not end here. The helpee learns from acting and the cycle of exploration – understanding – action is repeated in many different ways and in many different problem areas. At all points the helper works in such a way as to give the helpee the best chance of succeeding. At all points the helping process tries to get the helpee to act on his understanding. When he acts, he learns new things and opens up new areas. When he explores these

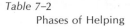

Table 7–2

Phases of Helping

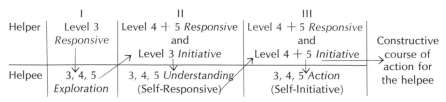

	I	II	III	
Helper	Level 3 *Responsive*	Level 4 + 5 *Responsive* and Level 3 *Initiative*	Level 4 + 5 *Responsive* and Level 4 + 5 *Initiative*	Constructive course of action for the helpee
Helpee	3, 4, 5 *Exploration*	3, 4, 5 *Understanding* (Self-Responsive)	3, 4, 5 *Action* (Self-Initiative)	

new areas he comes to new understanding and then acts again in a new and more effective way.

In order to accomplish this the helper must himself be understanding and acting in effective ways. The helper must be able to demonstrate that if he were in the helpee's shoes he could have found a way to handle the helpee's problems. If he cannot demonstrate this then there is no reason for the helpee to seek his help. The helper must be able to let the helpee know that there are ways of doing things that are different and more effective than the way the helpee has been doing them. In order to do this, the helper must himself be involved in a lifelong helping or learning or growing process; for that is what helping is—learning and growing. If the helper is not learning and growing himself, he cannot help others to learn and grow.

AN OVERVIEW OF HELPING OPERATIONALIZED

The forgoing guide was designed for the functional professional, whether lay or professional. It provides an approach to helping and human relations which is testable in experience and experimentation. It is based upon the author's direct experiences in thousands of cases in guidance, counseling, psychotherapy, education, and human relations. It is based upon his vicarious experiences in listening to thousands of other helping cases. It is based upon process and outcome research of the effectiveness of still more thousands of helping cases. It is based upon the application in thousands of cases of training of the learnings from this experience and experimentation. Finally, it is based upon modifications of our learnings from our assessments of the process and outcome of thousands of cases subsequent to training.

The operationalization of helping and human relations does away with the mysteries and the rituals of an earlier stage of development, the vestiges of our ignorance. It makes available for one and all the modalities of helping, to be employed as they are helpful, to be reoriented to increase their helpfulness, to be discarded when they are not helpful. Without filling in the content, the operationalization of helping provides a functional map to guide the losers, the lost, and the misled, the wanderers and the beginners. At each stage both helper and helpee are oriented toward functional criteria of the helping process. If the helpee cannot explore himself in the areas of relevant concern, he cannot understand himself in these areas; if he cannot understand himself, he cannot act effectively in his life. If the helper is not responsive enough to elicit self-exploration, he cannot move toward additive levels of understanding; if he cannot understand the helpee at deep levels, he is not able to initiate communications and actions based upon his own experience. Finally, if helper and helpee are unable to accomplish these delimited functional goals, then they cannot, together, develop effective courses of action. At each stage of helping, each party to the process has a job to do. If they do it, both parties benefit. If they do not do it, both parties deteriorate—or, in some instances, worse yet, remain the same.

Thus far we have focused upon the helping process. Indeed, it is traditional for the professional to emphasize the helping process. Yet what is done outside of the interaction between helper and helpee—by helper as well as helpee—is far more important than what transpires within the helping process. The helping interaction only sets the stage for how both helper and helpee live outside of helping. In this context, _no helpee_—indeed, depending upon the helper's level of development, no helper—_should leave the helping session without specific homework assignments_. The discharge of these responsibilities should mark the beginning of the next session. To be sure, the next session should be contingent upon the fulfillment of the homework assignment. It is easy to do if we know what we are doing.

In this regard, our operationalization of helping and human relations as a means to develop the effective person can be extended further to the development of a prototypical master plan for helping to be modified in the individual instance. (See Table 7–3.) First, let us recognize that helping is a multifaceted process. Second, let us acknowledge that _the helping process incorporates activities within and without the helping session._ As has been made clear in the development of effective courses of action, effective helping incorporates physical and intellectual as well as the emotional-interpersonal components emphasized in the guide. Accordingly, the most effective helping processes must be seen most broadly. Again, the criteria are functional.

The physical aspect of the helping process must be functional. Rather than both fat and skinny moving toward some statistical mode, all persons must move toward greater functionality. Physical functionality will depend in part upon the goals of helping. This could be quite clear in many areas of physical rehabilitation. In addition, in the instance of the helpee with intense fears of physical harm the physical program might involve a build-up of physical functioning to the point where the fear no longer dominated his existence. However, it is not always so clear with most cases off the streets. The variations in programs may become very subtle. Thus, for example, a persevering, enduring type may wish to function with greater speed in preparation for living with greater immediacy; one who acts rapidly but cannot sustain his actions may wish to build up his endurance in order to share more fully in his life; one who is neither may wish to achieve both. Accordingly, physical programs calculated to achieve

Table 7–3
      Standardized Helping Program

Physical
      Optimum physical readiness attained by proper rest including periodic relaxation
        periods and diet including vitamin intake or therapy, etc.
      Optimum physical functioning attained by exercising body in making it functional
        for attaining intended goals, with particular emphasis upon those exercises such as
        running which influence most positively overall cardiovascular functioning.

Emotional-Interpersonal
      Optimum interpersonal relationships attained by training in interpersonal skills,
        with special emphasis upon responsive and initiative dimensions.
      Optimum constructive personality change attained by experience of helper(s) offer-
        ing high levels of responsive and initiative dimensions.

Intellectual
      Optimum development of intellectual powers attained by systematic reading in
        area(s) of specialized interest.
      Optimum development of effective, working cosmology attained by recording in-
        sights in a systematic manner in an intellectual journal.

physical functionality will be developed according to the functional goals.
These programs will involve diet, rest, and exercise of a number of different
varieties, according to individual needs, but emphasizing those related to overall cardiovascular functioning. Thus, running and a variety of related activities
will constitute the core of any physical exercise program.

In the intellectual realm, the helpee must be brought to a point where he
can think for himself and develop an effective working cosmology for himself.
Again, this is an active, action-oriented process as well as a receptive, responsive
process. A person more steeped in receiving others' writings and verbalizations
may be trained to develop his own; a person who has emphasized his own articulations may learn to attend to others; a person who has accomplished
neither effectively may be trained to do both. Thus, a program of reading in relevant areas could be accompanied by a program of writing. The writing makes
demands upon the person to recognize the gaps in his thinking and to bridge
these gaps. The writing would ultimately be geared to the helpee's recording
of his own insights and the systematic integration of these insights into an effective set of assumptions about himself. A working cosmology is open though
directionful. It allows the helpee to discern relationships and make accurate
predictions in his world. It enables the helpee to live effectively in his world
as a helper.

Of course, an effective cosmology, while designed by the intellect, is based
in the emotional experiences of the helpee. Per se these are perhaps the most
difficult to operationalize, and yet if we assume that to some high degree interpersonal behavior reflects intrapersonal phenomena, we can, as we have in the
preceding guide, operationalize the process by which an individual is helped
to emerge. Here the experiential base which we have emphasized is most criti-

cal. However, in the context of the experiential base, the modeling and didactic aspects have great effects. Most basically, then, who the helper is and how he lives is basic to providing the helpee with a model for effective living to imitate and emulate. What the helper has gleaned to be effective from his past life's experiences and how effectively he can transmit these to the helpee is the basis for the helpee's cognitive-emotional learning. In this regard, an effectively operationalized step-by-step series of progressive, reinforcing human experiences would be most effective. In other words, training in intrapersonal development and interpersonal skills can be seen as the preferred mode of emotional treatment. Specifically, for example, a fairly responsive person must be taught assertive behavior before he can accomplish and integrate both at high levels. Similarly, an assertive person may be taught responsive behavior before he can accomplish and integrate both at high levels. A person who can neither respond nor initiate effectively must be systematically trained to accomplish and integrate both.

Finally, the physical, emotional, and intellectual components must be integrated in one process and ultimately in one person, the helpee. Obviously, this is not possible without the helper being himself integrated and fully functioning in all spheres of existence. There is a great deal of empirical as well as experiential evidence to indicate the interrelationship of these areas of functioning; although, to be sure, an individual may be functioning at higher levels in one area than another, and the program may be modified accordingly. The products of an active intellect, then, are based as much in the emotional-interpersonal experiences of an individual as they are in his frontal lobes. The emotional-interpersonal experiences, in turn, are as sharp as the body in which they are housed is finely tuned. Each component is sharpened by the sharpness of each other component in the fully functioning person.

A comprehensive treatment program, then, would incorporate physical, emotional, and interpersonal components. In a master treatment program, a physical program of diet, rest, and a variety of exercises might be complemented by a training program incorporating helping, to the degree necessary, depending upon the helpee's level of development; both, in turn, might be integrated by an intellectual program emphasizing the systematic development of an effective, working cosmology in daily entries in intellectual journals. A treatment program that does not incorporate the physical, emotional-interpersonal, and intellectual components is simply not a fully effective treatment program. Again, all programs are to be modified by our experiences; they are to be modified by the feedback which we get concerning what has been most effective; they are to be modified by the continuously changing aims and goals of helping; they are to be modified according to the level of development of the helpee in any or all realms. However, our conclusion is that training is the preferred mode of treatment. Training in all realms—physical, emotional, and intellectual—is the preferred mode of changing helpees into helpers in a helper world. Training in all realms—physical, emotional-interpersonal, and intellectual—is the preferred mode of living.

REFERENCES

Berenson, B. G., & Carkhuff, R. R. *Sources of gain in counseling and psycho-therapy.* New York: Holt, Rinehart and Winston, 1967.

Carkhuff, R. R. *Helping and human relations: A primer for lay and professional helpers.* Vol. I. *Selection and training.* New York: Holt, Rinehart and Winston, 1969. (a)

Carkhuff, R. R. *Helping and human relations: A primer for lay and professional helpers.* Vol. II. *Practice and research.* New York: Holt, Rinehart and Winston, 1969. (b)

Carkhuff, R. R., & Berenson, B. G. *Beyond counseling and therapy.* New York: Holt, Rinehart and Winston, 1967.

Truax, C. B., & Carkhuff, R. R. *Toward effective counseling and psychotherapy.* Chicago: Aldine, 1967.

CHAPTER 8
Principles of Training

Most social action programs, as most educational programs, do not know where they are going or how to get there. At best, their success is random; at worst, it is absent; at the median, it is haphazard. The personnel are most often not selected by criteria that are relevant to the desired outcome. The personnel are most often not trained by criteria that are relevant to hoped-for benefits. The results, as we have too often seen, are downright disheartening.

The programs these personnel develop and perpetuate are most often developed and conducted with the same lack of concern for criteria of efficacy as was true of their own selection and training. As a result of their own experiences, they are directionless, ineffective, and frustrated, and if, despite their inadequacies, they continue to collect salary checks for too long a period of time, may become dangerous, for they must defend their own misrepresentations to the detriment of the clientele they are retained to serve. The agencies and the people in them become self-perpetuating, functionally autonomous monsters that feed impersonally on the humanness of their helpees.

What is the difference between effective and ineffective programs? The difference is that the effective programs know where they are going and they develop steps to get there. In more technical terminology, the effective programs have operationalized their goals to such a degree that they are attainable and they have set up progressive reinforcement experiences for attaining these goals. This is the essence of training, operationalizing the goals and the steps to attain these goals.

People must be trained in that in which they are to be proficient. The effective ingredient of effective people is training, for by and large people learn what they are trained to learn. There is no limit to what can be achieved with the development of appropriate training methodologies. There is no limit to what can be.

Training, then, is a key to effective social action programs. Training, it can be seen, is more broadly conceived than our usual considerations of teaching methodologies. It incorporates the concept of training for the trainer as well as the trainee and, indeed, insists that the trainer of trainers establish his own credentials of effectiveness. It incorporates concepts of the experiential and modeling bases of learning as well as the more traditionally didactic or pedagogic.

TRAINER AND TRAINEE FUNCTIONING

The principal ingredients of any training program include trainer, trainee, and program variables. The relevant dimensions of human relations training, we have found in research, are (1) the initial levels of interpersonal functioning of both trainer and trainee or, in other words, the effectiveness with which these persons relate to their worlds, and (2) the type of program developed to achieve effective human relations (Carkhuff, 1969a).

The level of trainer functioning is the key to all training programs. *If the trainer is functioning at high levels of the dimensions on which the trainee is being trained, the probability of the success of training with any trainee population is high. If the trainer is functioning at low levels of relevant dimensions, the probability of the success of training is low.*

The initial level of trainee functioning on the dimensions to be learned is critical only insofar as it interacts with the trainer's level of functioning. Low-functioning trainees stand to gain in skills with high-functioning trainers, while high-functioning trainees (infrequent) stand to lose in skills with low-functioning trainers. In between, little or no change in either direction can be expected from low trainees with low trainers, a fairly common instance in many training programs. Least common but often effective is the instance of high trainees with high trainers. Just turn them both loose!

These changes can be broken down a little more finitely. Where the trainer is functioning at levels higher than the trainees the following rule holds: *The greater the deviation between trainer and trainee level of functioning the greater the change on the part of the trainee.* Thus, it can be said that while all trainees may gain in interaction with trainers functioning at high levels of the relevant dimensions, those functioning at the lowest initial levels do, with the necessary duration and availability of preferred modes of treatment, stand to demonstrate the greatest degree of constructive change. The trainees functioning initially at higher levels, while they respond immediately and go on to function more rapidly at higher levels, simply do not demonstrate as great a degree of change.

Trainer and trainee functioning may be seen in another light, with the so-called experiential base of training relating to the trainee's experience of training, and the modeling base of training relating to the model for effective functioning which the high-level trainer provides. Of course, the trainee's experience of the trainer and the program is confounded by the trainee's level of functioning: initially low level functioning trainees make poor discriminations in their articulations of their experience; initially high level functioning trainees make fine discriminations. However, effective trainers and effective programs inevitably develop effective trainees. Thus, trainees at the termination of training will be equipped to accurately assess their experience and the level of functioning of significant persons in their lives. Finally, the training program itself may be equated with didactic procedures or procedures "shaping" effective behaviors.

Let us take another look at the three critical sources of learning in training. While in practice they are at once integrated and simultaneous, we will view these sources of learning individually.

THE EXPERIENTIAL BASE OF TRAINING

Again, the experiential base within which the program takes place is critical. The trainee's firsthand experience of the dimensions involved is most critical. Thus, if the training program is focusing upon the discrimination and communication of empathy, the trainee must also have had the experience of the trainer communicating a depth of understanding to the trainee. If the training program is focusing upon the discrimination and communication of confrontation, the trainee must also have had the experience of trainer confrontation of trainee. In this context the trainee has the experience of having his own communications understood in depth with a degree of accuracy that extends his communications and allows him to understand himself at deeper and deeper levels. In addition, the trainee has the experience of being the recipient of communications initiated by the trainer, as in the instance of confrontation and the experience of knowing firsthand the constructive personal effects of such communications when in the hands of a high level functioning trainer. Finally, such an experiential base enables the trainee to experiment with different modes of functioning in the hope of finding those that in interaction with particular situations are most appropriate and effective for him.

The experiential base must be real if the dimensions are real. The trainee must experience the dimensions as real, the trainer as genuine in his offering, or the training process cannot be effective. However, while the trainer focuses upon the experiences he does not do so exclusive of his own experience. Accordingly, with time and the development of the relationship between trainer and trainee, the trainer may become highly conditional as a function of either his own experience or of the standards of the program. Thus, the trainee can only trust that he will receive fully honest communications, responsive dimensions as they are appropriate, and initiative dimensions as they are appropriate.

THE MODELING BASE OF TRAINING

Perhaps the most significant source of learning is modeling, or imitation. Surely, the largest degree of learning that takes place with children involves the imitation of parents or significant others. Modeling continues to be most critical in any kind of training program, and the trainer is the key model. He lets the trainee know whether the goals of training can be achieved, that is, whether or not it is all possible. With regard to helping or human relations training, the trainer is either living effectively in all relevant spheres of his life or he is not. If he is, anything is possible. If he is not, nothing is possible.

The trainer, then, provides a model for the trainee to identify with and emulate. Without such a person there is no program. The trainer must be a person who is not only congruent and genuine but also one who has worked out an effective yet open-ended working cosmology. He must not only be sensitive but must also be able to act upon his fine discriminations. He lives responsively and responsibly, filtering through his own experience his experience of others and initiating his own direction based upon his understanding of both. He translates his deep respect for constructive forces in his nourishment of them and also in his commitment to the destruction of destructive forces, both within and without individuals. At the highest levels he lives his life with immediacy, living fully in every moment, draining each moment of its full meaning for himself and others involved. In summary, without a person who in his dedication to his own integration at the highest levels can provide an integrated learning experience that draws upon all significant sources of learning, the trainee would not know what could be achieved, what is to be strived for, and the effectiveness of the didactic training would be limited.

THE DIDACTIC BASE OF TRAINING

In the context of a real, sensitive, and appropriately lifelike experiential base and in conjunction with a real, sensitive, and life-full trainer, the structure and the content of the training program unfold. The structure and the content of training should be a function of a strong empirical base of research. The constructs validated in research must be transmitted in training. This is the program of teaching and learning, is it not? The teacher has the responsibility to pass on to the student all that he has found from previous experience to be effective. It is the student's task, in turn, to test out the learnings to find if, in fact, they are more effective. It is, in this sense, also the trainer's responsibility to assess, following training, the effectiveness of the effort and compare it with efforts that were conducted without training and/or with different training.

The essence of the didactic training program, then, is operational goals for which step-by-step procedures can be systematically developed. The trainee goes through a series of successive reinforcement experiences. If the training has any direction at all, the trainee knows at each stage that he has either achieved the intended goals or not. In the learning of complex behavior, as in human relations training, the training program may be multifaceted, with the trainee receiving the appropriate rewards or punishments for his functioning toward that goal. Ultimately, the program must put it all together, letting trainee, as well as trainer, know that the trainee can or cannot function effectively in the desired manner.

In the development of the didactic material, then, training emphasizes the systematic development of programs to attain specifiable goals. This makes the whole training program honest. *If the goals cannot be specified or if the means to achieve the goals cannot be developed, then there is no basis for training.* The following program illustrates multifaceted training in human relations skills developed specifically for functional professionals and modified according to the needs of a given program. It represents a formalization of a program developed over a number of years, with extensive supportive research evidence.

PROJECT 14

Training Program
in Human Relations Skills
for Functional Professionals*

PHASES OF HELPING

I. **Responding to the Helpee**
1. *Introduction: General introduction of helping and human relations (see Guide, Chapter 7).*
   Homework: Introduce intellectual journals with entries to be made daily based upon experiences.
   (a) Initial entries may be single insights into any area of human relations.
   (b) Ultimately must relate and integrate insights.
2. *Discrimination of helper empathy (E): Introduction.*
   (a) *Focus upon feeling only.*
   (b) *Interchangeable understanding (level 3).*
      1. Judgment of level 3 is made on basis of whether helper could have said what helpee said in terms of feeling and helpee could have said what helper said (see Scale 1, Appendix B, in Carkhuff, 1969b).
      2. Need helpee-helper (2) response sequence to make judgment.
   (c) *Additive and subtractive understanding.*
      1. Judgment of 1 and 2 or 4 and 5 is made on basis of effects upon the helpee, i.e.: Does the helper's response enable the helpee to go on to a deeper level of self-exploration and/or self-understanding?

---

*Originally organized and written in December 1968 by Robert R. Carkhuff for the Activities of the Human Relations Center, American International College.

2. Need helpee-helper-helpee (3) response sequence to make judgment.
3. Judgment of levels 4 and 5 reflects additive nature of helper response, i.e., it enables helpee to go on.
4. Judgment of levels 1 and 2 reflects subtractive nature of helper response, i.e., it holds helpee back.
5. Group rates helper from 1 (worst) to 5 (best).

(d) *Classwork:* Listen to tapes of helpee-helper response sequence.
  1. Rate helper response from 1 to 5.
  2. Formulate own responses to helpee expression and rate.

(e) *Homework:* Practice listening and rating responses of other people in daily living. *Do not attempt responses.*

3. *Communication of interchangeable empathy: Group practice.*

(a) *Classwork:*
  1. Set up trainees in helpee-helper roles.
  2. Helpee makes single expression.
  3. Helpee attempts to role-play material of other person's problems.
  4. Helper listens for minimum of 30 seconds.
  5. Helper makes single response to helpee expression.
  6. Helper attempts to formulate interchangeable response in terms of feeling and meaning.
  7. Helper begins response with "You feel . . ." indicating responsive mode.
     EXAMPLE: "You feel sad (happy, angry)."
  8. Group rates helper on whether response is interchangeable (level 3) or not.

(b) *Homework:* Pair off with partner from class and practice making responses that are interchangeable.

4. *Communication of interchangeable empathy: Advanced group practice.*

(a) *Classwork:*
  1. Set up trainees in helpee-helper roles.
  2. Helpee makes 2 expressions.
     (a) Initial expression.
     (b) Responds to helper's response.
  3. Helper makes 1 response.
  4. Helper follows program of Stage 3.
  5. Other trainees write down their responses to helpee and discuss.
  6. Group rates helper response at all levels.

(b) *Homework:* Practice making interchangeable responses in impersonal relationships.

5. *Discrimination of helpee self-exploration (Ex): Introduction.*

(a) *Openness to exploring self (level 3).*

    1. Judgment of level 3 self-exploration is made on the basis of whether helpee introduces personally relevant material on his own (see Scale 8, Appendix B in Carkhuff, 1969b).

    2. Higher levels (4 and 5) and lower levels (1 and 2) are dependent upon whether helpee is fully or only partially involved in self-exploration.

(b) *High self-exploration (levels 4 and 5)* involves the helpee exploring himself with the feelings that go with the material.

(c) *Low self-exploration* involves the helpee either avoiding self-exploration (level 1) or only exploring himself when the helper directs him to do so (level 2).

(d) *Classwork:* Continue practice as in Stage 4.

    1. Incorporate ratings on helpee self-exploration.

    2. *E* and *Ex* could diverge because of short-term nature of practice.

(e) *Homework:* Continue to practice interchangeable responses in an attempt to get impersonal others to explore themselves more in daily living.

6. *Communication of empathy: Ongoing group practice.*

(a) *Classwork:*

    1. Trainees in helpee-helper roles are allowed to practice extended communication.

        (a) Extended sequences of no less than 6 exchanges between helper and helpee.

        (b) Helper continues to focus upon an interchangeable level of empathy.

        (c) Helpee focuses upon personally relevant problems of little consequence to him.

    2. Helper's set is emphasized:

        (a) Helper relates to helpee's expressions of helpee's experience.

        (b) Helper does not attend to problem solution.

        (c) Helper responds to person—not problem.

    3. Group rates helper on modal level of empathy, that is, the level at which the helper is functioning most of the time.

    4. Group rates helpee on modal level of self-exploration.

(b) *Homework:* Practice interchangeable responses in extended interactions in attempt to elicit self-exploration with impersonal others.

7. *Discrimination and communication of respect (R): Introduction and practice.*

(a) *Openness to respecting (level 3).*

    1. Judgment of level 3 respect is made on the basis of absence of negative regard (see Scale 2, Appendix B, in Carkhuff, 1969b).

    2. Higher levels (4 and 5) and lower levels (1 and 2) are dependent upon the presence of positive regard or negative regard.

(b) *High respect (levels 4 and 5)* involves the presence of positive regard.

(c) *Low respect (levels 1 and 2)* involves the presence of negative regard.

(d) *Classwork:* Continue to practice and rate extended communication.

    1. Incorporate ratings of level of respect communicated by helper.

    2. Continue to rate *E* and *Ex.*

(e) *Homework:* Practice responses communicating respect, along with interchangeable understanding with impersonal others.

8. *Discrimination and communication of specificity or concreteness (C): Introduction and practice.*

(a) *Openness to being concrete (level 3).*

    1. Judgment of level 3 concreteness is made on the basis of absence of being abstract (see Scale 3, Appendix B, in Carkhuff, 1969b).

    2. Higher levels (4 and 5) and lower levels (1 and 2) are dependent upon the presence of concreteness (specificity) or abstractness.

(b) *High concreteness (levels 4 and 5)* involves the presence of specificity or concreteness.

(c) *Low concreteness (levels 1 and 2)* involves the presence of abstractness.

(d) *Classwork:* Continue to practice and rate extended communication.

    1. Incorporate ratings of level of concreteness communicated by helper.

    2. Introduce *personal meaning* to accompany feeling.

      (a) Meaning incorporates feeling and content.

      (b) Meaning reflects personal phenomenology, i.e., how person looks out and sees the world.

(c) Meaning converges with need for specificity.
EXAMPLE: "You feel sad because she was the most important thing in the world to you and now she's gone."
3. Continue to rate E, R, and Ex.

(e) *Homework:* Practice responses that are concrete, along with interchangeable understanding with significant others, i.e., teachers, classmates, friends.

9. *Discrimination and communication of genuineness (G): Introduction and practice.*

(a) *Openness to being genuine (level 3).*
1. Judgment of level 3 genuineness is made on the basis of absence of being phony (see Scales 4 and 5, Appendix B, in Carkhuff, 1969b).
2. Higher levels (4 and 5) and lower levels (1 and 2) are dependent upon the presence of real genuineness or real phoniness.

(b) *High genuineness (levels 4 and 5)* involves the presence of real genuineness.

(c) *Low genuineness (levels 1 and 2)* involves the absence of genuineness or the presence of real phoniness.

(d) *Classwork:* Continue to practice and rate extended communication.
1. Incorporate ratings of level of respect communicated by helper.
2. Introduce initiative statements.
EXAMPLE: "I feel sad (happy, angry) for/with you."
3. Continue to rate E, R, C, and Ex.

(e) *Homework:* Practice responses that are genuine, along with interchangeable understanding with significant others.

II. **Initiation by the Helper**

10. *Communication of additive understanding: Group practice.*

(a) *Classwork:*
1. Trainees function in helpee-helper roles.
2. Helpee shares personally relevant material.
3. Helper makes a minimum of 6 interchangeable responses before trying for additive response.
4. Helper makes additive response, i.e., "What this all adds up to for me . . ." or "What I hear you saying is . . .", etc.
5. Rate helper on level of understanding in the following manner:

(a) Rate the modal level of attempted interchange-able responses.

(b) Rate the level of the additive response.

6. Rate the helpee on the level of self-exploration in the following manner:

(a) Rate the modal level of helpee self-exploration as the helper attempted interchangeable responses.

(b) Rate the level of helpee self-exploration in response to the helper's additive response.

7. Each member of the group formulates in writing his own additive response to the helpee.

(a) Following rating each member offers his additive response to the helpee as if he were counseling the helpee.

(1) The group member-helper formulates the response in such a manner that the helpee can respond to the helper's response.

(2) The helpee assesses the effectiveness of the helper's response.

(3) The remaining group members assess the effectiveness of the helper's response.

(b) The group member-helper's additive response will be dependent in part upon how well the original helper laid the interchangeable base of communication.

8. *Steps 1–6 of Stage 10 will be repeated as necessary.*

(a) After demonstrating the ability to lay an interchangeable base of communication Stage 10 becomes the most significant aspect of helping.

(1) The effectiveness of depth reflections or moderate interpretations are contingent upon practice of this stage.

(2) The development of effective courses of action predicated upon the helpee's depth of self-understanding are contingent upon practice of this phase.

(b) Step 6 of Stage 10 becomes particularly critical to the helpee's personal development.

(1) As the helpee presents personal relevant material it becomes more critical that he receive the most effective responses.

(2) The group members are a resource for ef-

fective responses and serve, in effect, as
consulting helpers.

(c) As step 6 of Stage 10 is repeated the flow of
communication between group member-helper
and helpee can be extended.

(1) Effective helper responses can be allowed
to develop into an extensive helping interaction.

(2) In this manner the helpee makes maximum
strides toward personal understanding in
preparation for the development of his own
personal courses of action.

(d) The trainer has the responsibility for himself or
some group member-helper putting together all
of the responses which have been helpful for
the helpee.

(b) *Homework:* Practice laying interchangeable base and
making additive understanding responses with significant others.

11. *Communication of additive understanding: Individual
practice.*

(a) *Individual work:*

1. Pair helper and helpee to practice outside of group.
2. Helper and helpee reverse roles.
3. Instructors consult periodically.
4. Helper and helpee rate each other afterward.
5. Bring class together for critique and discussion.

(b) *Classwork:* Introduce rating helpee on same dimensions as helper while practicing extended communication.

1. Rate helpee on degree of self-understanding communicated.
2. Employ same scales for helpee as for helper (Appendix B, in Carkhuff, 1969b).

(c) *Homework:* Practice laying interchangeable base and
making additive understanding responses with spouse
or close partner.

12. *Communication of additive understanding: Advanced
individual practice.*

(a) *Individual work:*

1. Pair helper and helpee to practice outside of group.
2. Select most advanced trainees to be trainers and to
supervise each helper-helpee interaction.

3. Helper and helpee reverse roles.

4. Trainer remains the same.

5. Instructors consult periodically.

6. Bring class together for critique and discussion.

(b) *Classwork:* Continue rating helpee on same dimensions as helper while practicing extended communication.

1. Rate helpee on *R, C, G* as well as *E*.

2. Employ same scales (Appendix B, in Carkhuff, 1969b).

(c) *Homework:* Practice laying interchangeable base and making additive understanding responses with spouse or close partner.

13–14. *Communication of additive understanding: Advanced training and individual practice.*

(a) *Individual work:*

1. Same as Stage 12 with the exception of the following:

(a) Select new trainers.

(b) Have trainers, helpers, and helpees reverse roles.

2. Bring class together for critique and discussion.

(b) *Classwork:* Continue extended communication.

1. Rate helper and helpee on same scales (Appendix B, in Carkhuff, 1969b).

(c) *Homework:* Practice training spouse or close partner to communicate.

15. *Discrimination and communication of confrontation: Introduction and practice.*

(a) *Openness to confronting (level 3).*

1. Judgment of level 3 confrontation is made on the basis of the openness to confront (see Scale 6, Appendix B, in Carkhuff, 1969b).

2. Higher levels (4 and 5) and lower levels (1 and 2) are dependent upon whether or not confrontations are made.

(b) *High confrontation (levels 4 and 5) involves the act of confrontation of another.*

NOTE:

1. Remember to make the point that sometimes additive understanding leads directly to confrontation.

2. Remember to make the point that confrontation is like empathy—only empathic understanding is

communicated from within the helpee's frame of reference while confrontation comes from the helper's frame of reference.

(c) *Low confrontation (levels 1 and 2)* involves the absence of confrontation.

(d) *Classwork:* Continue to practice and rate extended communication.
   1. Include ratings of level of confrontation communicated by helper.
   2. Continue to rate responsive dimensions.
      (a) Give global rating for responsive dimensions.
      (b) Emphasize empathy ratings.

(e) *Homework:* Practice confronting after having established a relationship based upon an interchangeable and additive level of understanding with spouse or close partner.

16. *Discrimination and communication of immediacy: Introduction and practice.*

(a) *Openness to interpretations of immediacy (level 3).*
   1. Judgment of level 3 immediacy is made on the basis of the openness to immediacy (see Scale 7, Appendix B, in Carkhuff, 1969b).
   2. Higher levels (4 and 5) and lower levels (1 and 2) are dependent upon whether or not interpretations of immediacy are made.

(b) *High immediacy (levels 4 and 5)* involves interpreting the relationship between helper and helpee.

(c) *Low immediacy (levels 1 and 2)* involves the absence of interpretations of immediacy.

(d) *Classwork:* Continue to practice and rate extended communication.
   1. Include ratings of level of confrontation communicated by helper.
   2. Continue to rate responsive dimensions globally based on empathy.
   3. Rate helpees as well as helpers on initiative dimensions.

(e) *Homework:* Practice making interpretations of immediacy after having established constructive relationship with spouse or close partner.

17. *Development of Courses of Action: Introduction and practice.*

(a) Definition and description of problem area(s).

(b) Definition and description of direction and/or goal(s) dictated by the problem area(s).

(c) Analysis of the critical dimensions of these direction(s) and/or goal(s).

(d) Consideration of the advantages and disadvantages of the alternative courses.

(e) Development of physical, emotional-interpersonal, and intellectual programs for achieving that course with the most advantages and fewest disadvantages in terms of ultimate success in goal achievement.

(f) Development of progressive gradations of the programs involved.

(g) *Classwork:* Continue to practice extended communication.

   1. Helper develops courses of action for helpee.

   2. Helpee develops courses of action for self.

(h) *Homework:* Develop courses of action with spouse or close partner.

III. Putting It All Together

18. *The stages of development in helping: Practice.*

(a) *Individual work:*

   1. The goals of helping for the helpee.

      (a) First goal: Helpee self-exploration.

      (b) Second goal: Helpee self-understanding.

      (c) Third goal: Helpee action.

   2. Helper activities in achieving these goals:

      (a) First activity: Respond to the helpee with interchangeable understanding.

      (b) Second activity: Additive understanding and initiative dimensions.

      (c) Third activity: Development of courses of action.

   3. Practice putting complete helping process together in helper-helpee pairs (1 complete session).

(b) *Classwork:* Helpers and helpees pair off.

   1. Helpees practice being selves at earlier crisis point.

   2. Helper and helpee develop course of action for helpee.

(c) *Homework:*

   1. Develop courses of action for helpee in writing.

   2. Put entire helping process together with child.

19. *The stages of development in helping: Advanced practice.*

(a) Same as Stage 18 with the exception of the reversal of helper-helpee roles.

(b) *Homework:*

1. Develop courses of action for helpee in writing.

2. Put entire helping process together with child.

20. *Training in human relations skills: An overview.*

(a) An overview of the helping process.

(b) An overview of training techniques.

(c) *Homework:* Continual practice in real-life and entries in journal developing own cosmology in systematic manner.

AN OVERVIEW OF SYSTEMATIC HUMAN RELATIONS TRAINING

In addition to the many potential benefits of group processes in general (Carkhuff, 1969b), the group being the preferred mode of conducting training, there are many unique contributions of systematic training. First, and perhaps most important, systematic human relations training incorporates all of the potential benefits of all of the other approaches to therapeutic and training processes without the drawbacks of these many approaches. Second, it actualizes the potential benefits of the other approaches to a degree greater than these other approaches. For example, systematic training incorporates therapeutic benefits unheard of in traditional counseling and therapeutic orientations. For example, in Stage 10 of training, the key stage in movement toward higher levels of understanding for both helper and helpee, the helpee is potentially the recipient of untold benefits. If the trainer has managed to establish an atmosphere of trust during the earlier nine stages and the helpee, accordingly, feels free to share personally meaningful problems, then the helpee may have the benefits of multiple helpers, or in more traditional terms, multiple counselors or therapists or consultants. If the helper is effective in laying an effective interchangeable base of communication, then he not only increases the probability of making an additive response that can enable the helpee to move toward deeper levels of self-exploration and self-understanding but he also increases the probability of the other group members' making effective additive responses as in step 6 of Stage 10. Just as the helping interaction is allowed to run with the helper and helpee, so does each group member-helper, in turn, have the opportunity for a sustained interaction with the helpee. The helpee, then, responds according to how meaningful each successive response of each helper has been. In addition to the benefits to the helpee, each potential helper is systematically exposed to a variety of different responses by the other helpers. In this manner he has the opportunity to develop systematically the number and level of his own responses. Even here, however, we often find that if the trainer has brought the group along effectively there will be some common core of understanding of the helpee which the various group member-helpers share. In other words, the different additive responses which the different helpers share with the helpee constitute variations off a central theme rather than responses which go off in their own autonomous directions. It is the trainer's responsibility, initially, and the trainee's responsibility, ultimately, to put together for the helpee a total picture incorporating and integrating each of the various group member-helper's responses that have been helpful. In this manner, the helpee has the benefit of multiple helper-consultants and a master trainer, the most powerful therapeutic means available to man.

The systematic human relations training program is not rigid and inflexible. It can and has been modified to meet the needs of a variety of programs, from the training of teachers in educational settings to the training of police or correctional officers in law enforcement settings. It has a built-in flexibility which allows each program to be designed to meet the needs of the functional criteria which have been developed as the goals of that particular program. It leaves each program free to meet its own needs. Indeed, it equips each program with its own in-service training and supervisory capacities. While systematic training of this nature can be patterned to serve ongoing, viable organizations, it can at the same time provide a directionality for movement into those social and educational areas where current systems are not effective.

While systematic training can be designed to meet the needs of a variety of different institutions and programs involving people-to-people contact and treatment, then, there is a master plan that is overriding. This involves a process of operationalization of goals or the problems to be eliminated or ameliorated. This involves a step-by-step sequence of training emphasizing movement from the most simple to the most complex of all behaviors, the effective helping process. Thus, we find movement from the specific to the global; from a single statement to multiple statements; from a Helpee-Helper sequence to a Helpee-Helper-Helpee sequence to an extended interaction; from attention to a single affect to many different affects; from affect alone to the personal meaning, an abstraction of content and feeling, which complements the feeling; from a single response that is interchangeable in feeling to multiple responses that are additive in feeling and meaning; from helper responsiveness to initiative to responsive and initiative responses; from helpee self-exploration to self-understanding to action; from practice with types to role-playing to real-life experiences; from homework assignments in practice, first in impersonal relationships, then with significant others, moving gradually to spouse and children; from simple homework assignments involving recording single insights into human relations to the systematic development of an effective working cosmology; from a consideration of different courses of action in practice to the effective implementation of a working course of action in life. And finally, with the assistance of an able trainer, putting it all together in an effective helping process.

In other words, here is the most effective means known for the development of effective living, for both the actualization and the transmission of meaning in life. We train people in every other aspect of life except how to live with themselves and each other. We teach them how to employ proper grammar and we tutor them on how to dance; indeed, the more affluent, the greater the likelihood of tutoring in every necessary or desirable skill. Yet we do not explore the human and his relations with his fellow humans. We do not train the individual to understand his own behavior and the behavior of others—a sad omission, for it is behavior and not attitudes which make for growth or crises. Change the behavior, and the attitudes follow. And in changing behavior we leave a man with tangible and usable skills that he can sustain and retain for his own betterment and the betterment of those around him. Here now is a means available to every individual, rich and poor, black and white, to realize his own potential resources, and the potential resources of others. Then, and only then can he effectively enable another human to actualize his own resources.

REFERENCES

Carkhuff, R. R. *Helping and human relations: A primer for lay and professional helpers.* Vol. I. *Selection and training.* New York: Holt, Rinehart and Winston, 1969. (a)

Carkhuff, R. R. *Helping and human relations: A primer for lay and professional helpers.* Vol II. *Practice and research.* New York: Holt, Rinehart and Winston, 1969. (b)

CHAPTER 9
Principles of Selection

Most social action programs have not only not successfully trained their personnel but also in most instances they have not conducted meaningful selection of the personnel. Effective personnel require two phases of development, selection and training: selection on the basis of the characteristics which we wish our personnel to have; training for the increased effectiveness of those characteristics which we wish our personnel to have. Training without selection is uneconomical and inefficient and may, over a limited duration, be ineffective. Only over an extended duration of time, which we can often ill afford, can we promise maximal training benefits without selection. In the instance of human relations training we must make our greatest investment where it will offer the greatest return in terms of immediate benefits. Selection is directly implied.

Selection allows us to discriminate those persons who are living at the highest levels of the relevant dimensions. Training simply and directly intensifies the trainee's level of functioning on these dimensions. The fact that the trainee is functioning at high levels has implications not only for immediate benefits but also for long-term retention, for if he was able to accomplish a reasonable level of functioning on his own, he is likely over a given period of time to retain at least that level of functioning.

The first problem of selection, then, is to analyze the critical dimensions of our ultimate criteria of functioning. Thus, in helping and human relations, if we plan ultimately for the trainee-product to function effectively in helping relationships, we must first obtain an index of his present level of functioning in such a relationship. This informs us of the level of the learning structure which the trainee can employ as his base upon which to build in the training experience. It also tells us how far along the way to the goal the trainee-candidate is.

CANDIDATE'S LEVEL OF FUNCTIONING

We have seen that the level of trainer functioning is most critical to the training process; we have also studied the effects of the interaction of the trainee level with the trainer level (Carkhuff, 1969a). Thus, we have established

201

that the greatest possible changes on the part of the trainee are a function of the greatest possible discrepancy between the initial levels of functioning of trainer and trainee. Accordingly, if we wish to demonstrate the greatest changes over the course of training we might select those trainees who are functioning at the lowest levels. In interaction with high level functioning trainers they would demonstrate the greatest changes. However, except in instances of inpatient treatment programs this would not constitute a legitimate or valued basis for selection.

Since in most social action programs it is desirable to have the highest level functioning personnel in the most responsible positions, we wish to select those persons who at the cessation of training will be functioning at the highest levels. *Those trainees who are functioning initially at the highest levels will function finally at the highest levels.* This is not to say that no change will take place over the course of training. We have already seen that it will under specifiable conditions. To be sure, in interaction with trainers functioning at still higher levels the trainees will also demonstrate significant constructive change. Indeed, the basic rule of change still holds: the greater the discrepancy between trainer and trainee level of functioning the greater the change.

The ideal combination of selection and training programs, then, would seem to be the selection of both trainers and trainees at the highest level possible. If the trainees enter at relatively high levels, they can, in conjunction with trainers who are significantly higher, demonstrate constructive gains in the direction of the trainer. In summary, the problem of selection for social action programs is twofold: (1) select the highest level functioning trainers from among the trainer candidates; (2) select the highest level functioning trainees from among the trainee candidates. Hopefully, based upon the greater experience and learning of the trainer, there will be a discrepancy between them that will ensure significant increments of learning for the trainee. The means by which trainer and trainee will be selected must be elaborated at this point.

TRADITIONAL METHODOLOGIES OF SELECTION

Traditional selection indexes have failed in accomplishing their basic task of discriminating between effective and ineffective persons (Carkhuff, 1966, 1969a). Beyond a certain minimum level of functioning in the normal range, performance on intellective indexes has failed to predict anything but performance on intellective indexes. For example, in terms of grade point average, intellectual functioning in the primary and secondary grades predicts intellectual functioning in the college years and nothing else; intellectual functioning in college predicts intellectual functioning in graduate study and nothing else; intellectual functioning in graduate school predicts nothing. Therefore, unless we wish to predict intellectual performance on aptitude and achievement tests in later life—and not functional performance in real life—our traditional intellective indexes are of little or no value.

Studies of personality patterns of trainees have also failed to discriminate between effective and ineffective persons. In the helping professions, they have yielded what have been considered to be more feminine response patterns. That is, these trainees tend to assume a more responsive and nurturant stance toward life. These response dispositions are, to be sure, intensified over the course of training. They are reinforced by the trainers who selected them, no doubt for the same reasons that they were selected in the first place. Like begets like! More feminine helper-trainers tend to select more feminine helper-trainees —independent of their ability to function effectively in the helping role.

In summary, our traditional testing indexes are only effective if we are attempting to predict traditional testing indexes. I could not imagine a world less worthwhile. Where these tests are descriptive of personality characteristics of a given group of candidates they are unrelated to real-life indexes of functioning. At best, our traditional tests are irrelevant. At worst, they may be harmful in terms of pointing up self-perpetuating, functionally autonomous directions for our efforts, efforts which will, in the long run, be wasted.

Studies of the characteristics of effective persons, then, must be related to functioning on indexes related to the effectiveness of their functioning. For example, in the helping area, studies of helper functioning must be related to effectiveness in the helping role. In this regard, there are many helpers and helper trainees who do not exhibit the personality characteristics of the dominant grouping of helpers, yet whose success rate is as good or better than that of the dominant grouping. There is evidence to suggest that these persons may be more masculine in their response disposition, although not necessarily to the exclusion of a feminine response disposition. That is, those persons who demonstrate a directionful action-orientation in conjunction with a responsive stance are most effective. The task before us, then, is to discern and describe the characteristics of those helpers whose helpees improve on a variety of change or gain indexes. In general, we must study the effects of those persons involved upon the goals which we are attempting to achieve.

In this context, and with the hope of relating the selection of effective persons to indexes of their ultimate functioning, let us turn to the development of relevant and meaningful selection indexes.

EFFECTIVE SELECTION METHODOLOGIES

In our efforts to develop these selection indexes we have been guided by one principle. We term this principle the "principle of selection." The principle of selection is this: *The best index of a future criterion is a previous index of that criterion.*

The development of selection indexes necessitates an analysis of the future criterion for which we intend to prepare our candidate. Thus, for example, in helping, an analysis of the helper's contribution to the helpee's process and outcome is essential. If we want to predict effective helping, then, we need to obtain an index of the prospective helper trainee's level of functioning in the help-ing role. Again, *the best index of future functioning in the helping role is a previous index of functioning in the helping role.*

A number of selection indexes flow directly and readily from this basic proposition.

Staying in the helping area for a moment, we know that the level of com-munication of the helper is most critical to constructive helpee change or gain. Accordingly, an index of communication is a most important selection device. Thus, *the best index of future communicative functioning in the helper's role involves casting prospective helpers in the helping role in order to obtain a present index of communicative functioning in the helping role.*

Usually, the potential helpers are rated by trained raters who are them-selves functioning at demonstrably high levels of functioning. The evidence for the relationship between these objective ratings and a variety of helpee out-come indexes is solid. On the other hand, evidence for the relationship of helpee ratings of helper performance is variable. In general, the evidence for helpee ratings is positive when trained and high level functioning standard helpees are employed, and is negative (independent or negatively correlated) when real-life helpees are employed.

The ideal, then, is to approximate as closely as possible the real-life condi-tions for which we are attempting to prepare our candidate. With regard to helping and training for helping, this means of selection has been employed with a wide variety of lay and professional populations. The results of all of the studies are consistent with the model being explicated.

In training and treatment, the helpee's level of communication moves in the direction of the helper's level of communication. When the helper is func-tioning at a high level, the helpee tends to gain significantly and rapidly. When the helper is functioning at a low level, the helpee does not gain or he deterior-ates (Carkhuff, 1969a).

In turn, the helpee's initial level of functioning in both training and treat-ment is relevant. Thus, in general, those helpees who function initially at the highest levels function finally at the highest levels, especially over time-limited programs (Carkhuff, 1969a), and also retain their level of functioning over time (Collingwood, 1970; Holder, 1969). Those helpees who function initially at the lowest levels function finally at the lowest levels, especially over time-limited programs, and also tend not to retain their level of functioning over time. This last finding is qualified by the time-limited nature of the programs. Where an indefinite period of time is available and the discrepancy between a high-level helper and a low-level helpee is great, the helpee may gain and retain a great deal.

Thus, in interaction with each other, where both helper and helpee initial levels of functioning are high and a discrepancy between their respective levels of functioning exists, the gain for the helpee will be rapid and the retention stable. Where helper level of functioning is high and helpee level of functioning is low, and unlimited time is available, gains may be slow but large; in these instances retention will be more a function of final rather than initial level of functioning. Where both helper and helpee are functioning at low levels and little discrepancy exists in either direction, change will be minimal and possibly deteriorative for either or both of the participants.

Finally, in the worst of all circumstances, where the helpee is functioning at high levels and the helper is functioning at low levels and the discrepancies are significant, the consequences for the helpee may vary according to whether the helpee acknowledges the helper as an agent of the helpee's change. If the helpee cedes the helper the power in the relationship, we can only generate predictions of significant negative change for the helpee. If the helpee does not cede the helper the power in the relationship, and indeed neutralizes or even avoids the helper entirely, we can generate predictions of no change for the helpee.

Other selection indexes flow from this basic principle of selection. For example, in relation to training we can develop indexes of trainability: *The best index of whether a helper trainee can effectively employ the training experience involves an index of the prospective helper's present ability to employ an analogue of training.* This procedure simply involves presenting the prospective trainee with an analogue or representative aspect of the training program for which he is being considered and assessing the effects in brief training by pre- and post-testing of his functioning on relevant indexes. This procedure has been employed effectively in a number of human relations training programs in social action applications (Carkhuff and Griffin, 1970, 1971a, 1971b). While predictive validity studies were not possible because only those who demonstrated the highest level of functioning were retained, one important conclusion developed. *All of those trainees who demonstrated the highest level of functioning following the training analogue were functioning above minimally effective levels following the completion of training.*

In addition, a variety of other indexes of selection were tested and evaluated. In relation to helping, for example, the critical incident index has been found to be valuable: *The best index of the helper's future ability to handle helpee crises effectively involves obtaining an index of the prospective helper's present ability to handle crises.* Related procedures can be employed naturalistically from evaluations of functioning in response to crises in the relevant role, or experimentally by "programming" persons to present the candidate with crises. Experimental procedures have been developed and implemented in both treatment and training. The evidence suggests that high level functioning helpers mobilize their energies to act forcefully and decisively at crisis points, while low-level helpers are manipulated and thus helpless in the face of the crisis (Carkhuff, 1969a; Carkhuff and Berenson, 1967). All of this evidence generates predictions for the course of treatment and training over time. Persons functioning at high levels mobilize both their own resources and those of the helpee at crisis points, and a constructive directionality emerges; over time and with repeated crises, the process and outcome are positive. Persons functioning at low levels do not mobilize either their own resources or those of the helpee at crisis points, if they acknowledge the crises at all; over time, and with crises, whether acknowledged or not, a deterioration process ensues.

An index of treatability and trainability specific to helping is the index of self-exploration: *The best index of the helper trainee's inclination to explore himself in training or treatment involves an index of the prospective helper's present inclination to explore himself.* Simple procedures for obtaining indexes of self-exploration involve casting the candidate in the role of the helpee. This device can be utilized most effectively in conjunction with evidence on the candidate's functioning in the helper's role. Since self-exploration is critical to any kind of learning or relearning process, those candidates who explore themselves at the highest or deepest levels are the best candidates for the program, and those who are not so inclined are not. Evidence from evaluations of treatment and training programs suggests higher-level functioning persons are also disposed to exploring themselves at higher levels and that persons disposed toward exploring themselves most highly gain the most from a training experience (Carkhuff, 1969a, 1969b; Carkhuff and Berenson, 1967).

Another index where past performance predicts future performance is that of the work performance index: *The best index of a candidate's future work performance is an index of his past work performance.* This simply involves obtaining an evaluation of the candidate's work performance. This may involve objective measures of attendance and productivity as well as subjective measures such as the supervisor's evaluation where the supervisor's own level of functioning must be taken into consideration in evaluating his evaluation of the candidate. While the supervisor's index has received wide employment in business and industry, evaluations of its effectiveness are limited. In our own work we have employed it with meaningful results (Carkhuff and Griffin, 1971b). All of the candidates who had outstanding ratings on past work performance went on to demonstrate outstanding work records. However, this principle is to be qualified by the fact that social action programs are frequently geared toward servicing people who have little or no previous work history.

Thus, the evidence for the previous indexes of the criteria which we are attempting to predict provides us with a base upon which to build valid selection procedures. Unfortunately, a major problem associated with selection procedures involves the wide variability and lack of standardization. In relation to helping, the problem is particularly troublesome when, for example, there are large differences in the interview and extra interview behavior of the helpees employed. In this context, a corollary of the principle of selection is relevant: *The best index of a particular selection procedure is a brief, standardized index that represents all relevant aspects of that procedure.*

In an effort to standardize procedures, then, representative problems have been developed to assess the level of functioning of the candidate in the relevant area. In addition, standard responses, prerated by experts, have been devised to obtain an index of the candidate's discrimination of high, moderate, and low levels of functioning in the problem area: those candidates whose ratings agree closely with those of experts are considered good or high discriminators; those candidates whose ratings deviate greatly from the experts are considered low discriminators. Again, the evidence for indexes of discrimination and communication obtained by standardized excerpts is consistent: in general, the helpee's level of functioning moves in the direction of the helper's, with initially high level functioning helpees gaining most rapidly, and initially low level functioning helpees gaining the most over unlimited time periods in conjunction with high level functioning helpers (Carkhuff, 1969a). However, while related to discrimination among high-level communicators, communication was found to be independent of discrimination among moderate to low-level communicators. Thus, since the only extensive evidence available is for the communication of conditions, it would appear that discrimination is a necessary but not sufficient condition of communication.

Again, the first task is to analyze the goals involved into their critical dimensions. That is, the task is to develop representative samples of the problems to be dealt with or the goals to be achieved. These samples should typify the problems of the areas involved so that we may obtain an index of the candidate's level of functioning in this area. Simply stated, the assumption is that *persons who have learned to respond effectively, or at least more effectively, in the relevant area or areas are those who can employ training most effectively.*

Brief, representative problem expressions can be developed, then, to sample the potential responses of the prospective candidate. The candidate may be asked simply to respond in the manner that he considers most appropriate and helpful. The problem expressions may be administered by means of audio or audiovisual tapes or in written form. Similarly, the candidate may respond verbally or behaviorally; or he may respond in writing, which allows for group testing. The prospect's level of functioning is obtained from rating his levels of responses to the problem expressions.

Following the basic principle of selection, then, in the following research project we conducted a predictive validity study for developing functional professional correctional counselors and trainers.

PROJECT 15

*Development of Selection Indexes**

All 26 applicants for a month-long correctional counseling and human relations institute were accepted in order to conduct a study relating selection indexes to final level of trainee functioning. The candidates were front line officers from federal and state prisons around the country. They ranged

* Reprinted in part with permission of the *Journal of Counseling Psychology*, 1971, 18, where it first appeared as "The Selection and Training of Correctional Counselors on Physical, Emotional and Intellectual Indexes," by Robert R. Carkhuff, George Banks, Bernard G. Berenson, Andrew H. Griffin, and Ries Hall.

in age from their 20's to their 50's and in experience from 2 to over 20 years.

The first task was to develop a selection inventory. Since the goal of the institute staff was to produce a fully functioning correctional counselor and since the training program itself had physical and intellectual as well as emotional-interpersonal components, an inventory was developed to assess the candidate's level of functioning in the physical, emotional, and intellectual spheres.

With the primary emphasis upon functionality, the responses to the inventory appearing in Figure 9–1 were scored by trained raters on the

Figure 9–1

Correctional Counselor Selection Inventory

INTRODUCTION

To achieve the high objectives of the Institute of Correctional Counseling, rigorous intellectual, emotional, and physical demands will be made on the trainee. To function as a helper and trainer of helpers a person must be living effectively himself. He must disclose himself in a genuine and constructive fashion in response to others. He communicates an accurate empathic understanding and a respect for all of the feelings of other persons and guides discussions with those persons into specific feelings and experiences. He communicates confidence in what he is doing and is spontaneous and intense. In addition, while he is open and flexible in his relations with others, in his commitment to the welfare of the other person he is quite capable of active, assertive, and even confronting behavior when it is appropriate. The attached inventory (Table 9–1) has been designed to aid in the selection of trainees who naturally function well and can be trained to function at the high levels required of a helper.

NAME OF APPLICANT _____ TITLE _____

PLACE OF EMPLOYMENT _____

COMPLETE BUSINESS ADDRESS _____

NAME OF ADMINISTRATOR WHO WILL ATTEND

THREE-DAY ORIENTATION OVERVIEW _____

TITLE OF ABOVE NAMED ADMINISTRATOR _____

Responses to the following items will provide an index of functioning in the physical, emotional, and intellectual areas so that in the future, prospective correctional counselor trainers will be selected on the basis of their functioning in these areas.

I. PHYSICAL
    1. Height _____ 2. Weight _____ 3. Total number of sit-ups
    4. Time to run a mile _____   in a row _____
    5. List any special skills or competencies within physical area (sports, athletics, etc.) _____

6. *NOTE:* a. Please provide full-length picture of candidate.
b. Please provide physician's certificate of health.

II. EMOTIONAL-INTERPERSONAL
Provide responses to accompanying stimulus items (Table 9–1).
Describe characteristics of the effective correctional officer in a written paragraph of no less than 100 words or more than one page.
List any special skills or competencies within emotional-interpersonal area (special skills in counseling, child-rearing, teaching, coaching, etc.).

III. INTELLECTUAL
Describe the basic principles of how you see your world and your life in a written paragraph of no less than 100 words or more than one page.
List any special skills or competencies within intellectual area (special skills in psychology, sociology, education, etc.).
NOTE: Acceptance in program is no guarantee of completion. Completion is dependent upon performance. Certification as a trainer is dependent upon application upon returning to the prison.

basis of 5-point scales ranging from 5 (most effective) to 1 (least effective) with level 3 designated minimally effective. It is noteworthy that the time it takes an individual to run a mile in addition to the number of sit-ups an individual can do correlate most highly (in the .80's and .90's) with overall cardiovascular functioning. In this regard, ratings of physical functioning were modified according to age norms. Ratings on intellectual functioning were obtained from evaluations of the candidate's written assignments.

Ratings of emotional-interpersonal functioning were obtained by evaluating written responses to written human relations stimulus expressions. The stimulus expressions were drawn from 16 helpee stimulus expressions crossing different affect areas (depression, anger, elation) with different problem areas (social, vocational, child-rearing, marital, confrontation). Tables 9–1 and 9–2 present a sample of these stimulus expressions with responses systematically varied according to level of responsiveness and initiative (Carkhuff, 1969a). While these expressions and responses were employed because of the abundance of base rate and validity data, stimulus expressions and responses more relevant to correctional officers were also developed.

The base rate data on functionality appear in Table 9–3. As can be seen, the candidates were functioning at relatively higher levels in the physical realm, low in the emotional-interpersonal realm, and moderate in the intellectual realm. Thus, in the area for which they were being trained, the emotional-interpersonal, they were functioning at the lowest level. Nevertheless, the indications of support from the physical and intellectual variables were positive.

Table 9–1

A Sample of Standard Helpee Stimulus Expressions and Helper Responses

---

Excerpt 5

Helpee: Gee, those people! Who do they think they are? I just can't stand interacting with them anymore. Just a bunch of phonies. They leave me so frustrated. They make me so anxious. I get angry at myself. I don't even want to be bothered with them anymore. I just wish I could be honest with them and tell them all to go to hell! But I guess I just can't do it.

Helper: (1) They really make you very angry. You wish you could handle them more effectively than you do.

   (2) Damn, they make you furious! But it's just not them. It's with yourself, too, because you don't act on how you feel.

   (3) Why do you feel these people are phony? What do they say to you?

   (4) Maybe society itself is at fault here—making you feel inadequate, giving you this negative view of yourself, leading you to be unable to successfully interact with others.

Excerpt 11

Helpee: I'm so pleased with the kids. They are doing just marvelously. They have done so well at school and at home; they get along together. It's amazing. I never thought they would. They seem a little older. They play together better and they enjoy each other, and I enjoy them. Life has become so much easier. It's really a joy to raise three boys. I didn't think it would be. I'm just so pleased and hopeful for the future. For them and for us. It's just great! I can't believe it. It's marvelous!

Helper: (1) It's a good feeling to have your kids settled once again.

   (2) Is it possible your kids were happy before but you never noticed it before? You mentioned your boys. How about your husband? Is he happy?

   (3) Do you feel this is a permanent change?

   (4) Hey, that's great! Whatever the problem, and you know there will be problems, it's great to have experienced the positive side of it.

Excerpt 15

Helpee: Gee, I'm so disappointed. I thought we could get along together and you could help me. We don't seem to be getting anywhere. You don't understand me. You don't know I'm here. I don't even think you care for me. You don't hear me when I talk. You seem to be somewhere else. Your responses are independent of anything I have to say. I don't know where to turn. I'm just so— doggone it—I don't know what I'm going to do, but I know you can't help me. There just is no hope.

Helper: (1) I have no reason to try and not to help you. I have every reason to want to help you.

   (2) Only when we establish mutual understanding and trust and only then can we proceed to work on your problem effectively.

   (3) It's disappointing and disillusioning to think you have made so little progress.

   (4) I feel badly that you feel that way. I do want to help. I'm wondering, "Is it me? Is it you, both of us?" Can we work something out?

SOURCE: From Robert R. Carkhuff, *Helping and Human Relations: A Primer for Lay and Professional Helpers,* Vol. I: *Selection and Training* (New York: Holt, Rinehart and Winston, 1969), pp. 124–125.

Table 9–2
Key to Design and Ratings of Standard Helper Responses Sample

		DESIGN		
Helpee Stimulus Expressions	*Helper Responses*	*Responsiveness*	*Initiative*	*Rating*
V	1	H	L	3.0
	2	H	H	4.0
	3	L	L	1.0
	4	L	H	1.5
XI	1	H	L	3.0
	2	L	H	1.5
	3	L	L	1.0
	4	H	H	4.0
XV	1	L	L	1.0
	2	L	H	1.0
	3	H	L	3.0
	4	H	H	3.5

SOURCE: Reprinted from Robert R. Carkhuff, *Helping and Human Relations: A Primer for Lay and Professional Helpers,* Vol. I: *Selection and Training* (New York: Holt, Rinehart and Winston, 1969), pp. 124–125.

Table 9–3
Table of Means and Standard Deviations of Pre Measures of Emotional Interpersonal Functioning of Trainees

INDEXES OF FUNCTIONING							
Physical		*Emotional-Interpersonal*		*Intellectual*		*Overall*	
M	*sd*	*M*	*sd*	*M*	*sd*	*M*	*sd*
2.39	.72	1.44	.30	2.12	.57	1.98	.37

The training program was conducted by functional professionals—all black—trained by the staff at the Human Relations Center. Thus, the purpose of the program was twofold: (1) to train the correctional officers in counseling and human relations skills; (2) to demonstrate directly what systematically trained persons from the black community are able to do in a training capacity and, accordingly, to make the correctional officers sensitive to the black man's frame of reference in and outside the prison. The training took part over a month. During the first three days the trainees were accompanied by the top administrator, usually the warden of the institution involved, for purposes of orienting the highest level administrators. The trainees received approximately 80 intensive hours of training after which they worked on developing courses of action for the return to their institutions. During the final week, the trainees had a practicum experience at a nearby Federal Penitentiary during which they worked in counseling and training both staff and prisoners. Both the correctional counselors and a sampling of their helpees and trainees were pre- and post-tested in preparation for evaluating the training experience and the selection indexes.

PROJECT 16
Predictive Validity of Selection Indexes*

In order to assess the effectiveness of the selection indexes it was necessary that they be related to the measures of functioning following training. The pre- and post-measures of physical functionality combined ratings of physical exercise tasks. The pre- and post-measures of emotional-interpersonal functionality combined ratings of written responses to stimulus expressions. The additional post-measure of helping effectiveness reflected degree of change in helpee-trainees seen by the correctional counselor trainees over the week practicum experience. The pre- and post-measures of intellectual functionality combined ratings of written assignments.

As can be seen in Table 9–4, the training program was effective in producing significant gains in (1) the emotional-interpersonal functioning of the officer trainees and in (2) the emotional-interpersonal functioning of a sample of the helpee-trainees seen by the officer trainees. The gains of the helpee-trainees were not relatively as great as those of the officer trainees;

Table 9–4

Table of Means and Standard Deviations of Pre- and Post-Measures of Emotional-Interpersonal Functioning of Officer Trainees and Helpee-Trainees seen by Officer Trainees

Level of Emotional-Interpersonal Functioning	Pre-training		Post-training		Net Change	
	M	sd	M	sd	M	sd
Officer Trainee (N = 26)	1.4	.3	2.6	2.8	+1.2*	.5
Helpee-Trainees (N = 26)	1.4	.2	2.3	.6	+ .9*	.4

*Significant beyond .01 level.

this can be accounted for by the duration of the program, which involved two weeks of intensive training for the officer trainees (approximately 80 hours) and one week of regular training for the helpee-trainees (approximately 10 hours).

As can be seen in Table 9–5, the pre-measures relate to the post-measures. The pre-training measures of physical functioning are most highly related to the post-training measures of physical functioning and the pre-

*Reprinted in part with permission from an article in the *Journal of Counseling Psychology,* 1971, 18, entitled "The Selection and Training of Correctional Counselors on Physical, Emotional and Intellectual Indexes," by Robert R. Carkhuff, George Banks, Bernard G. Berenson, Andrew H. Griffin, and Ries Hall.

Table 9–5
Table of Intercorrelations for Pre- and Post-Measures of Physical, Emotional-Interpersonal and Intellectual Functioning of Trainees*

Indexes of Functioning	POST-TRAINING				
	Physical	Emotional-Interpersonal		Intellectual	Overall (P, E$_I$, I)
		I Officer Trainees	II Effects upon Helpee-Trainees		
PRE-TRAINING					
Physical	.92	.81	.74	.63	.67
Emotional-Interpersonal (I Officer Trainees)	.67	.63	.77	.62	.64
Intellectual	.66	.78	.72	.73	.63
Overall (P, E$_I$, I)	.81	.90	.81	.77	.77

*All correlations are significant at or beyond the .01 level.

measures of intellectual functioning are most highly related to the post-measures of intellectual functioning. However, the pre-measures of emotional-interpersonal functioning are not quite as highly related to the post-measures of emotional-interpersonal functioning as are other pre-measures. Contrary to our expectations and previous research, in this instance the best index of a future criterion was not a previous index of that criterion, although it was, to be sure, related. However, this finding may be accounted for by the restricted range of variability in the pre-measures of emotional-interpersonal functioning. The top-rated trainee initially, the only one rated over level 2.0, had received systematic training elsewhere prior to this training institute and he neutralized any high and significant relationship due to his relatively poor performance over the course of the institute. The remainder functioned within emotional-interpersonal ranges (1.0 to 1.8) analogous to neuropsychiatric patients during the pretesting and thus nullified the possibility of establishing high and significant relationships with the post-measures.

It should be emphasized that all candidates from a group functioning at low levels emotionally and interpersonally were admitted for emotional-interpersonal training. Had we drawn the overall discrimination line at high levels, we would have selected all four of the top trainee-products. In social action programs, as we shall see in the next section, this is precisely what we do: we select only the highest functioning, so that while we may lose a few candidates who might have made it successfully, a minimum of those in whom we invest our energies will fail.

SELECTION AND SOCIAL ACTION

Selection is meaningful only insofar as it prepares personnel efficiently for a more effective discharge of their responsibilities. We see readily how selection fits into the total scheme of programs of social action and the development of human resources.

We have seen that the socioeducational systems have not been serving many minority groups effectively. Indeed, these systems have led directly to the need for social action and social service programs on a great scale. The social action programs, in turn, we have found are successful to the degree that they can develop successful personnel to implement them. Often the personnel best equipped to surmount the barriers to helping are functional professionals, although not, to be sure, to the exclusion of effective professional workers.

We have found that not only can we understand the phenomenology of the effective person but that we can operationalize this effectiveness at emotional-interpersonal as well as physical and intellectual levels. We can operationalize this effectiveness in terms of the quantity and quality of responses in the individual's repertoire. In an attempt to achieve a high level of personal effectiveness we need both the effective personnel to provide the necessary learning experiences as well as the effective programs which constitute these learning experiences.

Accordingly, programs for helping and training for both lay and professional helpers have been developed. These programs provide guides for the development of the functional professional and for his functioning in his role of responsibility. However, by themselves they are inefficient and uneconomical and thus less effective than they might otherwise be. Programs for helping and training are incomplete if they do not involve assignment of the most responsible helping and training positions to those persons functioning at the highest levels.

Persons who have learned to respond relatively effectively in a given area are those who have been shaped effectively by the feedback which they have received for their behaviors. They have retained their more effective behaviors. They have extinguished their less effective behaviors.

It is assumed that those persons who are most effective in a given area are those who are best equipped to utilize a training experience in that area. In turn, it is assumed that those whose relative effectiveness is increased and intensified through training are those who will discharge their later responsibilities most effectively. They will help most effectively. They will lead most effectively. They will live most effectively.

In the development of human resources, then, selection of both the personnel to function as helpers and trainers as well as those to function as trainees for helping and training capacities is a necessary first step. Put another way, the first step in the development of human resources involves the discrimination of potential human resources. It is upon these potential human resources that we build the foundation for an effective world, a world in which each can actualize himself according to his potential, a world in which each can serve according to his ability. We have the resources for such a world.

REFERENCES

Carkhuff, R. R. Training in the counseling and therapeutic processes: Requiem or reveille? *Journal of Counseling Psychology,* 1966, **13,** 360–367.

Carkhuff, R. R. *Helping and human relations: A primer for lay and professional helpers.* Vol. I. *Selection and training.* New York: Holt, Rinehart and Winston, 1969. (a)

Carkhuff, R. R. *Helping and human relations: A primer for lay and professional helpers.* Vol. II. *Practice and research.* New York: Holt, Rinehart and Winston, 1969. (b)

Carkhuff, R. R., Banks, G., Berenson, B. G., Griffin, A. H., & Hall, R. The selection and training of correctional counselors on physical, emotional and intellectual indexes. *Journal of Counseling Psychology,* 1971, **18,** in press.

Carkhuff, R. R., & Berenson, B. G. *Beyond counseling and therapy.* New York: Holt, Rinehart and Winston, 1967.

Carkhuff, R. R., & Griffin, A. H. The selection and training of human relations specialists. *Journal of Counseling Psychology,* 1970, **17,** 443–450.

Carkhuff, R. R., & Griffin, A. H. Selection and training of functional professionals for the inner-city, pre-school. *Journal of Research and Development in Education,* 1971, **4,** 87–96 (a).

Carkhuff, R. R., & Griffin, A. H. The selection and training of functional professionals for Concentrated Employment Programs. *Journal of Clinical Psychology,* 1971, **27,** 163–165. (b)

Collingwood, T. Variables in the maintenance of interpersonal skills following training. Doctoral dissertation, State University of New York at Buffalo, 1970.

Holder, B. T. Variables in the maintenance of facilitative dimensions following training. Doctoral dissertation, State University of New York at Buffalo, 1969.

PART FIVE

The Development
of Human Resources

CHAPTER 10
Human Service as a Preferred Motive

Each immigrant group as it came over to America found certain avenues of achievement closed to it. Often there was not only no room at the top but no room at all for the novice. Each immigrant group, in turn, found areas where there was a need and nobody else wanted to go. A social system could not run without police, and a great Irish-American tradition in police and politics was initiated, culminating in the last decade in the achievement of the highest office in the land by a third-generation Irishman. A social system could not build without cement masons and laborers, and a great Italian-American tradition in the building trades was initiated, culminating in the last decade in the achievement of some of the largest construction companies since the building of the pyramids. Such was the case with other groups of immigrants.

If we conceive of the blacks—their three-hundred-year role in the building of this nation notwithstanding—as themselves being, in effect, immigrants from a foreign land, arriving without the skills of the lowliest peasant from Europe, then we may draw similar analogies. Most avenues of achievement are closed to the blacks. Almost all are closed at the top and many are closed to entry.

The one avenue that is open to the blacks is the one in which they have served most fully—the human services. As we stand on the verge of a great social service revolution, it is clear that the human service area is the one area that is open and competitive. There is room—all the way to the top there is room.

For the blacks the beauty of developing their thrust in the human service area is not simply the vast experience which they have in the area. To be sure, this could even work in the opposite way attitudinally in the sense that part of what the current generation of blacks is fighting is a conditioned disposition to be responsive to the needs of others. This has at once been their greatest strength and greatest weakness.

No, the beauty of the human service area is that for the blacks it combines an ethical motive with an economic motive. At the highest levels, in the ideals of the greatest leaders, the black revolution, as other revolutions before it, stands for the freedom and fulfillment of all men. The human service area dedicated to the actualization of human resources offers the most relevant, certainly the most unique, perhaps the only, outlet for this ethic.

On the other hand, the black revolution cannot succeed if it cannot fulfill the economic motive, if it cannot assure the survival that makes growth possible. Here, the human service area offers an unusual opportunity for exploitation in the most positive sense. Not only does the human service area offer the blacks the possibility of providing services to themselves and their brothers but also of providing employment possibilities in the process—employment possibilities with opportunities to develop to the extent of one's capacity.

HUMAN RELATIONS SPECIALISTS

A concept which combines both ethical and economic motives is that of human relations specialists. Human relations specialist positions can be developed in business and governmental systems as well as in educational and welfare systems. With proper selection and training, human relations specialists can function to provide services for populations to which they, themselves, are indigenous. They can serve as models for persons who are growing and "making it" for themselves—as human beings. They can provide experiences which facilitate the growth of others. They can help a man adjust to a new job. They can help a student adjust to an integrated school. In short, the specialists can provide those human experiences which enable a person to make the transition from the deprivation and debilitation of the ghetto to new educational and vocational growth experiences.

In addition, they can provide vocational positions for persons who are indigenous to the population being serviced. Of necessity, a deprived population does not produce the credentialed specialists necessary to service it. The concept of human relations specialists provides the outlet for persons with talents but without credentials for human services. In one thrust, it meets the needs of the community, while at the same time it creates positions of responsibility for members of the community.

In response to black students' need for "assistance in adjusting to the predominantly white social setting in their new schools" in Springfield, Massachusetts, a pilot program involving paid positions for 14 human relations specialists was developed in an amendment to the Project to Improve Education for the Inner City Child (Title IV, E.S.E.A.). The project activities called for included providing direct social counseling with black students and parents and providing assistance to the principal and school staff in facilitating student adjustment at the seven junior high schools to which the specialists were assigned. The qualifications specified included having an intimate knowledge of the Model Cities neighborhood and an ability to communicate and work with the different persons from the community and the School Department. Selection and training

were conducted by the Human Relations Center, American International College, in conjunction with the School Department and the Model Cities board.

The first task was the development of selection indexes, particularly standardized selection indexes which represented the kinds of problems the specialists would have to deal with.

PROJECT 17

*Standardized Problems and Responses in Racial Relations**

First, the goals had to be analyzed in terms of their critical dimensions.
In this instance the specialist positions were created because of a breakdown in racial relations. While the central focus of the specialists' jobs was
the difficulties which the ghetto students were having in adjusting to the
predominantly white schools to which they were bussed, adults, black as
well as white, were clearly the source of the difficulty. Accordingly, representative samples of prototypical kinds of racial problems for adults and
children, black and white, were developed to assess the candidate's level of
communication in the racial relations area. In addition, standard helper
responses, pre-rated by experts, were devised to obtain an index of the candidate's discrimination of high, moderate and low levels of functioning in
the problem area.

The following standard tape (Table 10–1) was developed, then, in
order to assess both the level of communication and discrimination of the
candidate.

The race of the presenters of the problems was not identified to the
prospective candidates. Indeed, in some projects, following presentations,
the candidates were asked to identify whether the person presenting the
problem was black or white. In addition, the responders to the problem
were not identified, although in every instance the responders were of a
different race from the presenters.

It should be emphasized that these problem expressions were designed
specifically for this and related projects. Other stimulus expressions were
designed for other kinds of projects. Thus, for example, we will see in Chapter 11 tapes designed specifically for recruiting and working with hard-core
unemployed.

While the communication levels are to be obtained from the ratings of
trained experts, and therefore no key can be presented, a key for the rationale and the experts' ratings for the alternate responses will serve to be
illuminating. Thus we see in Table 10–2 that the alternate responses in-

*Reprinted in part with permission from the *Journal of Counseling Psychology*, 1970,
17, 443–450, where it first appeared as "The Selection and Training of Human Relations
Specialists," by Robert R. Carkhuff and Andrew H. Griffin.

Table 10–1
Standardized Problems and Responses in Racial Relations

INSTRUCTIONS

Please formulate the most helpful responses that you can think of in response to the following helpee stimulus expressions. Following this, rate the helper responses to these stimulus expressions on a rating scale ranging from 1 (poor) to 5 (very good) with 3 minimally facilitative:

BLACK-WHITE INTERACTION TAPE

Excerpt 1
Helpee: What do I have to do before they accept me—as a man—with my own individuality—my resources, my strengths? Jesus, it's always they either let me in and they go overboard with all their phony gestures or they exclude me completely—and, you know, always reading me as a Negro and never letting me show what I can do as a person. How do I communicate to them that I want to be accepted as a person?

Responses to Excerpt 1:
Response 1
Helper: More important than anything else, you want to be seen as a man.
Response 2
Helper: It's not a matter of being black or white or man or woman. It's the person down in there that's crying out to be heard—to be seen, but if *they* won't hear and *they* won't see then you're gonna have to do it on your own.
Response 3
Helper: Racial prejudice is universally pervasive.
Response 4
Helper: All men are created equal. I can't understand why anyone won't recognize you as both a Negro and a man. Certainly, our country and our religion in its firmest foundations emphasize this.

Excerpt 2
Helpee: There's just something I can't understand about these people. I just feel they're different. They're too different from me—particularly the men, not necessarily the women, but with the men there's just a sense of danger when they're around. I just don't feel as comfortable. I just don't feel as strong. I don't feel the same.

Responses to Excerpt 2:
Response 1
Helper: Everybody's different from everyone else.
Response 2
Helper: You don't know why you feel the way you do but somehow you just feel uncomfortable in their presence.
Response 3
Helper: There's no need to feel this way. It's foolish to feel this way. Racial prejudice can be overcome by education and that's where you should go. You should go for more education to learn what you can.
Response 4
Helper: One thing is that at the deepest level they threaten your identity, your manhood, and you don't know where it comes from but one thing you do know is that you gotta do something about it.

Excerpt 3
Helpee: Every time we start anything and become involved in it, it seems like the

Table 10–1
Standardized Problems and Responses in Racial Relations *(cont.)*

power structure in some manner arranges to take it away from us or make it inadequate—they do something to make it a bad thing or completely stop it in some manner.

Responses to Excerpt 3:

Response 1

Helper: Well, of course, if you go into a thing like that expecting to be defeated you probably are bound to be. Do you expect it to be handed to you on a silver platter?

Response 2

Helper: Well, everyone, of course, fails at some things—sometimes.

Response 3

Helper: It's almost as if it's not worth trying anymore within their system. You've about come around to the place where you feel that if anything's going to be accomplished it's going to have to be from a new base.

Response 4

Helper: It's awfully discouraging—hardly seems like there's any sense in trying.

Excerpt 4

Helpee: I hear my mommy and daddy talking about the trouble between Negroes and whites, but I really don't understand what they're talking about.

Responses to Excerpt 4:

Response 1

Helper: It's just so hard to understand what all the talk's about.

Response 2

Helper: My dear, you're just too young to understand the problems that we adults have to work with. When you get a little older, things will clear up for you.

Response 3

Helper: It's just so hard to understand. You just wish someone would make it clear to you what's going on.

Response 4

Helper: You haven't been doing your job. You haven't been reading the newspaper, you haven't been paying attention in class. What does your teacher say about all this?

Excerpt 5

Helpee: Well, you know, I'm not prejudiced myself, and I wouldn't really mind if it was just for myself if those people move next door to me, but I wonder if they really aren't happier—you know—if it's not really kinder to them to have them and their children with their own kind.

Responses to Excerpt 5:

Response 1

Helper: You'd like very much to convince me and maybe even yourself, and yet you're telling these people where to go before you've met them.

Response 2

Helper: We all hope that whites and Negroes will get together some day.

Response 3

Helper: Hey, you really feel that their staying by themselves would be in their best interests.

Response 4

Helper: May I refer you to your Bible which is in complete agreement with you. The races shall stay separated and *must* stay separated.

Table 10–1
    Standardized Problems and Responses in Racial Relations *(cont.)*

Excerpt 6

When I was in school, I was going to my class, this kid called me a dirty name. I just wanted to beat his face in. There's this kid in school—he called me a nigger and I wanted to just beat his face in. I knew if I had to fight him I would get kicked out of school or something or even get the paddle. I don't want to fight the guy. But he kept on tempting me. I went to my next class all upset and everything. And I went home I was upset and nervous and just scared and I didn't know what to do.

Responses to Excerpt 6:
Response 1
Helper: If you wait, it'll blow over.
Response 2
Helper: You can't beat him up. And that means you have to go to the teacher to stop him from insulting you.
Response 3
Helper: You really didn't know which way to turn.
Response 4
Helper: You're not sure how to do it. But you know you have to get back at him some way—not just to stop him but for yourself—as a man.

volve a systematic variation of levels of responsiveness and initiative, although they are, to be sure, presented in a random order. That is, the responses to each problem expression include the following combinations of levels of responsive and initiative dimensions: high responsive–high initiative; high responsive–low initiative; low responsive–high initiative; low responsive–low initiative. As can readily be seen, where responsiveness occurs at high levels the ratings are higher than where initiative occurs at high levels. Thus, a high responsive–low initiative response receives a higher rating than a low responsive–high initiative response for direction without understanding is less effective than understanding without direction. Obviously, both understanding and direction are most effective when they occur simultaneously at high levels.

The potential applications of these special selection indexes are numerous. Thus, for example, in initiating a human relations specialist program for schools integrating ghetto children, it was important to have an idea of the base rate of functioning of the adminstration, the guidance counselors and teachers, and the parents of the children involved. It was important in terms of understanding where each in his turn "was coming from." It was important to understand the pluses and the minuses in the population being serviced, to be aware of the possible deficits as well as assets, the problems to be encountered as well as the sources of support. In the following project we will indicate the results of a pre-project survey of the human relations specialist school project. While many similar evaluations were conducted, this survey will serve to illustrate the pur-

Table 10–2
Key to Design and Expert Ratings of Helper Responses to Racial Stimulus Expressions

| Helpee Stimulus Expression | Helper Responses | DESIGN: Level of | | Overall Ratings |
		Responsiveness	Initiative	
I	1	H	L	3.5
	2	H	H	4.5
	3	L	L	1.0
	4	L	H	1.5
II	1	L	L	1.0
	2	H	L	3.0
	3	L	H	1.5
	4	H	H	4.0
III	1	L	H	1.5
	2	L	L	1.0
	3	H	H	3.5
	4	H	L	3.0
IV	1	H	L	3.0
	2	L	I	1.0
	3	H	H	3.5
	4	L	H	1.5
V	1	H	H	3.5
	2	L	L	1.5
	3	H	L	3.0
	4	L	H	1.0
VI	1	L	L	1.0
	2	L	H	1.5
	3	H	L	3.0
	4	H	H	4.0

poses and methodologies involved. In the present project, the black-white problem expression tape provided the basis for assessing the respective levels of functioning with the problems involved for large groups.

PROJECT 18
Racial Relations Responses in the School and the Community*

The purpose of the present survey was twofold: (1) to assess the differential levels of functioning of members of the school and the black community; and (2) to select from among the members of the black community those who were functioning at the highest levels.

*Reprinted in part from a research project conducted by Robert R. Carkhuff in February 1969.

Accordingly, groups of administrators, teachers, and counselors from the schools and groups of parents and volunteers for the specialist positions were presented with the six racial problem expressions and, following this, the racial expressions in conjunction with the alternate responses. The groups were instructed to formulate their responses to the expressions in writing. The level of communication was obtained by ratings of experts who had previously demonstrated a high degree of intra- and inter-rater reliability. The groups were then instructed to rate the alternative responses from 1 (least effective) to 5 (most effective) with 3 minimally effective. Level of discrimination was determined by obtaining absolute deviations (independent of direction) from the experts' preratings of the alternate responses.

The results appear in Table 10–3. As can be seen, with the exception of the specialists who were selected from the community volunteers all of the groups were communicating at a mean level of less than level 2 and discriminating at a mean deviation level of more than 1.

Both the representatives from the school and the community were functioning at levels of communication and discrimination far below what would be considered minimally effective. The low level of functioning of the school personnel appears to reflect a lack of systematic selection and training of these professionals. In this regard, while in general the school personnel are functioning at levels slightly higher than representatives of the community, personnel, as the specialists, can be selected at higher levels than the professional personnel.

The problem expressions can be broken down qualitatively as well as quantitatively. While the quantitative breakdown did not yield much variability at these low levels, a qualitative breakdown did. For example, many white male respondents found Excerpt 2, where a white male was describing his difficulties in relating to blacks, particularly black males,

Table 10–3

Level of Communication and Discrimination for Racial Relations Problem Expressions

Populations	Number of Subjects	Level of Communication		Level of Discrimination	
		Mean	sd	Mean	sd
School					
Administrators	20	1.6	.5	1.1	.3
Teachers	60	1.6	.5	1.2	.4
Counselors	40	1.8	.4	1.0	.3
Community					
Parents	60	1.5	.5	1.3	.4
Volunteers	52	1.5	.6	1.1	.4
Specialists (Selected)	14	2.0	.6	.8	.3

a difficult item to respond to: some actually could not hear it and others had difficulty formulating responses to it. In addition, many white respondents had difficulty identifying the race of the child as being white, whereas blacks indicated that the racial questions asked by the child were not the kind that the black child who already knew the answers asked. Many otherwise effective persons, black and white, found the white woman in the fifth excerpt most difficult to respond to because they wanted to confront her hostility rather than respond from within a base of understanding.

While the ratings for the community members might reflect a language handicap, this conjecture is not strongly supported by their low discrimination scores. However, sophistication in understanding of helping and human relations processes can yield some advantages to the scores. For example, the guidance and social adjustment counselors obtained communication and discrimination scores slightly higher than the other groups; indeed, they obtained scores very similar to advanced psychology students who have some knowledge of the areas.

In general, the responses of school personnel, while more intellectualized than those of the community representatives, emphasized response dispositions similar to those of the community personnel. That is, the responses of all groups tended to be directive, with questions and action oriented prescriptions and little communication of understanding. In this context, the discrimination of alternate responses can be broken down further. Here, again, the main finding is a tendency on the part of both black and white, sophisticated and naive, to prefer a directionful, action-oriented response. This finding is consistent with previous base rate evidence in this area.

The racial problem expressions and the alternate responses, it can be seen, can be extremely useful, not only in selection but also in giving us an index of the base rate of functioning of the populations involved. In surveying the school and community groups, we have found an extremely low level of functioning of school personnel would appear to compound rather than ameliorate the difficulties in communication and discrimination in this area that may have begun already at home. In this regard, it might have been helpful to obtain indexes of the children's base rate of functioning since they were the primary concern of the project. However, in the absence at home and school of adult models for effectiveness, it is highly improbable that they could produce results significantly different from those of their teachers. In any event, it was clear at this point that the tasks which lay ahead for the specialists were extremely difficult ones.

It is to be emphasized that the racial relations problem expressions constituted only one index in the selection of specialists.

PROJECT 19
Selection of Specialists*

The selection of the specialists took place in two phases in December, 1968. The first phase consisted of an elaborate selection procedure conducted by the A.I.C. Center. The second phase consisted of an approximately 5-minute interview conducted by a joint panel of School Department and Model Cities personnel in order to review prospective candidates.

The first phase of selection is based upon the most extensively validated selection procedures available. Based upon the selection principle that the best index of a future criterion is a previous index of that criterion, the procedures simply assess the candidate's present level of functioning in the types of activities in which they will be involved on the job.

The assessment devices included the following 6 devices falling into three categories:

A. Each candidate or prospective helper was cast in the helping role with a black helpee with instructions to "be as helpful as you can in aiding this helpee."
   1. *Objective ratings of verbal communication:* The sessions were tape recorded and the helper was rated by trained raters as to the level of empathic understanding he communicated and the level of self-exploration of the problem area which he elicited from the helpee.
   2. *Helpee's ratings of verbal communication:* The helpers were rated by the helpees as to how effectively the helpers were able to enter the helpees' frame of reference.
B. Each candidate formulated his written responses to a series of tape-recorded "stimulus expressions" specifically designed to tap his ability to function in the racial relations area. The excerpts included prototypical problems of white and black and male and female adults and children.
   1. *Objective ratings of written communication:* The candidates' responses were rated as to their level of communication of responsiveness and initiative or action-orientation.
   2. *Objective ratings of discrimination:* The candidates rated alternate responses (to each stimulus expression) varying level of responsiveness and initiative in random high (H) and low (L) combinations (HH, HL, LH, LL); discrimination scores

*Reprinted in part with permission from the *Journal of Counseling Psychology*, 1970, 17, 443–450, where it first appeared as "The Selection and Training of Human Relations Specialists," by Robert R. Carkhuff and Andrew H. Griffin.

were obtained by absolute deviations from the ratings of experts.

C. Each candidate for approximately one-half hour was interviewed and rated as to his potential level of functioning.

    1. Each candidate was interviewed and rated by a black expert.

    2. Each candidate was interviewed and rated by a white expert.

Sixty-five candidates, overwhelmingly black in number, completed the selection tests. Of these 18 were invited back. At this point a seventh selection index was employed. Operating with the assumption that the best index of how an individual trainee might utilize a total training program would be to obtain an index of how he utilizes an analogue of that training, the following additional selection procedure was employed:

D. *Trainer ratings of effects of training:* Each of the 18 candidates received 2 hours of training in empathy and was rated by the trainer as to his ability to utilize the training experience.

The AIC Center submitted a list of 14 primary and 3 alternate candidates, all black, to the director of the PACE project. The black candidates, perhaps due in part to the nature of the selection indexes based upon working with black students and racial relations problems, demonstrated a higher level of functioning than whites. In addition to servicing the students involved and making a massive infusion of black models, there were distinct advantages in opening employment opportunities for effective blacks.

At this point, the second phase of selection took place. In interviews described as lasting "approximately 5 minutes or less," two members of the School Department and two members of the Model Cities Policy Board screened the top 30 candidates. They rejected three of the primary recommendations, including the highest recommendation, and instituted three of their own choices, one of whom was from the alternate list and one of whom, a white woman, was near the bottom of the list of 30 candidates.

As can be seen in Table 10–4, the trainees selected were at significantly higher levels of overall functioning ($p < .05$) on all five rating in-

Table 10–4
Comparison of Selected and Nonselected Population Ratings

Population	Mean Objective Tape Ratings		Mean Interviewee Ratings		Mean Standard Tape Ratings		Mean Discrimination Standard Responses		Mean Interviewer Ratings	
	M	sd	M	sd	M	sd	M	sd	M	sd
Selected (N = 14)	2.0	.6	2.9	.5	1.9	.5	.8	.3	2.5	.4
Non-selected (N = 52)	1.5	.6	2.4	.6	1.4	.5	1.1	.4	2.0	.5

Table 10–5
Comparison of Selected and Deselected Groups' Empathy Ratings after Preliminary
Training

Population	Pre-testing Empathy Level		Post-Preliminary Empathy Training	
	M	sd	M	sd
Selected	2.0	.5	2.9	.4
(N = 11)				
Deselected	2.0	.6	2.4	.5
(N = 3)				

dexes, the objective tape ratings of the interviews conducted by the candidate, the standard counselee's evaluation of the candidates' functioning in
the interview, the ratings of the candidates' written responses to standard
tapes and their discrimination scores and the interviewer's ratings of potential. The discrimination scores of the selected trainees are lower or more accurate than those of the nonselected trainees, i.e. indicating less deviation
from the experts' ratings.

Table 10–5 describes the levels of empathy communicated by the
trainees where cast in the helping role with a standard counselee. The
deselected trainees, while originally not significantly different from the
trainees selected for advanced training, did not utilize the preliminary
empathy training most efficiently and effectively. The 11 selected for advanced training went to nearly minimally effective levels of functioning
on the empathy dimensions in only two weeks of training.

In preparation for the difficult tasks which lay ahead the characteristics
for which the specialists were selected were systematically developed in training.

PROJECT 20
Training of Specialists*

The training of the human relations specialists was conducted almost
entirely by the AIC Center. Although Pupil Personnel Services was man-
dated to offer their contribution this consisted of one 2-hour session on
rules, regulations and procedures. The training program consisted of two
phases. The first phase consisted of five weeks of training at 35 hours a
week for a total of 175 hours. The second phase consisted of follow-up
supervision of twice weekly 2-hour sessions which over a year have totaled

*Reprinted in part with permission from the *Journal of Counseling Psychology*, 1970, 17,
443–450, where it first appeared as "The Selection and Training of Human Relations Specialists," by Robert R. Carkhuff and Andrew H. Griffin.

200 hours. In addition, during this second phase the specialists have participated in three separate 2-week programs which totaled 130 hours.

The training which the specialists received may be termed systematic human relations training. The term derives from the systematic application to training of those ingredients or conditions found to be effective in all helping and human relationships. Basically, the model indicates that all human relationships, including counseling and teaching, may have constructive consequences. The dimensions which can be rated to account for human effectiveness include responsive conditions (responding to another person's experience) such as empathic understanding, respect and specificity of expression, and initiative dimensions (initiating from one's own experience) such as genuineness, confrontation and interpretations of immediacy.

Systematic human relations training, then, involves a systematic step-by-step succession of reinforcing experiences in which the trainee learns to communicate first the responsive dimensions then the initiative dimensions. The trainees also learn systematic problem-solving activities in order to enable them to help their helpees to develop courses of action.

It should be mentioned that after two weeks of training a series of incidents occurred which led to a stand by the AIC Center not to endorse three of the candidates for training. While the Center's stand risked its losing its training responsibility, it was not removed from this training capacity, and two of the candidates were replaced and a third was reassigned to Social and Psychological Services. Thus, 13 specialists functioned under the sponsorship of the AIC Center.

In the follow-up supervision phase the specialists have been supervised (1) in their casework activities and (2) in their adjustment to their roles as functional professionals in the Springfield School Department. In addition, the specialists have participated in formal graduate programs in (1) Education and Human Relations and (2) the Teaching of Black History and (3) a special program in the Development of Effective Courses of Action with School Children.

Thus, *in total the human relations specialists have received over 500 hours of training, most of it systematic, for the equivalent of over one full year's college training in helping and human relations skills.*

Table 10–6 describes the levels of trainee functioning on all dimensions when cast in the helping role with a standard counselee before, during and following training. The training program was effective in eliciting change in the level of interpersonal functioning of the advanced trainees. The advanced trainees' level of functioning in the helping role on all dimensions is significantly greater ($p < .01$) at the end than at the beginning of the 150 hours of training. In addition, as a group the trainees are functioning above minimally effective levels, with few falling below level 3.0 on any one dimension.

Table 10–6

Effects of Advanced Training in Interpersonal Skills upon Level of Interpersonal Functioning

	INTERPERSONAL DIMENSIONS					
	Responsive				Initiative	
			Concrete-	Genuine-	Confron-	
	Empathy	Respect	ness	ness	tation	Immediacy
	M sd	M sd	M sd	M sd	M sd	M sd
Pre-training (N = 13)	2.0 .5	2.0 .5	1.9 .6	2.2 .5	1.9 .6	1.7 .5
Post-Preliminary Training (N = 13)	2.9 .5	2.7 .5	2.2 .5	2.2 .5	2.0 .6	2.0 .5
Post-Advanced Training (N = 13)	3.2 .4	3.3 .5	3.1 .5	3.0 .4	3.3 .5	3.4 .3

The selection procedures in application projects are complex but, we believe, necessary, the basic assumption being that while any one measure may be inadequate, all together will yield relatively superior results in personnel. Thus, employing the principle of selection, that the best indices of future criteria are previous indices of those criteria, we have implemented several procedures. First, we have cast the candidate in the helping role with counselees with the kinds of problems that typify the particular setting involved. Second, we have assessed the counselee's experience of the candidate's level of functioning. Third, we have standardized these activities with representative counselee stimulus expressions. Fourth, we have standardized our indexes of discrimination of effective counselor responses, a necessary but not sufficient condition of communication. In addition, we have obtained estimates of potential from experienced counselor-trainers. Finally, employing the principle that the best index of how a trainee might utilize a total training experience will be how he utilizes an analogue of that experience, we have deselected on the basis of those least able to make effective use of the training.

While we research our applications, application differs from research programs. In preliminary phases of planning we are free to conduct predictive validity studies employing all candidates. In application we wish to minimize our losses or "false positives." It is noteworthy that while some trainees who were not selected may have gone on to function effectively, those who were selected all functioned at approximately level 3.0 on all dimensions following training.

In addition, while establishing the predictive relationship of any individual index with our final outcome measure, functioning in the helping role is not quite meaningful with this limited segment of the population; the objective ratings of functioning in the helping role and of responses to standard stimuli appear most related to ultimate functioning in the helping role. Again, the best index of future criteria are previous indexes of these criteria.

According to the principle of training, the best training program is one which trains the trainees on dimensions which have been related to the outcomes which we wish to influence. Here the most effective training program for helping is one which emphasizes the critical dimensions of these roles, and this appears to have validity for social action programs.

Most important, the specialists appeared to have the greatest impact upon the black students. One year after the inception of the program, the specialists function with the following responsibilities: (1) treatment: direct social counseling with student counselees in conjunction with movement into the home and school environment to counsel parents and teachers; (2) training: training in interpersonal skills for parents, students and teachers; (3) teaching: organizing the children and their parents in work-study groups emphasizing black culture and social awareness and consulting with teachers with an interest in these areas. Additional evaluations are currently being conducted to assess the treatment, training and teaching effectiveness of the specialists in these capacities.

PEOPLE ARE PRODUCTS

In any meaningful human resource development program the people are the products (Carkhuff, 1969a, 1969b). In the human relations specialist program not just the students and parents, and the teachers and administrators,[1] but the specialists themselves are the products. Not only are the specialists able to facilitate the adjustment and the effectiveness of the people with whom they are working but their own resources are developed. A new life unfolds for the specialist. He acquires new skills and develops new meaning in service. Human service is for him truly a preferred motive for life.

Unfortunately, not all systems are ready for such growth—especially from noncredentialed persons—especially from blacks. It is often not politically expedient for many systems to take the rational course, the effective course. Indeed, it is politically naive to act with constructive directionality in developing human resources. In a world where children with the "wrong" pigment are bussed from their own miserable neighborhood schools to someone else's miserable neighborhood school—it is even sillier to bus them both ways: the "right" pigment to the "wrong" pigment's miserable school and the "wrong" pigment to the "right" pigment's miserable school—it is time to call the politicians' hand. Politics as we know them today are nonfunctional archaic vestiges. The choice is a simple one: *either politics and politicians as we know them must go, or human resources and human beings must continue to die.*

[1] The effectiveness of the human relations specialists in treatment, training, and teaching is assessed in Chapter 14, "Functionality and Effectiveness."

PROJECT 21
Summary and Recommendations
for the Specialist Program*

No other specialty areas in education have been as systematically selected as the human relations specialists. One can become a teacher with a minimal interview beyond the establishing of formal college credentials. One can become a supervisor without establishing his level of functioning and outcome of his work in his specialty area. One can become a member of the School Committee with no relevant credentials at all.

No other speciality areas in education have been as systematically trained as the human relations specialists. Indeed, *it is doubtful that there are any teachers, counselors, or administrators who have amassed the number of hours of training specifically in helping and human relations skills.* A survey of 70 supervisory counselors, teachers, and administrators at the inception of the specialist program indicates that most are not functioning effectively in interpersonal areas, particularly those involving racial relations. The issue is one of functional professionalism; that is, can the person do what he is paid to do? Some credentialed professionals are functional professionals. Others can be trained to become functional professionals.

No other speciality areas in education have been as systematically assessed as the human relations specialists. In this regard, we understand that the School Department is again conducting still another evaluation. Translated, this means that the principals are asked how the specialists are doing. The principals, in turn, will solicit opinions from teachers and counselors. The point is this: *there would be no specialist programs if these personnel had been effective in discharging their responsibilities to minority groups in the first place.* The same people who have created the problems cannot constitute the court of last appeal for the solution of these problems. The people who are being serviced, particularly the students, black and white, must have a voice. In this regard, the original data of the interesting survey courageously conducted by one principal at one junior high school to assess the effectiveness of all school personnel should be made public and should be replicated at all schools. More relevant, any specialty's contribution should be translated into objective evidence of achievement. Future research programs could assess the effectiveness of counselors, teachers, and administrators in the same manner. *The final test of any program, of course, should be an empirical one: the differential effects of functional and credentialed professionals in different specialty areas of*

*Reprinted in part from a mimeographed paper entitled "Description and Evaluation of the Human Relations Specialist Program in the Springfield School Department," written in February 1970, by Robert R. Carkhuff, and presented before the Massachusetts Legislature Joint Subcommittee on Education in February 1970 by Andrew H. Griffin.

work with students might be studied. The results might encourage the School Department to collapse or expand the functional professional program, the latter course, if chosen, at great potential saving to the School Department.

No other specialty areas in education have demonstrated such dramatically positive results. The fact is that the specialists have done so with daily obstacles beyond those experienced by any other group of professionals. The fact is that they have done so with no public statements of endorsement from the school administration and School Committee, little remuneration and much abuse. However, on the evaluation in June of 1969, 6 of the 7 principals involved endorsed the program, adding individually that they felt that they had been fortunate in obtaining the best team of specialists, reflecting no doubt a bias against the possibility of success of the program. In the same evaluation, 6 of the 7 principals involved stated that they would take their specialists' teams with them if they transferred schools. Two such principals have made such a transfer and have taken their specialists' teams with them. Only one of the 7 principals has made public statements endorsing the specialist program. Perhaps it is time we addressed ourselves to evaluating a principal who can demonstrate success, instead of listening to the criticisms of a principal who cannot. Perhaps it is time that we studied winners, instead of losers. Perhaps it is time we evaluated the evaluators.

No other school system in America can claim a human relations program like Springfield's in spite of all the handicaps. No other *system* in America can claim the success of a human relations program like Springfield's in spite of all the handicaps. However, the low salaries are not conducive to the sacrifice which the specialists have to make. (Two have left their jobs for better-paying positions in the same area, one for marriage.) Vacancies have not been filled because of the alleged "need for evaluation." The up-and-out possibilities for supervisory roles and special assistant principalships (roles in which several specialists are periodically employed and one is continuously employed) have not been created. The program has not been expanded. Continuing as it is, with all of the success which it has demonstrated, it must collapse. And with it, the collapse of a principal means of not only ameliorating the racial tensions but also of increasing the quality of education for white as well as black and Spanish students, the only reason for the existence of all paid school department personnel.

REFERENCES

Carkhuff, R. R. *Helping and human relations: A primer for lay and professional helpers.* Vol. I. *Selection and training.* New York: Holt, Rinehart and Winston, 1969. (a)

Carkhuff, R. R. *Helping and human relations: A primer for lay and professional helpers.* Vol. II. *Practice and research.* New York: Holt, Rinehart and Winston, 1969. (b)

Carkhuff, R. R., & Griffin, A. H. The selection and training of human relations specialists. *Journal of Counseling Psychology,* 1970, **17,** 443–450.

CHAPTER 11
Internship as a Preferred Mode of Learning

The great "edge" that the upper class in its titular nobility has consciously held over the middle and lower classes has not been its bloodlines. Rather, it has been the system disposed to tutoring the children in everything from language through horsemanship and fencing to etiquette. The tutorial approach systematically increases the response repertoire of the learner and the resultant greater number of responses available to the individual learner has constituted his "edge" over other children, and later on, other adults. In adult life, the upper-class product interns in the same manner for a partnership in a law firm or the presidency of a corporation. The tutorial and internship systems are perhaps the most effective learning programs known to man in terms of the results they produce. Indeed, the resultant "edge" which we write of, while relative to others, most closely approximates an absolute sharpness.

Similarly, the middle class in its motivated ignorance acts unconsciously to maintain its "edge" over its lower-class counterparts. It can neither understand nor afford the true sources of effectiveness. But it defends its "edge" nevertheless! It defends its "edge" in favoring the status quo in the educational systems that "educate" its children. It defends the status quo—not because it is the most effective system available—indeed, in spite of the fact that its children will never actualize their own talents in such a system—but simply because the system is the source of its "edge," relative and tenuous though the "edge" be.

This is the "edge" system. Its methodologies were effective for accomplishing what was intended. Its methodologies can still be effective—only for different purposes. Now they can be put to the use of all, for the good of all.

The point is that we cut the Gordian knot of racial and class disharmony by instituting a system whereby the people at the top open up the possibility for the people at the bottom to learn in the same way that they did. This is the only real way. This is the only honest way. Open the system up and equip the individuals involved with the skills they need to compete in a free and open market.

The principle involved is one of internship, apprenticeship, or tutorial learning. The principle of internship simply means that the individual intern has the opportunity for close and intense study of the skills of his mentor.

The principle of internship does not mean that anyone is automatically eligible to intern for the presidency of a program. It does mean that internships will be opened up to anyone who is qualified. It does mean that there will be openings for internships at the different steps in the hierarchy that will qualify an individual for a particular internship. For example, a teacher or principal who qualifies on all counts may intern for the superintendency of schools. While there may never be an opening in the particular system involved, there may be openings in other systems, and when he is qualified he can apply for those positions. It would be analogous to the upward mobility of an unskilled worker to skilled worker: he starts at the bottom as an unskilled worker, and he qualifies for an internship at the next level only as he has mastered the skills at the previous level.

Now, no one is so naive as to believe that power willingly creates power. However, power threatened with the loss of power creates power. In the same context, while a man might not under ordinary circumstances train himself out of a job, in the most effective of systems this would be prerequisite to his moving on to the next position. That is, as he trains another, he is freed to engage in higher level activities, thus preparing him for acquiring the skills necessary to discharge the responsibilities at the next level of functioning.

TRAINING TRAINERS IN INTERPERSONAL SKILLS

The Springfield Concentrated Employment Program, Department of Labor, dedicated to preparing hard-core unemployed and underemployed for meaningful vocations, was staffed primarily by persons who were, themselves, drawn from the ranks of the unemployed and underemployed. While they were not operating with the benefit of internship with an existing and effective business or industry, within their own program, they struggled as best they could to prepare themselves for positions in business and industry. However, without the benefit of systematic training programs in definable skills we could not consider the greatest number of them to be functional professionals. The first step, then, was to equip key persons with the skills they needed in order (1) to function effectively on the job, and (2) to transmit the skills effectively to others, clientele as well as colleagues.

A training program in the interpersonal skills was necessary to effect constructive relationships with fellow staff members and clients. The next step was to equip the program with its own inservice training capacity, which required selecting and training trainers for this purpose. In effect, the task of the initial training agency, rather than continuing on the usual consultation basis, was to train itself out of a job and develop the consultation service within the employment program, utilizing the resources of the program.

Again, the first job in selecting from among 150 potential candidates was to develop standard indexes of prototypical employment problems.

PROJECT 22

Standardized Problems and Responses with Hard-Core Unemployed*

Two problems that presented particular difficulty for personnel in the Concentrated Employment Program were (1) the aggressive alcoholic, and (2) the reluctant streetwalker. Accordingly, representative stimulus expressions were developed (see Table 11–1). In addition, related helper

Table 11–1
Developing Standard Indexes of Hard-Core Employment Problems

INSTRUCTIONS

The following are a couple of typical kinds of situations that a counselor in CEP or some other kind of program might find when he's out on the job.

What we'd like you to do is try and make that kind of response that would be most helpful to the person involved. In other words, if you ran into this kind of person on your job, what kinds of things would you say to him in order to try and get him involved in the program that you're pushing?

HARD-CORE UNEMPLOYMENT TAPE

Excerpt 1

Helpee: You people are always coming around wanting me to work. I don't want to work. I don't need no job. Look at me. I don't feel like working. I got other things to do beside work and work just don't bother me and I don't bother work. I got children to take care of and I just don't need no job. You want to train peoples, and it'll never work out—just always out there—it ends up the same way like it starts and I don't need no job so go away—take it someplace else.

Trainer: Now, we would like you to listen to the following four different kinds of responses that might be made to this kind of a situation, and we would like you to rate them from 1–5 with 5 being the very best kind of response that you might have made and 1 being the worst kind of response that you might have made. Three would be something in between where it's a pretty good response but it's really not as good as it could be and 4 would be somewhat better than that and 2 would be somewhat worse than that. So you can rate it anywhere from 1–5 and if necessary you can split the gaps rating 1.5, 2.5, 3.5 or 4.5.

*Reprinted in part with permission from the *Journal of Clinical Psychology*, 1971, **27**, 163–165, where it first appeared as "The Selection and Training of Functional Professionals for Concentrated Employment Programs," by Robert R. Carkhuff and Andrew H. Griffin.

Table 11–1

Developing Standard Indexes of Hard-Core Employment Problems (*cont.*)

Helper:

Responses to Excerpt 1:

Response 1: You've had it with these guys. You're frustrated and you're tired of having them coming around to your place and offering you all these real plums or pies in the skies and nothing coming through.

Response 2: You know, what you're really telling me is that you're just like all the rest of the folk, you know, you're lazy and you're tired and therefore you gave up. Forget it. Right?

Response 3: Hey, what's the matter with you? Don't you recognize something good for you? Have you talked to your minister? Have you gone to get outside help? You have to get yourself together. Go outside and find out what's going on here.

Response 4: Look, baby, you're down—I know you're down because I've been that route myself—but I still see within you—I still see within you that piece of spark and that life that I know that you have, and I know that you want up and you want out and you want something for real.

Excerpt 2:

Helpee: Hi Dad! They tell me you have a job going down here, and I want me a job right now! And I want no mess. I'm ready to work and I can do anything anybody else can do. I can do your job just as good as you can do it—just give me the chance to get there. I'll get there. Just show me how to do it, and I'll do it. Look, I've been working hard ever since I was born and I know that if I get an opportunity that I can do it, but I want me a job where I don't have to get my hands dirty no more. Man, I have to go home and get my fingers cleaned out. I worked with the pigs and all that sort of stuff. Man, I don't need to work with no pigs no more. I want to sit behind a desk and relax, wear a tie, use a pencil. Now, you know me and I know you. We drank together, we played together, we went to school together. Now you got a job and I got nothing. I want the same thing you got.

Helper Responses to Excerpt 2:

Response 1: Look, man, I know one thing. The only reason you want to get behind this desk is because you think you can get up and get out there and chase those women and go to them bars whenever you want to.

Response 2: Look, man, what you're saying is this: You've been out there, you know what it's like and now you want back in.

Response 3: Look, man, you make me feel real good. It means you're ready to give up that street life and you're willing to pay the price—you're willing to work to come on home.

Response 4: Man, why do you come screaming on me? Why don't you go see your councilman, go see your senator, go see somebody up there in the big time. I only got a little job. Why are you going to scream on me now?

responses, pre-rated by experts, were designed to obtain an index of the candidate's level of discrimination.

Also, while the communication levels are obtained from objective ratings, a key for the rationale and the experts' ratings for the alternate responses will provide a basis for determining level of discrimination by obtaining deviations from expert ratings (See Table 11–2).

Table 11–2
Key to Design and Expert Ratings of Helper Responses to Employment Stimulus Expressions

Helper Stimulus Expression	Helper Responses	DESIGN: Level of Responsiveness	Initiative	Overall Ratings
I	1	H	L	3.0
	2	L	L	1.0
	3	L	H	1.5
	4	H	H	3.5
II	1	L	L	1.0
	2	H	L	3.0
	3	H	H	3.5
	4	L	H	1.5

It is to be emphasized again that standard employment selections were only one of many indexes used in selecting the employment trainers.

PROJECT 23

Selection of Employment Trainers*

Out of 150 employees of the Concentrated Employment Program, 72 completed the procedures employed for the selection of inservice trainers in interpersonal skills. First, the tasks of the employment program were surveyed in order to develop representative problems. Difficult situations developed to typify everyday work with people "off the streets" were twofold: (a) an aggressive and belligerent alcoholic male; and (b) a passive and despondent female streetwalker. Real helpees who typified these problems were selected and trained briefly to serve as standard helpees. The candidates, then, were tested on a variety of relevant indexes: (1) each was cast in the helping role on two separate occasions with each of the two standard helpees and the process was recorded and rated for the level of interpersonal functioning of the helper; (2) each standard helpee rated the candidate on his level of functioning as experienced by the helpee; (3) each candidate's written responses to tape recorded standard helpee stimulus expressions by the two helpees (see Table 11–1) were rated for level of interpersonal skills; (4) each candidate's ratings of four alternative helper

*Reprinted in part with permission from the *Journal of Clinical Psychology*, 1971, **27**, 163–165, where it first appeared as "The Selection and Training of Functional Professionals for Concentrated Employment Programs," by Robert R. Carkhuff and Andrew H. Griffin.

Table 11–3
Comparison of Selected and Nonselected Population Ratings

Population	Mean Objective Tape Ratings		Mean Interviewee Ratings		Mean Standard Tape Ratings		Mean Discrimination Standard Responses		Mean Interviewer Ratings		Mean Supervisor Ratings	
	M	sd	M	sd	M	sd	M	sd	M	sd	M	sd
Selected (N = 22)	2.0	.5	3.3	.4	1.8	.4	1.1	.3	2.8	.5	3.5	.4
Nonselected (N = 50)	1.4	.5	2.5	.6	1.3	.4	1.4	.4	2.0	.6	3.0	.4

responses (in which level of responsive and initiative dimensions were crossed at high and low levels) to each standard stimulus expression were scored for their deviation from the ratings of experts who had demonstrated the predictive validity of their ratings in previous studies (see Table 11–2); (5) each candidate was interviewed by two experienced staff members, one white and one black, and rated on his potential for functioning effectively; (6) each trainee was rated by his work supervisor on the basis of his past work performance. All ratings were done on 5-point scales ranging from level 5, which is most effective to level 1, which is least effective, with level 3 designated as minimally effective. The ratings on the six different indexes were simply averaged and the top 22 candidates were selected for training. A seventh index was introduced after ten hours of training at which point those trainees who demonstrated the least ability to make use of the training program were deselected or eliminated from training.

As can be seen in Table 11–3, the trainees selected were functioning at significantly higher levels ($p < .05$) of all six rating indexes, the objective tape ratings of the two interviews conducted by the candidate, the standard helpees' evaluation of the candidates' functioning in the interviews, the ratings of the candidates' written responses to standard tapes, the interviewer's ratings of potential and the supervisors' evaluations of past work performance. As can also be seen, the ratings of the interviewees, the interviewers and the supervisors were higher than the objective ratings of the

Table 11–4
Comparison of Selected and Deselected Groups' Empathy Ratings after Preliminary Training

Population	Pre-testing Empathy Level		Post-Preliminary Empathy Training	
	M	sd	M	sd
Selected (N = 14)	2.0	.5	2.7	.4
Deselected (N = 8)	2.0	.4	2.2	.5

candidates' functioning in the helping role or responses to standard stimulus expressions.

In Table 11–4 we see that the deselected trainees, while originally not significantly different from the trainees selected for advanced training did not utilize the ten hours of preliminary empathy training most efficiently and most effectively. The 14 trainees selected for advanced training went to nearly minimally effective levels of functioning on the empathy dimension in only ten hours of intensified training.

Again, the characteristics for which the candidates were selected, their interpersonal skills, were systematically intensified over the course of training.

PROJECT 24

Training of Employment Trainers*

All 22 trainees received ten hours of preliminary communication training in empathy, the key helping ingredient. After the tenth hour those trainees who demonstrated the highest levels of empathic communication in the helping role were retained while the remainder were deselected. The 14 trainees (all were black) who were retained completed 100 hours of systematic training divided into two phases: the first focused upon those skills necessary to implement an effective helping process; the second focused upon those skills necessary to train others to be effective helpers. The helping skills included advanced training in the operationalization of empathy, respect, concreteness, genuineness, confrontation and immediacy as well as the development of effective courses of action. The training skills included practicum experience in transmitting the helping skills.

In the context of high levels of conditions offered by the trainers, the training utilized the scales that had been employed in assessing helping outcome to shape trainee functioning: trainees received immediate and concrete feedback in the form of ratings of their helping effectiveness by the trainers and other trainees in the group. For example, the first goal of empathy training was to establish an interchangeable base of communication (level 3) in which the helper accurately expresses at least the feeling and personal meaning which the helpee has expressed. At higher and lower levels, there would be indications from the helpee's response to the helper's offering that the helper had been additive (levels 4 and 5) or subtractive

*Reprinted in part with permission from the *Journal of Clinical Psychology*, 1971, 27, 163–165, where it first appeared as "The Selection and Training of Functional Professionals for Concentrated Employment Programs," by Robert R. Carkhuff and Andrew H. Griffin.

Table 11–5

Effects of Advanced Training in Interpersonal Skills upon Level of Interpersonal Functioning

	Empathy		Responsive Respect		Concrete-ness		Genuine-ness		Initiative Confron-tation		Immediacy	
	M	*sd*	*M*	*sd*	*M*	*sd*	*M*	*sd*	*M*	*sd*	*M*	*sd*
Pre-training (N = 14)	2.0	.5	2.1	.6	1.8	.5	2.1	.4	2.0	.5	1.5	.6
Post-Preliminary Training (N = 14)	2.7	.5	2.5	.5	2.0	.4	2.1	.5	2.0	.4	1.9	.5
Post-Advanced Training (N = 14)	3.3	.5	3.2	.5	3.0	.4	3.3	.4	3.4	.4	3.2	.4

INTERPERSONAL DIMENSIONS

(levels 1 and 2) in his communication, i.e. that the helper had enabled the helpee to explore, experience and understand himself at deeper levels or he had held the helpee back from doing so. Other dimensions were operationalized in a similar manner. At the beginning and end of training all advanced trainees were assessed on their level of functioning on all relevant dimensions. The training was conducted by two high level and experienced helper-trainers (a mean level of functioning of 4.0 across all dimensions).

The final outcome criteria was the level of effective functioning in the helping role with helpees with problems typical of that setting. This index was obtained by objective ratings of the taped sessions. Ratings of communication level were accomplished employing the same scales by experienced raters of demonstrated rate-rerate reliabilities who exhibited Pearson product moment inter-rater reliabilities in the .80's and .90's for all dimensions. Functioning in the helping role was the goal of training and the prerequisite for being effective trainers. In addition, the outcome criteria had been most extensively related to helpee change or gain.

As we note in Table 11–5, the training program is effective in eliciting change in the level of interpersonal functioning of the advanced trainees. The advanced trainee's level of functioning in the helping role on all dimensions is significantly greater ($p < .01$) at the end than at the beginning of the 100 hours of training. In addition, as a group the trainees are functioning above minimally effective levels, with very few falling below level 3.0 on any one dimension.

Beyond training trainers for transmitting interpersonal skills, the employment program was further utilized for training hard-core unemployed for new careers in human services. Thus, following the selection and training of the employment trainers we now focus upon the functioning of some of the trainers in training others.

PROJECT 25
Internships
in Human Services*

The six highest of the 14 functional professional trainers who completed advanced training were assigned to conduct a New Careers program, one as liaison between the Human Relations Center and the New Careers project, one as coordinator of the program and four as teacher-counselors. The New Careers project was a full-time program developed to prepare approximately 60 unemployed or underemployed people every six months for careers in the human service areas for nonprofit agencies, i.e. positions such as casework aides in welfare agencies. The New Careers trainees were assigned by a component of the Concentrated Employment Program after brief screening interviews conducted largely by other graduates of the training program.

The mornings of each week were organized around training in interpersonal skills or, as it was known, systematic human relations training, while the afternoons were organized around remedial skills. Thus, if a trainee attended sessions regularly, half of his total of nearly 1,000 hours was spent on human relations training. The training program implemented was the same as that accomplished with the functional professional trainers, an integrated didactic and experiential approach in which the functional professional trainers now systematically shaped interpersonal skills employing previously validated rating scales. The functional professional trainers received five hours' group supervision time weekly from the Human Relations Center staff. The New Careers trainees were tested in the helping role at the beginning and at the midpoint of the training period.

Those six New Careers trainees who functioned at the highest levels at the midpoint testing were assigned to the functional professional trainers as assistants or interns, one each to the liaison person, coordinator and the teacher-counselors, with the functional professional trainers functioning in effect as overall consultants. In addition, the next twelve highest level functioning trainees were assigned to the four teacher-counselors, three as interns or assistants, to each one of the teacher-counselor interns, with responsibilities for tutoring and counseling within the same training program those assigned trainees who had demonstrated less expertise in human relations skills. Thus, 18 of the trainees now became part of the staff.

In effect, the project underwent a decentralization process with each teacher-counselor now responsible for his own training operation. Potential

*Reprinted in part with permission from the *Journal of Counseling Psychology*, 1971, 18, 147–151, where the article first appeared as "Principles of Social Action in Training for New Careers in Human Services," by Robert R. Carkhuff.

benefits could accrue not only to the interns but also to the teacher-counselors who were now able to share directly the responsibility for the students' experience of the program. In addition, both the functional professional trainers and the interns continued to receive five hours weekly group supervision from the Human Relations Center. The New Careers trainees who had not succeeded in demonstrating high levels of expertise were tested again at the end of the six months' training.

As trainees functioned at minimally effective levels and as job positions opened, the trainees were assigned to the positions. The positions were with social service agencies in the local community. At first the trainees worked one day a week and were trained the other four days; gradually as they demonstrated improved functioning they worked two, three, four and finally full-time, five days per week. Weekly supervision was maintained. At the end of training all of the trainees who successfully achieved minimal levels of functioning were awarded 12 college credits in human relations by agreement with American International College.

The level of functioning of the trainers and trainees when cast in the helping role can be seen in Table 11–6. As can be seen, the levels of interpersonal skills at the midpoint or three-month testing are significantly greater ($p < .05$) than at the beginning of training, thus indicating the effectiveness of lay trainers for many of the trainees. As can also be seen the 18 trainees selected as interns were functioning at levels significantly higher ($p < .05$) than the population of trainees from which they were drawn, thus indicating the basis for their selection as trainer-interns. Finally, the post-testing results indicate that the tutored trainees established levels significantly higher ($p < .05$) than at the midpoint testing, thus indicating the effectiveness of the intern program in eliciting change over and above that originally elicited by the lay trainers.

Let us review the projects according to the principles of social action. First, indigenous lay personnel may be effectively utilized in social action programs. The literature indicates that functional professionals do as well as or better in both the training and the practice of helping than credentialed professionals. This project supports the efficacy of employing lay personnel as trainer-helpers. The natural outlet for credentialed professionals is to create, plan, develop and assess programs in which lay personnel may be effectively utilized.

Second, systematic selection and training procedures are most effective. Here the evidence is again consistent with the literature. The systematic selection and training procedures employed have demonstrated their effectiveness. The principles of selection and training, both based upon functional criteria and methodologies, have been successful in translating their procedures to tangible human benefits.

In this regard, it is clear that not all candidates can be eligible for the responsibilities as functional professional trainers. Success was built in by

Table 11-6
Effects of Training upon the Levels of Interpersonal Functioning of Trainers, Interns, and Trainees

		DIMENSIONS					
		Responsive			Initiative		
		Empathy	Respect	Concreteness	Genuineness	Confrontation	Immediacy
Population	Testing Period	M sd	M sd	M sd	M sd	M sd	M sd
Functional Professional Trainers (N = 6)	(Pre)	3.4 .4	3.3 .3	3.2 .4	3.3 .5	3.4 .4	3.2 .4
New Careers Trainees (N = 63)	(Pre)	1.4 .5	1.4 .6	1.5 .5	1.6 .5	1.5 .6	1.3 .5
New Careers Trainees (N = 45)	(Mid-Pt)	2.1 .5	2.2 .5	2.3 .4	2.0 .5	2.1 .5	1.9 .6
New Careers Trainer-Interns (N = 18)	(Mid-Pt)	2.9 .4	2.8 .4	2.8 .3	2.8 .4	2.9 .5	2.7 .4
New Careers Trainees	(Post)	2.5 .5	2.5 .4	2.6 .5	2.5 .4	2.6 .5	2.5 .5

selecting and training only those who were functioning at the very highest levels of those skills which they were to employ in training others. A critical difference between social action programs developed to meet crises and the pilot projects that were conducted in preparation for the social action projects is that the former cannot afford the luxury of not selecting and conducting predictive validity studies: too much is at stake and the highest level functioning persons available must be employed. Those who were trained by the functional professionals, in turn, the New Careers candidates, were not selected as systematically or as stringently, for they represented more fully the population from which they were drawn, the hard-core unemployed.

Third, social action programs equipped with their own inservice training capacity are most effective. Not only does this make the knowledge of the professionals directly available but also gives the lay personnel training responsibilities as functional professionals. In addition, the recognition that the trainer is, in effect, training himself out of a job offers the professional an opportunity to bridge the gap between the advantaged and the disadvantaged. Of course, all of this does not exclude periodic supervision and other contacts which were maintained throughout the duration of this program.

Finally, the principle of an internship for every job has functional utility. Not only does the intern prepare himself for his supervisor's job but also does the supervisor have the opportunity to extend himself into new areas of creativity and responsibility. In addition, the internship principle offers the program the possibility of replacement of personnel at any point should a position open up due to new job opportunities. Not every position in every operation can have an internship at every point in time due to the level of expertise required. But every operation can work toward developing personnel who qualify to meet the standards of the position. Obviously, this principle has broad implications for the upward mobility of the indigent within different employment programs.

It is important to note that 55 of the trainees successfully completed training and were awarded 12 college credits. One year later almost all of these persons retain the positions to which they were originally assigned. Many have gone on to enroll for further college training on a part-time basis and at least two are full-time college students. While the written feedback from supervisors is most laudatory and while in one instance one New Careers casework aide has even been assigned to train five professional caseworkers in one Welfare agency this feedback is anecdotal and current studies are under way to assess the effectiveness of New Careers workers. Nevertheless, we believe that the results as stated are significant when we consider that the population was one identified as hard-core unemployed. Indeed, many of the current welfare casework aides were welfare recipients prior to their training, and for a year of the training they received less payment than they had received on welfare. The next major task would appear to be to persuade the social service agencies to adopt an "up and out" employment program.

In summary, the project successfully implemented a program in which professionals systematically selected and then systematically trained indigenous lay personnel as functional professionals who, in turn, conducted successful training programs and developed interns for their own positions. Such programs can be effectively accomplished in the social action sphere, particularly the human service area, and indeed other areas of industry, business and government.

WELFARE OR WARFARE?

Lest the reader think that the tasks of human resource development are easily accomplished, particularly when they are of demonstrable success as the programs which we have illustrated, it would do well for him to understand the behind-the-scene difficulties. While the empirically based social activist must believe in the power of productivity—*and he must believe in the power of productivity; he must believe this if there is to be a world for human life*—he continually finds his work neutralized or overwhelmed by the power of politics.

Every program which we touched —and I daresay the same goes for any potent social programs anywhere—was actively thwarted, undermined, and in some instances, crippled by the change resisters—the militant "status quoers." The story of 22 New Careers graduates who were prepared for positions as Social Service Technicians for the Massachusetts Department of Welfare is just one story of wasted time, talent, and energy spent in surmounting barriers and climbing obstacles. It is worth telling because it illustrates the toil and travesty of social action.

The Welfare story began in February, 1969 when the Springfield Welfare Service Center accepted 22 on-the-job trainees from the New Careers program with a commitment to hire those trainees who successfully completed the course of training. In July, 1969 the trainees assumed full-time positions at the Welfare Department.

At the time that the trainees assumed their duties with the Welfare Department, the Massachusetts State Legislature had not established the positions; indeed, the positions requested were stricken from the budget by the legislature. Trainees who had increased their on-the-job-training schedule from two to three days a week, now began to work a full 5-day week for the Department but continued to receive only a modest training allowance from the New Careers program.

As a result of an intensive effort on the part of those concerned, a supplementary budget was passed allocating to Springfield 60 positions—30 Case Aide positions and 30 Social Service Technician positions, subject to Civil Service provisions. At this point lobbies resisting the innovation, particularly those most intimately involved, were able to influence the political sources sufficiently to establish questions for the New Careers trainees. One question was whether the technicians could be appointed provisionally prior to taking an examination for the position, as was originally guaranteed by agreement. Another question was whether or not such an examination would be given as a promotional examination limited only to those already officially on the staff of the Welfare Department. The technicians were informed that while they might take an open, competitive examination, no appointments would be made from the open list until the promotional list was exhausted.

The New Careers trainees were placed in the ironical position of being excluded from the positions which were created specifically for them.

In spite of a bill (Chapter 549, effective July 23, 1969) on provisional appointments passed to enable the disadvantaged to qualify for positions, the trainees were to be denied the temporary appointments.

In spite of the positions which were created for the disadvantaged the trainees were to be denied an open, competitive Civil Service examination for the positions.

The following quote written at the time is from a letter by an assistant administrator of the Welfare Department:

> This action constitutes, in my opinion, a shameful betrayal of trust. . . . Seventeen people remain in the program (five having dropped out prior to July 1 because of the fog of uncertainty which obscured their prospects). . . . These seventeen have given unstintingly of themselves to the Department in the firm expectation that they would be given a fair chance to win their jobs in open competition. They have been performing social work tasks and doing so in splendid fashion, while receiving a stipend which is barely half that of a social worker. . . . They have maintained an air of poise, dignity and restraint through times of extraordinary turmoil and in circumstances of great discouragement. I cannot conceive how this office could have traversed this time of chaos without their steady help.
>
> These trainees have never shrunk from the necessity of proving their mettle in open competition—even with persons who had the advantage of many years service with the Department. But for them now to have to confront the all-too-familiar fact of their second-class citizenship is a blow too cruel to accept without outcry.
>
> For years, public outrage against welfare has centered about the need of persuading people to seize opportunities to improve themselves and move towards self-sufficiency. Well, here we are! We have seventeen people who have done just that. At considerable sacrifice to themselves and their families, they have devoted their time and energies to the tasks of education and training to qualify themselves for some sort of decent employment. Can we now tell them that the promised jobs are reserved

for others? Certainly, of all agencies, public welfare can least afford to rationalize this sort of gross discrimination against the poor.

It is my conviction that just a little judicious consideration must convince the administrators of the Department of Public Welfare and the Civil Service Commission that the proposed action on this examination is cruelly discriminatory against the very people we are sworn to help and is therefore completely indefensible.

The New Careers trainees continued to work. To be sure, they function as full-fledged social caseworkers and, in some instances, are actively employed in training new caseworkers.

Finally, due to enormous pressures brought by those who made the program possible, including several bus trips to Boston involving the entire group of New Careers trainees and staff, a decision was made to create 30 Social Casework Clerk positions at the same level as the 30 Social Casework positions. While the technicians were originally to have been appointed in July, after bureaucratic and budget delays and other red tape, the trainees were finally appointed December 29, 1969.

Technically, then, the jobs did not exist until December 29. The New Careers program carried the trainees until they were officially appointed, even though the workers were performing their actual duties for the Welfare Department since July and should have been paid accordingly. During the time the workers were carried as trainees they earned $78 per week, $40 less than the Technician position, and received no state fringe benefits such as vacation build-up, sick leave accrual, medical insurance, and other benefits.

Perhaps more important, *some of the trainees received significantly less during the year that they were in training for casework technician positions than they would receive if they, themselves, were welfare recipients.* It is difficult, indeed, to argue that recipients would not welcome the opportunity to be gainfully employed, particularly in the human service areas.

With all of this effort, they are not "home free." They have been subjected to extensive humiliation and abuse. Investigations of the Welfare Department have centered around providing the technicians with access to files and the ability to authorize payments. Jobs have been in jeopardy due to past criminal records—when rehabilitation of the hard-core unemployed was the very purpose of the program!

The technicians have received training and accreditation from a recognized educational institution and yet they are treated as if they are incompetent.

They have learned to be proud of their skills and their personages and yet they are treated as if they were not human.

In this context, the director of a local community action program notes:

Persons who never before have been able to influence their own lives due to a lack of hope and skill have now achieved self-confidence and an awareness of their capabilities; they have achieved a skills level needed to sustain themselves and their confidences; and they have done so in the belief that they would be rewarded with justice and encouraged by recognition of their efforts by agencies, both public and private, of our State and local communities. But, to date, they have been rewarded with what appears to be deception and obstructionism. It is my hope that we—all State agencies included—will see these problems as an opportunity to make significant contributions to the agencies and institutions and the people of our Commonwealth.

The chances, it is clear, are as good that there will be no such Technician Program, particularly in its effective form, a year hence as that there will be.

There are larger issues—much larger issues. If minority groups, black and Spanish, are to get on their own feet, then they must be provided with the opportunity to pull themselves up by their own bootstraps. In order to do so, they need men of competence, men of commitment, to teach them the tangible skills which they need to effect their own constructive change. They do not need men of influence, men of power, men of politics because these men respond only to influence, power, and politics. The days of providing positions for people of privilege in poverty and welfare programs are numbered if the programs are to be effective.

Comfortable people should not be allowed to make a living off other people's misery, especially when they are not themselves effective with the people they are supposed to serve.

The story of Otis tells much of this tale:*

> Otis is a black man.
> His future got lost somewhere before his past.
> His present bubbled in a bottle.
> To say he was unemployed would be an understatement.
> He could not believe his eyes the first day of class. There before him, teaching his class, was a black man "off the streets" like he was. Imagine, someone who just a few months before was as lost as he was, was now suddenly transformed into his teacher. He looked at his teacher and wondered. "Maybe there is hope," he thought.
> To many blacks, to the poor blacks, to the down-and-out blacks, hope was a lie. Over and over, each hope was a lie. He had hoped and nothing had happened. But now he hoped again. He hoped against hope that maybe, maybe he could do like the teacher in front of him.
> This time there was something different. There was a black man up there. There was a new ingredient. Maybe, maybe!

*Mimeographed manuscript written and published by Robert R. Carkhuff in November 1969.

Now Otis works at Welfare.
He could have gone there as a recipient.
But instead he works there.
He could have made more as a recipient.
But instead he works there.
He takes home $63 per week.
Hardly enough for a man to live on.
But he hopes again—never quite believing—but always hoping!

Otis is a graduate of the New Careers program. It is a program dedicated to developing new careers in the human services for hard-core unemployed. He now has 12 college credits in helping and human relations skills. Imagine, 12 college credits for someone who never even made high school.

"Those teachers sure were 'heavy,'" he thought. "Someday, that's what I want to be, 'heavy' like they were."
The program pushed him. It pushed him hard. It pushed him intellectually. It pushed him emotionally. It pushed him physically.
But now he was "together." He had skills—salable skills. He knew how to help people. He had been helping people at Welfare. He knew it. They knew it.

Otis and 16 of his fellow graduates have performed the duties of Social Service Technicians with the Welfare Department since the Spring of 1969. Together, they have discharged their responsibilities far beyond the call of duty. Everyone knows that.
They were performing the duties of Social Service Technicians—but they were not Social Service Technicians.
They had been promised the opportunity to become Technicians. Indeed, the Bill to make them Technicians was a community action effort on behalf of the New Careers trainees.
They had been promised a two-year provisional appointment as Social Service Technicians in preparation for an open, competitive Civil Service examination. Upon satisfactorily passing the test, they were to be made Technicians.

Now that was all over. Different pressure groups had reached the political sources. The New Careers graduates were to be denied inclusion of professional status pending examination. They were to be denied the opportunity for taking an open, competitive examination.

Otis goes through the motions. He sees the clients. And they still love him. But it all feels hollow.
His future gets lost again on him once in a while.
He feels helpless in the face of it all.

He must depend on the people who created the positions in the first place.

He must depend on the integrity of politicians.

But he hopes—never quite believing—but still hoping against hope![1]

Areas such as social welfare are not substantive areas. Other than an elite core of high-level trainers and consultants, with demonstrated competencies, this profession should serve only for the creation of positions for the people who are themselves being serviced by welfare and who have the resources and disposition for such work. At that, these positions should be transitional, with each group of former recipient technicians serving, in turn, to help to get the present welfare recipients on their feet so that they can become technicians while the former technicians move on up into government, education, and private industry.

People, comfortable or not, should not be allowed for long to make a living off other people's misery, *even if they are effective* with the people they serve.

The pyramid of learning is the pyramid of internship.

The pyramid of responsibility is the pyramid of growth.

REFERENCES

Carkhuff, R. R. Principles of social action in training for new careers in human services. *Journal of Counseling Psychology,* 1971, **18,** 147–151.

Carkhuff, R. R., & Griffin, A. H. The selection and training of functional professionals for Concentrated Employment Programs. *Journal of Clinical Psychology,* 1971, **27,** 163–165.

[1]A footnote to this particular program is that an open Civil Service examination for social casework technicians was finally administered and all but three of the New Careers graduates passed the exam with all distinguishing themselves by their superior performance from among approximately 100 applicants. Two of the three who failed were Spanish speaking and had difficulty with the written language of the exam. Nevertheless, the technicians' jobs remain in jeopardy. In spite of passing the exam, some of the graduates are scheduled to be precluded from the positions that were created for them.

CHAPTER 12
Training as a Preferred Mode of Helping *

In a very real sense we might say that the concept of training as a preferred mode of helping had its origins in Little Hans and Peter and the Rabbit. Sound allegorical? Well, it is not! Freud, in the early 1900s, introduced what we know today as "filial therapy" by training the father to carry out the treatment of Little Hans (1959). Jones extended Watsonian behaviorism to the modification of human behavior in his systematic desensitization of Peter to the fear of rabbits (1920).

Adler, also in the early 1900s, furthered this concept of training by introducing programs to develop the therapeutic skills of resourceful persons without medical credentials. The impetus for client-centered developments in training as treatment was provided, interestingly enough, by Rogers' daughter; with training from her father, she was able to help her daughter to overcome a toilet-training problem (Fuchs, 1957).

With the exception of the case of Peter, each of these instances of training as treatment has dealt primarily with "significant others" or symbionts in the client's or helpee's life. The primary emphasis in the research literature has also been upon parents and school or other institutional personnel, involving both authority and peer figures. Professional helpers, it has been assumed, can most effectively discharge their responsibilities by training persons most intimately involved in the helpee's welfare, providing them with the skills necessary to effect the helpee's optimum functioning. Another modality of training as a preferred mode of treatment is to directly train the one person most intimately involved with the helpee's welfare—the helpee himself. Training significant others and training helpees directly, then, are the two modalities of training as a pre-

*Reprinted in part with permission from the *Journal of Counseling Psychology*, 1971, 18, 123–131, where it first appeared as "Training as a Preferred Mode of Treatment," by Robert R. Carkhuff.

ferred mode of treatment, with the former more heavily emphasized in child treatment, although not to the exclusion of direct training. It is to be emphasized that neither modality operates to the exclusion of the other. Indeed, the two may be most effectively integrated in programs where symbionts are trained to train the helpees involved.

TRAINING SIGNIFICANT OTHERS

The two broad categories of therapeutic treatment, the so-called insight therapies and the behavior modification approaches, converge upon the training of significant others as a preferred mode of client treatment. Although parent involvement in therapeutic treatment of the child continues to be incorporated by psychoanalytic and egoanalytic practitioners, the main thrust in the development of training of significant others among the insight therapies has come from the client-centered orientation.

Building upon the work of Rogers (1951, 1967), Baruch (1949), and Moustakas (1955), and emphasizing play therapy conducted in the home by the parents, Guerney (1964) and his associates formalized the concept of "filial therapy." Filial therapy involves training parents in small groups to conduct play sessions with their own emotionally disturbed children, using an orientation and methodology modeled after client-centered play therapy. The child's play sessions and the parent's training are conducted with Rogerian emphasis upon the experiential source of learning; they attempt to (1) correct the child's distorted perceptions of the parents, (2) allow the child to communicate his own experiences, and (3) facilitate the development of the child's feelings of self-respect, self-worth, and self-confidence. Promising demonstrations have been shown (Guerney, 1964; Guerney, Guerney, and Andronico, 1966), and some research (Stover and Guerney, 1967) has produced positive results indicating that parents can learn to modify their pattern of interaction with their own emotionally disturbed children, in the direction of the role behavior of client-centered therapists. Variations of the filial therapy theme have been recommended for teachers (Andronico and Guerney, 1967) and have been attempted with college students (Stollak, 1967) with positive results.

In our own work we have added counselor-initiated dimensions to the counselor-responsive conditions and have developed systematic training programs in interpersonal skills, in eclectic extensions of Rogers' "necessary and sufficient conditions of therapeutic personality change." Whereas the client-centered approach, at least theoretically, relied exclusively upon the experiential sources of learning, these training programs emphasized the didactic and modeling sources of learning in shaping effective trainee responses in the context of a relationship emphasizing high levels of trainer-trainee communication. Extensions to the systematic training of parents of emotionally disturbed children have been made. The assumption, as with filial therapy, is that the children's responses are at least in part a function of the quality of the interpersonal relationship between parents and between parents and children.

PROJECT 26
*Training Parents as Helpers**

In developing effective treatment procedures we must first consider the conditions which are conducive to the development of difficulties in living or psychopathology and then relate these conditions to the conditions of helping. Our attempt to translate our constructs to tangible human benefits begins with the helpee himself and his difficulties in living. The helpee is, at least in part, a product of his many relationships with significant persons in his environment, past and present. His present relationships reflect the difficulty of his past relationships. He has learned to respond to others in ways that significant others have responded to him. The helpee, then, is a product and a promulgator of his experiences, and the critical core of these experiences involves relationships with other human beings.

The body of evidence leading to the development of training as a preferred mode of treatment has been summarized in propositional form: (1) The core of functioning or dysfunctioning (health or psychopathology) is interpersonal; (2) The core of helping processes (learning or relearning) is interpersonal; (3) Group processes are the preferred mode of working with difficulties in interpersonal functioning; (4) Systematic group training in interpersonal functioning is the preferred mode of working with difficulties in interpersonal functioning. Thus, systematic group procedures can be constructed to achieve operational treatment goals by progressive step-by-step gradations of interpersonal experience.

In the present study an attempt was made to incorporate systematic group training in interpersonal skills as the core of the treatment program for parents of emotionally disturbed children. While the focus of the study was upon training, three different treatment groups conducted by high-, moderate- and low-functioning counselors and one time control group were incorporated in the study.

METHODOLOGY

Trainees

Twenty-one sets of parents ($N = 42$) of children ($N = 21$) designated as "emotionally disturbed" on the basis of destructive behavioral patterns were taken in sequential order from a waiting list of approximately one year's duration and offered different modes of treatment. Thus, the helpees selected were as random as helpees enrolling themselves for clinical help. The couples were from all walks of life and the husbands' occupations

*Reprinted in part with permission from an article in the *Journal of Counseling Psychology,* 1970, 17, 157–161, entitled "Training as a Preferred Mode of Treatment of Parents of Emotionally Disturbed Children," by Robert R. Carkhuff and Ralph Bierman.

ranged from laborers to business executives. The couples ranged in age from 30's to 50's.

Procedure

The five couples of the training group met in a group once or twice weekly over a several-month period for 25 hours of systematic training (Group I). Both parents and children were pre- and post-tested on a variety of different testing indexes, including real-life indexes assessing the parents' interpersonal functioning with each other and with their children. Three traditional treatment groups involving four sets of parents each ($N = 8$) of therapists functioning at High (Group II), moderate (III) and low (IV) levels of interpersonal skills and one time control group of the same composition (V) were employed as controls. The treatment groups met over a period of months for a total of 25 hours of training. Thus, in total, ten helpees (and their five children) were involved in the training proper while 24 helpees (and their 12 children) were involved in traditional treatment groups and 8 helpees (and their 4 children) comprised a time control group.

Group Training of Helper Parents

Based upon the assumption that the child's disturbance is a function of the level of interpersonal functioning between parents and between the individual parents and the children involved, an integrated didactic and experiential program was devised for Group I, the training group, in the following sequence: (1) communication between members of different families and different sexes; (2) communication between spouses in the same family unit; (3) communication between members of different families and sexes with each, in turn, role-playing their children; (4) communication between members of the same family with each, in turn, role-playing their child; (5) one practice session focused upon communication between the parents and their children. While the responsive dimensions of empathy, respect and concreteness and the initiative dimensions of genuineness, confrontation and immediacy were incorporated in training, the dimension of empathy was emphasized throughout.

Empathy training was operationalized as follows: (1) *Discrimination training:* Trainees were first taught to discriminate levels of empathy according to whether or not the helper's responses were interchangeable (level 3) with the helpee's expressions in terms of the feeling and personal meaning expressed, i.e. the discrimination of interchangeability was made on the basis of whether the helper had expressed the feeling and meaning that the helpee expressed; trainees were then taught to discriminate whether, if the responses were not interchangeable, they were additive (levels 4 and 5) or subtractive (levels 1 and 2) according to the effect of the helper's response upon the helpee's subsequent response, i.e. could the helpee utilize the helper's response to enable the helpee to go on to explore and understand himself at deeper levels. (2) *Communication training:* The initial goal of communication training, the formulation of interchangeable responses, served as the basis for the later shaping additive responses; at all times the other trainees plus the trainer offered immediate and concrete feedback in terms of empathy ratings. The trainer had ten years of experience and was functioning at high levels of facilitative and action-oriented dimensions (well above the level 3.0 overall designated as minimally effective).

Group Treatment of Helpee Parents

The three treatment groups were conducted by therapists of a Child Guidance Clinic. While each had psychoanalytically oriented training, all were quite eclectic in practice. The therapists averaged more than ten years of experience, much of it in group treatment of parents. The group therapists were functioning at the following overall levels based upon submitted tapes and tapes from a standard group situation: high, an average of 3.0 overall; moderate, 2.2 overall; low, 1.5 overall.

Testing

Each parent responded to 16 standard helpee stimulus expressions and pre-rated alternate responses prior to and following training. The stimulus expressions were designed to cross different affect areas (depression-distress; anger-hostility; elation-excitement) with different problem areas (social-interpersonal; educational-vocational; child-rearing; sexual-marital) plus a silence. The alternate responses were designed to cross level [High (H) and Low (L)] of facilitation or responsiveness with level of action-orientation or initiative in random combinations (i.e. HH, HL, LH, LL). In addition, each parent was cast in the helping role with his spouse, and both parents conducted a play session with their child. Ratings of both the tapes of the interviews and the written responses were conducted by two trained raters who had demonstrated Pearson r rate-rerate and inter-rater reliabilities in the .90's in previous studies and who were themselves functioning at high levels of the dimensions involved. A relationship inventory assessing the level of communication of all responsive and initiative dimensions between parent and child was filled out by each parent. A constructive personality change index of the MMPI, i.e. only those items on which the examinee could change constructively, with those items on which he could not change eliminated, was taken by the parents while the Child Adjustment Index was administered to the children.

RESULTS

The results of the effects of training upon the overall level of communication and discrimination appear in Table 12–1. There was a significant

Table 12–1
Parent Level of Interpersonal Skills in the Helping Role

| | OVERALL COMMUNICATION | | | | DISCRIMINATION | |
| | Written Responses | | Helping Role | | (Deviation from Experts)* | |
	M	sd	M	sd	M	sd
Pre-training (N = 10)	1.5	.6	1.5	.6	1.5	.5
Post-training (N = 10)	2.7	.5	2.9	.4	.8	.4
Change	+1.2 p < .01	.3	+1.4 p < .01	.3	−.7 p < .01	.3

*The lower the score the more accurate the discrimination.

improvement in the level of communication in response to helpee stimulus expressions and in the helping role with spouse. In addition, there was a significant improvement in the level of discrimination, with post-training ratings of alternative responses significantly more accurate when compared to the expert ratings than the pre-training ratings. However, while there are significant parents' perceived parent-to-child relationship inventory changes ($p < .05$), the pre-post training changes of parental functioning in a play situation were not significant, thus suggesting limited generalization to functioning in an experimental play situation. In general, there were slight non-significant trends by two-tailed randomization tests for matched pairs for mothers to become more passive and fathers to become more active. The parents' pre-post changes on the constructive personality change index and the children's pre-post changes on the child adjustment index were not significant.

A comparison of training and treatment group means by Duncan's Multiple Range Test yielded the following results: (1) the final mean level of communication in the helping role (2.9) by the training group I was significantly greater than treatment control groups III, IV and V ($p < .05$), each with means of 1.5, although not significantly greater than group II with a mean of 1.8; (2) the final mean level of parent-to-child communication change as indicated by the relationship inventory indicated that while training group I was not significantly different from groups II, III and IV, groups I and II alone were significantly different ($p < .05$) from control group V; (3) while none of the experiences was particularly successful in effecting the constructive personality change index, the parents' mean adjustment changes indicated that group III was significantly higher ($p < .05$) than groups I and II while groups IV and V were not significantly different from the others; (4) there were no significant differences between any groups in the mean level of child adjustment changes.

The Pearson product moment intercorrelations of the indexes of parental functioning appear in Table 12–2. The results indicate a high relationship between pre- and post-training measures of communication and discrimination. Indexes of both communication and discrimination were good predictors of final level of communication while only the personality index was related to that change index. In general, a particular pre-training index was a good predictor of the same index after training. Although there may have been an overall group change, the parents apparently maintained the same relative positions within the group.

DISCUSSION

The results support the efficacy of training as a potential preferred mode of treatment with important qualifications. In terms of critical changes in functioning which the training set out to effect there was evidence of significant constructive change or gain in level of communication and discrimination in general and in communication between parents specifically. However, while the parents perceived themselves as communicating at a higher level with their children, there was little evidence to support this from play sessions with their children. While the experimental nature of the play situations may have had a neutralizing effect upon the parents' functioning, the fact that there was very little practice in the play situation seems most salient. In general, this study supports the proposition that _people learn best what they practice most_. Indeed, it suggests that if we wish to effect changes in play situations we ought to devise methodologies where we train parents specifically and progressively to understand and work with their children in these situations. A number of such projects, where parents are trained directly with their children to interpret and facilitate constructive play and helping interactions, have already grown out of this research.

Concerning the comparative effects of training and treatment, it is important to note that in a relatively brief period systematic group training

Table 12–2
Intercorrelations of Pre- and Post-training Indexes of Parental Functioning
(N = 10)

	POST-TRAINING		
	COMMUNICATION		DISCRIMINATION	PERSONALITY
	Helpee			_Constructive_
	Stimulus			_Personality_
	Expressions	_Helping Role_	_Alternate Responses_	_Change Index_
PRE-TRAINING	_(HSE)_	_(HR)_	_(AR)_	_(CPCI)_
HSE	.73*	.71*	−.21	−.25
HR	.69*	.85*	−.45	−.02
AR	−.71*	−.76*	.31	−.15
CPCI	.45	−.08	.09	.91*

*Significant at the .05 level.

can effect changes in interpersonal skills that traditional counseling groups cannot. Here it is noteworthy that the clients of the traditional therapist functioning at the highest levels (Group II) demonstrated the highest level of functioning following therapy; however, it was not nearly as high a level of functioning as the trainees of the training group achieved in the very limited time period. It is noteworthy, though, that while the training group was successful in effecting changes in interpersonal functioning, none of the groups were particularly successful in effecting constructive personality and adjustment changes of parents and children. Again, if this is a goal of helping, we ought to devise methodologies to effect such changes.

In regard to the indexes involved, it appears again that the best predictors of future criteria are previous indexes of those criteria. Communication in the helping role is the best predictor of communication in the helping role. Ratings of written responses to standard helpee expressions constitute a good index of functioning in the helping role. In addition, while previous research indicates a lack of relationship between discrimination and communication, in this instance, discrimination appears a good predictor of future functioning in the helping role, perhaps reflecting the naive or unsophisticated nature of the population.

Together, then, the results suggest two directions for the development of effective training and treatment methodologies: (1) the best index of a criterion which we wish to achieve is an operational index of that criterion; (2) the best means for attaining that criterion is to develop step-by-step gradations of success experiences leading to that criterion. Again, if we wish to affect significantly the level of communication between parents, then we must practice communication between parents as we have done in this project. If we wish to affect significantly the level of communication between the parents and their children, then we must practice communication between parents and their children, something we did not do sufficiently in this project. If we wish to accomplish both, then we must incorporate both experiences in the training program.

In summary, the results support the concept of training as a preferred mode of treatment. Training does not operate to the exclusion of the more therapeutic or experiential learnings; rather it incorporates these experiences within a work-oriented structure which leaves the trainee-helpee with tangible and usable skills.

While the results indicate that the program was successful in directly effecting changes in the interpersonal behavior of parents, there was no tangible demonstration that the effects were achieved with the children. A longer-term program which focuses not only upon changes between parents but also between the parents and their children is necessary. The work of Santilli (1969), growing out of this original work, focused directly upon the interaction between parent and child: parents were systematically taught how to understand and relate to their children in play situations with demonstrably positive effects.

In our own work at the Center, we have set up an experimental situation in which we reconstituted families. In one instance, for example, we treated interpersonal problems within the family simultaneously with difficulties in racial relations by setting up a training group of two families without fathers, one white and one black, conducted by a black man and a black woman as parental surrogates. Many other variations of the training theme are possible. In addition to parents' groups, children's groups at different age levels, mothers' groups and fathers' groups are all meaningful possibilities. Any combination of persons may be brought together for training programs tailored to the participants' individual needs. In this regard, we are limited only by the helpee's needs and our own imagination.

Perhaps most important, the implications for the prevention of problems —not simply the rehabilitation of problems—in child-rearing is the greatest potential contribution of a training approach. Parents must learn effective child-rearing skills in the same manner that they learn to play a musical instrument or to sew or play baseball.

The results suggest that training significant others in relationship conditions can have a demonstrably positive effect upon the development of both client and his symbiont. For our purposes it should be emphasized, however, that the *training was much more effective in effecting gains in interpersonal communication than traditional parental counseling groups conducted by high level as well as moderate and low level functioning therapists.* Follow-up studies emphasizing direct training in parent-child relations (Carkhuff, 1969a; 1969b) and play sessions (Santilli, 1969) promise positive results. Further, in the only studies comparing experiential training with systematic training in experiential dimensions (Berenson, Carkhuff, and Myrus, 1966) and systematic training as treatment with experiential counseling (Carkhuff and Bierman, 1970), the results strongly favor the systematic approaches.

The interesting transition from a program beginning with an exclusively experiential emphasis to one emphasizing a systematic approach to communicating experiential dimensions is an interesting one. The shift was accomplished simply by modifying the program according to the feedback obtained from studies of the effects upon the behavior of the trainees. While the behavioristic approaches were not capable of discerning and describing experiential dimensions, once this was accomplished, the systematic approaches were clearly superior to the experiential approaches in achieving the communication of experiential dimensions.

The behavioristic approaches, spurred on by Wolpe's translations to human behavior modification (1958), developed variations on the themes of instrumental and classical conditioning (Krasner and Ullmann, 1965; Ullmann and Krasner,

1965). Succinctly, these approaches simply attempt to help an individual to behave in a desired way and to see that the behavior is sustained. The distinctive contributions of the behavior modification approaches has been their systematic methodologies and their resultant ability to demonstrate tangible evidence of human behavior change and its sustenance after relatively short periods of treatment (Carkhuff and Berenson, 1967).

The behavior modification approaches are simple, direct, and concrete. They require no understanding of complex causes and psychodynamics. In these respects, they are ideally suited for training noncredentialed personnel in their implementation. Applications in training significant others are, therefore, natural extensions of the behavior modification approaches.

Particularly in relation to child treatment, parents have been trained in the methodologies needed to identify and reinforce the child's adjustive behavior (Krasner and Ullmann, 1965). One such program taught parents of disturbed children operant behavior principles (Walder, Cohen, Breiter, Daston, Hirsch, and Liebowitz, 1969). In an attempt to restructure the home so that it resembled more closely the controlled environment of the laboratory, group meetings were held training the parents in the following: (1) the accurate observation of behavior and recording data; (2) the identification of the contingencies of behavior; (3) the shaping of behavior; and (4) the procedures of behavior control.

Wahler and his associates (Wahler, Winkel, Peterson, and Morrison, 1965) trained mothers as behavior therapists for their own children. The researchers attempted to modify the deviant behavior of the children by producing specific changes in the behavior of their mothers. They demonstrated that a mother's social behavior may function as a powerful reinforcer for her child's deviant as well as normal behavior. It was also demonstrated that a mother's reactions to her child's behavior may be systematically modified within the confines of an experimental setting and that these modifications may produce marked changes in her child's deviant behavior.

Extensions of this work (Hawkins, Peterson, Schweid, and Bijou, 1966; O'Leary, O'Leary, and Becker, 1969; Shah, 1969) demonstrated an experimental modification of the mother-child relationship in the home with mother as therapist. In general, the child's objectionable behaviors were observed to change in frequency and topography as a consequence of the treatment and appeared (1) to generalize from the experimental hour to the remaining hours of the day and (2) to hold on follow-up.

In an extension of his earlier work in which he trained parents as co-therapists, Patterson (Patterson and Brodsky, 1966) employed a kind of "total push" treatment program for children. Different conditioning procedures were employed for different deviant behaviors by parents, teachers, and peers as well as the experimenters. Fear reactions were counter-conditioned while cooperative behaviors were operant-conditioned with highly positive results.

In a similar vein, the child's academic self-concept and actual academic achievement were modified successfully. Parents were trained simply to communicate that they thought their children were capable and ought to achieve at higher levels (Brookover, Erickson, Hamachek, Joiner, LePere, Paterson, and Thomas, 1969). The failure of either counselors or experts to induce similar changes suggests that working through an already established significant other is more likely to be effective than developing a new significant other.

Laboratory findings concerning those factors determining social reinforcer effectiveness in modifying children's behavior (Horowitz, 1963) were extended to the classroom. Problem behaviors were successfully eliminated when the teachers ignored them and also gave approving attention for verbal and self-help behaviors (Harris, Wolf, and Baer, 1964; Wolf, Risley, and Mees, 1964) and when they removed social consequences of the behavior (Zimmerman and Zimmerman, 1962). The combination of ignoring deviant behavior and reinforcing incompatible behavior appears critical (Becker, Madsen, Arnold, and Thomas, 1967). In addition, it has been demonstrated that select students (Davison, 1965; Kreitzer, 1969) and nurses (Ayllon and Michael, 1959; Bachrach, Erwin, and Mohr, 1966) can be taught in a short time to execute a behavior-control program that requires the application of learning principles to the acquisition or elimination of the client's "target" behaviors.

Interestingly enough, while the experiential approaches were, in effect, becoming more behavioristic, the behavioristic approaches were becoming more experiential. There was a growing recognition on the part of many behaviorists that the behavior schedule or program was not enough. Indeed, there was a recognition that the effects of the behavior program were to some great degree dependent upon the relationship established between the counselor and the client. Wolpe, himself, has conceded that as much as 60 percent of the effectiveness of the counter-conditioning process may be due to "non-specific relationship factors." Thus, while the relationship researchers moved toward specifying and operationalizing these "non-specific" variables, the behaviorists moved toward acknowledging the necessity for incorporating the experiential frame of reference into the total treatment process.

It is a singular tribute to the methodology of science that investigators beginning from diverse and seemingly antithetical viewpoints do converge in their explorations and their findings, if they are shaped by the results of their efforts and their inability to account for the major part of the variability in change indexes.

DIRECT TRAINING OF HELPEES

We take a shortcut in our efforts when, instead of training counselors to treat helpees, we cut out the middleman and train those most directly involved in the helpee's welfare. It is a further step in the direction of efficiency and effectiveness to directly train the helpee himself. The most direct form of treatment, then, would be to train clients and patients in those skills necessary to function effectively in society.

Assuming the necessity of interpersonal skills for getting and staying out of the hospital, the following program employed systematic training in interpersonal skills with a group of chronic neuropsychiatric patients who were not otherwise being seen in treatment.

PROJECT 27
*Training Helpees as Self-Helpers**

There is a great deal of evidence in the literature correlating positive outcome in therapy, teaching, and child rearing with the personally facilitative dimensions of empathy *(E)*, positive regard *(R)*, genuineness *(G)*, and concreteness *(C)*. Briefly, empathy consists of the ability to recognize, sense and to understand the feelings that another person has associated with his behavioral and verbal expressions, and to accurately communicate this understanding to him. Respect, or positive regard, consists of expressing to a second person an honest concern that what he does is of real importance to the first person. Genuineness means that the first person expresses what he truly feels in a nondestructive manner without insincere professional role playing. Concreteness involves the first person helping the second person to explore and develop fully in definite and specific terms, the areas of life which are important to him.

The efficacy of training people to function more constructively on these dimensions in a relatively brief time using an integrated didactic and experiential approach has also been established with students, housewives and hospital attendants. This approach essentially involves the trainees experiencing highly constructive levels of these conditions while at the same time being shaped didactically to respond more appropriately. To date, however, no one has provided a test of this approach by training those judged by society to be most severely disturbed, namely psychiatric inpatients. If this population can be trained to function in a more facilitative manner, then any other less disturbed group might also be amenable to training. In addition, there are potentially profound implications for traditional counseling and therapeutic approaches; for example, it is the purpose of this study to examine the feasibility of psychiatric patients improving on the interpersonally facilitative dimensions of *E*, *R*, *G*, and *C* through training and to compare these results with those obtained by the more traditional approaches.

*Reprinted in part with permission from the *Journal of Counseling Psychology*, 1969, **16**, 295–298, where it first appeared as "Teaching Facilitative Interpersonal Functioning to Psychiatric Inpatients," by Richard Pierce and James Drasgow.

METHOD

Training Group

The Ss were 7 male psychiatric inpatients, selected at random from a group of 14 patients who had not been assigned to individual or group therapy, since it was believed they could not meaningfully participate in, or benefit from, such programs. They ranged in age from 21 to 55 years and had been hospitalized from one to four times. Five of the patients were diagnosed schizophrenic and two as having psychiatric difficulties associated with chronic brain syndrome. The training group met 5 days per week for 1½ hours per day for a total of 20 hours. The integrated didactic and experiential approach was used, where the trainees experienced high levels of E, R, G, and C, while their responses were being shaped through practice in discrimination and communication. However, the approach was modified to emphasize a behavioristic shaping to essentially reconstruct the communication process as follows: Patients were first given a verbal listing of common feelings, that is, anger, depression, joy, etc. They then heard one sentence from either one of the trainers or a fellow patient and were asked to identify the feeling in one word. This was then built into a response in a sentence such as, "You feel happy," "You feel sad," or whatever the appropriate feeling was. The patient was then encouraged and differentially reinforced to shape two-sentence interactions, then three and so on up to sustained 15- or 20-minute interactions with one patient assigned to be the "listener" and the other the "talker." Using previously validated research scales for E, R, G, and C, assessments were made of the patient's functioning prior to training by asking each one to respond "as helpfully as you can" to three separate taped excerpts expressing depression, anger and elation. Their responses were then rated on the scales. The tape was prepared specifically for this study and used content material about hospital life, being discharged, etc. It was derived from earlier tapes developed to assess communication level. The posttraining assessment measures consisted of two parts: (a) "responding as helpfully as you can" to the same tape used in the pretraining measure, and (b) a taped interview with a standard patient whom none of the Ss knew and for which they were also given the set to be as helpful as they could. The responses to the tape were then rated, as well as three 2-minute excerpts from the interview. In addition, the standard interviewee was asked to rate the patients on their helpfulness to him on a scale where Level 1 was unhelpful; Level 2, somewhat helpful; Level 3, more helpful than unhelpful; Level 4, almost always helpful; and Level 5, always helpful.

Control-Control Group

The control-control group consisted of the seven male psychiatric inpatients not included in the random selection for the training group. These patients received either drugs, and individual, or group treatment during the control period. They received pretesting and posttesting around a 4-week time interval of exposure to their treatments.

Medicine Treatment Control Group

The medicine treatment control group also consisted of seven male psychiatric inpatients who were receiving only drug treatments. They had been in the hospital for an average period of 4 months with a range of 1–9 months. This group received only the post-measures of the taped expressions and standard interview.

Individual Treatment Control Group

The individual treatment control Ss were seven male psychiatric inpatients who had received an average of 45 hours of individual therapy with a range of 20–150 hours. The group also received the post-measures of tape responses and interviews.

Group Treatment Control Group

The group treatment control group consisted of five male and two female psychiatric inpatients who had received an average of 76 hours of group therapy with a range of 20–150 hours. They, too, received only the post-measures of tape and standard interviews.

Trainers

The trainers were two experienced therapists who in previous research had been shown to be functioning at high levels across the facilitative conditions of E, R, G, and C. One trainer averaged 4.0 across conditions and the other 3.0 as measured by the scales.

Raters

The raters were two experienced researchers whose previous ratings had been shown to be correlated with other measures of outcome in previous research. In the present study their interrater reliabilities were as follows: E, .96; R, .92; G, .91 and C, .84.

Standard Interviewee

The standard interviewee was a psychiatric inpatient who was known to one of the trainers. He was found to be functioning at level 2.15 on an overall rating of the facilitative dimensions when responding to the taped excerpts. He did not know who had received training and was simply instructed to share a problem that he had with each S and then give his rating of their helpfulness to him.

RESULTS

The results are summarized in Tables 12–3 and 12–4. The Wilcoxon paired-comparison signed-ranks test was used to analyze the within-S data for the training group and the control-control group. The analysis revealed that the training group demonstrated significant changes from the pretape measures on both the posttape and standard interview ($p < .02$), and no significant differences between the two post-measures. The control-control group showed no significant differences between the post-measures and the pre-measure nor any differences between the two post-measures.

The Tukey two-sample test was used to analyze the data between groups. The results indicated that the training group's pretape was not significantly different from any of the four control groups' measures. The posttape and interview of the training group were significantly different from all three control-control group measures, the two medicinal treatment measures, the individual treatment tape, and the group treatment tape at the .001 level. The training group post-measures also differed significantly from the individual treatment interview and the group treatment interview ($p < .01$). There were no differences among any of the control groups on any measure.

In addition, the interviewee's mean ratings on helpfulness to him, with the standard error, were as follows: training group, 3.43, $\pm$ .43; control-control group, 1.80, $\pm$ .90; medicinal treatment group, 1.67, $\pm$ .25; individual treatment, 2.08, $\pm$ .33; group treatment, 1.86, $\pm$ .28. The training group differed from the control-control, medicinal treatment, and group treatment ratings at the .01 level of significance and from the individual treatment ratings at the .05 level. None of the control groups differed significantly from each other. A Spearman rank-order correlation between the

Table 12–3

Means and Standard Errors of Facilitative Conditions for the Training and Control-Control Groups

Measure	Empathy M	SE	Regard M	SE	Genuineness M	SE	Concreteness M	SE
Training group (pretape)	1.19	.07	1.17	.07	1.26	.09	1.14	.04
Control-control (pretape)	1.14	.06	1.12	.05	1.20	.07	1.10	.04
Training group (posttape)*	2.55	.12	2.46	.13	2.46	.10	2.60	.13
Control-control (posttape)	1.23	.07	1.16	.06	1.15	.06	1.25	.08
Training group (post interview)*	2.31	.17	2.36	.15	2.40	.15	2.33	.13
Control-control (post interview)	1.32	.06	1.23	.07	1.25	.08	1.21	.06

*Different from the training group pretape measure at the .02 level of significance on all variables.

Table 12–4

Overall Means and Standard Errors for the Training Group and All Control Groups

Measure	Training group		Control-control group		Medicinal treatment		Individual treatment		Group treatment	
	M	SE	M	SE	M	SE	M	SE	M	SE
Pretape	1.19	.06	1.14	.06	—	—	—	—	—	—
Posttape	2.53**	.12	1.20	.06	1.26	.07	1.33	.07	1.29	.12
Post interview	2.35*	.15	1.25	.08	1.28	.07	1.55	.12	1.38	.09

*Significantly different from the individual treatment interview and the group treatment interview at the .01 level.
**Significantly different at the .001 level from all three control-control group measures, the two medicinal treatment measures, the individual treatment tape, and the group treatment tape.

standard interviewee's rating and the expert ratings yielded a correlation of .628 ($p < .01$).

Finally, it was found that the training group's level of functioning prior to treatment and the level of functioning of all control groups was in line with other data available on patient level of functioning. For example, the assessed functioning of psychiatric outpatients previously reported agreed with the levels found in the present study.

DISCUSSION

The results indicate rather conclusively that psychiatric inpatients can significantly improve their level of interpersonal functioning in the brief time of 20 hours. Furthermore, the major implication for traditional therapy is that progress in improving interpersonal relations must be taught directly and systematically since none of the control groups' final levels were given near the final level of the training group. While there is some evidence that the patients of high-level therapists in individual therapy do gain on these interpersonal dimensions, the individual therapy gains they report are not as great nor as efficient in terms of therapy hours.

The low level of facilitative conditions offered by patients in general indicates that the possibility of their helping each other in a group context or in the wards is very slim. If one wants patients to function more effectively with each other, one must train them to do so. The standard interviewee judged his fellow patients in the control groups to be between "unhelpful" and "somewhat helpful" to him whereas the trained patients were rated between "more helpful than unhelpful" and "almost always helpful." This may indicate that untrained patients may have at best a neutral effect and at worst a potentially negative effect on each other. Thus if one wants to create a truly therapeutic atmosphere in either group therapy or on the wards, one must train the patients since they do not exist in isolation from each other but rather are a major part of each other's environment. Potentially the patients are also learning to function more facilitatively with significant others outside the hospital and to the extent that other people are involved in their lives, this type of treatment could bring added benefits and hence become a major goal of therapy.

In summary, while training in interpersonal functioning appears to constitute a potential preferred mode of treatment with neuropsychiatric patients, future research needs to focus not only on the generalizability of the results but also on their duration, as well as the effects of this type of training on the psychological problems that bring a patient to a hospital, clinic, or private practitioner.

It is clear that the training group demonstrated significant improvement and was found to be functioning significantly more effectively than groups receiving drugs, individual therapy, or group therapy. While the study established the benefits to the patients themselves, including a significantly greater discharge and maintenance rate on follow-up, it is a logical extension of this work to train the patients to help other patients as well as themselves.

The results were again overwhelmingly in favor of training when compared with the different forms of treatment. *The training group members demonstrated significant improvement and were found to be functioning at significantly higher levels interpersonally following treatment than the members of the other groups.* In addition, follow-up research indicated that the training group members got out and stayed out of the hospital with greater frequency than the treatment group members.

A replication of the pioneering work by Pierce and Drasgow (1969) was incorporated into a program which was searching to extend the earlier work by investigating the range of client changes produced by training. Incorporating group therapy and nonspecific treatment control groups, Vitalo (1971) found that systematic human relations training was nearly six times more effective than modeling in group therapy, in demonstrating neuropsychiatric patients' improvement in interpersonal functioning. Further, the skills acquired during training were employed by the patients in relationships outside of the immediate group setting, and there was evidence of the patients' improved social functioning.

Again, it was most significant that just as in the Carkhuff and Bierman and Pierce and Drasgow studies, *the training group was significantly more effective than all other forms of treatment, particularly on those dimensions which the training was calculated to effect.* With the replication of these results with other populations, it becomes increasingly clear that training approaches appear to be the most direct, economical, and effective mode of helping.

A generalization to other learning areas appears in the work of Minuchin,

Chamberlain, and Graubard (1967), who made direct attempts to change the learning behavior of disturbed, delinquent children. It was assumed that the child's difficulty in school behavior and learning was related to (1) a difficulty in focusing attention, (2) a communications style that handicapped the child in the enlistment and ordering of new information, and (3) the child's search for a solution to conflicts with the teacher. The authors therefore designed an intervention curriculum to instruct the children in the communications system used in school and to train them in observation of others as well as in self-observation. Each session was structured in the form of games and the sessions were built systematically around the following skills: listening, the implications of noise, staying on a topic, taking turns and sharing in communication, telling a simple story, building up a longer story, asking relative and cogent questions, and categorizing and classifying information and role-playing. There was a marked improvement in attention, style of communication, and cognition.

In a similar manner, Gittleman (1965) trained aggressive, acting-out children in the skills that they needed to handle interpersonal situations effectively. The method involved the use of role-playing or behavior rehearsal, whereby various instigatory situations are played out by the child and other group members. While the techniques were similar to psychodrama, desensitization procedures were incorporated.

The most direct form of training as treatment, then, is to train the helpee himself in the skills which he needs to function effectively.[1] The culmination of such a program is to train the helpee to develop his own training programs. To say, "Helpee, heal thyself!" and to train him in the necessary skills is the most direct—and also the most honest and most effective—form of treatment known to man.

TRAINING AS A PREFERRED MODE OF HUMAN RELATIONS

Still other applications of training as treatment extend into problems between people. The same principles which hold in individual and group treatment may hold for treating large segments of society in dealing with social problems. For example, systematic training programs in interpersonal skills have been conducted to facilitate the relations between races and between generations. One such project involved black parents and white teachers. Viewing racial relations problems in the broader context of human relations problems, members of each subgrouping were trained first to learn to communicate effectively with each other. Only then were they trained to communicate effectively with members of other subgroupings. Thus, black (white) adults worked first with black (white) adults, and only upon successful completion of this stage did they move to work with other races and the younger generation.

[1] Comprehensive training programs that integrate training in interpersonal skills with systematic desensitization and systematic training in training helpees to devise their own training programs are described in Chapter 14.

PROJECT 28
Training in Relations
Between Races and Generations*

A major problem of this or any age is the inability of one segment of a society to communicate effectively with another. Nowhere is this more evident than in the problems between representatives of a majority-dominated system and minority groups within that system, as with white and black Americans. The question for the helping professions is what tangible offerings do education and psychology, counseling and psychotherapy have to facilitate communication leading to constructive resolution of the difficulties between these segments. These problems are intensified in counseling relationships between white counselors and black counselees where the little research evidence which is available suggests the differential effects of race.

As with any helping process, the real tasks are twofold: (1) to operationalize goals involving tangible benefits or skills that can lead to the amelioration of the difficulties between the individuals and the groups involved; (2) to develop empirically based programs in systematic step-by-step progressions in such a manner as to insure the ultimate success of the program. The goal of establishing effective relations between races may be operationalized by assessments of the level of communication between representatives of these races. The means for attaining effective communication will involve successive reinforcement experiences in communication developed in such a manner as to shape the most effective final level of communication.

In the present study, relations between white teachers and black parents, an area of intense conflict in urban areas around the country, are emphasized. In addition, these difficulties are compounded by difficulties in communication between generations so that, for example, the white helper or teacher may have even greater difficulty in communicating with the black child than with the parents of that child. Accordingly, relations between generations as well as between races are attended.

METHODOLOGY

Trainees

Fourteen teachers enrolled in a program in interpersonal skills and ten Negro parent volunteers from the black community adjacent to the

*Reprinted in part with permission from the *Journal of Counseling Psychology*, 1970, 17, 413–418, where it first appeared as "Training as a Preferred Mode of Facilitating Relations Between Races and Generations," by Robert R. Carkhuff and George Banks.

college were involved. The teachers ranged in experience up to ten years and in age to their 50's. They included eight females and six males. The community volunteers were all females and also ranged in age to their 50's. All but two of the mothers were the sole means of support for their families.

Procedure

The teachers and parents met every morning for a total of 20 hours over a three-week period. In broad outline both teachers and parents were pre-, mid- and post-tested on a variety of real-life indexes of interpersonal functioning. Specifically, the ten parents and 14 teachers were subdivided into two groups matched on the basis of the results of the pre-testing. One group was assigned a white trainer for the first ten hours of training and a black trainer for the second ten hours and in the second group the order of trainer race was reversed.

Training

The primary purpose of the program was to effect positive changes in relations between races. A secondary purpose was to effect positive changes in relations between generations and races. Thus, for example, the specific goals for the professional helpers, the white teachers, were twofold: (1) improved communication between white teachers and black parents; (2) improved communication between white teachers and black children. The training program, based upon extensive research concerning the process and outcome of effective helping relationships, involved the following behavioral sequence of learning experiences: (1) communication between adults within racial groups, i.e. white teachers with white teachers and Negro parents with Negro parents; (2) communication between adults of different races; (3) communication between generations within races involving white (black) adults alternately role-playing white (black) children; (4) communication between generations and between races, i.e. between white (black) adults and black (white) role-playing children; (5) communication between generations both within and between races, i.e. between white and black parents and white and black children who were brought into the program.

The training program employed rating scales of the following helper-offered dimensions related extensively in previous research to the constructive change or gain of persons seeking help: empathic understanding, respect, specificity or concreteness, genuineness, confrontation and immediacy. The training was developed in step-by-step progressions from simple to complex responses with trainees role-playing both helper and helpee. The trainees first learned to communicate effectively in terms of the dimensions which were *responsive* to the helpee's expressions (empathy, respect, specificity). For example, on empathy the trainees first learned to make responses that were interchangeable with the helpees in terms of the affect and meaning which the helpee was expressing, following upon which they learned to make additive empathic responses which went beyond the helpee's expressions and enabled the helpee to explore and understand himself at deeper levels. Then the trainees learned to communicate effectively in terms of the dimensions which were *initiated* from the helper's experience (genuineness, confrontation, immediacy). For example, in confrontation the trainees first learned to indicate to the helpee an open-ended awareness of discrepancies in the helpee's behavior following upon which the trainees learned to confront the helpee with specific discrepancies in the helpee's behavior. At each stage as the trainees assumed the role of helper they were constantly given feedback in terms of ratings on the scales from all members of the group and its leaders in a process of "shaping" effective responses.

Both the black and white trainer were experienced trainers and counselors, the black in his 20's and the white in his 30's, with the ages reflecting relatively greater experience of the white, and both were functioning at high levels of facilitative and action-oriented dimensions (above 4.0 overall dimensions).

Testing

Before and after the first phase of training and following completion of the program, the trainees were tested with the ratings of the following standard indexes: (1) *an index of communication* based upon (a) trainee responses to 16 standard helpee expressions crossing different affects (depression-distress, anger-hostility, elation-excitement) with different problem areas (social-interpersonal, educational-vocational, child-rearing, sexual-marital, confrontation) and (b) trainee responses to five racial relations items designed specifically for the program in which black and white males and females and an unidentified child presented typical problems; (2) *an index of discrimination* based upon ratings of alternative responses (crossing level of responsiveness of facilitation with initiative or action-orientation) to both the (a) standard stimulus expressions and (b) the racial relations items.

In addition, each trainee was cast in the helping role with a set to be "as helpful as possible" in order to maximize the conditions for his demonstrating his highest level of interpersonal skills. Thus, each trainee's *level of functioning in the helping role* was assessed by interviews before and after training with the following four helpees: (1) a Negro adult; (2) a white adult; (3) a Negro child; (4) a white child. The children were in their early teens.

Finally, in order to assess the possible differential effects of white and black trainers who are functioning at high levels upon white and black trainees, an intermediate testing following the first phase of training and involving interviews with both white and black adults was conducted.

Ratings of communication level were accomplished employing the same scales by experienced raters of demonstrated rate-rerate reliabilities

Table 12-5

Pre- and Post-training Differences on Communication and Discrimination for Black and White Trainees

Communication	PRE-TRAINING		POST-TRAINING	
	Black	White	Black	White
Standard Tape	1.46	1.44	2.31	2.56
Racial Tape	1.44	1.33	2.30	2.54
Black Adult	1.53	1.38	2.53	2.59
White Adult	1.41	1.48	2.39	2.63
Black Child	1.49	1.34	2.07	1.86
White Child	1.42	1.49	2.04	1.99
Discrimination*				
Standard Tape	1.51	1.20	.92	.69
Racial Tape	1.52	.94	.84	.54

*The lower the discrimination scores the more accurate the rater.

who exhibited Pearson product moment inter-rater reliabilities in the .80's and .90's for all dimensions. Discrimination scores were obtained by the absolute deviations from the pre-ratings of experts different from those accomplishing the communication ratings.

RESULTS

The overall mean levels of interpersonal functioning (combining levels of all dimensions) of both white and black trainees for the pre- and post-training indexes of communication and discrimination may be seen in Table 12–5. The results are very similar to the tables for the individual dimensions. As can be seen from examination of the communication data, whites and blacks, beginning from very similar levels, both demonstrated gains in interpersonal skills, with the white teachers tending to gain more with the adults on the standard and racial indexes and with the black parents tending to gain more with the children. In discrimination the table indicates that both black and white improved: the blacks, beginning from relatively poor levels of discrimination, exhibited more accurate post-training levels of discrimination, especially on the racial items while the white teachers, beginning from relatively accurate discriminations, became even more accurate on both standard indexes.

Analysis of the data was in three phases. First, a repeated measurements design to test pre-post differences for blacks and whites separately on all of the individual dimensions for all of the six indexes of communication and the two indexes of discrimination was employed. The F tests were all significant at or beyond the .01 level. Thus, the training did effect significant changes in the levels of communication and discrimination in both black and white trainees.

Second, an analysis of covariance on post scores of blacks and whites was conducted in order to compare blacks and whites. The trainee's initial levels of functioning were used as the covariates. The results indicated that only on the standard and the racial indexes were there significant differences, with the whites receiving higher ratings than the blacks. There were also significant differences on the standard discrimination index, with the whites receiving more accurate scores than the blacks.

Finally, a two factor (one within S's and two between S's) design was employed to test the first half of training versus the second half of training (within S's factor) and to test the effects of the race of trainer (between S's factor), with the dependent variable being the change scores of the black and white trainees in response to black and white adults. The results indicate the uniformly significant differences between the first and second half of training with the first half of training effecting the greater changes. The race of trainer was uniformly not a significant source of effect, although the white trainer did tend, in general, to elicit slightly greater changes in the trainees than the black trainer. While an interaction of trainer race and phases of training was significant for the white trainees with white adults, the "t" tests were not significant.

DISCUSSION

The pre-training data suggest that difficulties in racial relations may be part of a larger human relations problem. Both blacks and whites tend to communicate at low levels with other whites and blacks. Put another way, not only is there a lack of effective communication between blacks and whites but also between blacks and blacks and whites and whites of the same and differing generations. The pre-data are particularly significant when we consider (1) that the teachers are paid professionals whose effectiveness is contingent upon their interpersonal skills and (2) that trained teachers do not differ significantly from untrained parents.

With regard to discrimination, the pre-training data are consistent with previous evidence indicating a lack of significant relationship between discrimination and communication among low-level communicators. The whites, while they were able to discriminate fairly accurately, were unable to communicate effectively. Indeed, if anything, they evidenced a pronounced tendency in communication to give advice without taking the helpee's expressions into consideration. The blacks, in turn, while they discriminated poorly, did not communicate significantly different from the whites.

The post-training data suggest that the systematic training was effective in eliciting higher levels of functioning in interpersonal skills. Both blacks and whites gained significantly over the course of training, with each tending to do slightly better with members of their own identity groups, a finding consistent with previous evidence. That is, the whites tended to function at slightly higher levels with white adults and children while the blacks demonstrated a similar tendency with black adults and children. Similarly, the adults tended to function at higher levels with adults than with children. This result was consistent with the pre-data and reflects perhaps some generalized greater facility in communication with persons who are similar in characteristics.

However, in general the blacks tended to do relatively better with children than with whites while the whites tended to do relatively better with adults, perhaps reflecting some tendency for the more educated whites to emphasize adult and verbal communication while the blacks emphasized the words and feelings that communicated to the children. This interpretation is buttressed by the results of the written responses to the standard and verbal stimuli where the whites indicated a greater utilization of the training experience as reflected in the higher ratings of their responses. With regard to discrimination, while both groups demonstrated significant improvement, the black gains were relatively greater. However, the whites in their increasing accuracy may have reached a point of "diminishing returns."

With regard to the effect of trainer level of functioning, it is important to note that while previous literature indicates the differential effects of helper race, trainers of one race functioning at high levels can effect significant gains in trainees of the same and different races. In terms of the white trainer this means that above a certain level of functioning he has as great a chance of effecting constructive changes in blacks as black trainers. This remains qualified by the fact that while all trainees gained the most during the first half of training, the white trainees did tend to function at higher levels with white adults under the white trainer's tutelage than under the black.

Systematic training in interpersonal skills, then, was effective in "shaping" higher and more effective levels of communication and discrimination between races and with the younger generation, although the greatest changes took place where there was the most practice, with the adults.

The most difficult and final stage, as we have seen, that of enabling the white teacher (black parent) to communicate effectively with the black child (white child), was accomplished with a high degree of success because success was built into the project by making movement to the next stage contingent upon satisfactory performance at the last stage.

There are many variations on this basic training theme. For example, the whites and blacks might have been trained separately in preparation for meeting and communicating with each other. This may be essential in some crisis situations when there is enough time and when a further breakdown in relations cannot be tolerated. In addition, the youth, white and black, may be trained, separately or together, in preparation for the adult, white and black.

Bringing together black and white in this fashion has been a theme of many of the programs at the Center. Masters degree candidates were recruited from among black and white leaders in the community. The black educators group developed and trained a white educator auxiliary group. White volunteers were systematically trained in preparation for functioning as helpers on community projects.

More behavioristic programs have been instituted in training civil rights workers in passive resistance (Belfrage, 1965) and in preparing black children for entry into desegregated schools by subjecting them systematically to a hierarchy of provocation and abuse which they might expect upon entering school (Gittleman, 1964).

With the application to problems between people, entire communities may be developed or rehabilitated. Indeed, the problems of society at large may be treated by training, so to speak. In this context, the development of the social action concept of functional professionals has been a natural extension of training as treatment.

The results have indicated the enormous success of functional professional programs in social service spheres of functioning. In the social action area, the direct implications for the credentialed professionals are twofold: (1) to acquire the skills necessary to establish their own functionality and (2) to elevate their levels of responsibility to consultancy levels involving designing, training, and researching the effects of functional professional programs.

At another level, systematic training provides the opportunity for the most potent form of traditional psychotherapeutic treatment. For example, at one advanced stage of systematic training in interpersonal skills, a trainer may explore and experience real problems at the most intense levels for the following reasons: (1) all trainees, including the helper-trainee working directly with the helpee-trainee, are functioning at high levels of interpersonal skills; (2) following the therapeutic interaction with the helper-trainee, the helpee-trainee may select from among the responses of multiple trained helper-trainees in the group, and he may interact extensively with those helper-trainees who are most effectively "tuned in" on his problem. Thus, the trainee with a problem has the benefit of numerous trained and high level functioning helpers right within the context of the training group. The probability for improvement is increased accordingly.

Again, it is to be emphasized that training programs should be developed, as we have seen, in all spheres of functioning—the physical and intellectual as well as the emotional-interpersonal—in order to effect maximum benefits for the individual involved. Thus, for example, the emotional-interpersonal program should be accompanied by systematic training programs in the physical realm (development of an exercise program to improve cardiovascular functioning or to acquire physical skills, etc.) and in the intellectual realm (systematic development of intellectual journal entries into effective working cosmology as well as productivity and creativity in intellectual areas, etc.) (Carkhuff, 1969a).

Perhaps the major conclusion which we can draw from our development of the concept of training as a preferred mode of helping is that effective helping is a function of an effective helping relationship and an effective helping program. When either the relationship or program is effective, benefits accrue. When both the relationship and program are effective, maximum benefits accrue.

The helping relationship is critical because it is the vehicle by which the helper becomes both agent and model for the helpee. An effective relationship enables a low level functioning helpee to function at higher levels in critical areas of functioning. Given an effective helping relationship, the most direct and effective modality for accomplishing this is to train the helpee directly in the conditions necessary to function at higher levels in these areas.

In turn, an effective relationship establishes the helper as a potent reinforcer for the helpee, so that he may involve the helpee in programs that will influence the helpee constructively—whether in the elimination of distressing symptomatology or in the attainment of desirable goals. Again, the most direct and effective modality for accomplishing these functions is to train the helpee directly in the methodologies necessary to develop and to implement such programs.

The professional trainer, then, whether he is working directly with the helpee or training a symbiont to work with the helpee, must first himself establish a relationship with the helpee or symbiont so that he can institute his training program. In this regard, a comprehensive program of training as helping may be defined by the following operations: (1) training in the interpersonal and other skills necessary to function effectively; (2) training in the methods of discerning and developing effective courses of action; and (3) training in the means and modalities necessary to implement the resultant programs. The effectiveness of these three facets of training has been demonstrated extensively.

Individually, then, training programs in each of these areas have demonstrated a clear superiority to any and all other training and treatment control programs. *Together, in an integrated training program, they constitute the most comprehensive and effective form of helping available to man.*

Training is truly the preferred modality for effecting therapeutic change or gain.

REFERENCES

Adler, A. *The individual psychology of Alfred Adler: A systematic presentation in selection from his writings.* H. L. Ansbacher & R. R. Ansbacher (Eds.). New York: Basic Books, 1956.

Andronico, M. P., & Guerney, B. G. The potential application of filial therapy to the school situation. *Journal of School Psychology,* 1967, **6,** 2–7.

Ayllon, T., & Michael, J. The psychiatric nurse as a behavior engineer. *Journal of Experimental Analysis of Behavior,* 1959, **2,** 323–334.

Bachrach, A. J., Erwin, W. J., & Mohr, J. P. The control of eating behavior in an anorexic by operant conditioning techniques. In L. Ullmann & L. Krasner (Eds.), *Case studies in behavior modification.* New York: Holt, Rinehart and Winston, Inc., 1966.

Baruch, Dorothy. *New ways in discipline.* New York: McGraw-Hill, 1949.

Becker, W. C., Madsen, C. H., Arnold, C. R., & Thomas, D. R. The contingent use of teacher attention and praise in reducing classroom behavior problems. *Journal of Special Education,* 1967, **1,** 187–307.

Belfrage, S. *Freedom summer.* New York: Viking Press, 1965.

Berenson, B. G., Carkhuff, R. R., and Myrus, P. The interpersonal functioning and training of college students. *Journal of Counseling Psychology,* 1966, **13,** 441–446.

Brookover, W. B., Erickson, E., Hamachek, D., Joiner, L., LePere, J., Paterson, A., & Thomas, S. Self-concept of ability and school achievement. In B. G. Guerney (Ed.), *Psychotherapeutic agents.* New York: Holt, Rinehart and Winston, 1969.

Carkhuff, R. R. *Helping and human relations: A primer for lay and professional helpers.* Vol. I. *Selection and training.* New York: Holt, Rinehart and Winston, 1969. (a)

Carkhuff, R. R. *Helping and human relations: A primer for lay and professional helpers.* Vol. II. *Practice and research.* New York: Holt, Rinehart and Winston, 1969. (b)

Carkhuff, R. R. Training as a preferred mode of treatment. *Journal of Counseling Psychology,* 1971, **18,** 123–131.

Carkhuff, R. R., & Banks, G. Training as a preferred mode of facilitating relations between races and generations. *Journal of Counseling Psychology,* 1970, **17,** 413–418.

Carkhuff, R. R., & Berenson, B. G. *Beyond counseling and therapy.* New York: Holt, Rinehart and Winston, 1967.

Carkhuff, R. R., & Bierman, R. Training as a preferred mode of treatment of parents of emotionally disturbed children. *Journal of Counseling Psychology,* 1970, **17,** 157–161.

Davison, G. C. The training of undergraduates as social reinforcers for autistic children. In L. Ullmann and L. Krasner (Eds.), *Case studies in behavior modification.* New York: Holt, Rinehart and Winston, 1965.

Freud, S. Analysis of a phobia in a five-year old boy. In *Collected papers.* New York: Basic Books, 1959, pp. 149–289.

Fuchs, N. R. Play therapy at home. *The Merrill-Palmer Quarterly,* 1957, **3,** 89–95.

Gittleman, M. Report on the work of the Medical Committee for Human Rights in Mississippi. Paper read at Albert Einstein College of Medicine in New York, November, 1964.

Gittleman, M. Behavior rehearsal as a technique in child treatment. *Journal of Child Psychology and Psychiatry,* 1965, **6,** 251–255.

Guerney, B. G., Jr. Filial therapy: Description and rationale. *Journal of Consulting Psychology,* 1964, **28,** 304–310.

Guerney, B. G., Jr., Guerney, L. F., & Andronico, M. P. Filial therapy: A case illustration. *Yale Scientific Magazine,* 1966, **40,** 6–14.

Harris, Florence, Wolf, M., & Baer, D. M. Effects of adult social reinforcement on child behavior. *Young Children,* 1964, **20,** 8–17.

Hawkins, R. P., Peterson, R. F., Schweid, E., & Bijou, S. W. Behavior therapy in the home: Amelioration of problem parent-child relations with the parent in a therapeutic role. *Journal of Experimental Child Psychology,* 1966, **4,** 99–107.

Horowitz, F. D. Social-reinforcement effects on child behavior. *Journal of Nursery Education,* 1963, **18,** 176–184.

Jones, M. C. A laboratory study of fear: The case of Peter. *Pedagogical Seminars.* 1924, **31,** 308–315.

Krasner, L., & Ullmann, L. *Research in behavior modification.* New York: Holt, Rinehart and Winston, 1965.

Kreitzer, S. F. College students in a behavior therapy program with hospitalized emotionally disturbed children. In B. G. Guerney (Ed.), *Psychotherapeutic agents.* New York: Holt, Rinehart and Winston, 1969.

Minuchin, S., Chamberlain, P., & Graubard, P. A project to teach learning skills to disturbed delinquent children. *American Journal of Orthopsychiatry,* 1967, **37,** 558–567.

Moustakas, C. E. The frequency and intensity of negative attitudes expressed in play therapy: A comparison of well-adjusted and disturbed young children. *Journal of Genetic Psychology,* 1955, **86,** 309–325.

O'Leary, K. D., O'Leary, S., and Becker, W. C. Modification in deviant sibling interaction pattern in the home. In B. G. Guerney (Ed.), *Psychotherapeutic agents.* New York: Holt, Rinehart and Winston, 1969.

Patterson, G. R., & Brodsky, G. A behavior modification program for a child with multiple problem behaviors. *Journal of Child Psychology and Psychiatry,* 1966, **7,** 277–295.

Pierce, R., & Drasgow, J. Teaching facilitative interpersonal functioning to psychiatric inpatients. *Journal of Counseling Psychology,* 1969, **16,** 295–298.

Rogers, C. R. *Client centered therapy.* Boston: Houghton Mifflin, 1951.

Rogers, C. R., Gendlin, E., Kiesler, D., & Truax, C. B. *The therapeutic relationship and its impact.* Madison, Wisconsin: University of Wisconsin Press, 1967.

Santilli, Muriel. Training parents in play-specific interpersonal skills. In R. R.

Carkhuff, *Helping and human relations.* Vol. I. New York: Holt, Rinehart and Winston, 1969.

Shah, S. A. Training and utilizing a mother as a therapist for her child. In B. G. Guerney (Ed.), *Psychotherapeutic agents.* New York: Holt, Rinehart and Winston, 1969.

Stollak, Gary E. The experimental effects of training college students as play therapists. Paper presented, Midwestern Psychological Association, Chicago, Illinois, 1967.

Stover, L., & Guerney, B. G. The efficacy of training procedures for mothers in filial therapy. *Psychotherapy: Research and practice,* 1967, **4,** 110–115.

Ullmann, L., & Krasner, L. *Case studies in behavior modification.* New York: Holt, Rinehart and Winston, 1965.

Vitalo, R. Teaching improved interpersonal functioning as a preferred mode of treatment. *Journal of Clinical Psychology,* 1971, **27,** 166-170.

Wahler, R. G., Winkel, G. H., Peterson, R. F., & Morrison, D. C. Mothers as behavior therapists for their own children, *Behaviour Research and Therapy,* 1965, **3,** 113–124.

Walder, L. O., Cohen, S. O., Breiter, D. E., Daston, P. G., Hirsch, I. S., & Liebowitz, J. M. Teaching behavioral principles to parents of disturbed children. In B. G. Guerney (Ed.), *Psychotherapeutic agents.* New York: Holt, Rinehart and Winston, 1969.

Wolf, M., Risley, T. R., & Mees, H. L. Application of operant conditioning procedures to the behavior problems of an autistic child. *Behaviour Research and Therapy,* 1964, **1,** 305–312.

Wolpe, J. *Psychotherapy by reciprocal inhibition.* Stanford, Calif.: Stanford University Press, 1958.

Zimmerman, E. H., & Zimmerman, J. The alteration of behavior in a special classroom situation. *Journal of the Experimental Analysis of Behavior,* 1962, **5,** 59–60.

CHAPTER 13
Training as a Precondition for Teaching

It is absurd to argue that a white child has a response to a given item that a black child does not have, or that a white child has three responses and the black child two, when, given appropriate teaching and training programs, each may have the potential for 20 or 30 or 40 or 50 or an indeterminate number of responses.

This point is underscored when we realize fully the physiological implications of systematic stimulation and training. Intelligence as we know it is a function of memory traces or the structural changes that are brought about in the nervous system through stimulation, largely occurring in early childhood. The absolute differences in these memory traces in infancy are compounded geometrically through childhood, adolescence, and adulthood. Thus, the child with few memory traces falls progressively further behind the child with many who is putting the traces together in new permutations and combinations. In summary, early stimulation and training experiences translate to anatomical terms that dictate the restrictiveness or expansiveness of learning throughout life.

Indeed, if we accept these propositions concerning early environmental stimulation or training, the implications for the black child are profound. If intelligence is a function of structural changes in the nervous system brought about through stimulation and if, as the American Association for the Advancement of Science Study (Chapter 3) implies, many black children are superior in terms of the responsiveness of their nervous systems, then with adequate training these children should become superior achievers.

The key is training!

The key is always training!

Training, to be sure, involves not only the intellectual skills described here nor the emotional-interpersonal skills emphasized in this book. Training involves all of the spheres of human functioning—the physical, the emotional, and the intellectual. Indeed, the fact that the emotional-interpersonal realm, the most difficult to operationalize, *can be* operationalized has implications for the systematic development of training programs in the intellectual and physical spheres of functioning.

Each realm of functioning, we have seen, is integrally related to the other. Together, they define the fully functioning person, the effective man—his health, his productivity and creativity, his essence as a man and a human being.

No one who would live life fully can do less than he is capable of. And systematic training programs make delivery possible at each level and in every sphere of endeavor in life.

The best of men—whatever their field of endeavor—are in constant training or, if you will, always learning to sharpen their skills. The athlete or soldier who has a broad base in the intellectual and emotional as well as the physical sphere can make the sharpest thrust in his efforts. The scholar or teacher who is broadly based in physical and emotional as well as intellectual development can produce his works in sharpest relief. The parent or therapist who has a broad base in physical and intellectual, as well as emotional and interpersonal, development can listen and hear and communicate and act most sensitively and most accurately.

Traditional education and traditional treatment, as we have known them, are processes, more or less random, that we engage in when we do not know what we are doing.

Training is what we do when we know what we are doing.

TRAINING AS ACHIEVEMENT

In the same manner that parents learn child-rearing skills, teachers can learn and transmit those skills associated with effective learning. Whether they involve the substance or method of education or the interpersonal skills needed to transmit the substance and method, the learning programs must be systematic. They can be systematic only to the degree that teachers are able to describe their goals or, in other terms, to the degree that they know what they are doing.

In effective programs, then, both the teachers and the students are trained systematically to acquire the skills which they need to function effectively. The teachers are trained systematically in their course matter and in the different methodologies to teach the course matter. The students, in turn, are trained systematically in their course matter and in the different methodologies needed to learn the course matter. Students and teachers are viewed in new roles: the teachers as master trainers and the students as trainees.

This approach does, to be sure, run counter to many of the approaches favored today. "Learning by discovery," for example, is a frequently heard phrase. In the hands of a master trainer who knows what he wishes to accomplish and reinforces the student's behavior according to the student's movement toward that goal, this can be a powerful learning device. Again, unfortunately, most teachers have not defined their objectives so precisely that they are able to accord their reinforcements so accurately.

Cultural enrichment is another catchword in education. The children in Springfield, as in many communities, are so culturally enriched that their high points are in capitalization and spelling and their low points in reading and arithmetic concepts and problems, all this with the black students significantly behind the white! Cultural enrichment is a fraud if it is not based upon the systematic acquisition of skills. One cannot be a good artist or anything else if he is not broadly based in tangential areas as well as deeply rooted in his speciality area.

In lieu of these approaches teachers and students may, in effect, learn together. For example, the teacher learns association methods so that she can transmit the principles of association or similarities to the students. Equipped with the necessary methodological skills, the students can "learn by discovery." Indeed, except in preliminary skills "shaping" programs, there is no meaningful "learning by discovery."

With the established relationship between the communication level of the teachers and the achievement of the students, the colleges have been remiss in developing systematic programs for interpersonal skills. Colleges, particularly departments of education, have been the last haven for the ineffectual, and the more the programs they sponsor are open-ended, absent-minded, random, and directionless, the greater the likelihood that the ineffectual will not be exposed. Unfortunately, the teachers in the primary and secondary schools are in the front lines, on the firing lines, and they, not their mentors, are the ones who suffer and become disillusioned and leave because of educational inadequacies.

Current trends converge in emphasizing the need for more systematic teacher training. One is that the educational field is quickly shifting from a seller's to a buyer's market. The colleges and universities, as is their wont, are not only irresponsible in producing inadequately prepared teachers but also in producing an overwhelming surplus of them. If there is one time in history to exert quality control over teachers, it is now. If the colleges do not do so—and this begins with the staffs themselves—the crisis-ridden schools must do so. With the abundance of applicants the schools can now afford to do so. Indeed, they cannot afford not to do so.

The teacher, then, must become an all-purpose person. He must acquire and put "on the line" not simply his teaching skills, but his helping skills as well. We must extend the designations for all public officials to include the notion of "helper." Thus, the teacher becomes a helper-teacher, just as a policeman becomes a helper-cop.

While our immediate concern is with the goals of teaching student achievement in specific areas, we can best effect gains in all areas by training the teachers in the necessary skills to effect the desired gains. In the following study, a group of teachers were systematically trained in interpersonal skills, and their effects upon student achievement and a variety of other indexes were studied in comparison to the effects of untrained teachers.

PROJECT 29
*Training Teachers
as Teachers**

The educational literature has repeatedly referred to the importance of interpersonal variables in the teaching process. A number of theoretically oriented papers have appeared, as well as several reports of research on various factors hypothesized to be of importance. However, little systematic work has been done to translate any specific and meaningful relationships involving these variables to actual teaching and teacher-training situations.

The current research was conceived within the theoretical framework linking certain process variables found by psychologists (Carkhuff and Berenson, 1967) to have apparent relevance for all human relationships. Preliminary investigations in the educational context (Aspy, 1969; Aspy and Hadlock, 1967; Kratochvil, Carkhuff, and Berenson, 1969; Truax and Tatum, 1966) have indicated in general that the more accurate a teacher's understanding of his or her pupils (empathy), the higher the commitment to bringing out their full potential (respect). And the better the communication of this understanding and respect to them, the more the students learn.

The present investigation was undertaken in order to further clarify the important variables, to investigate their role in the preparation of teachers, and to verify their relationship to pupil achievement. It was expected (a) that participants in an interpersonal process training program would experience more significant gains in their ability to discriminate facilitative and destructive teaching situations and to communicate facilitatively with their classes than would non-participants in such a program; (b) that quality of interpersonal processes to which teacher-trainees are exposed during their practicum experiences would relate positively to their own interpersonal functioning; and (c) that quality of interpersonal processes occurring in the classroom would relate positively to pupil achievement.

METHOD

Subjects

Subjects were 16 graduate students, 15 experienced teachers, and 99 students in classes taught by them. All of these people were involved in an M.A.-level teacher preparation program at a school for the deaf in Buffalo, New York. The 16 graduate students comprised the entire 1968–1969 teacher training program, with the exception of two trainees who were unable to participate in the research. The 15 experienced teachers

*Reprinted in part with permission from the *Journal of Research and Development in Education,* 1971, 4, 52–69, where it first appeared as "The Effects of Systematic Human Relations Training upon Student Achievement," by Thomas J. Hefele.

were all selected on the basis of their each having at least one assigned teacher-trainee for a six-week practicum from mid-February until the end of March. The 99 students were included in the study on the basis of their membership in the classes normally taught by the critic-teachers.

Procedure

The total research effort was divided into a Process Phase and an Outcome Phase. The Process Phase involved the measurement of variables relevant to teacher and teacher-trainee interpersonal functioning. It also involved investigation of the impact of a special interpersonal process training program on an experimental group of teacher-trainees. The Outcome Phase involved study of the relationships between pupil achievement criteria and teacher interpersonal functioning predictor measures.

Process phase. Three videotape recordings of one-half hour teaching sessions of the teacher-critics and teacher-trainees were made (in November, February, and April) and were rated on levels of facilitative functioning by a pair of experienced raters (rate-rerate $r = .63$). Ratings were made during the first, fourth, and sixth five-minute segments of the films.

The children in each of these videotaped lessons were also rated by the same pair of raters during the second, third, and fifth five-minute segments of the films. Mean pupil involvement scores were computed for each five-minute segment thereby providing a score representative of overall classroom atmosphere. Although the reliability of these ratings was relatively low, they were tentatively retained due to the important relationships which they had with the other variables.

The functioning of two teachers who declined to be filmed and their respective classes was assessed on the same scales and according to the same half-hour format. Two different raters whose ratings were determined to be highly correlated with those of the pair of videotape raters secured these ratings by sitting in on actual classes.

Just prior to the February filming, each of the sixteen teacher-trainees was assigned to each of fifteen experienced critic-teachers (two of the trainees, however, being assigned to one critic). All of the trainees then observed and taught daily under their respective critic teachers during a six-week period in February and March.

Outcome phase. The achievement measurement was two-fold. In the first section, the three Department Supervisors at the school—one for the Primary grades (up to and including Grade 2B), one for the Intermediate grades (up to and including Grade 6), and one for Junior High and High School grades (up to and including Grade 9)—were asked in both January and May to rate each of the children ($N = 99$) in the classes involved in the research according to their level of achievement. In general, the supervisors were asked to make a judgment as to whether or not the child involved was performing at the level of competence they would expect for a child with his abilities and at his grade level. They were then to make a determination as to how far above or below expectation he was performing by indicating on the rating scale for each nine-point achievement category the level of his achievement (each point representing one month, September through May) and also by indicating on the five-point scale their judgment as to the overall satisfactoriness of the pupil's performance.

In order to insure that the supervisors were rating essentially the same factors, they were asked to meet with one another to discuss and agree upon the criteria. Rate-rerate reliability figures for these criterion variables ranged from .75 to .92.

In the second section, grade level scores from the Reading, Arithmetic, and Literature sub-tests of the various forms of the California Achievement Tests used at the school for the deaf were collected for those children (N = 29) who (a) were rated by the supervisors; and (b) had been tested both in March of 1968 and in February of 1969. Differences (in months) between the 1968 and 1969 grade level equivalents on each of the three sub-tests constituted the three dependent variables used in this section of the achievement measurement. It was assumed that, although a four-month period of school time had elapsed between the 1968 testing and the beginning of the current academic year, for which no information was available on the classroom situation, it would be a worthwhile endeavor to look also at the relationships between these three criteria and the teacher functioning predictors. It was unfortunate that the nature of the C.A.T. and the primitive state of achievement measurement in deaf education precluded availability of C.A.T. scores for all ninety-nine of the children. However, it was expected that analysis of the limited data would yield useful additional information about the relationships between pupil achievement and the teacher interpersonal functioning predictors.

RESULTS

The results of a regression analysis of the pre-measure (trainee functioning in November) on the four dependent variables, viz., (a) trainee functioning in February, (b) February functioning of critic-teachers selected by the trainees, (c) involvement of the children when taught by the trainees, and (d) involvement of the children when taught by their regular classroom teachers were such (F-ratio in multivariate association test = 7.29, df = 4/42, $p < .0002$) that it was decided to use the pre-measure as a covariate in subsequent analyses.

The multivariate analysis of covariance on outcome of the interpersonal process training yielded a significant multivariate F-ratio ($p < .0007$) and significant univariate F-ratios for all four dependent variables. Inspection of the means and standard deviations (Table 13–1) for the February ratings on each of these variables pointed out that all of the differences were in the expected directions and that the interpersonal training participants had secured higher ratings. Indeed, the covariance analysis, insofar as it adjusted for the November difference between the training and control groups, indicated even more dramatic differences between them than suggested by the February means of Table 13–1.

These results indicated that participants in the interpersonal process training, when compared with non-participants: (a) communicated with their classes at significantly higher levels of facilitative interpersonal functioning ($p < .0037$); (b) selected teacher-critics as practicum supervisors who were functioning at significantly higher levels ($p < .0192$); (c) succeeded in eliciting higher levels of involvement from their students ($p < .0501$); and (d) chose to work in classes where there was a normally high level of process involvement by the students ($p < .0001$).

The means and correlations (Table 13–2) show that all of the trainees and critics responded considerably to one another during the six-week practicum period. Although the major change in mean level of classroom functioning during the practicum appeared to occur in the teachers, this was a mutual change in which the teachers and their trainees became like one another in mean functioning level. The progressive change in the significant correlations (Table 13–2) between critics and trainees (November $r = -.29$; February $r = .19$; and April $r = .65$) showed this change most clearly.

In order to further specify the most important factors in these interpersonal changes, a series of stepwise regression analyses was undertaken. In both sets of analyses the predictor variables were added to the regression singly or in groups, and in various orders, according to logical expectations

Table 13–1

Means and Standard Deviations for Teacher, Trainee, and Pupil Variables

Variable	Mean	sd
Nov. Trainee Functioning (TRNNOV)	2.75	.75
Nov. Pupil Functioning With Trainee (TRNCNV)	3.10	.46
Nov. Teacher Functioning (TCHNOV)	3.27	.81
Nov. Pupil Functioning With Teacher (TCHCNV)	3.35	.39
Feb. Trainee Functioning (TRNFEB)	3.02	.68
Feb. Pupil Functioning With Trainee (TRNCFB)	2.89	.51
Feb. Teacher Functioning (TCHFEB)	3.46	.77
Feb. Pupil Functioning With Teacher (TCHCFB)	3.36	.45
Apr. Trainee Functioning (TRNAPL)	3.04	.74
Apr. Pupil Functioning With Trainee (TRNCPL)	3.00	.56
Apr. Teacher Functioning (TCHAPL)	3.26	.94
Apr. Pupil Functioning With Teacher (TCHCPL)	3.15	.55

Table 13–2
Intercorrelations of Teacher and Trainee Functioning

	TRNNOV	TCHNOV	TRNFEB	TCHFEB	TRNAPL	TCHAPL
TRNNOV**	1.00					
TCHNOV	—.29	1.00				
TRNFEB	.56*	—.08	1.00			
TCHFEB	—.11	.58*	.19	1.00		
TRNAPL	.15	.07	.44*	.33*	1.00	
TCHAPL	—.08	.47*	.35*	.70*	.65*	1.00

*p < .05 (two-tailed).
**See Table 13–1 for complete names of variables.

as to their relative contributions. Predictors based on the pupil involvement variable were also included in these analyses because of their potential influence on the teachers and trainees.

The nine predictors accounted for a substantial portion (59 percent) of the variance in April trainee functioning ($R = .76, p < .0001$). Furthermore, the stepwise procedure showed that both trainee level of functioning in February (TRNFEB) and critic functioning in April (TCHAPL) accounted for significantly larger portions of the residual criterion variance than did the other seven predictors. Although the first two predictors (TCHCNV and TCHCFB) were not expected to be important, the F-ratio bearing on the significance of their contribution was substantial ($p < .0306$). However, the high correlation (Table 13–2) between teacher and class in November ($r = .78$) and that between teacher and class in February ($r = .63$) suggested that the first and second steps in the regression could have been interchanged, thereby according prime importance to the direct measures of teacher functioning (TCHNOV and TCHFEB). These results, in conjunction with the lack of significant contribution by November trainee functioning (TRNNOV), demonstrated clearly that teacher functioning was the better predictor of eventual trainee functioning.

The seven predictors used in this analysis correlated very highly with the criterion ($R = .86, p < .0001$) and accounted for seventy-five percent of the variance in April teacher functioning. Here, the two predictors involving the children's classroom functioning when taught by the trainee (TRNCNV and TRNCFB) were eliminated because they were not logically related to the present criterion. As could be expected, the best predictor of April teacher functioning was April trainee functioning. However, consistent with the previous analysis, the functioning of teachers and their classes in November and February (TCHNOV, TCHFEB, TCHCNV, and TCHCFB) predicted ultimate teacher level (TCHAPR) much better than did previous trainee functioning (TRNFEB and TRNNOV) ($p < .0004$ and $p < .0107$ versus $p < .5713$ and $p < .0008$). Indeed, this relationship existed even though the contribution of November and February trainee functioning was accounted for first. The results of this analysis, in conjunction with those of the previous one, suggested strongly that, although critics and trainees became progressively alike, the greatest change, as expected, was in the trainees.

Concerning the results of the multiple correlation and stepwise regression analyses of teacher level of functioning on the supervisory achievement criteria, the teacher level of functioning predictors were found to relate significantly to the group of ten achievement measures ($p < .0001$). Of the thirty possible correlations among predictors and criteria, nine were significant ($p < .05$, two-tailed).

With regard to the results of the multiple correlation and stepwise regression analyses of teacher functioning in November and February on the California Achievement Tests scores, it was found that, although the predictors and criteria in the three regression equations, considered jointly, were significantly related ($p < .0001$), only the correlation ($R = .79$) of the predictors with Reading Achievement was significant. A step-down analysis indicated that the correlation with the Arithmetic Achievement score was also significant ($R = .43$, $p < .0092$), thereby substantiating a negative Pearson r ($-.43$) between November teacher functioning and Arithmetic Achievement. However, it was noteworthy that his correlation accounted for only 19 percent of the Arithmetic criterion variance whereas teacher functioning accounted for 62 percent of the variance in the Reading criterion.

DISCUSSION

All of the above analyses were in strong agreement with the principal predictions of the study.

The interpersonal process training was found to have had a significant impact on the ability of teacher trainees to both recognize and implement those aspects of good teaching which are defined by high levels of interpersonal variables. The trained group picked critic teachers who, on the average, were significantly more empathic, genuine, and confident in their own ability and that of their pupils than were those picked by members of the control group. As has been noted, the mean level of functioning of the critic teachers for the trained group was more than one-half a level higher than that for the control group. Examination of the teacher functioning scale further emphasizes the importance of this difference. This result indicated that the trained group was able to select teacher-critics who could best teach them the special methodology of teaching the deaf. Moreover, in the above-noted analysis of covariance, it was also found that the trained group succeeded in communicating at significantly higher levels with the children they were teaching. Not only were members of the trained group able to pick good supervisors, but they were also able to begin their practicum experiences as more effective teachers. Both of these findings were in remarkable agreement with the findings of Carkhuff and Berenson (1967) concerning the ability of people both to discriminate effective living and to communicate effectively with one another. In general, the results clearly indicated that the interpersonal process training did have a highly significant and important impact on the trainees.

The finding that the teachers and trainees subsequently exerted a reciprocal impact on one another during the six-week practicum period was of equal interest. The twenty-hour interpersonal training program was actually a sort of "pre-training" period. It prepared the trainees for the practicum but did not in any way focus on teaching the specialized skills and methods needed for teaching the deaf. That was expected to occur during the practicum. Insofar as the goal of any teacher-training program is changed trainee teaching style, the finding that the greater change in interpersonal functioning during the practicum occurred in the trainees pointed clearly to its efficacy. However, the additional aspect of that finding which pointed to a deteriorative change in average level of functioning of the practicum supervisors clouded the efficacy issue somewhat. Indeed, in view of this second distressing finding, some serious questions must be raised concerning this interpersonal influence process.

On the one hand, some teacher deterioration from mid-year onward may reflect an unfortunate phenomenon which characterizes the average teacher. It may be that the less than maximally functioning teacher becomes much less effective as the school year progresses and that this substantial decline, when averaged with the functioning of the best teachers, creates a false picture of an overall deterioration. On the other hand, this deterioration may denote an idiosyncrasy of critic teachers which can be due to their working with trainees who function, on the average, at levels lower than their own. This second explanation would be partly consistent with Carkhuff and Alexik (1967) who showed that the functioning level of low- or moderate-functioning counselors tended to vary with the behavior of their clients.

Of anecdotal interest in clarifying this phenomenon are two cases involving high-functioning critic-teachers and low-functioning trainees. In one case, a low-active, moderately high-facilitative teacher and a high-active, low-facilitative trainee, who had responded poorly to the interpersonal training, both plummeted in level of functioning while they were working together. In the other situation, a very low-functioning trainee who had made very small but positive gains in the interpersonal training exhibited a gain of over two levels while working with a teacher who was functioning consistently around level 4.5. Both of these situations suggested that the type and magnitude of discrepancy between a teacher and trainee may, for yet to be determined reasons, be a highly significant determinant of the direction and magnitude of teacher and trainee change. The active-passive dimension in human relationships (Carkhuff, 1969a) may be critical. It may also be that brief training has a potentiating effect on the destructive capacities of some trainees. Some people seem to be able to learn to recognize effectiveness, and then seek to neutralize or destroy it in order to protect themselves against exposure. A moderately effective teacher who isn't quite sure of herself may be particularly vulnerable to a trainee thus potentiated.

How true!

Perhaps those persons who are perceived as responding poorly to training should not be allowed to enter a practicum lest they harm the teacher-critic and her class! Or, it may be that a more efficient solution would be to train both trainees and critics so that critics would be better prepared to survive the practicum.

Concerning the relationship between the quality of personal relationships and academic achievement, on the basis of the available data, it was reasonable to conclude that reading and arithmetic as well as other achievement areas were definitely related in a positive fashion to level of teacher interpersonal functioning and that other undifferentiated achievement areas were also related in a significantly positive fashion.

In retrospect, the most effective course of action appears to involve both selection and training. In order to maximize the academic achievement of students, deliberate efforts must be made to select only those teachers, and prospective teachers, who are interpersonally competent. Systematic interpersonal communication training programs need to be provided to all parties concerned in order to maximize their interpersonal levels. Courage is also demanded for the task of excluding from teaching positions those persons who are unwilling or unable to respond to the training. Retention of ineffectuals can only yield harm for their colleagues and students. Having implemented these practical steps, concomitant research needs to be conducted in order to continually assess the effects of the programs and to help sustain the high functioning levels of trainees, of teachers, and, most importantly, of the children.

Again, quite clearly, the systematically trained teachers were more effective than untrained teachers in translating their efforts to student benefits. The control group of teachers were not, to be sure, untrained. They were trained by traditional teaching methodologies and were, therefore, trained as randomly as those methodologies function. Nevertheless, important methodological questions might be asked about the results. In the following project, a number of training control groups are incorporated in order to control for other sources that might account for some or all of the effects of the systematic training.

PROJECT 30
Training Teachers as Helpers*

In recent years, the concept of the role of the teacher has undergone several significant changes. While these conceptions may vary, the influx of research literature on the mental health and counseling aspects of classroom teaching represents one dominant trend. The impact of this interest has reached the teacher training institutions as evidenced by the large-scale response to a U.S.A.E. request for innovative teacher education programs and several projects funded by N.I.M.H. Many of the submitted proposals include provisions for flexibility training, empathy training, and other similar techniques designed to improve the teacher-trainees' sensitivity in dealing with children.

Several researchers have reported studies of the effects of a mental health approach to teacher education which have achieved varying degrees of effectiveness. Taylor (1967) reports higher scores on the M.T.A.I., after a two year program, and a greater capacity for status favoring the experimental treatment while control group demonstrated significant gains on a number of variables measured by the C.P.I. This program built around the identification and solution of teaching and personal problems failed to produce significant differences on the Manifold Interest Schedule and the Teacher Education Examination. A program sponsored by the N.I.M.H. was designed to explore the differential effects of a concept-centered, case-study, and learner-centered approaches to teacher education. The data from this project revealed no evidence that the classroom communication behavior of the subjects was related to the communication behavior of their college instructors in any of the experimental treatments. A follow-up study of the same students during their first year of teaching yielded similar results.

Whiteis (1962) identified significant differences favoring a "therapeutic education" program on the criteria of grade point average, program completion, attendance and indices of mental health. Jones (1962) replicated these findings and added improved self-acceptance.

Hough and Ober (1967) utilized five combinations of dyadic programmed instruction and theory training in human relations with skill and theory training in Flanders' system of classroom interaction analysis with 420 student teachers. In simulated classroom conditions, the student teachers who were trained in the use of interaction analysis in addition to read-

*Reprinted in part with permission from the *Journal of Research and Development in Education,* 1971, 4, 70–85, where it first appeared as "The Effects of Systematic Human Relations Training upon the Classroom Performance of Elementary School Student Teachers," by David H. Berenson.

ings on the theory and classroom application of human relations concepts used significantly more praise and encouragement and questions during their teaching. Students who received skill training in interaction analysis in addition to the dyadic case study technique used significantly more accepting and clarifying behaviors and generated more pupil-initiated talk and fewer teacher-initiated responses.

Still another approach taken to train teachers for greater sensitivity in dealing with children is reported by Joyce (1968). In a flexibility training program, the students used the observation of coping behaviors as a method of increasing their awareness of the children's frame of reference. They also practiced modifying their teaching strategy in response to differing pupil cognitive and affective orientations. The research conducted to study the effects of this training reported no increase in the use of questioning or in sensitivity as measured by Hunt's Communication Task. The author also reported no significant differences between the trainees' reactions under simulated and normal conditions.

An implicit assumption underlying many of these programs and investigations is that there is a relationship between some interpersonal variables and pupil performance. The evidence supporting this assumption may be found in the research on the effects of specific dimensions of interpersonal skills on productivity and constructive change.

Teacher warmth, for example, has been found to be related to pupil-initiated work, general achievement, and learning in American Government classes. Dixon and Morse (1961) found empathy related to positive pupil and supervisory perceptions. Teachers identified as "more open" were perceived by their pupils as significantly more student-centered—empathic, congruent, and unconditional in their level of regard.

Truax and Tatum (1966) reported that pupils receiving high levels of empathy and positive regard demonstrated greater adjustment to school, teachers and their peers. Aspy (1969) extended these findings, noting that pupils of teachers offering high levels of empathy, warmth and genuineness demonstrated a mean gain of 1.6 years in reading achievement over a group of comparable pupils of teachers offering low levels of these conditions. A similar study (Aspy and Hadlock, 1967) indicated pupils gained 2.5 years in reading achievement with teachers functioning at high levels of these conditions as compared with a gain of 0.7 years for children receiving low levels of these conditions.

Several investigators have addressed themselves to the question of training teachers in these dimensions. Hefele (1971) reported a positive relationship between the offered level of interpersonal skills of student teachers and the academic achievement of deaf pupils.

The present study was conducted to explore the effects of a human relations training program on the classroom performance of elementary school student teachers.

METHOD

Subjects

To achieve the purpose of this study, 48 students were randomly selected from the senior population of elementary education majors at a coeducational, suburban state college. Since the nature of this population is predominantly female, only female student teachers were included in this study. The student-trainees were randomly assigned to four treatment groups: the experimental group (E_x), the training control group (C_t), the Hawthorne Effect control group (C_h) and the control group proper (C_p). Thus, each treatment group consisted of 12 female teacher-trainees.

Materials

The trainee level of interpersonal functioning is determined by ratings of written responses to helpee stimulus expressions on the Student Form of the *Communication Index of Interpersonal Functioning* (Kratochvil, Carkhuff, and Berenson, 1969). Rating of overall functioning is a composite assessment of the dimensions of accurate empathy, positive regard, genuineness, concreteness, immediacy, significant other reference and confrontation. These dimensions are operationally defined on the *Scales of Assessment of Interpersonal Functioning* (Carkhuff, 1969a, 1969b) which demonstrate the range of functioning from level I when none of these conditions are communicated to any noticeable degree to level V when all of the conditions are fully communicated simultaneously and continually. Level III on these scales is considered minimally effective.

The *Student-Teacher Competency Rating Scale* (STCR) is a locally constructed device designed on a five-point scale to yield information concerning the student teacher's rated competencies as a person, teacher, staff member, member of the teaching profession, classroom manager, and knowledge of the teaching-learning process and of children. For the purpose of this study only total competency and those subscales relating to classroom performance were utilized.

The *Teaching Situation Reaction Test* (T.S.R.T.) (Duncan and Hough, 1966) is reported to measure written reactions to teaching situations related to planning, management and teacher-pupil relationships. The testee is asked to rank-order four options for each of 48 questions relating to a teaching situation. Scores on this device have been found to be related to scores on the *Minnesota Teacher Attitude Inventory*, the *Dogmatism Scale* and the *Relationship Inventory*.

Amidon and Flanders (1967) describe Interaction Analysis as a "feedback system designed to supply to the teacher objective and reliable information about his role in the classroom." All events occurring in the classroom are tabulated in sequence on a 10×10 matrix. Teacher behaviors are categorized as direct or indirect influence. The former category includes lecturing, giving directions and criticizing or justifying authority. Indirect teacher influence consists of accepting pupil feelings, praise or encouragement, accepting and using pupil ideas and asking questions.

Pupil comments made in the classrooms fall into two categories: teacher initiated or pupil initiated. In addition, there is a category in which moments of silence or confusion may be tabulated. Any statements, made by the teacher or the pupils occurring longer than seconds are tallied on the matrix where the row and column converge for that category. These are referred to as continuous talk categories.

Procedure

Three weeks preceding the student teaching period, the subjects in the experimental group (E_x) received 25 hours of training in the discrimination and communication of the interpersonal conditions of accurate empathy, positive regard, genuineness, concreteness, immediacy, significant other references, and confrontation. The training procedure which utilized the integration of the didactic, experiential and modeling sources of learning, was conducted by a trainer who was functioning well above the level 3.0 overall, on a five-point scale designated as minimally effective.

Twenty-five hours of didactic training in human relations was given to Ss in the training control group (C_t) but did not incorporate the quasi-therapeutic experience or the use of the *Scales of Assessment of Interpersonal Functioning*. Ss in the Hawthorne Effect control group (C_h) were informed of their participation in a study to determine the effects of the pre-student teaching workshop on their performance in the classroom and on their relationships with the pupils. These instructions were given at the beginning of the first, third, fifth and seventh week of the student teaching period. Since all measures utilized prior to student teaching were applied to all seniors, Ss in the randomly selected control group proper (C_p) had no knowledge of their participation in the study.

Data Collection

Student teachers in all four treatment groups were tested for overall level of interpersonal functioning prior to and after the human relations training period (Communication Index) and were randomly assigned to classroom and college supervisors. During the final two weeks of student teaching, all subjects were instructed to tape-record two, twenty minute lessons.

At the completion of eight weeks of student teaching, classroom supervisors and college supervisors were requested to rate the student teacher on the competency rating device. The student teachers also used this scale as a self-report. Additionally, classroom supervisors' ratings of 12 randomly selected teacher trainees from each of the three semesters preceding this study were collected. This provided three rating control groups (C_r). The T.S.R.T. was also administered to the four study groups at this time.

RESULTS

Level of Interpersonal Functioning

The student teachers' written responses to the helpee stimulus expressions presented in the Communication Index were rated independently by two raters. The Pearson r interrater reliability on the C.I.I.F. for the two raters on pre- and post-training measures ranged from 0.855 to 0.96 ($p <$ .01).

The student teachers' scores on the C.I.I.F. before training reveal no significant differences among groups (Table 13-3). Post-training scores significantly favored the E_x student teachers over C_t ($p <$ .001), C_h ($p <$ .001), and C_p ($p <$ .001). After training, the mean scores on the Communication Index for the four treatment groups were $E_x = 2.663$, $C_t = 1.871$, $C_h = 1.696$, and $C_p = 1.738$. Differences among the three control groups were not significant.

Competency Ratings

As can be seen in Table 13-4, the classroom supervisors rated the E_x student teachers significantly higher than each of the control groups in total competency rating ($p < .001$), general teaching competency ($p <$ .001), classroom management ($p < .001$), understanding of the teaching-learning process ($p < .001$) and understanding of children ($p < .001$). There were no significant differences in competency among the three control groups of student teachers as judged by the classroom supervisors.

In general, the college supervisors' competency ratings of the student teachers in this study yielded significant differences in favor of the E_x

Table 13-3

Means and sds of the Pre- and Post-Training Scores on the Communication Index of Interpersonal Functioning

			GROUPS		
	I	II	III	IV	F
Pre-Training					
Mean	1.717	1.658	1.642	1.721	0.213
sd	0.345	0.221	0.216	0.348	
Post-Training					
Mean	2.663	1.871	1.696	1.738	16.163*
sd	0.577	0.219	0.273	0.305	

*Significant at $p < .001$.

Table 13–4

Means and sds for All Student Teacher Competency Ratings

	GROUPS							
	E_x		C_t		C_h		C_p	
Source	Mean	sd	Mean	sd	Mean	sd	Mean	sd
Class								
Super.								
Total***	172.333	7.284	140.583	17.956	140.500	23.810	134.083	28.582
I***	39.083	1.320	31.167	4.394	32.083	5.314	29.417	6.551
II***	24.583	.862	17.500	2.466	18.500	3.708	18.583	5.107
III***	14.667	.850	10.750	1.534	11.750	2.350	10.583	3.616
IV**	19.583	.759	16.917	2.361	16.250	2.890	15.917	3.121
College								
Super.								
Total*	156.250	14.777	128.833	31.953	118.667	30.324	133.417	33.225
I	34.667	3.771	28.667	7.409	28.250	6.697	29.833	7.381
II	21.333	2.779	17.250	4.474	16.917	3.989	17.500	5.424
III*	13.500	1.384	10.500	2.930	9.750	2.803	10.500	3.476
IV	17.500	2.327	14.417	3.904	14.250	3.700	15.000	3.488
Student								
Self-Rating								
Total	159.583	10.452	153.583	19.581	155.083	12.751	155.083	25.250
I	35.917	3.148	34.500	4.481	34.000	3.000	33.583	6.512
II	22.000	2.345	21.333	2.560	20.667	2.528	20.833	4.687
III	13.833	1.067	13.667	1.795	13.250	1.422	13.500	2.217
IV	17.917	1.552	17.833	3.287	18.750	1.362	18.333	1.886

* = F. significant at $p < .05$
** = F. significant at $p < .01$
*** = F. significant at $p < .001$

group. In total competency, E_x students were rated significantly higher than C_t ($p < .01$), C_h ($p < .001$) and C_p ($p < .025$). The E_x students were rated higher in general teaching competency than C_t ($p < .025$), C_h ($p < .001$) and C_p (p not significant). The same students scored higher in rated understanding of the teaching-learning process than C_t ($p < .01$), C_h ($p < .001$) and C_p (p not significant). The E_x group demonstrated significantly greater understanding of children as judged by the college supervisors when compared with students in C_t ($p < .001$), C_h ($p < .001$) and C_p ($p < .01$). E_x students were also rated significantly higher than C_t ($p < .025$), C_h ($p < .01$) and C_p ($p < .025$) in classroom management.

It was also noted that the student teachers' self-ratings on the competency scale did not differ significantly. In general, all student teachers rated themselves high: ($E_x\bar{X} = 159.583$, $C_t\bar{X} = 153.583$, $C_h\bar{X} = 155.083$, and $C_p\bar{X} = 155.083$). The F-ratio of 0.230 was not significant.

When the classroom supervisors' ratings of the experimental subjects were compared with the ratings of three randomly selected samples from previous semesters, C_r, significant differences were noted. E_x student teachers were rated higher than all C_r groups in all subscales of less than the .001 level except classroom management ($p < .01$).

Teaching Situation Reaction Test

The mean scores on the T.S.R.T. were $E_x = 217$, $C_t = 187.67$, $C_h = 169.17$, and $C_p = 169.83$. An analysis of variance yielded an F-ratio of 13.562, significant at $< .001$, which warranted further analysis. The t tests for significant differences indicated that the student teachers in E_x demonstrated significantly higher scores than C_t ($p < .001$), C_h ($p < .001$) and C_p ($p < .025$). Differences in C_h and C_p scores failed to achieve significance.

Classroom Interaction Analysis

A Pearson r of 0.979 was computed as an assessment of the interrater reliability of the two observers using Flanders' Interaction Analysis. Ratings on the revised i/d ratio (categories 1,2,3,6, and 7) were utilized for this purpose.

Means and standard deviations on the thirteen subscales of the interaction analysis are presented in Table 13–5. It can be noted that E_x student teachers were significantly more indirect in their approach to motivate and control (i/d ratio) than C_t ($p < .01$), C_h ($p < .001$) and C_p ($p < .001$). The E_x group placed less emphasis on content than C_t ($p < .01$), C_h (not significant) and C_p ($p < .01$). Differences among the control groups were not significantly different for the i/d ratio or content emphasis.

Differences favored E_x student teachers over C_t ($p < .001$), C_h ($p < .025$) and C_p ($p < .001$) on the extended use of indirect influence. That is, not only did the experimental group accept pupils' feelings and ideas and encourage them, but did so over extended periods of time. The E_x students also used less extended direct influence than C_t ($p < .05$), C_h ($p < .025$) and C_p ($p < .05$). Thus the student teachers in the experimental group spent fewer extended periods of time criticizing and giving directions to their pupils.

With reference to the question of how the student teacher responds to pupil comments, Table 13–5 also shows E_x using significantly more indirect pattern than C_t ($p < .025$), C_h ($p < .025$) and C_p ($p < .05$). The kinds of pupil talk in the classroom do not appear to differ significantly among the four treatment groups ($F = 0.829$, n.s.). That is, pupils in all classrooms spend about the same amount of time responding to the teacher and reacting to each other.

Classroom behaviors which occur for extended periods of time (longer than three seconds) are tallied in the diagonal cells of the interaction matrix. An analysis of those cells related to this study are also reported in Table 13–5. Student teachers in the E_x group accepted and clarified the pupils'

Table 13–5

Means and sds for All Student Teachers on the Tape Ratings Using Flanders' Classroom Interaction Analysis

DIMENSION	GROUPS							
	E_x		C_t		C_h		C_p	
	Mean	sd	Mean	sd	Mean	sd	Mean	sd
i/d ratio**	70.367	8.109	52.175	22.051	44.583	15.163	50.525	18.345
Content	28.058	5.900	35.983	8.016	32.717	9.029	38.525	12.213
Ext. indirect influence**	5.886	2.438	2.388	2.175	3.068	3.313	1.671	1.628
Ext. direct influence	2.370	1.929	4.150	2.406	4.965	3.087	5.230	5.008
Response to pupils*	1335.583	1704.279	284.592	267.085	294.475	288.033	323.667	187.913
Kind of pupil talk	140.900	60.339	134.260	150.383	191.450	131.845	115.393	111.018
Continuous Talk								
Accepts feelings***	1.600	1.796	0.029	0.097	0.000	0.000	0.000	0.000
Praise	0.898	0.685	0.403	0.354	0.477	0.798	0.365	0.254
Accepts ideas***	2.870	1.710	0.252	0.271	0.653	0.995	0.551	0.903
Commands	1.050	1.218	2.717	2.140	2.223	1.696	3.124	3.101
Criticism	0.571	0.416	1.161	1.929	1.239	2.011	2.026	2.098
Teacher-initiated pupil talk	5.993	3.163	5.986	5.168	4.984	4.554	8.254	7.987
Pupil-initiated talk**	6.666	3.358	2.492	2.743	0.407	0.863	6.455	7.076

$*$ = F. significant at $p < .05$
$**$ = F. significant at $p < .01$
$***$ = F. significant at $p < .001$

feelings significantly more than C_t ($p < .001$), C_h ($p < .001$) and C_p ($p < .001$). It is also noted that, in 40 minutes of teaching, there were no instances of student teachers in the C_h and C_p groups taking longer than three seconds to accept or clarify the feelings of their pupils. E_x students utilized significantly greater use of extended praise and encouragement than C_t ($p < .025$), C_h ($p < .05$), and C_p ($p < .01$). They also spent more extended periods of time accepting and clarifying pupil ideas than all control groups ($p < .001$). C_h and C_p were rated higher in this area than C_t ($p =$ n.s.).

In the two categories comprising the student teachers' extended direct influence, the differences were not as clearly defined. E_x students gave fewer directions and commands than C_t ($p < .025$), C_h ($p < .025$) and C_p ($p < .025$). While achieving significance only over C_p ($p < .025$), percentages did demonstrate that the experimental students used less criticism than C_t and C_h students.

Pupils in the classes of the four treatment groups did not differ significantly in extended response to their student teachers ($F = 0.695$, n.s.). E_x did, however, spend significantly more time voluntarily responding to the teacher and interacting with each other than pupils in C_t ($p < .001$) and C_h ($p < .001$). C_h pupils responded to each other significantly less than pupils in C_t classes ($p < .01$) and C_p classes ($p < .025$).

Factor Analysis

Raw scores for the six central outcome variables (classroom and college supervisors' and students' total competency ratings, T.S.R.T scores, level of functioning and i/d ratio) were submitted to a principle component analysis and subsequent varimax rotation. For this sample, only factor pattern scores exceeding .50 are considered significant.

In the component analysis for all groups combined, *Factor I,* accounting for 58 percent of the total variance, indicated the student teachers' self-ratings in competency represent an isolated factor (loading $= 0.958$). All other scores and ratings load significantly in Factor II (14 percent variance), suggesting a possible best-worst factor, that is, agreement is achieved among ratings and scores on either all high or all low scores.

The factor patterns for combined control groups and the experimental group are as follows:

Experimental group. Factor I (47 percent variance). Classroom supervisors' ratings of the E_x subjects appear as a significant and isolated factor, that is, unrelated to any of the other measures utilized in this study.

Factor II (20 percent variance). College supervisors' ratings load significantly (0.923) and appear to be strongly related to the student teachers' use of indirect patterns in the classroom.

Factor III (14 percent variance). High scores on the T.S.R.T., Flanders' i/d ratio, C.I.I.F. load significantly and are strongly related to E_x student teachers' self-ratings.

Control groups, combined. Factor I (49 percent variance). While classroom and college supervisors' and student teacher self-ratings load significantly on this factor, inspection of the mean scores indicates that this agreement holds true for low ratings. That is, all sources of ratings concur on low competency.

Factor II (15 percent variance). Scores on all external indices (T.S. R.T., C.I.I.F. and i/d ratio) load significantly and are strongly related to the classroom supervisors' total competency ratings of the control groups.

DISCUSSION

This study appears to support the efficacy of a human relations training program in a teacher education context. Specifically, training which focuses on the conditions of empathy, positive regard, genuineness, concreteness, immediacy, significant other references, and confrontation and which systematically employs the experiential, didactic and modeling sources of learning has been shown to be significantly related to a wide variety of desirable outcomes for teacher trainees.

The analysis of the data on pre-training level of interpersonal functioning is consistent with previous research with comparable samples (Carkhuff and Berenson, 1967; Carkhuff, 1969a). Lay and professional helpers in training appear to function between 1.5 and 2.0 on a five-point scale. The pre-training mean level of functioning for this study was 1.684. The mean gain in functioning after the training period was approximately one full level for students in the experimental group (E_x), 0.21 for the training control group (C_t) and 0.016 for students in the control group proper (C_p). It may be concluded that the methods used in this study to create a Hawthorne Effect (C_h) and the didactic training procedure (C_t), failed to produce a constructive effect upon the interpersonal skills of students in these groups.

As to the question of the outcomes of training used as the experimental treatment, the following results appear to be warranted. (1) Student teachers can be trained in relatively short periods of time, to function at significantly higher levels on dimensions which have been shown in previous research to be significantly related to constructive gains in other helping relationships and in teaching. (2) Classroom and college supervisors perceived student teachers who are functioning at higher levels in interpersonal skills to be more competent in their classroom performance than student teachers who are functioning at lower levels of these skills. (3) Student teachers functioning at higher levels of interpersonal skills appear to be more capable of solving teaching problems related to planning, management and teacher-pupil relationships (T.S.R.T.) than those teacher trainees functioning at lower levels.

Utilizing the analyses of the taped classroom recordings, it is possible to describe the teaching patterns utilized by the student teachers in this study. The following generalizations were drawn from this data.

Student teachers functioning at higher levels of interpersonal skills appear to utilize (1) a greater incidence of positive reinforcing behaviors, such as praise and encouragement, accepting and clarifying pupils' feelings and ideas; (2) less criticism of the pupils; and (3) less emphasis on subject matter content. The pupils of student teachers offering higher levels of interpersonal skills appear to (1) feel free to volunteer information and ideas to the teacher even during lectures; (2) interact more with their peers; and (3) become more extensively involved in classroom activities when stimulated by their peers than by the teacher. The classroom behaviors of student teachers in the control groups were characterized by (1) a more direct approach to motivation and control, that is, the use of significantly less positive reinforcement; (2) a greater emphasis on subject matter content; and (3) a greater use of commands and criticism. The pupils of the control group classes generally responded more to their teachers than to their peers.

Thus, classes conducted by teacher trainees offering high levels of human relations skills demonstrated significantly greater use of teaching patterns which have been shown in previous research to be positively related to pupil growth (Amidon and Flanders, 1967).

The principle component analyses suggest the following generalizations. (1) Classroom and college supervisors can discriminate low-level functioning student teachers. (2) While student teachers' ratings are generally equivalent, training forces low-functioning students to confront their lowness and highs to rate themselves at a level commensurate with external criteria. (3) All external criteria used in this study appear to be measuring similar or related variables.

SUMMARY AND IMPLICATIONS FOR TEACHER EDUCATION

This study was conducted to examine the effects of an integrated didactic and experiential human relations training program on the classroom performance of elementary school student teachers. Subjects were randomly selected and assigned to the experimental treatment group ($n = 12$), training control ($n = 12$), Hawthorne Effect control ($n = 12$) and control group proper ($n = 12$).

After 25 hours of training, the experimental subjects were rated significantly higher in interpersonal functioning, were rated by their college and classroom supervisors as more competent in the classroom, scored significantly higher on a situation reaction test and utilized significantly more positive reinforcing behaviors in their teaching.

The results appear to suggest several implications for teacher education. First, the student teachers' level of interpersonal functioning appears to be highly correlated with several desirable outcomes of teacher training. This index should be further examined as a selection device for teaching candidates. Secondly, unlike many programs which are designed to improve the quality of the teacher-pupil interaction by focusing upon the discrimination of desirable teaching behaviors, the training procedure used in this study focused upon practice in the communication of desirable teaching behaviors. Previous research (Carkhuff, 1969a) has demonstrated there can be no assumption of the transfer from discrimination to communication. Put another way, if it is desirable that teachers be capable of offering appropriately high levels of the conditions of empathy, regard, concreteness, genuineness, immediacy and confrontation then learning the communication of these conditions must be included in their professional preparation.

As in the Hefele study, *the systematically trained teachers were signifi-cantly more effective in bringing about changes on desired indexes than all other forms of traditionally trained or "educated" groups of teachers.* Training programs systematically shape more competent and more positively reinforcing teachers who, in turn, shape more competent and more effectively achieving students. Put another way, students can effectively learn more of the skills es-sential to their effective functioning if they are taught—or trained—by teachers who have themselves effectively learned the skills essential to their effective functioning. There are indeed, as Berenson suggests, important implications for the selection and training of teachers.

SELECTION AND TRAINING OF PARENTS AND TEACHERS

Selection and training of teachers, then, are the effective ingredients of effective educational processes. If we can select those teachers who are func-tioning at the highest levels of those dimensions related to student development —and if we can intensify these dimensions over the course of training—then we can produce the most effective agents of change possible and exercise the privilege of truly "educating" our children.

Similarly, if we could select and train parents for the privilege of rearing children we might make another step toward order in an otherwise disorderly world. It is not an alien concept to train people for the discharge of lesser responsibilities. And it certainly makes good sense in those areas such as child placement and adoption where we can exercise our ability to discriminate those who can most effectively discharge their responsibilities to children from those who cannot.

In an attempt to develop valid selection procedures for developing effec-tive teacher-helpers, a number of different selection indexes were related to a variety of indexes of functioning in the helping role following training. It was found that functioning in the helping role prior to training was the best predictor of functioning in the helping role after training (Carkhuff, 1969c). Level of re-sponsiveness to standard stimuli was highly and significantly related to the post-training indexes. Level of discrimination was unrelated to the post-training indexes.

Again, we found that those teachers who were functioning at relatively the highest levels initially tended to both (a) function at the highest levels finally and (b) gain the most in interpersonal skills over time-limited training. The im-plications for selected persons who are themselves functioning initially at high levels are indeed profound. Our task is one of selecting those persons function-ing at the very highest levels and intensifying their skills in training before we entrust them with the solemn responsibility of educating our children. All this— no less—for the welfare of our kids and the future of mankind. In this context, selection and training, the heart of rehabilitating the educational programs that have contributed to our social problems, also constitute, as we shall see in the next project, the heart of the social action programs which are calculated to compensate for our educational and social problems.

In this regard, it is appropriate to think of the parents once again assuming the reins of responsibility for teaching their children. If the teachers cannot or will not do it, let the parents do it. Put another way, with appropriate selection and training, parents can do anything that teachers can do—and more! They can learn, particularly at the earliest level of development, what is important for the learning and development of the child. They can learn to start the child and themselves off in a lifelong training and learning process.

Programs such as Head Start are meaningful to consider in this context. Here the teachers are frequently indigenous functional professionals. Here parents can teach and train their own and neighborhood children. If properly selected, trained, and supervised, they can do much to initiate the training and learning process in the home as well as the school, for themselves and their families as well as others.

PROJECT 31
Training Parents
as Teachers*

A central contribution of social action programs for the disadvantaged lies in the utilization of indigenous lay personnel as functional professionals. By functional professionals we mean lay persons who have completed helper training programs, who have professional responsibilities with regard to helpees, but who do not have professional credentials. In the present context "functional professional" is employed to designate lay teacher-helpers in Project Head Start who have received certificates as specialists in helping and human relations skills.

The effectiveness of any social program, then, is contingent upon the selection and training of the lay personnel. The evidence concerning the effective ingredients of counseling and psychotherapy has been helpful in developing selection and training methodologies. In this regard the communication of certain core interpersonal dimensions which cut across all approaches to helping have been found to be related to a wide variety of indexes of constructive change or gain on the part of the helpee.

The responsive dimensions emphasize the helper's sensitive communications to the helpee and in this respect they focus upon the helper's responsiveness to the experience of the helpee. They include empathic understanding, respect or regard and concreteness or specificity of expression.

*Reprinted in part with permission from an article in the *Journal of Research and Development in Education*, 1971, 4, 87–96, entitled "The Selection and Training of Functional Professionals for the Inner-City Pre-School," by Robert R. Carkhuff and Andrew H. Griffin.

The initiative dimensions emphasize the helper's assertive or initiative behavior in developing a direction for the helping process and in this sense they focus upon the helper's experience as the origin of this initiative behavior. They include genuineness or congruence, confrontation and immediacy.

These responsive and initiative dimensions may be employed in the selection and training of lay personnel to become functional professionals. For selection, prospective candidates may be cast in different situations related to helping problems in their setting and their levels of responsive and initiative communication assessed. Training programs, in turn, can be built systematically around learning to discriminate and communicate those responsive and initiative dimensions related to the constructive change or gain of the helpees involved.

The purpose of the present paper is to report on a project for the selection and training of trainers in human relations skills in a Head Start program for pre-school children in the inner city of Springfield, Mass. The human relations skills involved working with the families as well as the pre-school children. The trainers were simply lay teacher helpers who had received advanced human relations training and who were trained to conduct training for other lay personnel. The ultimate purpose of the project was to enable the Head Start Program to conduct its own in-service training. To accomplish this we (a) selected the most promising trainees and (b) trained them in the helping and training roles.

METHOD

Selection Indexes

The first phase involved pre-testing the candidates on a variety of relevant indexes. Twenty-three teachers, twenty-two women and one man, the entire staff available from three Head Start Pre-School Centers, participated in the pre-testing on the following indexes: (a) each candidate was cast in the helping role with an adult with child-rearing problems and rated on level of communication of responsive and initiative dimensions; (b) each candidate's written responses to four taped, standard helpee stimulus expressions crossing affect (depression and anger) with problem area (educational and child-rearing) were rated for their level of communication of responsive and initiative dimensions; (c) each candidate's ratings of four alternate helper responses (in which level of responsive and initiative dimensions were crossed at high and low levels, i.e. high-high, high-low, low-high and low-low) to each standard stimulus expression were scored for their deviation from the ratings of experts who had demonstrated the predictive validity of their ratings in previous studies. The ratings of the candidates' communication in the helping role and in response to the taped stimuli were accomplished by two trained raters (different from the trainers) who had demonstrated Pearson r inter- and intra-rater reliabilities in the .90's for both ratings on the individual dimensions involved and for overall functioning. Each of the 23 candidates then participated in a preliminary training phase after which they were post-tested in order to determine the degree to which they effectively utilized the training experience.

Rating Scales

The scales for the responsive dimensions initially received their impetus from the work of Rogers et al. (1967), Truax and Carkhuff (1967), and Carkhuff and Berenson (1967), while the scales for the initiative dimensions were developed with the work of Carkhuff and Berenson, (1967), and Carkhuff (1969a, 1969b) with historical roots in a variety of sources. Carkhuff serves as the best source for integrating and fully describing the dimensions.

The scales ranged from 1 to 5 levels. In general, level 3 indicates an openness to communicating at higher levels and is termed minimally effective while levels 4 and 5 indicate the presence of the particular dimensions involved and levels 1 and 2 indicate an absence of the specific dimensions. Thus, for example, with empathy, level 3 indicates the interchangeability of the helper's communication with the helpee's in terms of feeling and meaning; at higher levels the helper's responses are additive in such a way that they enable the helpee to explore and understand himself at deeper levels; at lower levels the helper's responses are subtractive in that he subtracts significant affect and meaning from the communications of the helpee. Similarly, at level 3 of respect there is an openness to communicating respect while at higher levels there are communications of positive regard for the helpee's worth and at lower levels there are indications of negative regard. At level 3 of concreteness there is an openness to specificity while at higher levels there is specificity in personally relevant communications and at lower levels there are communications of vague and anonymous generalities only. At level 3 of genuineness there is an openness to being genuine while at higher levels there are communications of spontaneity and genuineness while at lower levels the helper is inauthentic. At level 3 of confrontation the helper demonstrates an openness to confronting the helpee while at higher levels he actively confronts the helpee with discrepancies in the helpee's behavior and at lower levels he disregards these discrepancies. At level 3 of immediacy the helper indicates an openness to interpreting the immediate relationship while at higher levels he actively relates the helpee's expression to the helper-helpee relationship and at lower levels he does not do so.

Preliminary Training

Preliminary training focused exclusively on the discrimination and communication of empathy, the key helping ingredient. In the context of a program conducted by two experienced trainers offering the helper-trainees high levels of these dimensions, the trainees participated in a systematic sequence of human relations training. The same scales which had been related to helpee gains in studies of helping were employed in training. Thus, employing 5-point scales, the trainees first learned to discriminate levels of empathic understanding. The trainees practiced listening to tapes and rating responses from 1 (worst) to 5 (best). The immediate goal of preliminary communication training, in turn, was to establish an interchangeable base of communication (level 3) in which the helper-trainee accurately expressed the feeling and personal meaning which the helpee had expressed. At first, the trainees responded to taped material and then they were organized for empathy communication training within the group. With the interchangeable base of communication continuing as the goal, the communication process was gradually constructed in a step-by-step training sequence. Finally, the communication process was gradually built up until it was allowed to flow in an interactional sequence.

Advanced Training

Those trainees who demonstrated the highest level of functioning on the basis of the results of preliminary training were selected for advanced training. Advanced training emphasized the skills necessary (a) to be an effective teacher-helper and (b) to train others to be effective teacher-helpers. It included training in the previously described dimensions and the development of effective courses of action. For example, after the trainees were introduced to the remainder of the responsive dimensions, respect, and concreteness, in a manner similar to that described for empathy in preliminary training, the trainees were introduced to communications initiated by the helper. Following this phase, individual pairing and practice in helpee-helper interactions were emphasized and the initiative dimensions of genuineness, confrontation and immediacy introduced in a manner similar to the responsive dimensions. In addition, initially the most advanced trainees were selected to function as trainers to supervise the helpee-helper interactions. Thus, concurrent with the development of the helping process, the trainees' experience as trainers of others was initiated. Next, the concept of the development of courses of action was introduced and implemented. At the end of their advanced training the trainees' level of communication was again assessed on the six dimensions in the helping role with parents with school-related problems and with pre-school children. The ratings were again made from taped sessions by the same trained raters.

Outcome Criteria

The principal outcome criterion following both preliminary and advanced training was the level of communication in the helping role with helpees with child-rearing and educational problems. This index was obtained by objective ratings of the taped sessions. Ratings again were made by the same trained raters. Functioning in the helping role was the goal of training and the prerequisite for being effective trainers. In addition, this index has been related most extensively in the literature to helpee change or gain. The standard taped stimuli and alternate responses were also employed following preliminary training.

RESULTS

Preliminary Training

The results of the preliminary training are shown in Table 13–6. Improvement in functioning is reflected on all three measures: helping role, standard taped stimuli and standard taped alternate responses. There is an improvement in the level of communication reflected in the helping role and standard measure. There is improvement in the level of discrimination reflected in the decrease in deviations from expert ratings. The mean differences are significant at the .01 level and all trainees improved on all measures.

Of the six trainees rated as communicating initially at level 1.5 and above in the helping role, five finished the preliminary training at 2.5 or above while of the 17 functioning initially below 1.5 only two finished above 2.5 (see Table 13–7). On the written responses to standard tapes, all five rated as communicating initially at level 1.5 or above finished at level 2.5 or above while only two of 18 functioning initially below 1.5 finished above 2.5.

Table 13–6

Effects of Preliminary Empathy Training upon the Communication and Discrimination of Empathy

	COMMUNICATION				DISCRIMINATION	
	Helping Role		Standard Stimuli		*Standard Responses* (Deviations from Experts)	
	Mean	*sd*	*Mean*	*sd*	*Mean*	*sd*
Pre-training (N = 23)	1.3	.5	1.2	.4	1.2	.3
Post-training (N = 23)	2.1	.4	2.4	.5	.5	.2

Table 13–7

The Relationship of Different Selection Indexes to Communication in the Helping Role Following Preliminary Training

MEASURE 1

Post-test Communication in Helping Role

	Ratings	2.5 and above	Below 2.5
Pre-test Communication in Helping Role	1.5 and above	5	1
	Below 1.5	2	15

MEASURE 2

Post-test Communication in Helping Role

	Ratings	2.5 and above	Below 2.5
Pre-test Responses to Standard Tape	1.5 and above	5	0
	Below 1.5	2	16

MEASURE 3

Post-test Communication in Helping Role

	Ratings	2.5 and above	Below 2.5
Pre-test Discrimination of Standard Responses	Less than 1 level deviation	1	0
	More than 1 level deviation	6	16

Advanced Training

The seven candidates functioning above level 2.5 on the post-preliminary training helping role measure were invited for advanced training; one was unavailable and six received advanced training. A comparison of Tables 13–6, 13–7 and 13–8 shows that the six trainees did better prior to their preliminary training than the group of 23 candidates as a whole. Table 13–8 shows that on all six dimensions the levels after preliminary training were significantly higher ($p < .01$) than before such training. Similarly, after advanced training the levels were significantly higher ($p < .01$) than before such training. At the end of advanced training all participants had achieved levels higher than 3.0 (considered to be minimally effective) on all dimensions.

DISCUSSION

The results indicate that the selection and training procedures employed are effective for the development of lay personnel as functional professionals. The two communication selection indexes were effective in predicting those trainees who would be functioning at the highest absolute levels following preliminary training. The discrimination index was not a successful predictor. In general, those trainees who were functioning above 1.5 prior to the preliminary training were functioning above 2.5 after the preliminary training. While the 23 candidates did not as a group achieve minimally effective levels of communication (3.0) in the ten hours of preliminary training, the training did serve as an introduction for those not selected. As well, it served as a fourth selection index to enable the trainers to further discriminate those who could most effectively utilize the training to function at the highest absolute levels. Thus, while the best index of functioning in the helping role is present functioning in the helping role, the best index of the ability to utilize an extensive training experience may be an index of the trainee's ability to utilize a delimited training experience.

It is to be emphasized that the systematic training program was employed in the context of a relationship offering high levels of these dimensions. Thus, the trainers not only offered the trainees the experience of high levels of responsive and initiative dimensions but also served as models of effective helpers for the trainees. However, we believe that a systematic

Table 13–8

Effects of Advanced Training in Interpersonal Skills upon Level of Interpersonal Functioning

	INTERPERSONAL DIMENSIONS					
	Responsive				Initiative	
	Empathy	Respect	Concrete-ness	Genuine-ness	Confron-tation	Immediacy
	Mean sd	Mean sd	Mean sd	Mean sd	Mean sd	Mean sd
Pre-training (N = 6)	1.6 .6	1.5 .5	1.5 .4	1.6 .5	1.4 .6	1.2 .5
Post-Preliminary Training (N = 6)	2.7 .5	2.4 .5	2.0 .4	1.6 .5	1.5 .5	1.7 .4
Post-Advanced Training (N = 6)	3.7 .4	3.6 .5	3.1 .4	3.5 .4	3.5 .5	3.6 .4

didactic program based upon a step-by-step succession of reinforcement experiences makes significant contributions over and above those made by those other sources of learning in training. Thus, in the hands of high-level functioning trainers the training can be replicated with significant results.

SUMMARY

Working with indigenous, lay personnel of a pre-school (Head Start) program, it was found that selection and training based upon the measurement of six interpersonal dimensions were effective. The dimensions, empathy, respect, concreteness, genuineness, confrontation and immediacy, are described as are the methods by which persons may be trained in them. The trainees who demonstrated the highest levels of communication following a 10-hour preliminary training program for teacher-helpers were selected for 100 hours of advanced training in communication to become trainers of teacher-helpers. All six participants of the advanced training achieved a minimally effective level of interpersonal functioning in these dimensions. The results indicate that social action programs can use procedures herein described for conducting their own in-service training which should greatly aid in carrying out the spirit and practice of their function.

Other larger-scale programs for entire Head Start programs were also implemented (Bierman, Carkhuff, and Santilli, 1969). The general point is simply this: the parents must not allow themselves to be shoved into the background. They are human beings, and at many levels they are as capable of being trained and, in turn, of training, as any other group, professional or otherwise. The Head Start Program is just one example of an outlet for concerned parents; it is as well a possible demonstration, with selection and training, of the potential functional utility of the efforts for everyone concerned with life and learning. The program offers the children a "head start" and the parents the possibility of a "fast finish." Indeed, the "head start" as well as the "fast finish" of the children may be integrally bound to the "fast finish" of the parents.

Again, all this is not to say that we do not equip both parents as well as teachers with the necessary programs in learning the skills which they and their children will need to get an "even start" if not a "head start." Systematic programs in learning the specific physical, emotional, and intellectual skills necessary to function effectively in the world are the essential complements of effective agents of change. In this regard, there are current and significant developments in individualized, programmed instruction in a variety of areas. Perhaps the most dramatic example of the potency of effective people plus effective programs has been the work of Allen (Glaser and Ross, 1970) in which trained teachers offer programmed instruction in a variety of academic areas to individuals or small groups of learners. For example, a group of several learners may function at a learning machine with no one member able to proceed to the next item until every member in the group has learned the correct response to the last item. Thus, helper-leaders emerge in the group. Indeed, for the person having the greatest difficulty in learning a response to a given item, there are, in effect, 4 teacher-helpers available. The potential applications for school and family learning projects are numerous. In this manner, combining effective teachers and effective social reinforcement from peers in combination with effective teaching programs, the students are able to achieve literally years of academic growth in only weeks of systematic study.

TRAINING AS A PREFERRED MODE OF LIVING

Both education and treatment are, as they are usually employed, nonfunctional terms which incorporate all the things we do when we do not know what we are doing. They are random and inefficient and therefore ineffective. If we are to develop new and effective concepts of education and treatment, we must define these terms as systematic training to increase the repertoire and quality of related reponses.

Again, we may summarize the potential benefits of training in both systematic and experiential terms.

First, we must consider the unique contributions of systematic training to helper as well as to helpee. By unique contributions, we mean simply those contributions to the helpee's change or gain over and above those accounted for by the helper's level of functioning on the critical responsive and initiative dimensions.

The unique contributions of systematic approaches to the student, trainee, or helpee may be summarized as follows (Carkhuff, 1969b): (1) systematic approaches provide the trainee with an understanding of the helping program and his role in it; (2) systematic approaches provide the trainee with a concrete awareness of his level of progress in the helping program; (3) systematic approaches provide the trainee with a useful knowledge of the history of the reinforcements that have created and sustained his difficulties in living; (4) systematic approaches provide the trainee with knowledge that the trainer is guided by trainee feedback insofar as it fits the trainer's system; (5) systematic approaches provide the trainee with an opportunity to actively accelerate the helping program; and (6) systematic approaches provide the trainee with the assurance that the helping program is resolving the difficulties that it set out to resolve.

In regard to the unique contributions to the teacher, trainer, or helper, systematic approaches accomplish the following: (1) systematic approaches provide the trainer with a system of well-defined procedures; (2) systematic approaches provide the trainer with a well-defined role; (3) systematic approaches provide the trainer with a high and extremely useful level of confidence in what he is doing and where he is going; (4) systematic approaches provide the trainer with the means to become meaningfully involved beyond the helping program per se; (5) systematic approaches provide the trainer with an opportunity to make translations from the helping program to life; (6) systematic approaches encourage the trainers to attend fully to nonverbal cues; and (7) systematic approaches provide the trainer with a specific behavioral base for understanding trainee behavior.

The number of unique benefits of systematic training may be summarized as follows (Carkhuff, 1969b): (1) systematic approaches are goal-directed and action-oriented; (2) systematic approaches emphasize practice in the behavior which we wish to effect; (3) systematic approaches leave the trainees with tangible and usable skills; (4) systematic approaches promote longer retention of learned skills; (5) systematic approaches enable us to make systematic selection of trainees; and (6) systematic approaches offer a built-in means of assessing the effectiveness of the program.

The limitations of systematic approaches for both trainee-helpee and trainer-helper are primarily a function of the rigid employment of the programs. If the trainer-helper is not shaped or influenced by the feedback which he gets from the helpee concerning what is most effective for the helpee, and if he does not modify his treatment procedures accordingly, the program, as any, can be as harmful as helpful.

Again, spontaneity and creativity are not possible without a basic repertoire of responses. And the trainee-helpee learns most efficiently and effectively to be spontaneous and creative when he has a model in his trainer-helper, one who employs his basic response repertoire spontaneously and in creative combinations.

If we define training more broadly, in experiential terms, then, it may be viewed as the most effective means available for the development and sustenance of effective living. We are limited only by our own creativity in the number of different applications which might be made. Again, the system is simply to define the goal in a way that it can be achieved and to develop the appropriate programs to achieve it.

If we define training broadly, it may be viewed as a most effective way of life.

Training is in a true sense an adventure, where new experiences and new learning continually unfold themselves. As an adventure it is not free of risk to the adventurers, trainer as well as trainee. The trainer must put his theories and his research on the line. He is courageous to do so. And yet, compared with the dangers for the trainees, the adventure seems relatively comfortable. If the project fails, *it* has simply failed. The adventurer can modify his theories and develop new programs of research.

For the people "off the streets," those involved in the projects recorded in this book, everything is at stake—their physical, emotional, and intellectual beings. If they fail, *they* fail. They return to a life of survival in a world of urgent nothingness. It is as if they have never lived.

Survivors know nothing of growth and are vulnerable to its introduction. Growth is what is on the other side of a great chasm—a yawning void whose endless echoes tell of the fate of those who leap and miss or those who cannot put the last plank in their carefully constructed bridges. Yet only survivors can grow. Real growth is only possible when survival is assured. Those who cannot survive cannot grow, for the risks in growth are such that they throw the grower periodically back upon his survival instincts.

This is a great price to pay—to risk all for growth. And those who would demand to risk it are demanded of themselves. If the people must risk, the teachers must risk. It the people must put themselves "on the line," the teachers must put themselves—not their theories or their research—"on the line." If the people must learn of growth, the teachers must learn once again of survival, and in doing so, broaden the base for their own growth. This is the real struggle —between the grower and the survivor—where each "sticks" the other with what he has to teach, where both enter a world of endless reverberations of learning culminating in the actualization of each man's resources.

REFERENCES

Amidon, E. J., & Flanders, N. A. *The role of the teacher in the classroom.* (Rev. ed.) Minneapolis, Minn.: Association for Productive Teaching, 1967.

Aspy, D. The effect of teacher-offered conditions of empathy, positive regard, and congruence upon student achievement. *Florida Journal of Educational Research,* 1969, **11,** 39–48.

Aspy, D., & Hadlock, W. The effects of high and low functioning teachers upon student performance. In R. R. Carkhuff & B. G. Berenson, *Beyond counseling and therapy.* New York: Holt, Rinehart and Winston, 1967.

Berenson, D. H. The effects of systematic human relations training upon the classroom performance of elementary school teachers. *Journal of Research and Development in Education,* 1971, **4,** 70–85.

Bierman, R., Carkhuff, R. R., & Santilli, Muriel. The effects of a basic orientation program in interpersonal skills upon Head Start teachers. In R. R. Carkhuff, *Helping and human relations,* Vol. II: *Practice and research.* New York: Holt, Rinehart and Winston, 1969.

Carkhuff, R. R. *Helping and human relations: A primer for lay and professional helpers.* Vol. I. *Selection and training.* New York: Holt, Rinehart and Winston, 1969. (a)

Carkhuff, R. R. *Helping and human relations: A primer for lay and professional helpers.* Vol. II. *Practice and research.* New York: Holt, Rinehart and Winston, 1969. (b)

Carkhuff, R. R. The prediction of the effects of teacher-counselor training: The development of communication and discrimination selection indexes. *Counselor Education and Supervision,* 1969, **8,** 265–272. (c)

Carkhuff, R. R., & Alexik, M. The differential effects of the manipulation of client self-exploration upon high- and low-functioning therapists. *Journal of Counseling Psychology,* 1967, **14,** 350–355.

Carkhuff, R. R., & Berenson, B. G. *Beyond counseling and therapy.* New York: Holt, Rinehart and Winston, 1967.

Carkhuff, R. R., & Griffin, A. H. Selection and training of functional professionals for the inner-city pre-school. *Journal of Research and Development in Education,* 1971, **4,** 87–96.

Dixon, W. R., & Morse, W. C. The prediction of teaching performance: Empathic potential. *Journal of Teacher Education,* 1961, **12,** 323–329.

Duncan, J. K., & Hough, J. B. *Technical review of the teaching situation reaction test.* Unpublished manuscript, Ohio State University, 1966.

Glaser, E. M., & Ross, H. L. *An evaluation of the effectiveness of the Allen Teaching Machine at the Federal Correctional Institution, Lompoc, California.* Washington, D.C.: Federal Prison Industries, Federal Bureau of Prisons, 1970.

Hefele, T. J. The effects of systematic human relations training upon student achievement. *Journal of Research and Development in Education,* 1971, **4,** 52–69.

Hough, J. B., & Ober, R. The effect of training in interaction analysis on the verbal teaching behavior of preservice teachers. In E. Amidon & J. B. Hough (Eds.), *Interaction analysis: Theory, research and application.* Reading, Mass.: Addison-Wesley, 1967.

Jones, R. M. The role of self-knowledge in the educative process. *Harvard Educational Review,* 1962, **32,** 200–209.

Joyce, B. R. *The teacher-innovator—A program to prepare teachers.* Final Report, 1968, Teachers College, Columbia University, OE-58021, Project #8-9019, U.S. Department of Health, Education and Welfare.

Kratochvil, D. W., Carkhuff, R. R., & Berenson, B. G. Cumulative effects of parent and teacher offered levels of facilitative conditions upon indices of student physical, emotional, and intellectual functioning. *Journal of Educational Research,* 1969, **63,** 161–164.

Rogers, C. R., Gendlin, E. T., Kiesler, D., & Truax, C. B. *The therapeutic relationship and its impact.* Madison, Wis.: University of Wisconsin Press, 1967.

Taylor, B. L. An exploratory study of teacher education and mental health. In Association for Student Teaching, *Mental Health in Teacher Education.* Iowa: William C. Brown, 1967.

Truax, C. B., & Carkhuff, R. R. *Toward effective counseling and psychotherapy: Training and practice.* Chicago: Aldine, 1967.

Truax, C. B., & Tatum, C. R. An extension from the effective psychotherapeutic model to constructive personality change in preschool children. *Childhood Education,* 1966, **42,** 456–462.

Whiteis, U. E. Poor scholarship in college—two interpretations and an experimental test. *Harvard Educational Review,* 1962, **32,** 3–38.

PART SIX
Functionality and Change

CHAPTER 14

Functionality
and Effectiveness

.

When Dr. John C. Houbolt of Langley Research Center, Virginia, part of the National Aeronautics and Space Administration (NASA), developed the concept of the lunar-orbit rendezvous, he separated the lunar-landing mission into precise functions to which specific spacecraft parts could be assigned. Thus, he operationalized putting a man on the moon—a product of man's most vivid imagination.

Concretizing the goal in terms of its operations made the moon venture possible. The goal could be seen in dimensions that could be achieved. Specific steps could be worked out to achieve these dimensions. Finally, everything could be put together to achieve the final criterion—putting a man on the moon.

In a similar way goals in any area of endeavor may be operationalized and the means to achieve them developed systematically. Indeed, the goals are seen in terms of the operations employed to achieve them. These operations incorporate the functions of the final goals and, when achieved, we say that our outcome or product has functionality. *Functionality*, then, is a term which we employ to define the accomplishment of goals which have been operationalized in terms of their functions.

In short, *functionality is effectiveness.*

SOCIAL SIGNIFICANCE OF FUNCTIONALITY

The special significance of the issue of functionality in the human service areas is that it addresses itself to the questions, "Can they do what they claim to do?"; "Do they make delivery for promises made?" By operationalizing the goals of the various social services we can answer whether educators educate and rehabilitators rehabilitate. We can operationalize our goals by assessing increments of achievement and growth, rates of improvement, cure and recidivism. Programs that achieve high levels of success by these criteria have functionality and are considered effective. Those that do not are neither functional nor effective.

Clearly, as we have seen through the pages of this book, those programs that have analyzed their goals into their functional dimensions and established progressive gradations of reinforcing experiences for accomplishing them have been effective in terms of meeting the functional criteria. Those that have not systematically related their programs to their goals have not been effective in meeting functional criteria.

The social significance of functionality is twofold: (1) it provides a means by which the persons supposedly being serviced may assess the effectiveness of the different social service agencies; (2) it provides a means by which persons being serviced may themselves be developed to provide their own social services. In the first instance, for example, inquiry is no longer defeated by the concept of education as the vague, amorphous term which connotes the kinds of things that children do when they go to school. Education may be assessed by situation-specific questions, "How many months reading growth did my second grade child achieve over the course of the academic year?" *Teachers may be selected, hired, rewarded, and fired on the basis of their credentials of functionality in their different roles.*

In the second instance, the helpee may become helper. With the knowledge of the precise functions of the goals, to continue the example, the helper may be trained in the kinds of operations necessary to enable his child, himself in a functional professional capacity, and other children to achieve high levels of achievement in reading or in any other area. The implications for all other social service functions are similar.

For the black and minority movements in 1971 what this means is that one way or the other, by the first or the second method, people can assure themselves that the deliveries to them are being made. If the credentialed professionals are not, in the first instance, making the delivery, then indigenous personnel may be selected and trained, in the second instance, to make the delivery. But the delivery must be made!

In a healthy society, then, people are measured by what they can do, by criteria of competency, by functionality, by effectiveness. Each, with work, can have a place, but only so much of a place as he has earned by the power of his productivity. A working concept of functionality, alone, can equalize the opportunity and justice necessary for each to determine the extent of his contribution.

DEVELOPMENT OF FUNCTIONAL PROGRAMS

The real value of functional programs is that they make deliveries at every stage of the program. *Every stage of development is a stage of delivery.* With the step-by-step progressions of accomplishment, there is no waiting until some final day for benefits. Indeed, any program that promises no delivery until its end is a lie, for it is based upon the methodology of miracle rather than achievement. Thus, en route to the moon, satellites became weather-gathering and TV relaying stations. The moon venture itself and the valuable information that may be gained from it will constitute not an end but a link in man's endless chain into the heavens.

Criteria of functionality, then, may be developed by concretizing the critical dimensions of otherwise abstract goals. In this regard, a full definition of the goal is not possible without an understanding of the need or problem which led to the goal (Carkhuff, 1969a, 1969b). To be sure, we must emphasize that the goal is simply the flip side of the problem to be solved. The goals, in turn, can be analyzed into their critical dimensions, with the primary emphasis upon the potential achievability or attainability of these dimensions. *Abstract goals are not helpful in attaining concrete realities. Concrete realities are helpful in attaining abstract goals.*

A number of different courses of action may be available for the attainment of these critical dimensions. A consideration of the advantages and disadvantages of each alternative course of action will lead to the one that offers the highest probability of success for the overall effort.

PROJECT 32

*Consideration of Alternate Courses of Action**

In the process of consulting with the Concentrated Employment Program in an attempt to make it more functional, one regulation which proved to be a morale depressor, that of requiring all staff members to punch the time clock, was considered in detail. It should be emphasized that while the staff members hoped to become functional professionals, many were themselves "off the streets," having been hard-core unemployed or underemployed persons like the clientele they were servicing. Punching the clock had been instituted after repeated instances of tardiness on the part of many employees. Table 14–1 depicts a consideration of the advantages and disadvantages of alternate courses of action involving just one problem, the time clock.

As can be seen, in spite of the fact that many employees verbalized an interest in no clock it was found, when considered in depth, that the clock was preferable to no clock, with Course I having more advantages and fewer disadvantages than Course III. A variation of using the clock involved having the clock for a probationary period after which the employee need

*Reprinted from mimeographed materials prepared in January 1970 for the Concentrated Employment Program, Springfield, Mass., by Robert R. Carkhuff.

Table 14–1

A Consideration of Alternate Courses of Action

1. *Problem:* Resentment against punching time clock a morale factor.
2. *Goal:* More effective effectuation of punctuality.

3. *Courses of Action*	I *Clock*	II *Clock Probationary Period*	III *No Clock*	IV *No Clock Rating of Effectiveness*	V *No Clock Clock if abuse*
A. Consideration of advantages and disadvantages on following criteria:					
1. Treatment as professionals	−	− +	+	+ +	+
2. Administrative control	+	+ −	−	− −	− +
3. Supervision	+	+ −	−	+	+
4. Assignment of penalties	+	+ −	−	−	+
5. Relation to over-all effort	+	+	−	+	+
	4+ 1−	5+ 4−	1+ 4−	4+ 3−	5+ 1−
B. *Amendments*					
1. Differential treatment of supervisory staff	Sign-in Sign-out	Sign-in Sign-out	None	Supervisor is rater	Supervisor assigns clock
2. Period of grace	5 minutes	5 minutes	——	None	None
3. Modify penalties	No suspension	No suspension	——	Fire low-rated	Fire if tardy after on clock

no longer punch the clock unless he abused the privilege (Course II). While it had more advantages than Courses I and II, however, it tended to neutralize itself, having as many disadvantages as II and more than I. Course IV concentrated most upon the overall effectiveness of the employees, incorporating punctuality in the ratings of individual effectiveness. Finally, Course V, involving the use of the clock only upon the abuse of the no clock privilege, seemed to offer the most advantages and the fewest disadvantages to the overall program.

The programs to implement the courses of action are dictated by the programs chosen. The programs are developed in the same manner as the courses. Those programs that offer the greatest prospect for successfully implementing the course of action are chosen. The programs will be developed in successive gradations in order to ensure the success of the program.

In the following problem-solving program, the purposes were twofold: (1) to develop effective courses of action for the Concentrated Employment Program; (2) to train the trainees to be able to develop effective courses of action. That is, the trainees were both working on immediate problems to make the overall program more effective and to understand how to develop effective courses of action with their own groups in the future. The prerequisite to training was the selection of the most effective workers, independent of rank, to participate in the program.

PROJECT 33

Development of Effective Courses of Action*

FORMAT FOR SESSION #1

A. **Initial Problems of Program:**
1. Poor morale
2. Ineffectiveness
3. Lack of direction

B. **Initial Goals of Program:**
1. Work effectiveness
2. Preparation for up and out
3. Personal development

C. **Goals of Training:**
1. Effectiveness in working with individuals
2. Effectiveness in working with groups
3. Effectiveness in developing courses of action

D. **Steps of Training:**
1. Focus on responding effectively to others
2. Focus on initiating effectively "Telling it like it is"
3. Development of effective courses of action:
    (a) Develop goals that can be achieved
    (b) Consider alternate courses of action
    (c) Develop programs to achieve the goals
4. Principles of effective courses of action:
    (a) Divide programs down into progressive step-by-step experiences
    (b) Movement is from simple to complex

*Reprinted from mimeographed materials prepared during the Fall of 1969 for the Concentrated Employment Program, Springfield, Mass., by Robert R. Carkhuff in conjunction with Bernard G. Berenson, Andrew H. Griffin, and George Banks.

(c) Movement to next step only when previous step is accomplished

(d) At failure, return to previously mastered step

(e) Principles of differential reinforcement

1. Reward—positive reinforcement
2. Punishment—negative reinforcement
3. Leaving alone—extinction

5. Development of goals:

(a) Assessment should be based upon publicly observable behavior

(b) Goals should involve changes in behavior rather than attitudes, etc.

(c) Develop specific courses of action for each person

REVIEW OF SESSION #1

A. **Emphasis of Session:**

1. Focused upon input of CEP Leaders into development of present program
2. Human Relations Center Staff focused upon responding to CEP leaders' feelings and ideas about problems and goals at CEP

B. **Summary of Problems:**

1. Principle problems:

(a) Lack of morale

(b) Lack of hope for future of CEP

2. Source of Problems:

(a) CEP personnel who are doing it are not getting rewarded

(b) CEP personnel who are not doing it are not getting punished

3. Consequence of Problems:

(a) Ineffective people pull effective people down rather than effective people pulling ineffective people up

(b) Initiative of effective people is not encouraged

(c) Politicking of ineffective people is encouraged

C. **Homework assignment:**

1. Further summarize problems and boil them down
2. Start to look for ways to define goals

FORMAT FOR SESSION #2

A. **Review homework assignments**

B. **Develop goals of program**

1. Goals flow from problems

      (a) If we understand problems we can formulate goals

      (b) Therefore need to focus on understanding first

  2. Develop goals in ways that can be achieved

C. **Establishment of Goals:**

  1. If problem is lack of reward for effective personnel

    Then

    Goal is developing a system for rewarding personnel

  2. Similarly, if problem is lack of encouragement for initiative

    Then

    Goal is developing a system for encouraging initiative

  3. Similarly, if problem is lack of punishment (or at least no rewards) for ineffective people

    Then

    Goal is developing a system for punishing (or at least not rewarding) ineffective people

D. **Means to Achieve Goals:**

  1. Focus of next session

  2. See points 3, 4 and 5 of Steps of Training

E. **Development of Professional Role:**

  Model

  1. Focus of next sessions

  2. Development of code of conduct

REVIEW OF SESSION #2

A. **Emphasis of Session:**

  1. Further study of problems in order to boil the problems down into their critical dimensions

  2. Tentative probing to develop goals

B. **Summary of Problems:**

  1. Problems of CEP take place at three different levels:

      (a) Between CEP and outside agencies and community

      (b) Within CEP between the different staff members and groups of staff members

      (c) Within each individual staff member at CEP

  2. Further breakdown of problems:

      (a) The problems between CEP and outside agencies reflect CEP's inability to sell itself as a professional agency

      (b) The problems within CEP reflect the fact that CEP does not treat its own staff members as professionals in addition to the points made in Session #2

      (c) The problems within each individual reflect the fact that individual staff members do not see themselves as professionals

3. All of these areas require further examination
C. **Tentative Goals Suggested:**
    1. Development of functionally professional models
        (a) Development of functionally professional image for CEP
        (b) Development of functionally professional policies within CEP
        (c) Development of functionally professional models within CEP
    2. Develop new job concepts
    3. Develop new programs
    4. Develop new industries
    5. Develop new work/study concept
    6. Develop guide for personal and professional conduct
D. **Homework**
    1. Establish goals in achievable terms
    2. Establish goals based upon an understanding of problems

FORMAT FOR SESSION #3

A. Review homework assignments
B. Develop goals of program
C. Develop sub-goals that can be achieved
D. Consider alternative ways of attaining the sub-goals and final goals
E. Consider the advantages and disadvantages of alternative ways of attaining goals
    1. Long-term advantages
    2. Short-term advantages

REVIEW OF SESSION #3

A. Emphasis of Session:
    1. Organizing problems into broad categories
        (a) Problems *between* CEP and outside world
        (b) Problems *within* CEP
        (c) Personal or individual problems
    2. Assessing significance of different categories of problems
B. Summary of Problems:
    1. *Between* CEP and outside world the problems include:
        (a) Need for public relations
            1. Education
            2. Communication
        (b) Need to sell CEP to business and industry
            1. Particularly need to sell staff

           2. Need to sell new concepts

      (c) Need to acquire basic skills

           1. For CEP as a unit

           2. For individual staff within CEP

      (d) Need to learn how to fully utilize community resources

    2. *Within* CEP the problems include:

      (a) A definition of CEP:

           1. Definition of goals

           2. Definition of means

      (b) Problem of morale:

           1. Encouragement and reward of initiative

           2. Guidance and counseling services for individual problems

      (c) Functional professionalization

           1. Code of conduct

           2. Personal professionals

      (d) Communication

           1. Information

           2. Race Relations

           3. Comprehension of meaning

      (e) On-going in-service training and schooling

           1. Acquisition of skills

           2. Credit for education

    3. Personal or individual problems

      (a) Physical

      (b) Emotional

      (c) Interpersonal

      (d) Discipline

      (e) Work skill

C. Tentative understandings reached:

    1. All programs begin with persons or individual

      (a) Must get own house in order

      (b) Then work on problems within CEP

    2. Main concentration of this program will be upon problems within CEP

      (a) Must get CEP house in order

      (b) Then work on problems between CEP and outside

D. Homework:

    1. Develop personal program for self

    2. Define goals of CEP

FORMAT FOR SESSION #4

    A. Review homework assignments

    B. Begin to concentrate upon problems within CEP

REVIEW OF SESSION #4

A. Emphasis of Session:
    1. Consider individual programs of action
    2. Consider goals of CEP

B. Summary of Problems:
    1. Individual program of action
        (a) Begin with physical programs
        (b) All other programs depend upon physical energy
    2. Goals of CEP
        (a) CEP's commitments are multiple:
            1. To clients
            2. To staff
            3. Program includes clients and staff
        (b) Commitment to hard core:
            1. Find out where he is at
            2. Find out what he can do
        (c) Develop employment opportunities
            1. Obtain employment
            2. Sustain employment
        (d) Staff development and placement
        (e) Develop concept of functional professional

C. Tentative understandings reached:
    1. If we define our own effective program, then we are defining goals of CEP
        (a) Individual who is personally effective is what CEP seeks
        (b) The whole concept of functional professional is the goal of CEP
    2. We do not help clients simply by finding and sustaining employment
        (a) By concentrating upon where client is and what he wants to and can do we provide him a model for somebody who is employed yet is doing something important
        (b) By concentrating on his feelings we give him a feeling of self worth
    3. Biggest morale problem at CEP will be take-over of DES
        (a) Most ineffective component will be supervising activities of most effective—coaching
        (b) Issue of whether we can work out a program to provide guidance, consultation, training for DES

D. Homework:
    1. Concentrate upon problems within CEP, particularly rela-

tionship between functional professionalization and definition of CEP goals

FORMAT FOR SESSION #5

A. Review all previous sessions
B. Study relationship between definition of CEP goals and functional professionals
C. Develop code of conduct for functional professionals to achieve CEP goals (described above)
    1. Include:
        (a) Personal code
        (b) Code within CEP
        (c) Code between CEP and outside

The essence of effectiveness in achieving any goal, then, is the operationalization of the ends and the means to attain the ends. In this instance the ends were both the programs that were produced by this series of problem-solving conferences and the knowledgeability of the trainee on how to solve problems effectively. The conferences involved four separate committees of approximately five staff members and a consultant each. They included the following breakdown of groups: functional professionalism; communication; morale; inservice training. The culmination of the problem-solving involved the programs that were produced entirely by the lay personnel of CFP's staff.

PROJECT 34
*Designs for Functional Programs**

GROUP I: FUNCTIONAL PROFESSIONALISM

A. Goals:
    1. Definition of Functional Professional
        (a) Specified skills and services
        (b) Code of conduct
            (1) Self
            (2) Clients
            (3) Community
            (4) Colleagues

*Reprinted from mimeographed materials prepared during January and February of 1970 for the Concentrated Employment Program, Springfield, Mass., by Robert R. Carkhuff, Bernard G. Berenson, Andrew H. Griffin, and George Banks.

        (c) Educate for concept within and outside of CEP

2. *Definition: A Functional Professional is a person, independent of formal credentials who possesses those characteristics and skills directly related to performing the essentials of a position or service to a high level of effectiveness.*

3. *Code of Conduct:*
   - (a) Identification of unique skills, talents, values of subcultures, then systematize them for transmission within and without
   - (b) Maximize potential
   - (c) Specific skills and services
   - (d) Demand and development of effective leadership
   - (e) Effective and functional selection—periodic assessment for both those assessed and the assessors
   - (f) Reinforcement of effective people—salary, responsibility, recognition, trust, independence, decision making within area of expertise
   - (g) Built-in up and out for all levels within CEP and outside

4. *Copies of code of conduct should be printed and circulated and explained throughout CEP and the community.*
   - (a) *Self:*
     - (1) Development of specific skills and services
     - (2) Commitment to maximizing human potential
     - (3) Commitment to one's own physical, emotional and intellectual growth
     - (4) Demand for maximum performance at all levels
   - (b) *Colleagues:*
     - (1) Demand and development of effective leadership
     - (2) Effective and functional selection
          Code for Functional Professionals should be understood and endorsed by all potential FP's
     - (3) Periodic reassessment of functional professional and FP assessors (committee)
     - (4) Internship systems
     - (5) Reinforcement of effective people
          Salaries, responsibilities, trust, recognition, independence, authority
     - (6) Certification of functional professionals by FP's
     - (7) On-going consultation
     - (8) On-going problem-solving committees for morale, communication, on-going training and functional professionalization, ethics

(9) Demand highest level of functioning from all colleagues

(c) *Community:*

    (1) Up and out policies at all levels

    (2) Development of new jobs, services and industries

    (3) Communicate the concept of functional professional

    (4) Develop and implement new concepts of education and training

(d) *Client:*

    (1) Internship systems

    (2) Credit programs taught by FP's

    (3) Systematize identification and transmission of unique skills, talents, values and aspects of sub-cultures

    (4) Commitment to maximizing human potential

    (5) Confidentiality should be practiced by both clients and staff

    (6) On-going problem-solving committees for morale, ethics, functional professionalism and communication

    (7) Communicate the concept of functional professional

    (8) Continuous assessment of new systems, equipment or concepts to be used for the benefit of clients

    (9) Do whatever is in best interest of the client's emotional, physical and intellectual progress

   (10) Respond to client before recommending courses of action

   (11) There are no full time students or clients (everybody is teaching something and learning)

B. Program:

1. Meetings to interpret and review Code of Conduct to staff for endorsement
2. Periodic meetings for staff and clients for review and alterations
3. Part of orientation of new clients and staff will include copies and discussion of code of conduct
4. All components alter code to fit individual demands of that component
5. Copies to community leaders, business-industry and professionals with follow-up meetings

GROUP II: COMMUNICATION

A. Goals
   1. *Communication*
      (a) Between staff and administration
      (b) Between components
      (c) Within components
      (d) Between component and clients
      (e) Administration and client
      (f) Between clients
      (g) Improvement of race relations

B. **Program:**
   1. *Between staff and adminstration*
      (a) Any program or idea affecting a component's behavior, attitudes and curriculum should have representation of that component, i.e. the coordinator or his designated representative
      (b) Verification via memo of agreements or business
      (c) Standard agenda provided for each weekly coordinator's meeting, including assessment of coordinators (point system) and reason
      (d) Weekly assessment of component and reason
      (e) Periodic visits of administration to component
      (f) Feed-back on visit to component—comments should be positive or negative reinforcement
   2. *Between components*
      (a) Feed-back, i.e. interchange or referral of any information relating to another component
      (b) Meeting between affected component coordinators for plan of action or presentation (before attending in-house or outside program sessions)
   3. *Within components*
      (a) Minutes of coordinators' meeting read at weekly inter-componental staff meeting which is held weekly after coordinators' meeting
      (b) Staff meeting after 4:00 P.M. daily for evaluation of work day (wherever feasible, i.e. components with clients)
      (c) Weekly assessment of staff by coordinator—reason. Several low assessments warrant follow-up by coordinator
      (d) Continued bi-monthly reports which are to be assessed by development services director

Factors to be considered:
(1) Punctuality
(2) Content
(3) Additives, such as solutions to problems or at least suggestions

4. *Between component and client*
    (a) Any decision involving client should be clearly understood, read, discussed, put in writing
    (b) Opportunity for expression—possibly part of class session
    (c) Complete and continued information of concept of CEP and its functions
        Indoctrination of what component offers presented verbally and written
    (d) Knowledge of grievance procedure
        (1) Procedure
        (2) Training of supervisors and coordinators for handling grievances

5. *Administration and client*
    (a) Monthly meetings (assembly)
    (b) Newsletter

6. *Between clients*
    (a) Newsletter
    (b) Outstanding client of the month chosen
        Possible categories:
        (1) Attendance
        (2) English
        (3) Math
    (c) Class picture—before job orientation instruction
    (d) Growth chart in classroom

7. *Improvement of race relations*
    (Seeking better understanding of race relations and culture)
    (a) Reports and memos to be in Spanish and English whenever feasible
    (b) Planned and organized cultural programs initiated and implemented through clients and staff aided by development services, such as getting films and speakers
    (c) Interpreter should have material context of speech beforehand
    (d) Packaged report of materials and knowledge obtained from successful programs visited
    (e) Cultural experience to be derived in environment,

utilizing all Spanish organizations and Black organizations

(f) Newsletter in Spanish and English

(g) Human relations staff member (Spanish)

GROUP III: MORALE

A. Goals:
1. To have different policies for staff and clients
2. To have a clear basis for rules and regulations for all
3. To set staff up as models
4. To get the best people to the top

B. Program:
1. *Conditions of reward other than pay and promotions*
   (a) Encourage use of suggestion box by:
      (1) Awarding best suggestion of the month—2 days off with pay
      (2) Awarding second best suggestion—1 day off with pay
      (3) Awarding third best suggestion—½ day off with pay
      (4) If unacceptable—alternate awards
         (a) Dinner with director
         (b) Trip with director—for exposure to inner workings
   (b) Special projects and/or trips
      (1) Effective people assigned special tasks to work on
         (a) Follow through on ideas for change
         (b) Trips for exposure to inner workings and plans for CEP
      (2) Effective people sent to conferences
      (3) Establish a speakers' bureau
         (a) Only effective people allowed to take paid engagements
   (c) Open door policy of personnel office
      (1) Handle personal problems of staff within CEP
      (2) Handle personal problems of staff outside CEP
      (3) Make referral to outside community agencies when necessary
2. *Create program within the program*
   (a) Component Representative Advisory Committee (CRAC)
      (1) One representative elected by each component

will serve on this committee (would be like a shop steward)

 (2) The representative will seek to resolve problems presented within component, if possible

 (3) Representative is to "weed out" unnecessary problems before they reach committee

 (4) If unable to solve problem, he will bring it to the committee, along with the person concerned

 (5) Committee hears problem, *recommends* courses of action to Administration

 (6) If committee's recommendation is vetoed more than three or four times: A closer look at Administration

(b) Recreation committee (personnel office)

 (1) Promote outside activities for personnel

  (a) Bus trips

  (b) Sporting events

  (c) Plays

 (2) Set up lunch-time activities

 (3) Create better relations with clients

  (a) Invite clients to participate in recreation programs

  (b) Set up programs to include clients

3. *Develop a criteria of effectiveness*

 (a) 5-point rating system for each position

  (1) Each component sets guidelines for effectiveness within itself

  (2) Each employee graded as to effectiveness

4. *Differential reinforcement*

 (a) Divide staff into three categories

  (1) Effective personnel—rewarded

  (2) Middle group—left alone

  (3) Low group—punished

   (a) If warnings are not producing—immediate termination

 (b) Time clock

  (1) Change penalty

5. *Hiring of public relations man*

 (a) Main function—publicize good aspects of CEP

  (1) Newspapers

  (2) Television

  (3) Radio

 (b) Enlighten community agencies

(1) Speaking to agencies

(2) Invite community to CEP

   (c) Enlighten business and industry

(1) Speaking engagements

(2) Invite business and industry to CEP

GROUP IV: INSERVICE TRAINING

A. Goals:

1. *Start with what you have:*

   (a) Recognize the skills the staff has and use them

2. *Strengthen old and develop new capabilities*

3. *Human relations training for all staff*

4. *On-going training for all staff*

5. *Coordinators should utilize other resources within CEP*

6. *Build-in a consultation registry of personnel and resources in CEP*

B. Program:

1. *Provide skills training:*

   (a) Have a strong person from this group, picked by one of the leaders to represent his component and teach the staff and clients what CEP is all about

   (b) Public relations for all staff

2. *Visit other programs:*

   (a) Coordinators should bring back materials so their staff can use it

3. *Establish a sub-college within CEP*

   (a) Staff to get credits while working within CEP

   (b) Have other teachers from different colleges to come and assist staff in teaching CEP students

   (c) Clients within CEP will receive certificates upon completion of courses

4. *Proposal: Work-Study College as part of CEP*

PROPOSAL: WORK-STUDY COLLEGE[1]
CONCENTRATED EMPLOYMENT PROGRAM

A. General:

That the existing structure of the Concentrated Employment Program staff in conjunction with consultation services be utilized for

---

[1] The ideas from this proposal were combined with ideas emanating from the Masters program in Human Relations and Community Affairs, and under the leadership of Louis Frayser and Leonard Lockley the Springfield Free University was initiated.

implementing a new careers program in educational and vocational development for the staff and clientele of CEP.

B. **Specific:**

(1) That an educational program serving CEP and the black community be superimposed upon the existing CEP structure.

(2) That programs be developed to deal systematically with improving skills in present service areas and in areas of future interest to staff and other personnel.

(3) That faculty be recruited from within CEP and from credentialed and functional professionals in surrounding communities.

(4) That college credits be awarded under the auspices of the Work-Study College on the basis of the credentials of the staff.

(5) That simultaneous with academic program job development for staff members be accomplished as part of an up-and-out staff policy.

(6) That the Work-Study College take place on a Monday-Wednesday-Friday schedule at 3–5 P.M. on a voluntary basis.

(7) That a credentialed professional be appointed as provost of the college that operates within CEP.

(8) That a dean and a business manager be appointed from within CEP to coordinate the program.

(9) That New Careers become the central training agency for helping and human relations skills for staff in addition to continuing present responsibilities.

(10) That students pay \$1.00 per credit academic credits for expenses and overhead of the college.

(11) That college run on a quarterly basis with each course worth three credits for once a week meeting for three months.

(12) That each student take no more than 9 academic credits a quarter, thus no more than a total of 36 for a year.

(13) That each enrolled student receive an equivalent amount of internship credits for successful demonstration of effectiveness on the job; and demonstration of successful completion of on-the-job project; thus, no more than a total of 36 for a year.

(14) That a student be graduated with 126 credits, thus a minimum of 7 quarters at 9 academic credits and 9 internship credits (total 18) a quarter.

(15) That functional professional teachers be reimbursed in academic and internship credit for teaching.

C. Courses and Sequence:

Quarters	Physical	Emotional-Interpersonal	Intellectual
1	*Physical Fitness	*Helping and Human Relations Skills	*Historical and Contemporary world
2	*Nutrition	*Black Culture	*English
3	Survey of Biological Sciences	*Spanish Culture	Mathematics
4	The Human Body	Marriage and Family	Survey of Social Sciences
5	Prenatal and Infant Care	Child-rearing and Education	Survey of Physical and Engineering Sciences
6	First Aid	Community Relations	Business and Consumer Skills
7	Physical Education	Community Organization	Technical-Industrial Management

Electives for Majors:

A	Recreation	Mental Health Counseling	Creative Problem Solving
B	Coaching	Development of Human Resources	Technical & Creative Writing
C	Officiating	Principles of Social Service	Fundamentals of Research

*Required

D. Appendages:

(1) Three elective courses may with permission from Dean replace three courses from one of each of physical, emotional-interpersonal and intellectual areas for those students who intend to major in the speciality area.

(2) Students may with permission from Dean replace courses with successfully completed courses in skill areas at other colleges.

(3) Course organization: Professors will be encouraged to organize their courses as follows:

(a) Succinct summary of literature with reading assignments
(b) Emphasis upon skill acquisition
(c) Assignment of specified projects demonstrating skills
(d) Rotation of related experts through course

(4) Professors will volunteer their time for a quarter of 12 weeks with reimbursement for travel only.

The staff teams were then assigned to the various components of the organization to report and solicit feedback from its members. Thus, in the following order the teams rotated through the different components: functional professionalism; communication; inservice training; morale. The program was then finalized and incorporated into the organizational structure, to be modified as new learnings were acquired and as the feedback of what was effective and what was not was introduced.

These programs are the products of only ten weekly 2-hour conferences and one 10-hour conference, that is, a total of 30 hours of intensified problem-solving activities. The outcomes of these programs are in process. The ends, it is anticipated, will have functional utility. The test is whether they do or not.

A number of other specific programs evolved and were elaborated upon in some detail from these basic formats.

CRITERIA OF FUNCTONAL UTILITY

We have also operationalized the means by which the human relations specialists in our various programs have been developed. Since these are now relatively long-standing programs, we can turn to them for assessment. We must put them to the test of functional utility. Do they accomplish what they set out to accomplish? Are they functional?

These are not questions that credentialed professionals in the educational and social service professions ask of themselves. But they are questions that must be asked, for only then can we be shaped by the feedback to become more effective.

Of course, there are the usually anecdotal critiques from supervisors within the program or from evaluators from outside the program. Thus, for example, there are the following tributes to the human relations specialist program in the school department from outside experts such as the Field Supervisor for the State Department of Education: ". . . I was very impressed . . . reflected careful planning . . . I saw teachers, students and specialists actively involved in the teaching-learning process . . . congratulations to all on a job well done."

Clearly, however, these tributes, while reinforcing, are not enough to assess the functionality of the specialists. Neither are the negative reports adequate for assessments of effectiveness, for many of these may have a large political dimension.

Assessments of functionality can best be accomplished by breaking the specialist's job down into its various components and assessing the specialists' relative effectiveness on each of these dimensions. We have done this in various ways. (See our assessments of the effects of training in Part Five, where we reported the effects of our selection and training programs upon specialists' level of functioning.) We must now study the specialists' effects upon others in their translation of their learned skills to functioning on the job.

One program which we can study systematically in this regard is the program of the human relations specialists in the school department. Their functions, as we have seen, can be broken down into the three Ts: Treatment, Training, and Teaching. Let us assess the effectiveness of their functioning in each of these areas. But first let us look at a cross-section of the clientele seen by the specialists.

PROJECT 35
Human Relations Specialist Activities*

Table 14–2 presents the quarterly report of the specialists' work for the Fall of 1969.

As can be seen, the main emphasis — as it should be — is upon the number of children and the characteristics of the children seen by the specialists. Involvement with members of the school department and community is recorded primarily in terms of referral and consultation.

Table 14–2
Human Relations Specialist Activities

Quarterly Report, All Schools   Date 1/22/70
September, October, November, December

Grade Breakdown	Initial Interview	Terminal Interviews	Returnees	Ongoing	Contacts
7	229	93	27	263	595
8	433	68	43	476	947
9	235	114	31	242	665
G. A.	27	20	21	112	133
Parents	251	41	6	143	400
Teachers	190	35	11	96	453
Total	1365	371	139	1332	3193

*Reprinted from mimeographed table of quarterly data prepared December 1969 by Andrew H. Griffin and Robert R. Carkhuff.

Table 14-2
Human Relations Specialist Activities *(cont.)*

Ethnic Breakdown of Students		Contacts	Subject Area Due to Overt Misbehavior	
Black	962	1900	English	177
Puerto Rican	14	31	Reading	183
White	157	318	Mathematics	90
Total	1133	2249	Science	53
			Social Studies	148
Problem Area			Gym	108
			Music	152
Home	459		Art	77
Social	241		Foreign Lang.	4
School	723		Homeroom	2
Racial	514		Other Teachers	4
Economical	260			
Sexual	16			
Vocational	81			

Referred by		Agency Referrals	Student	Parent
Principal	153	Big Brothers	1	
Asst. Prin.	97	CEP	1	
Counselor	60	Dunbar	8	
Teacher	184	Family Center	5	2
School Nurse	12	Juvenile Court	25	5
Student	398	Legal Services	2	1
Community	60	NES	53	
Himself	123	PACE	1	
		Urban League	8	1
		Welfare	4	1
		YWCA (PAGE)	4	1
		Y.O.C.	3	
		NYC	1	
		Salvation Army	3	1
		Public Defender	3	
		District Court	10	
		School Dept.	12	
		Suspendee Program	3	
		Headstart		1
		Youth Aid Bureau	1	
		Total	148	13

As can also be seen the specialists are quite busy. But, again, we must ask, how effectively do they discharge their responsibilities?

The next task, then, is an assessment of the specialists' level of functioning in making these human contacts.

PROJECT 36

*Level of Judged Effectiveness**

The general level of effectiveness of the specialists in all areas of contact in the school was assessed by teams comprised jointly of two representatives of the school department and two representatives of the Human Relations Center staff.

Table 14–3 summarizes the evaluations of the level of functioning of the specialists in various spheres of endeavor. The estimates, while made by the evaluators, were based upon extensive interviews with those persons who had been most intimately involved with the specialists' efforts.

As can readily be seen, in the area of their principal emphasis—working with the school children, themselves—the specialists were judged most effective. The interviews with students indicated that the students felt that the specialists were most effective, with the general comment being that the specialists were more understanding and more responsive to the students' needs than any of the credentialed professional staff. While, quantitatively, the contacts with white students were not as numerous, qualitatively, the interviews with them yielded similar responses. In this regard it is important to note that white gang leaders who were interviewed acknowledged readily that they utilized the black specialists to avoid eruptions of violence between white and black students.

With the exception of one school the specialists were also generally regarded effective by the principals, administrators, counselors, and teach-

Table 14–3

Ratings of the Effectiveness of Human Relations Specialists in School Settings I

Source of Ratings	I	Specialists*		III	IV	V	VI	VII
		#1	#2					
Students	4.0	4.0	4.0	4.5	4.5	4.5	4.0	4.5
Principal and Administrative Staff	3.0	1.0	3.0	3.0	4.5	3.8	3.5	4.0
Teachers	2.0	1.0	2.5	4.0	2.5	3.5	4.0	4.5
Counselors	1.0	1.5	3.0	X	4.0	4.5	5.0	X

*Specialists = Human Relations Specialists broken down into individual ratings due to unique interaction of specialist #1 and principal at school II.

*Reprinted in part with permission from the *Journal of Counseling Psychology,* 1970, 17, 443–450, where it first appeared as "The Selection and Training of Human Relations Specialists," by Robert R. Carkhuff and Andrew H. Griffin.

Table 14–4
Ratings of Effectiveness of Human Relations Specialists in School Settings II

| Source of Ratings | SCHOOLS | | | | | | |
	I	II	III	IV	V	VI	VII
Students	4.3	4.5	4.5	4.0	4.3	4.5	4.6
Principal and Administrative Staff	3.0	3.0	4.5	3.0	4.3	1.5	4.6
Teachers	3.5	3.0	3.5	2.5	4.0	4.0	4.0
Counselors	4.0	1.0	3.0	4.5	4.0	3.5	3.5

ers. The comments were generally favorable and ranged to the utilization of the specialists by teachers for the benefit of the teacher's own growth. The depressed ratings at the one school were a function of a personality clash between the male specialist and the male principal of the school. By the time the second, and follow-up evaluation, was conducted, the specialist had been reassigned to another school and the ratings were elevated accordingly (see Table 14–4).

However, even these positive subjective evaluations were inadequate to measure the functionality of the specialists. What was needed was some objective measure of their effectiveness in specific treatment functions. The specialists' unique contribution to treatment was viewed as follows: first, social and adjustment counseling with students; second, movement into the school and community environment to increase the probability of successful treatment; third, systematic development of courses of action for the students. One index that was continuously employed during the early stages was ratings of taped, role-played, and live sessions with the students. Here, the specialists demonstrated above minimally effective levels of functioning and involved their helpees in intense and meaningful self-exploration and self-understanding. But even this was not enough to demonstrate their capability to make full delivery to the helpees. For one thing, no evaluations were made as to whether the helpees had reached some objective criterion of outcome. The following project involves all three treatment functions in assessing the outcome of courses of action developed for ghetto children who were having great difficulty adjusting.

PROJECT 37

*Level of Treatment Effectiveness**

To meet the needs of young black students in integrated junior high schools, an experimental program assigning school positions for adult black human relations specialists was developed. The specialists were lay persons who were systematically selected and systematically trained as functional professionals according to selection and training programs based upon extensive research evidence. Assessments of their effectiveness indicate that the specialists were functioning in the helping role above levels determined to be minimally effective and were highly rated by students, principals and administrative staff, teachers and counselors.

The programs upon which the selection and training methodologies are based were developed from the evidence indicating a relationship between helper-responsive (empathy, respect, specificity) and helper-initiated (genuineness, confrontation and immediacy) dimensions and a variety of indexes of helpee process movement (self-exploration, self-experiencing of relevant problems) and helpee outcome (self-understanding, constructive action). The specialists were selected on the basis of their ability to offer relatively high levels of responsive and initiative dimensions in a variety of critical incident type situations. The training, in turn, was based upon developing proficiencies in communicating still higher levels of the responsive and initiative dimensions by systematically expanding the quantity and the quality of the responses in the specialists' repertoire.

An important part of training involved the systematic development of effective courses of action and programs to implement these courses of action. In each instance, the courses of action developed came out of the helpee's frame of reference. Experientially, the specialists had the opportunity to develop their own courses of action and programs. Didactically, the specialists were taught to be able to develop courses of action for their helpees.

The present study was conducted to assess the specialists' ability to develop and implement effective courses of action for the ghetto school children.

METHODOLOGY AND RESULTS

For a two week summer program designed to develop effective teamwork between specialists and school personnel, twelve ghetto school children, six male and six female, who had been transferred to predominantly

*Reprinted in part with permission from *Psychology in the Schools,* 1970, 7, 272–274, where it first appeared as "The Development of Effective Courses of Action for Ghetto School Children," by Robert R. Carkhuff.

white junior high schools upon the closing of a ghetto junior high school, were selected on the basis of their inability to adjust to the new environment. Twelve specialists were designated team leaders of twelve guidance or social adjustment counselors and twelve teachers in such a manner that one specialist, one counselor and one teacher were assigned as a team to each of the ghetto children. Where possible, all school personnel were from the same school as the students.

Under the leadership of the specialists the helping relationship with the children was developed so that courses of action could be established. The development of courses of action was based upon the stages designated in Table 14-5.

Based upon the exploration of personal problems by the children, group and, in some instances, individual, goals were established. Due to the time-limited nature of the program the group goals could be supervised more readily. In addition, they provided a standard index for assessment at the conclusion of the program. One problem common to all of the children was their inability to speak freely in their predominantly white classes. Thus, a course of action was developed, i.e. a program to achieve this goal was developed for each child.

The group goals for the black students were concretized in achievable terms. Systematic step-by-step programs were worked out to achieve these goals. The problems were first discussed in imagery, then role-played and finally enacted in real life. While the programs designed by the teams to achieve these goals were tailored to the students' individual needs, a typical program was as follows: (1) first, the student explored in imagery with a friend, then with peers, then with the specialist, his problems in class; (2) then he role-played as a student with his fellow black students; (3) then he role-played as a teacher with his black students; (4) then he role-played as both student and teacher, with the specialists serving as coaches; (5) then he functioned, with the specialists as coaches, as a student when white

Table 14-5

The Stages of Implementing a Course of Action in Helping

  I. The definition and description of problem area(s)
 II. The definition and description of direction(s) and/or goal(s) dictated by the problem area(s)
III. An analysis of the critical dimensions of these direction(s) and/or goal(s)
 IV. A consideration of the alternative courses of action available for attaining the dimensions of the direction(s) and/or goal(s)
  V. A consideration of the advantages and disadvantages of the alternative courses of action
 VI. The development of physical, emotional-interpersonal, and intellectual programs for achieving that course with the most advantages and fewest disadvantages in terms of ultimate success in goal achievement
VII. The development of progressive gradations of the program involved (Carkhuff, 1969a)

teachers and counselors made class-room presentations; (6) then with the specialists serving as coaches he made his own presentation to the teachers and counselors; (7) finally, on his own, he made his presentation to the class of teachers and counselors.

At each stage of the program the experiences progressed from least difficult to most difficult and they were repeated until the student successfully accomplished his sub-goals. Thus, for example, as a student, initially he simply listened and received the presentation, then he raised questions in consultation with the specialists; then he raised questions on his own; then he presented alternate ways of viewing the issues presented in consultation with his coaches; then he presented alternate views on his own.

At the end of the two-week period, the black students conducted an entire day of classes in the area of their own interests for the white counselors and teachers. They were rated by the class with 5-point scales for their level of functioning in their classroom presentation and interaction with the class. In addition, they were rated by an outside expert from the State Department of Education.

The results indicate that all twelve students successfully conducted classes made up of white teachers and counselors on the final day. With scales ranging from level 1 (ineffective) to level 5 (most effective), with level 3 designated minimally effective, all students received a mean rating above 3 from the teachers and counselors and the rating by the expert for all twelve students was 4.0. In addition, the students experienced themselves as having successfully completed the experience, with their composite rating of their own performances slightly under level 4.

DISCUSSION

It appears that a systematic development of courses of action and programs to achieve the goals involved can be effective in ameliorating or eliminating some of the school problems of ghetto youngsters.

Of course, the effectiveness with which the course of action is developed is contingent upon how well the helpee's frame of reference is developed. The degree to which a student explores himself is in part a function of how effectively the helper is able to establish a relationship with the student. This relationship, in turn, is in part a function of how effectively the helper can respond to the helpee's experience and initiate communication from his own experience.

In this context the teachers and counselors were neither systematically selected nor trained on the basis of their ability to communicate, although their effectiveness is, to be sure, in part a function of this ability. In addition, they were not functioning at nearly as high levels as were the trained specialists. Here it should be noted that all twelve students preferred the specialists over the teachers and counselors. While this preference may be a consequence of racial differences, it may also be a consequence of the specialists' ability to function at higher levels with the children.

All this is not to say that white teachers and counselors cannot be selected and trained to function effectively with ghetto children. Indeed, systematic human relations training should be required for all school personnel. It is to say, however, that those best equipped to reach the children should also be equipped to provide means to establish and the means to achieve constructive goals for the children.

In conclusion, it appears that black human relations specialists, selected on the basis of their communications skills and trained to intensify these skills, may have a distinct contribution to make to the welfare of these children in a school setting. There are systematic techniques available to enable indigenous lay personnel to be effective in developing and implementing effective courses of action for the students. The results suggest further that the functional professionals are not simply a measure of last resort, but, rather, when appropriately employed, may be a preferred mode of treatment, constituting the human link between society and the person in need of help.

In addition, and throughout the school year, the specialists developed individual courses of action for more personalized problems, particularly those related to school adjustment. For example, in one instance, a black student had had a traumatic experience with a particular white teacher. The specialist handled the problem in the following manner.

Betty had a problem. Betty was a junior high school student who was bussed out of her home area to one of the outlying junior high schools. She had a serious problem with one of her teachers, a problem which seemed to get in the way of her making progress in other areas of her school work. Miss B, a human relations specialist with the school department, worked with Betty on this problem.

Miss B was leader of a team involving a guidance counselor and a teacher. In conjunction with the counselor and teacher, Miss B worked out a course of action with Betty.

There were several important differences between Betty and her teacher. Betty was young and her teacher was older; Betty was black and her teacher was white; Betty felt her teacher could not understand her.

Miss B had Betty relate her difficulties with the teacher verbally over and over to different people until she felt comfortable with each; first, to a fellow black student from the ghetto; then to Miss B, who is also black; then to another black female human relations specialist; then to a white teacher who was dissimilar from the teacher with whom Betty had difficulty; then to a white teacher who was similar to the final teacher.

Next, Miss B had Betty go through a role-playing situation in the classroom with fellow students portraying members of the class. Betty went through each scene time and again until she felt comfortable: first, with a fellow black student as teacher; then with Miss B as teacher; then with another black female human relations specialist as teacher; then with a white teacher who was dissimilar to the problem teacher; then with a white teacher who was similar to the teacher.

The final phase was similar to the first phase with the exception that the comments made by the listener became strongly negative over repeated listening. First, Betty related the incident to a fellow student with gradually increasing negative comments from the students; then to another student; then to Miss B; then to another specialist; then to a white teacher dissimilar from the problem teacher; then to a white teacher similar to the problem teacher.

Finally, Betty related the incidents to the teacher with whom she had difficulty. She did so successfully and teacher and student reached a degree of understanding and rapport which they had never had.

It is to be emphasized that at the same time the specialist was preparing Betty for the teacher, she was preparing the teacher for Betty in the same systematic manner, working through ideationally and in action with persons of progressively increasing similarity with the characteristics of Betty which dominated the teacher's perception of the girl.

A lot of work? Certainly! But no more than is necessary to build in success for one girl's school life. No more than is necessary to illustrate the value of systematically trained specialists and their employment, where appropriate, of systematic treatment programs.

The real learning is that *the development of effective courses of action is itself a study of functionality.* That is, functional goals were established and functional means developed to achieve these individual and group goals. The achievement of the final goal was contingent upon the achievement of progressively difficult subgoals. In this manner, success was built in rather than out. The fact is that functional criteria can be established and reached with the systematic operationalization and implementation of courses of action. The fact is that the human relations specialists could demonstrate their effectiveness in all three treatment functions: the counseling upon which the courses of action were predicated; the preparation and manipulation of the environment, in this instance, the school environment; and the successful accomplishment of the course of action developed.

The specialists were also involved in training functions with parents and students as well as teachers. That is, individual specialists conducted training programs in interpersonal or human relations skills geared to the needs of the particular groups involved. The following studies assess a sampling of those programs conducted by the specialists.

PROJECT 38

Level of Training Effectiveness*

While there is evidence to indicate that lay persons can be trained to function effectively on the responsive and initiative conditions of communication related to constructive helpee change or gain, there is only limited evidence to demonstrate that trained lay persons can, in turn, be effective trainers. That is, can trainees be trained to be effective trainers? The only extensive study involved training of an essentially unselected group of 55 hard-core unemployed by six systematically selected and trained functional professionals. In this study the trainees demonstrated significant gains in their level of functioning as a consequence of training exclusively by lay trainers. However, the fact that lay personnel can be trained by trained lay personnel does not establish sufficient generalization for the effectiveness of training by lay trainers. The effects of training by lay trainers must be studied on populations other than those to which the trainers were indigenous.

In five separate programs the human relations specialists were assigned training responsibilities with the following trainee populations: (1) parents; (2) students; (3) teachers; (4) teachers and counselors; (5) correctional officers.

METHODOLOGY

Study 1

Two human relations specialists were assigned as trainers for ten parents in a special 20-hour program in interpersonal skills, particularly those relating to family relationships (Group I).

Study 2

Two human relations specialists were assigned as trainers for ten junior high school students in a special 30-hour program in interpersonal skills, particularly those relating to classroom adjustment, for 30 hours of training (Group II).

Study 3

Thirteen human relations specialists were assigned as trainers for thirteen teachers in a graduate education course. The specialists were assigned roles as trainer and co-trainer and paired in teams of two with two teachers to receive 20 hours of systematic human relations training (Group III).

*Reprinted from mimeographed manuscript prepared August 1969 by Robert R. Carkhuff.

Study 4

Twelve human relations specialists were assigned as trainers for teams of guidance counselors and teachers in a summer practicum on "The Development of Effective Courses of Action for Ghetto Children." Each specialist was assigned as a trainer for each team of one counselor and one teacher for 10 hours of preliminary empathy training.

Study 5

Six human relations specialists were assigned as trainers for 26 front-line correctional officers from the Bureau of Prisons in a special month-long project involving 80 hours of training for the Department of Justice. The specialists functioned individually as team leaders of small groups of correctional officers (Group V).

Outcome

In all instances an index of the trainee's level of functioning prior to and following training was obtained from responses to a tape of five standard stimulus expressions in the racial relations area. The responses were rated by trained and experienced raters who had demonstrated high inter-rater and intra-rater reliabilities in previous studies.

RESULTS AND DISCUSSION

The results appear in Table 14–6. As can be seen, the lay trainers were able to effect significant changes in the level of interpersonal skills of the different trainee groups involved. The degree of change, it appears, was related to the duration of training.

The results demonstrate the effectiveness of trained lay personnel as trainers in interpersonal skills of different populations. In addition, they suggest that the gains achieved by the trainees were in part a function of the duration of the program. That is, the longer the trainees were in training, the greater the gain in their level of functioning.

Table 14–6
Effects of Lay Trainers upon Groups of Professional Trainees

Overall Ratings	GROUPS									
	I Parents (N = 10) (20 hours)		II Students (N = 10) (30 hours)		III School Staff (N = 24) (10 hours)		IV Teachers (N = 20) (20 hours)		V Officers (N = 23) (80 hours)	
	Mean	sd	Mean	sd	Mean	sd	Mean	sd	Mean	sd
Pre-training	1.5	.5	1.4	.4	1.8	.6	1.6	.4	1.4	.5
Post-training	2.2	.5	2.2	.5	2.3	.5	2.3	.4	2.6	.4
Net Gain	+.7	.4	+.8	.3	+.5	.4	+.7	.3	+1.2	.3

It is noteworthy that in the instances of the professional programs the credentialed white trainees were being trained by functional professional black trainers. A side benefit of the learning of interpersonal skills, then, was the learning of skills for communication between races.

The functional test, then, was whether the specialists, having themselves been trained in interpersonal skills, could, in turn, effectively train others to function effectively interpersonally. The answer is emphatically, Yes! This is one of the unique benefits of systematic human relations training. People who are themselves trained to function at high interpersonal levels can train others to do likewise, independent of previous education and professional status. Or, in sequence, people who are functioning at high interpersonal levels may, with the assistance of a systematic program in interpersonal skills, train those who are functioning at low levels to function at high levels so that they, in turn, can train others who are functioning at low levels to function at high levels.

Finally, the specialists also developed an expertise in teaching functions, particularly black history and related areas of social awareness. Now, this is a more difficult area to assess. Nevertheless, in a special summer program an attempt was made to do just that. The specialists in the following program had teaching responsibilities for educating teachers as well as inner-city children from a neighboring city summer school program.

PROJECT 39
Level
*of Teaching Effectiveness**

Springfield, like all other American cities, is finding that what passed for an "excellent school system" twenty years ago must now institute some radical changes if it is to recapture that title honestly. The most salient deficiencies, as events of recent weeks in the Springfield schools have indicated, center around the whole area of serving the students of the inner-city adequately and the relationship of the educational structure to the city's racial injustices in general.

Since the teachers are the members of the educational institutions who most closely and significantly are involved with the students it is obvious to us that any attempt to reach the "unreachables" and teach the "unteachables" in the inner-city must begin with the teachers. In the first place, there is a notable dearth of black teachers and administrators in the Springfield school system. This very serious shortage of real black models

*Reprinted from an article entitled "Inner-City Workshop for Better Schools," *American International College Alumni Magazine*, Fall 1969, by Andrew H. Griffin and George Banks.

for black students to identify with, leads us to the assumption that black lay people, if trained, may be excellent as "extra-teachers" in the inner-city schools. Furthermore, if the traditional methods of training white teachers were on the mark the chances are that the city's schools would not have reached a point of total breakdown and all students would benefit.

AIC, as an urban college located in the middle of Springfield's black community, has the opportunity and responsibility to do something concrete to change the direction of teacher training and evaluation. The College has one immediate goal, to throw out the long-held tenet that teaching black children is the same as teaching white children. It is time to impress all those who will come in contact with school children that ghetto children are unlike suburban children. As soon as teachers start finding out who that ghetto child really is and what factors are working on his life, then the white teacher can begin to alter curriculum so that it means something to the inner-city child. The children in turn will then have something real to identify with and use. The following is a description of a course designed to provide some real training for teaching in the inner-city schools.

"Teaching in the Inner-City School," a two week workshop held at AIC this past summer, has opened new worlds to the twenty-one participants by providing new experiences. The course served a twofold purpose: to break down old myths surrounding the ghetto students and open new doors to a better use of individual skills in the classroom. We hoped in this workshop format to find an innovative and systematic approach to tackle the ways by which dedicated white teachers could "deprogram" themselves to the place where they can more fully understand the world of the black child, while also showing how irrelevant most of the conventional courses in teacher education are when it comes to reaching real students, especially those of minority groups.

There was a concomitant goal which was to prove empirically that lay people can be trained to teach without having previously had teacher education courses or other professional or college training. This goal was achieved, as well as its corollary which is that, because of the present irrelevant selection methods, there are teachers in the system who have closed minds and should not be allowed to touch the lives of any children.

The first week of the workshop heavily emphasized the background of the black—his world and his heritage, as well as the white world he lives in. By comparing what a ghetto child might see at home—e.g. cramped quarters, no books, debris, and rats—with what a white middle class child of the same age might see—e.g. adequate space, recreational facilities, grass, well-kept buildings—the point was emphasized that these two worlds are in no appreciable way alike, and if a teacher is not familiar with both worlds she is really not equipped to teach, no matter how much concern she has about the racial crisis.

During the first week black myths were attacked—myths which become so much a part of the white subconscious as to be unknown to his conscious self but which influence his performance in the classroom in such a way that he unwittingly holds back black students from realizing their real potential in the classroom. Such ideas as the natural inferiority of blacks, the Christian justification for slavery in America, the smaller mental capacity of blacks, were discussed along with the myths of the usual American heroes such as George Washington and Patrick Henry, who both were slave owners during the period of white America's struggle for independence. The discussions of the black experience and the white power structure which continues to say one thing and do another were very informative to the human relations specialists as well as to the white and black teachers, but the discussions were especially jarring to the whites, who were finding themselves the natural underdogs, having always before been the comfortable overprivileged.

The general study of "the black experience in a white world" also included lessons in African history. One of the human relations specialists taught short lessons out of one of the course texts, *Poverty, Education and Race Relations,* to give him the experience of standing in front of a class as teacher. Subjects from this book included poverty, social services, and social change; education, employment, and civil rights for Negro youth; and the magnetic teacher. This phase of the workshop proved very beneficial to the specialists' understanding of the job of the teacher—the importance of preparation and unmeasurable ingredients of good teaching. A further opportunity to gain this type of experience occurred the following week when each class member was responsible for teaching one chapter of Lerone Bennett's *Before the Mayflower,* to a small group of his classmates. In general, this is the basic outline of what happened from 9 A.M. to 1 P.M. the first week of the Inner City Workshop, but what happened out-of-class contributed as much as the concentrated classroom studies to the students' total awareness of the ways in which the white power structure is making sure they keep control over the destinies of black people.

After class each day, the students were assigned certain agencies to visit and conduct interviews in and write up as comparative studies, describing the activities and noting the racial breakdown of clientele and personnel, the attitudes of the interviewees toward the agency, co-workers, the people served, and the interviewer. For example, one day three public housing projects were assigned—one a garden-type duplex project for mostly whites which is very attractive and boasts a good setting, while another was a similarly constructed project but on a busy flat street with virtually no planting or recreational facilities which was for blacks primarily, and the other—Riverview Project—which is 95% non-white and one of the worst projects anywhere in the country. Comparisons of these housing projects are painfully obvious, but the knowledge of them all escapes the majority of Springfield citizens who will never visit them unless a professor assigns such field trips.

Another day the class members visited (visits were not made as a class, but on an individual basis) the Springfield YMCA, the Springfield Boys' Club, and the Family Center, the first two of which are located in new buildings harboring locked rooms and serving very few indigent children, while the latter with the smallest amount of space serves many times the number of children, all from the inner-city neighborhood, and nearly all black. The Family Center, however, is assigned a disproportionate number of white staff members.

In general, all the off-premise assignments led the class members to the conclusions that those agencies designed to help disadvantaged people find better employment, housing and recreational facilities are, as a rule, not hiring any more than a token number of blacks while the bulk of the clientele is black (as in the Welfare Department on State Street where the majority of the recipients are black and regular high-level black employees are almost non-existent). Another conclusion which was very easily arrived at is that agencies serving whites are better equipped (such as the South End Community Center which does not even have an on-premise summer program and has two trampolines in a locked gym, compared to Dunbar Community Center which has a six-week daily program and doesn't even have a ping-pong table). The eyes of the workshop students were further opened by these interviews to what the black experience is in the white world of Springfield, Mass.

Throughout the first week a constant subject of discussion was the variety of techniques which can be used to make school relevant and interesting to ghetto as well as all other students, with a heavy emphasis on the overall goal of becoming creative teachers who recognize the on-the-spot teachable moments and have enough confidence in themselves to deviate from a lesson plan to take advantage of such a challenge.

The second week of the workshop found the students with the opportunity to put to work what they had been talking about. Approximately 40 students each who regularly attend day sessions at the Family Center on Acorn Street were brought to Reed Hall, where the workshop was held, by class members who had teamed up in twos (usually a teacher and a human relations specialist under the leadership of the specialist). Each team then taught a week of lessons from 9:30 to 10:30 each morning on the general subject of helping each child achieve a more positive self-image. The teachers thus had a concrete experience with children who were products of the world they had been analyzing for a week and the experience was profound in a number of ways.

Teaching these classes helped underline the basic tenet that all children are *not* equal and must not be approached as equal marbles all in one bag. This may be the most salient contradiction presented to the students who are already teaching in the system. The oft-heard position of "I treat all my students as equals," is the most cleverly disguised "cop-out" for the teacher who only knows one type of experience himself and refuses to push out his own experiential boundaries to learn enough about different children, cultures and modes of treatment, educational techniques and philosophies to begin to know how to deal with children in the way that will best help them all equally to learn to push out *their* own boundaries to new learning and experiences. To learn as much as possible about the children, the workshop students were asked to visit all the homes and write short analyses of what the home was like, whether the appropriate agencies are playing any constructive role in helping the family solve its problems, if any, and whether the child is, in fact, developing a realistic view of himself. This practice of visiting students' homes is essential whether the unit is concentrating on the development of a positive self-image or not. Teachers *must* become familiar with the environment of their students.

The point was often made during the workshop that, like it or not, the teacher is a model to his or her students, which is not to say that he craves imitation, but that he maintains the attitude and sensitivity which will enhance the learning and growth of all his students. This idea of the teacher as model is not a concrete formula and is very difficult for materialism-oriented Americans to grasp, as is the whole idea of the so-called contracts or roles assumed by black men and women in dealing with white men and women. In the cases of the teaching teams which paired blacks and whites one of the profound learning experiences was the playing out of these "contracts" and, in the cases of three, the course took on the added dimension of the struggle to work out the conflicts inherent in the unwritten contract, conflicts such as who should lead and who follow when there is no rapport or meeting of minds about purpose, techniques, etc. Should a white woman take control of the situation if the partner is a black man, no matter how weak? or vice versa?

A concrete learning experience which was one of the highlights of the workshop was acted out by class members and further struck fear into white hearts in the AIC community by the sight of interracial couples. The class paired off into seven black/white couples to attend the AIC Summer School picnic on Tuesday of the second week of the workshop. Two whites refused to take part but the other couples were the objects of innumerable poorly-disguised stares and open comments of disbelief and disapproval. A liberal-talking psychology professor couldn't hide his discomfort and a table of nuns made angry comments when they caught sight of the couples. One couple was a pregnant black woman, another was a white man and black woman with five small black children, another was a dashiki-clad bearded black man and white woman, two others were a white woman and a black woman from the class who switched husbands for the "happening." Another principal in the cast was the closed-circuit TV photographer who caught for posterity some of the looks of surprise and dismay on the faces of even the young liberal student crowd who were present. The liberal party line is easy to manage in the protected confines of the classrooms, but apparently not so easy to handle in a real-life confrontation.

We have found out what we need to do, what we need to be, if we expect to tackle the most important job in America today—teaching all the children to be the best they can be. We have also learned that taking regular education courses doesn't make us teachers, and that the kids in the ghetto are not only as intelligent as any other kids, but they bring a beautiful world into the classroom which will be to everyone's benefit to know about, if only the teacher will bring it out in the open and build on it. Since traditional educational institutions are reluctant to change themselves, it looks like it is up to educators to do what needs to be done and that means to work like we never dreamed of working before.

We, through our workshop sessions at AIC this summer, had a successful beginning in a venture in teaching teachers to do their job better. It was proved not only that established white teachers but that previously academically untrained lay community people can be trained to teach inner-city children effectively.

Indeed, *to a child, all 40 children involved expressed that this had been the best "school" experience that they had ever had and that the community teachers (the human relations specialists) were the reason for this good experience.*

We also proved that black children, who are fortunate enough to have a teacher who understands both himself and who his students are, and one who will then know how to introduce materials which are relevant to the true education of these students, will have an infinitely greater chance of developing a positive self image which will free them to realize their full potential as individuals—the only important reason for a school's existence.

As can be seen, the human relations specialists demonstrated a high level of expertise in the discharge of their different treatment, training, and teaching functions. They could demonstrate the improvement of their helpees on specific and definable tasks. They could train others in the skills necessary to discharge their respective responsibilities. They could teach the students, white as well as black, black history, an area that has become increasingly important to the students.

In addition, the subjective evaluations of the specialists' functioning are high. *The students are believers!* The evaluations of the teachers reflect the specialists' value as consultants in areas of racial relations and black history.

The principals and administrators utilize the specialists. Again, of seven junior high school principals, six have expressed that they would take their specialists with them if they were reassigned different schools, and two principals have, in fact, done so. The guidance counselors, those who had to experience the greatest threat to job security, acknowledged, reluctantly or otherwise, a high level of effectiveness in many instances.

Sadly, while all of the evaluations, systematic and otherwise, are basically positive the specialists are not seen for who they are. The topic has fallen into the realm of political controversy, for many white parents do not want black students receiving differentially positive attention; this, in spite of the differentially negative attention which the black student has received in the past; this, in spite of the fact that the specialists work increasingly with white as well as black students; this, in spite of the fact white students have made very favorable evaluations of the specialists, rating them above all other personnel at the only school where a poll of the entire student body was taken; this in spite of the fact that the human relations specialist program has been successfully replicated in other large urban communities (Griffin, Tamagini, and Carkhuff, 1971).

The program has not been expanded in Springfield, *although ultimately the human relations specialist program in one form or another must be expanded throughout the country.* The only real resource for black staff members is from among uncredentialed personnel. The salary remains little, less than $6500 after a year of work. There is no "up-and-out" promotional policy in spite of the fact that the specialists are utilized as assistant principals at some of the schools. There is no reward for educational attainment shy of the bachelors degree, in spite of the fact that specialists have gone on to earn college credits.

Thus, we find that the criteria of functionality conflict with the criteria of political expediency. While it is true that no healthy society that is not predicated upon the criteria of functionality can flourish and emerge, it is also true that no unhealthy society, community, or school can survive without the criteria of political expediency. Or, put another way, any society, community, or school that operates primarily in terms of political expediency is doomed.

These, then, are the steps by which the most effective programs are developed. In this regard, those programs that are most effective are also most economical and efficient. They are most economical and efficient because the people involved know where they are going and what they are attempting to do. They are most effective because they set out systematically to accomplish their purposes.

Any program worth doing is worth doing now. Long-term benefits are comprised of short-term gains.

Any mode of solution makes delivery as it is implemented. Each stage of process is also outcome.

Any program that cannot bring immediate results in a crisis situation is not worth doing!

In summary, any goal that can be operationalized can be achieved. Man's goals in space or on Earth are curtailed only by the boundary of his intellect.

Hopefully, he will not forego his home on Earth prematurely.
Hopefully, he will reach for the stars here on Earth.

REFERENCES

Carkhuff, R. R. Training in the development of effective courses of action. Chapter 15 in *Helping and human relations: A primer for lay and professional helpers.* Vol. I. *Selection and training.* New York: Holt, Rinehart and Winston, 1969. (a)

Carkhuff, R. R. Integrated approaches to behavior change. Chapter 9 in *Helping and human relations: A primer for lay and professional helpers.* Vol. II. *Practice and research.* New York: Holt, Rinehart and Winston, 1969. (b)

Carkhuff, R. R. The development of effective courses of action for ghetto school children. *Psychology in the Schools,* 1970, **7,** 272–274.

Carkhuff, R. R., & Griffin, A. H. The selection and training of human relations specialists, *Journal of Counseling Psychology,* 1970, **17,** 443–450.

Griffin, A. H. & Banks, G. Inner-city workshop for better schools. *American International College Alumni Magazine,* Fall 1969.

Griffin, A. H., Tamagini, J., & Carkhuff, R. R. The selection and training of human relations specialists for the inner-city high school. *Journal of Clinical Psychology,* 1971, **27,** in press.

CHAPTER 15

Planning For Constructive Change

The simple message of this volume has been this: we can develop programs to maximally develop human resources. But these must be systematic programs which "build in" success. They are the programs of "winners"—not "losers" who in their initial denial and ultimate panic over crises cannot collect themselves to do anything positive. They are the programs of "winners"—not the "losers" who would rather risk death than be exposed as the ineffectuals and incompetents that they are.

The failures of our past have been calculated. The successes of our future can be calculated.

The problems, of course, are apparent in every field of endeavor—not just the school and the community. The prospects of slow death by pollution—of quick death by the Bomb—pervade our every movement. As these outer physical forces close in on us, we have deteriorated from the inside—finding ourselves unable to deal with any problems of life and death urgency. Indeed, the outer forces of death reflect the inner turmoil of a people who do not know whether they want to live or die.

When I treat an individual and sense this life and death struggle I work to nourish and develop the life forces and destroy the death forces (Carkhuff and Berenson, 1967).

When we treat a nation with this life and death struggle we must work to nourish and develop the life forces and destroy the death forces.

An individual who can learn to cope with and conquer his inner problems can learn to cope with and conquer his outer problems.

A nation which can learn to cope with and conquer its inner problems can learn to cope with and conquer its outer problems.

EDUCATION AND URBAN REVITALIZATION

Unfortunately, in this life and death struggle there is little agreement upon the sources of these problems—the blacks and the students, or the inequities which they protest. The essential legitimacy of the student's concern derives from another man's cause. In his searching adolescence he comes closest to meaning in his protests over the lack of relevancy of educational programs to the current problems of our time. The remainder of the students' protests revolve around alleged inquities to them which the poor, the black and the needy would experience as privileges when compared to their own conditions of deprivation and exploitation.

Again, unfortunately, the students' mentors have, in one way or another, confirmed the accusations by abdicating their responsibilities for anticipating and educating. Those hailing the students as the "hope of the future"—which indeed they are—do not realize that if there is no hope for the father, there is none for the child. Those vigorously reaffirming academic freedom with the rationale that society's expectations for the college are unrealistic (American Council on Education, 1969) do not recognize that educational programs—especially at the college level where leaders and teachers are trained—are the most basic sources of social change as well as social failure. The psychopathic defense of impotency typified in the view of the college as social critic is not at all dignified by the stature of the men who make it.

Instead, the first task is to accept responsibility for failure—*healthy adults can do this*—and rework the structure of the principal sources of social failure—the institutions of alleged higher learning—to make them functional, to make them effective, to make them sources of truly constructive and demonstrable social change.

It is in this context that a functional reorganization of our colleges and universities must be considered. However, organization or reorganization is never, per se, the answer. The equation for effective outcome relies primarily upon effective people and effective programs. *Effective organization is simply a means for relating effective people to effective programs in the most expeditious manner.* From another perspective, effective organization is not possible without effective people with effective programs who can be creative in meeting the daily crises of change.

PROJECT 40
The Functional Reorganization
*of Urban College Programs**

It is ironical in a nation that has long been equipped with the technical knowledge necessary to handle its mechanical problems, that at that moment in time when science first enables us to analyze the sources of constructive and deteriorative effects in human systems we are confronted with apparently unmanageable human problems. These human problems have been most intensely experienced in those quarters to which, ostensibly, we are to turn for leadership, the academic community, the colleges and universities of our nation. The academic community has failed to deal with the sources of current conflict by extending them yet controlling them in a constructive fashion. It has failed to anticipate the problems of the future. It has failed to assume bold initiative in leading us to the frontiers of a brave, new world. It has brought staid, old concepts and methodologies to bear upon burning, new problems. Its institutions have not reflected the level of development of learnings produced from within its walls.

It is in this context that the present plan for a functional reorganization of the urban college is offered. It is an organization based upon criteria of functional utility. It is an organization that deals with all of the major problems that we can anticipate in the 1970's and 1980's.

THE CURRENT PROBLEMS IN BRIEF

The problems currently confronting the academic community and, indeed, the nation are well documented *everywhere*. Briefly, the major apparent problems involving student dissatisfaction with the current state of affairs may be summarized as follows: a growing frustration with adults who are unable to anticipate and, indeed, who all-too-often precipitate the major problems of our times including the wars at home and abroad; and relatedly, in this context, their frustration with their inability to influence and shape their own destinies. In addition, there are many other problems with which college leadership has failed to cope. These include, among others, providing leadership in responding to the problems of the community-at-large, particularly those not-unrelated problems of the poor, the black, and the city. In addition, there has been little recognition of and outlet for the responsible and competent members of the academic community, those who have a significant and constructive contribution to make

---

*Reprinted from a mimeographed manuscript entitled "The Functional Reorganization of the Urban College," prepared and submitted in April 1969 by Robert R. Carkhuff and adapted by American International College, in August 1969.

and whose efforts deserve differential attention and reinforcement if we are to preserve the richer aspects of the academic tradition. Finally, there are the not-unrelated increasing financial problems of our academic system, particularly those of small colleges with little endowments who can no longer thrive on tuition payments.

A FUNCTIONAL ORGANIZATION

To meet the challenges of the 1970's and 1980's the urban college must be functionally organized into three colleges: (1) the student or academic college; (2) the college of community and educational services; (3) the faculty college.

Briefly, the student or academic college will be the college much as we know it now, concentrating upon the academic curriculum for undergraduates. The college of community and educational services will concentrate upon providing services to the community-at-large. The faculty college will concentrate upon the intellectual development of those members of the faculty and student body who have demonstrated the very highest levels of excellence in their chosen areas.

The faculties and student bodies of the three colleges will be interrelated with a given faculty or student body member serving to function in any one, two or all three of the colleges at any given point in time. All colleges will award bachelor's degrees in speciality areas, with only the faculty college awarding degrees indicating advanced or graduate training and only the community college offering associate degrees and certificate programs. A student will receive his degree in that college in which he invests the majority of his study, with special provisions being made for his major area of study. Thus, for example, a student may receive his degree from the community or the student college, with a faculty degree at the same time indicating excellence in his major area.

The Student College

The student or academic college is based upon the precept that any qualified student is entitled to higher education. While the student college will be conducted in much the same manner as the present college is conducted, it will have several distinct advantages. The student college will be administered by a dean and a senate comprised of eligible faculty and students who have made their major investment in the undergraduate academic affairs of the college. Thus, the faculty will be oriented to the teaching of undergraduate curricula although not to the exclusion of scholarly research and community concerns. The students, in turn, will, in conjunction with the faculty, have an opportunity to share the responsibilities and the authority for the development of their programs and curricula. Such an organization deals with the need for communication between faculty and students. It deals with the legitimate gripes of students that they have not had an opportunity to assume responsibilities in developing their own programs. It offers the student the opportunity to develop his level of basic skills in many of the traditional academic areas while not excluding the incorporation of academically substantive programs and courses.

The Community College

The college for community and educational affairs is based upon the precept that any person is entitled to an advanced education. The community college would be oriented toward providing services to the community-at-large. As such, it would be conducted by a dean and senate comprised of eligible faculty and regularly enrolled students. It would emphasize human service programs, including teacher education and training in various social service and human relations capacities. It would provide internship credits for persons now functioning effectively in many social service capacities and provide a credited outlet for their teaching skills in their areas of expertise. It would incorporate remedial skills programs and, in addition to its bachelor degree program, would respond to the needs for new community service programs in its certificate and associate degree programs. It offers the distinct advantage of flexibility in making the transition toward the development of constructive directionality in community programs. It offers an opportunity for the student who is impatient with traditional academic skills and who wants to go directly into the community. It provides programs of learnings which make direct translations to human benefits possible.

The Faculty College

The faculty college is based upon the precept that anyone demonstrating a high level of expertise should be provided with an opportunity for the pursuit of further excellence. The college, as the others, is conducted by a dean and a faculty-student senate. Only those who have demonstrated excellence in their areas of study will be appointed to the faculty college. Thus, faculty members who have demonstrated credentials in scholarly research, teaching, administration and other related pursuits shall be eligible. Students who excel not only in their course work but in projects that demonstrate creativity and productivity shall become eligible at any time in their careers in the student or community college. They must be voted by the faculty of the college. Upon entry into the faculty college the student may be enrolled in advanced speciality courses at the undergraduate level or in graduate courses. Conceivably, a student functioning at a high enough level academically may be enrolled for graduate study during his first year in college, thus providing the flexibility for gearing programs to facilitate in the most economical, efficient and effective manner the development of those with the greatest potential. Thus, the faculty college offers an academic outlet for the high achieving faculty and student body. It also offers an incentive for students in the academic and community college for further effort. It also provides the opportunity for junior faculty members to study with distinguished senior colleagues. It offers an inexpensive mode of conducting graduate study, for any member may, in conjunction with his colleagues, award graduate degrees to the level of his own attainment. It offers an interdisciplinary opportunity for the pursuit of academic excellence for both student and faculty.

A SUMMARY STATEMENT

Much of the confusion on the academic scene today is due to the potpourri of interests and the inability to differentiate them functionally. For example, there are many students and some faculty members who have no interest whatsoever in pursuing traditional academic programs, and they would change the programs of those students and faculty who are so interested. A functional reorganization would allow for each group to pursue the area of their special interests without excluding acquiring the knowledge and the skills of the other areas. There are many students and many faculty members who feel that their real resources are not tapped and developed at the highest levels while there are others who seek only the minimal skills necessary to secure them the credentials which secure them positions. A functional reorganization would provide for the differential reinforcement and development of these persons according to the level of their demonstrated abilities. There are many students and faculty members as well as community members who feel that they have not had the opportunity to share in the development of their own educational destinies. A functional reorganization provides for the opportunity of students and faculties in each of the three colleges to share in the responsibilities and the authority for the development of their own programs.

A functional organization is just that, an organization tailored to the functions which it seeks to discharge and which is governed by the criteria of functional utility in this discharge. While there is an exchange and interchange of faculty and students between the various colleges, however, it is not for the members of one college to develop functions duplicating the efforts of another. Thus, it is not for the members of the student college to emphasize community services but rather, if they choose, individually, to seek membership in the community college. Similarly, it is not for the members of the student or community college to develop advanced programs in academic areas. Rather, it is for them to conquer the basic skills at a demonstrated level of excellence and seek membership in the faculty college.

A functional organization such as this provides mechanisms to cope with the problems of the 1970's and 1980's without excluding the development of new functional divisions. Each college is free to evolve in its own manner according to the goals of achievement which it prescribes. It does so in a manner that is most economical, most efficient and most effective. It provides a mechansim which can deal with the major problems of our time and the future for some time to come.

The two unique aspects of the functional reorganization are the college for community and educational services and the faculty college. A figure on the organization of the substance of the programs of the community college would be illuminating at this point (see Figure 15–1). As can be seen, the college for community and educational services is more broadly conceived than the traditional community colleges. It ranges broadly from undergraduate programs in human and educational services and urban planning to the most basic certificate programs in subsecondary remedial education and contemporary problems. It offers an opportunity to the members of the community to acquire skills commensurate with their needs and levels of development. Persons holding responsible positions in the community—at any level—can earn credits for their work and their teaching about their areas of responsibility as well as their areas of learning.

The faculty college is just as important to the community of the poor and the black as it is to high level functioning members of the academic community. Where the community college offers an opportunity to the members of the community to acquire skills that will facilitate their development at primary, secondary, and undergraduate levels, the faculty college takes the lid off the level of educational attainment for community leaders with college degrees. While it offers them an opportunity to acquire higher level skills in their areas of endeavor, it also stamps them with the label of the highest level of approval and rationalizes their ability to secure the highest level positions within the system, particularly those servicing their own communities.

Finally, the academic or student college offers an opportunity for those who would choose a more traditional academic program—and in many instances that is most appropriate. While it is open to modification from within, it is restricted from evolving into a college for community and educational services. While students are free to choose their colleges and, indeed, to take programs in either, they must choose their major areas and in so doing they cannot make traditional programs "relevant" and, for that matter, relevant programs, traditional. The legitimate sources of much of the current strife on the campus scene would be put to rest. And, unless I am badly mistaken, many, if not most of the "students for relevancy," will choose their majors in more traditional areas that will enable them at a later point to fit more easily into the system.

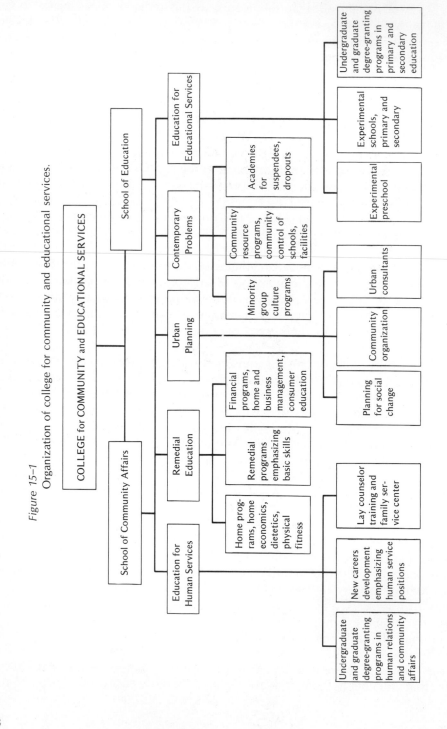

Figure 15–1
Organization of college for community and educational services.

In this regard, the college for community and educational services runs the danger of producing graduates who have no definable area of competency. This is a real danger, for while we do not know the duration of the current crises we may be producing people who need crises in order to make a contribution. Better to have an engineer who is a community organizer and who can return to his trade when he is no longer needed than to have a man whose major area is community organization who would be lost with the resolution of the crisis. Human relations is not a substantive area. It is only a means to an end which, when achieved, eliminates the necessity for emphasis upon human relations.

Any functional organization should converge with structural planning. A functional reorganization of the urban college, of necessity, involves a physical involvement with the surrounding urban community. Rather than to protect itself from the community-at-large, the college should reach out physically into the community, not just architecturally in its own buildings, but in jointly sponsored community facilities designed to serve community needs and to stimulate community redevelopment (Educational Facilities Laboratories, 1968). Thus, the college may develop community buildings and sponsor community agencies that would provide educational experiences for its students as well as service to the community. The college may sponsor businesses which could provide internships for community residents as well as for students with interests in business. The college may sponsor social service agencies which could provide internships for community residents as well as for students with interests in the social services. In short, each would be serviced by the other, the college by the community and the community by the college. In this manner, the urban college serves most fully the society which rationalizes the existence of our educational institutions.

However, just as the urban college is reorganized, so also must the urban community be reorganized. Initially, this can be done simply by coordinating the various agencies dedicated to the development of human resources. Building upon competencies already existent in the agencies, a central coordinating vehicle can provide direction and develop efficiency and effectiveness in the various efforts.[1] Ultimately, however, all city government agencies must be functionally reorganized upon the basis of demonstrated competencies and deliveries, for they now rank among the least functional archaic vestiges of once functional town meetings.

Again, the urban college can provide leadership in the implementation of such reorganization. Indeed, the urban college can be the instrument for the revitalization of the urban community.

With its emphasis upon the development of human resources, the urban college can become a central resource for the development of urban resources.

[1] A formal proposal to this effect was prepared and submitted to the mayor of Springfield in October 1969 by Robert R. Carkhuff.

Redefining itself as a work-study center dedicated to the growth and emergence of all members of the community, almost any agency in the community becomes potentially a satellite or subcollege. Thus, housing projects and hospitals, employment programs and schools, each become work-study centers whose educational and training programs are coordinated by the urban college.

Work-study programs may be developed in all current crisis areas. Projects that are currently considered deficits may be turned into assets.

Thus, for example, *public welfare programs may be conceived of as transitional educational and vocational experiences for their recipients.* It is the only moral usage of such an agency for the 5 to 10 percent of its recipients who are employable and for the up-to-40 percent on aid to dependent children who are capable. Welfare's fate is intimately bound to education, with welfare often constituting the next to final receiving agency for the educational system's worst mistakes. The "employables" are often "burned out," near illiterate, and "messed up" on some addiction. This generation of welfare children will be the next generation of recipients if they are not provided intensive educational support, and if parents are not provided educational, vocational, and other kinds of services to help them become models and agents for constructive citizens for their children. Welfare's fate, then, is directly related to the effectiveness of the local education system. Welfare can be functionally reorganized to provide child-care educational centers for the children which serve at once as a service to the mothers and their children and as a first step on a career ladder for the mothers. Services such as health and counseling centers and medical and drug centers can additionally provide trainee-recipients vocational internship experiences leading to positions as caseworkers coordinating the different functions within the system for the other recipients. In addition, other kinds of physical, emotional-interpersonal, and intellectual training experiences would be provided trainee-recipients. Learning and training experiences can be provided those populations such as the medically disabled and the geriatric so that their energies may be translated into constructive endeavors. In the process of such a functional reorganization, education has become relevant and welfare has become meaningful. In effect, the welfare system would itself at all levels become a work-study satellite center leading to the autonomy and accreditation of that part of its membership which is capable of further educational and vocational experiences. The agencies would be conducted by master trainers and master consultants who themselves are in a transitional two- or three-year vocational experience. These master trainers may be drawn from the graduate programs leading to degrees in the human service areas. Ultimately, if successful, the master trainers will be drawn from the ranks of former recipients.

Further examples of the untold benefits of the functional reorganization based upon the work-study satellite program are available in almost every public service area.

Federal housing projects which were poorly conceived, and even more poorly implemented, may be reorganized to have functional utility for all of their residents.[2] In a total push program involving human, educational, and vocational services, residents may live in the project on a transitional basis. Parents will be trained in all the skills, nutritional as well as interpersonal, which they need in order to live and work effectively with one another and their families. Projects would be staffed, also on a transitional basis, by candidates for advanced degrees at the urban college and by personnel from the community, with already developed areas of expertise. Thus, two internship experiences would run simultaneously. Staff members would receive practicum experiences in managerial and social service positions and at the same time provide internship experiences for their resident-trainees. All positions, then, would automatically involve career ladder opportunities. In a step-by-step program of educational and vocational training residents would move progressively through higher and higher levels of expertise in positions ranging from custodial through management positions and including all of the physical facility and human service positions. At the highest levels, the programs would both involve and produce credentialed persons with expertise in physical and human engineering so that future housing projects may be designed functionally.

In a similar manner the now crises-ridden urban hospitals may be developed into work-study centers which not only expand the quantity and quality of service to the community but also build in the kinds of educational and interpersonal training experiences that produce productive agents in the community. Thus, the entire staff may be selected and trained systematically to provide patients and others the kinds of experiences that make medical services effective. In addition, the work-study center would provide a career ladder moving, as appropriate, from custodial work through attendant, nurse, medical assistant and technologist, practical physician, and finally physician. Training in skills at each level will be contingent upon the success in mastering the skills at previous levels. Accreditation will be a function of a working relationship with the urban college and other medical centers. Such a program, then, provides not only more effective services to the community but an opportunity for those with the human resources but not the financial resources to advance to the highest level of functioning in a human service profession.

Similarly, employment programs such as the aforementioned Concentrated Employment Program may be incorporated within the urban college structure as subcolleges.[3] Staff members as well as clients may work and study at the same time, accumulating the skills and the credits which enable them to prepare themselves for progressively higher levels of functioning. We have already noted how we trained and credited trainers and how we systematically devel-

[2] A formal proposal to this effect was prepared and submitted to the Springfield Redevelopment Authority and American International College in October 1969 by Andrew H. Griffin in conjunction with Robert R. Carkhuff and Bernard G. Berenson.

[3] A formal proposal to this effect was prepared and submitted to Concentrated Employment Program and American International College in January 1970 by Bernard G. Berenson, Robert R. Carkhuff, and Andrew H. Griffin.

oped and implemented courses of action for the program. It is only a small step to impose an educational superstructure on such a vocational program, with credits assigned according to the level of accomplishment in all the skills demanded of each man in his respective position. Such an integrated program would provide a working vehicle for a partnership not only between the community and the Establishment in the form of the college and business and industry involved but also between all levels of race and background. In addition, it would provide a vehicle for a large-scale application of the concept of functional professionality with all of its attendant skills and methodologies.

INDUSTRY AND THE DEVELOPMENT OF HUMAN RESOURCES

In regard to the relationship between community and industry, there are a growing number of businessmen who recognize the need for a new partnership. In the decade since 1960 the black revolution and business and industry have gone through three separate but parallel phases. While the black community was going through a period of awakening, business and industry were, generally speaking, apathetic toward social problems. With the outbreak of violence following a smoldering frustration with the lack of social progress, business was ushered into the phase of concern for the "new" environment affecting or potentially affecting its profit structure. This concern on the part of management produced some of the worthwhile corrective industry-wide programs now in effect, but still failed to lay the groundwork for effective, functional social action on the part of individual business concerns. Finally, as the black community achieved maturity with responsible leadership redirecting efforts to self-determination for social improvement, the business community floundered in a phase of uncertainty, acknowledging that its lack of expertise in the "new" human relations and a failure to produce an organized procedure for social involvement had left it unable to keep pace with the growing need for social action.

The alternatives facing the business community are eminently simple: either the business community rebuilds and reinforces the social structure within which it operates or the crumbling social structure will destroy private enterprise as we know it today. This testimony is heard in louder and louder voices in higher and higher places. Charles B. McCoy, president of E. I. du Pont is relevant: "No business can operate successfully over a long period of time in a crumbling social structure—or in a society that is hostile to enterprise" (1968). George Champion, Chase Manhatten Bank, is expansive: "Improving the quality of our society is simply another step in the process of taking a broader gauged view of return on investment . . . the destruction between capital investment and social investment is much more a difference of degree than of kind" (Hopkins, 1968).

Management personnel are proclaiming their mandate to business, asking that the duties of management be broadened to encompass social reform:

". . . the public has set a very definite agenda before management, asking for leadership in such areas as eliminating depressions, rebuilding our cities, wiping out poverty and race prejudice" (Special report, *Newsweek,* 1969). If business management fails in this mandate, it must eventually answer to "the people" —and the people are its stockholders who will show little patience with dwindling profits and the eroded capital investment that are bound to result from a "business as usual" attitude in what we now clearly know to be a most unusual period in the growth of our economic, social, and political lives.

Roger Lewis (1969), president of American Dynamics Corporation, in his address "Business Leadership for Urban Affairs," stated a threefold responsibility of business: (1) "We must dispose of the notion that change is a process that alters the tranquil status quo—because in the area of social change there is no tranquility left"; (2) "Business and industry must stand up and be counted as good examples of community citizenship"; (3) "It is absolutely necessary to bring more of our underprivileged minority groups into the mainstream of American economic life without further delay, and thus forestall further corrosive effects from these neglected problems in the American society at large."

It would seem, then, that if business is to continue to make progress as it has been known to do in the past, it must marshal its best brains and largest resources in an organized effort to improve the environment in which the companies can flourish: "Desperate problems demand desperate remedies, and businesses, given the will, are best equipped of all American groups to change their environment" (Letrachman, 1968).

The business approach has always been effective in delivering financial profits. Only now it is being asked to deliver human profits.

PROJECT 41
*Social Action and Profit Action**

While there is ample evidence that the business community is stepping up its involvement with the black community, witness, for example, the National Alliance of Businessmen program of JOBS (Job Opportunities in the Business Sector), there are cautions being articulated. Howard J. Samuels, a businessman who was administrator for the Small Business Administration, has warned repeatedly against trying to turn our social problems over to private enterprise as if it had some magic formula for success (Wright, 1969). Although Samuels praises the concept of business-govern-

---

*Reprinted in part with permission from the summary of a chapter entitled "Industry and the Development of Human Resources," by Robert R. Carkhuff and J. Walter Reardon, in *Progress in Clinical Psychology* (New York: Grune & Stratton, 1971).

ment partnership to provide housing, jobs, and to meet other social needs, he contends that government still must provide the leadership and financial backing.

POSITIVE MANAGEMENT ATTITUDES

Others feel more strongly positive. The President of American Oil Company, L. W. Moore, expressed this sentiment in a recent address, "It is just plain good business to make the 10.5 million households now living in poverty a productive market for the wares of business" (1967). In another address, Robert C. Tyson, Chairman of the Finance Committee, United States Steel Corporation, expressed the business attitude of the future in this manner, "Free enterprise is our greatest weapon in the war on poverty. The tremendous productivity of free enterprise is made possible precisely because enterprise is free—because products are at once both the means and ends for progress" (1965).

A new kind of businessman is taking off his blinders. He is aware of what's happening—and he is sufficiently motivated to recognize the need for a coalition of thought and action between black minorities and the present business establishment. Darwin W. Bolden, Director of the Interracial Council for Business Opportunity, suggests that black America is roughly analogous to an underdeveloped country with a lack of control over its governmental and economical processes and recommends that new models for economic development involving community participation in ownership be explored (1970). In the same vein, John W. Gardner, former Secretary of Health, Education and Welfare, states that the coalition principle requires that minority groups be represented in the effort to solve community problems: "If there is to be fruitful collaboration between black and white leaders, it must begin and be tested in a non-crisis atmosphere" (1968).

It appears, then, that there has never been a greater opportunity for business management to insure the perpetuation of the free enterprise system, and at the same time there has never been a greater threat to its continuity. The present generation of top business management is being called on at this very minute to make that most fateful decision. Fortunately, there is evidence that enough of top management truly recognize the fact that social action is one of today's greatest markets, and for this reason alone there is reason to believe they will enter this marketplace with the same deliberation they have entered new fields in the past.

Although there is controversy, then, over the leadership role of government and the influence of the minority group communities, the commitment to meet the challenge of social action is being met—at least in attitude. With regard to any inferiority feelings that the business community might have about government leadership, let it be noted that while the federal government is terribly good at collecting monies and funding agencies, it is terribly poor in spending monies and effecting leadership for social change. It remains for the business community to accept the responsibilities for effecting the changes in problems that it has in large measure contributed to creating. With regard to the involvement of the black and Spanish communities let it be emphasized that we cannot develop potential if we do not provide it the opportunity to develop.

Perhaps the most important question has not been asked. How can the business community commit itself to the development of human resources in such a way as to build success into its programs?

BUILDING-IN SUCCESS

While this entire paper has devoted itself to elucidating the sources of human development and the principles of helping and social action, there are several of these principles worth reiterating as means to making the combined business-social action effort come off successfully.

The efforts within the corporations should be to open up jobs to the deprived. This means not only providing positions for the previously unemployed or underemployed but providing training for those who do not have the skills and providing the possibility for upward mobility of those with the capability. In this regard, let us consider a few of the principles that build success into the venture.

Perhaps the most important principle of human resource development as well as human relations in this context is that we are interested in behavior change—not attitude change—on the part of both the old as well as the new employees. Attitude change follows behavior change! Behavior change does not follow attitude change! With this principle as a guideline, top management, after establishing its goals in conjunction with the minority communities, can set up its differential reinforcement programs for shaping the behavior of its employees. Just as with profit action for the benefit of a select group so also with social action for the benefit of a neglected group, value judgments are made in establishing goals and reinforcing their achievement.

In this context, behavioral training in human relations and other skills is necessary from top to bottom in every corporation. Training at the top echelon convinces the management of the utility of the program and insures its success in implementation. Indeed, any program that does not (1) begin at the top and cannot (2) convince top management of the functional utility of the skills transmitted is suspect. However, training top echelon management is not enough. First line supervisors in particular must be trained in the skills necessary to bring off the program: "Do not leave minority hiring and training to subordinates. You, yourself, must demand that your supervisors down to the most junior level are provided meaningful guidance and advancement opportunities" (Goldfarb, 1969). The supervisors, then, must be guided in their human relations activities and they, in turn, must supervise the activities of the employees. The benefits that accrue will not occur solely in the social action realm. There is extensive evidence to indicate that really effective human relationships facilitate learning and productivity of all kinds.

A variation on the theme of creating an internship for every job is to create new positions for human relations specialists drawn from the ranks of effective persons who are indigenous to the minority populations being serviced and who have made it successfully in business and industry. For example, the federal government's energetic new welfare proposals are accompanied by concurrent job training opportunities designed to succeed where schools and industry have failed. As they are designed, they cannot succeed. To offer jobs where the foreman (even trained in human relations skills) is the husband of the same teacher who failed the welfare recipient is not new. There is no effective transitional phase for the job candidate. There are no effective transitional experiences for the job candidate. Most critical, there are no effective transitional personnel. Beyond preparing the foreman and workers, then, we must prepare personnel who are indigenous to the population being serviced, personnel who have themselves surmounted the numerous obstacles to effective education and employment, personnel who have, themselves, been selected and trained for the necessary helping and human relations skills that make the success of such programs possible.

These are just a few of the principles which we can employ to build in success where failure is otherwise dictated. These principles surmount the kinds of obstacles that are reflected in the supervisor's and workers' reluctance and lack of enthusiasm for training programs for minority group employees. In addition, they bridge the gap between emotional commitments to self-help and individualism and corporate philanthropy and progressivism (Goeke and Weymar, 1969).

SIMULTANEOUS PROGRAMS

These programs alone, however, cannot accomplish the ends of corporate effectiveness in social action. A number of other programs must be carried on simultaneously in order to further build in success.

At the broadest possible level, business and industry must assume a new leadership role in the development of human resources at two levels. At the local government level, they must influence and adhere to a need priority in housing, education and police-community relations. At the federal government level, they must influence the need priorities and the funding thereof, encouraging the development of local programs and initiative for the alleviation of social problems.

At both the local and federal levels, *they must insist upon the utilization of persons of high levels of expertise in the areas involved.* This is perhaps the most important principle. In this context, the federal government sets an example for the kind of talent that is being utilized in the social action area. At that, the federal government sets a poor example, for the best men in their various disciplines do not get to the top. Political expediency can no longer subordinate the loss of human resources and human lives!

In addition, there are a variety of other programs which the businessmen must develop in order to insure the success of their human resource efforts. They must work for and reinforce a responsible press—both local and national—by using advertising muscle. They must insist on a proper allocation of needs by the community's social agencies, including the united giving approach. They must support those school and educational programs that will produce the professionals—both functional and credentialed—needed to properly do the necessary jobs. They must use their purchasing power to plug in minority business and see to it that the companies' suppliers adhere to a positive concept in regard to social action. They must explore new forms and models for our economic development to provide community participation in ownership. They must explore the possibility of getting wider economic benefits to the black community through a significant profit-sharing plan.

In addition, and perhaps most critical for the individual corporation, management must establish company policy, directing the responsibility, scope and organizational structure of a company's corporate relations activities. At least one innovating corporate relations program currently being developed at Massachusetts Life Insurance Company may serve as a model (Reardon, 1970). The corporate relations division incorporates responsibility for civic and community affairs in its community relations program along with advertising and publications in its traditional public relations program. The distinct advantage of developing a corporate relations policy is that it makes all levels of management aware of a definite company policy that includes, among others, human resource goals. The establishment of a separate division reporting directly to the president places the communication activities at the corporate level where it can better serve the company as a whole.

Additional action programs designed to strengthen the position of a specifically structured corporate relations department are as follows: initiating a program of special training for those company officials dealing in corporate and urban affairs; establishing an urban affairs task force that will report to the urban affairs committee those innovative programs generated by the black community; establishing a contributions committee with authority to disburse company funds to those areas of social action which are in the company's best interest; establishing a political action committee whose purpose it will be to work for good government at the city, state and federal level; establishing a committee of local black leaders to form a coalition with the company's urban affairs committee for the purpose of maintaining up-to-the-minute and accurate communication; establishing the company's urban affairs committee to act as an honest broker in bringing together the necessary parties to make any specific action program workable.

In summary, the goal for business and industry would be to become the catalystic agent of those forces that can influence social action on both a local and national level. The means would include developing within industry a cadre of functional professionals trained to interact with those forces effecting social action. Additional means involve providing the necessary funds to act as an "exciter" for the necessary programs to implement desired social action. Finally, business and industry would attempt to harness and direct those controllable forces which can be used to influence government policy in favor of social action.

Unfortunately, with few notable exceptions, corporate leaders have so far devoted only the barest fraction of their resources to the development of human resources. Accordingly, their efforts have been uncoordinated, spasmodic and generally left to untrained second and third line management.

In the vacuum created by a lack of coordination and coalition, the authority to negotiate and resolve social issues could drift from black and white men of essential good will to those who are less patient and increasingly more angry. In this context, the attitudes of minority groups toward businessmen are relevant:

> Realize that for the foreseeable future "liberals" are irrelevant in the ghetto. Black men and Latin want to negotiate with those who control jobs and venture capital and have the authority to implement massive urban change. The conservative businessman is more welcome and trusted than the powerless liberal who seeks brotherhood (Goldfarb, 1969, p. 144).

While our social system is on a collision course due to inequities in opportunity, our economic system is on a collision course due to discrepancies in delivery. At time of crisis, spiraling costs and diminishing returns mark the contributions of professional educators and helpers. Reared in environments devoid of demands for delivery, their answers to problems at least in part resultant from their abdication of responsibility have been simply to ask for more money. Any businessman who has spent $50,000 training or, more appropriately, "retraining" the college product, knows that it is not product at all—but raw material—that he is working with: college has not prepared its graduate to be functional in a world demanding delivery.

Business must develop new models in order to survive. At a minimum, it must see community, educational, governmental and service agencies as extensions of its interests. It must evaluate the leaders of these agencies in the same manner that it does a division manager—on the basis of delivery. It must influence its environment by differentially reinforcing agencies in its environment. It must actively support those enterprises that are producing a significant return on human potential—not the Ivy League type colleges that flourish because of high input but the colleges that effect high output to input ratio (Astin, 1968)—and actively not support those institutions that do not effect any output-input ratio. But it must not simply support the progressive institutions. It must further influence these institutions to functionally reorganize themselves to become still more effective. At a maximum, in the absence of effective institutions, it must consider creating its own educational and service institutions. Historically, where high costs and low returns exist in public agencies, those industries that can improve returns and reduce costs move in.

Top management must prepare itself for the fact that future profits are indeed directly related to the whole environment surrounding its business enterprises. The need is now for industry to approach and solve its community's social problems with the same surgical precision with which it attacks any outside influence that threatens its profit structure. The Standard Operating Procedure is the same in every industry: that is, establish the result which you wish to achieve, determine what means are needed to achieve the desired result, set up one or more action programs to solve the problems and place your best men in charge of it. Given a model to follow, then, business and industry will attempt to handle the social problems with the same degree of success with which they have met other challenges in the past.

The greatest potential for growth and planning, as well as for contracting what people desire, today lies with the great corporations. They pay enormous taxes, often spend millions on foundations and civic good works—but they do not yet seem prepared for the idea that the business of business could do for the overall good without loss of profits—on the contrary, with a certainty that profits would in the long run increase (Special report, *Time*, 1969).

In this regard, James F. Oates, Jr., Chairman of the Board and Chief Executive Officer of the Equitable Life Assurance Society, notes the three basic assumptions of private enterprise: "(1) Every business enterprise operates to meet human needs through the use of capital; (2) human needs change as social values change; (3) business succeeds to the degree that the changes in social values are recognized and the resulting new or changed human needs identified and served" (1969, p. 3).

The message of this paper has been that there are, in addition to historical and philanthropic reasons, reasons of profit, of a progressive image, and, more basically, of survival for business and industry to enter the social action sphere and commit themselves to the development of human resources. Thus far, while the attitudes are right, for the most part there has been much talk and little delivery, perhaps because businessmen have felt uncomfortable in this area and in so doing have deferred to the social activists and educators who for the most part, while well intentioned, know nothing themselves about producing results and, indeed, because of this are responsible in large part for the problems which they are now attempting to resolve. Too many of those people who have chosen to earn their livings in educational and social services have done so precisely because of the difficulty in assessing the outcome of their efforts. The readers of this paper now know more about what is known with a certainty that can be replicated about the sources of human development, the nature and effects of training and the principles of social action. It remains for them, in true business fashion, to set the goals and institute programs to achieve them. The methodology of business is more relevant than the eloquence of protest!

What is different about this crisis from every other crisis in American history is that everybody's on the line—whites as well as blacks, governors as well as governed, teachers as well as students, police as well as community, social workers as well as clients, businessmen as well as consumers.

PLANNING FOR EDUCATIONAL CHANGE

Just as satellite programs can be accomplished in employment, social service and housing areas, so also can they be developed in educational areas. For example, one area which has received a great deal of attention has been the issue of community control of schools. By and large the programs which have been implemented have been spasmodic in nature and mixed in consequences. By contrast, programs for the recommended model schools (Coleman, 1966; Eaton, 1969; National Advisory Commission on Civil Disorders, 1968) can be systematically developed and the community can be systematically prepared or weaned via the internship principle to influence the adminstration of school programs.[4] Teachers, counselors, and administrators can be systematically selected on the basis of their interpersonal skills and their knowledgeability in their substantive areas. Parents and students as well as school personnel can be systematically trained in the human relations and other necessary helping skills which they require for the discharge of their respective responsibilities. Parents and students as well as school personnel can be systematically trained in the different teaching methodologies and the conditions under which they can be successful or not in the different learning areas.

In this regard, and in keeping with the philosophy of this book, there is tentative evidence to indicate that the more different methodologies employed in teaching a student solutions to given problems in a given subject area, the greater likelihood of the student excelling in that subject area (Berenson, 1969). Again, the larger the repertoire of responses, the higher the quality of responses and the more creative the problem-solving. Learning is not simply a matter of learning by discovery, thereby stimulating greater interest in learning. Learning is a matter of systematic programs training the student in the basic skills which

[4] Formal proposals on model ghetto elementary and preschools to this effect were prepared and submitted to the Springfield School Department and the School Committee in August 1969 by Andrew H. Griffin.

he needs to learn by discovery and then systematically reinforcing and expanding the creative applications of these skills by the student. The student who is taught associative learning systematically, for example, can most effectively make creative applications of associations.

Again, it is to be emphasized that the model schools are not based solely and exclusively upon systematic or programmed instruction. Instructional programs presently being introduced may cause just as great difficulty in the ghetto youngster's learning as the previous nonsystematic programs—but for different reasons. Experts who have emphasized mechanistic approaches have de-emphasized humanistic approaches and thus have not reaped the full benefits of their mechanistic approaches. And vice versa. The point is that *systematic programs employed in the context of a high level of interpersonal skills employed by teachers systematically trained in these skills are the most effective modality of learning known to man.* The reason no one "knows how to make a ghetto school work" (*Newsweek,* 1969) is because no one has been able to put these two basic principles together: (1) systematic programs in the context of high levels of interpersonal skills; and (2) fully functional programs in the hands of fully functioning helpers.

Unfortunately, most educational programs are not planned to prevent crises or even to anticipate them. Most innovating programs are considered after the fact of the crisis. They are rehabilitative in nature and, as such, encourage further failure. Instead of having the children on the schedule of healthy and directionful adults with the hope that the children may themselves be healthy and directionful, rehabilitative educational programs frequently place the adults who develop them on the schedule of undeveloped and directionless adolescents who have been involved in violent and disruptive activities. The following training program was presented for approximately a year preceding the outbreak of violence in the local high school. It was formalized in the present document following that outbreak of violence.

PROJECT 42

Training for Urban Teachers*

This paper will take the following form: a consideration of the need for training in helping and human relations skills; assessment of the types of training available; the development of the most effective training programs; the structure of the training program; simultaneous programs and reorganizations; options available to the school department; follow-up consultation and evaluation.

*Reprinted from a mimeographed proposal entitled "Human Relations Training for the Springfield School Department" prepared and submitted to the School Committee January 1970, by Robert R. Carkhuff. Printed in part in the *Springfield Union* newspaper.

NEED FOR HUMAN RELATIONS TRAINING

The need for helping and human relations skills on the part of school department personnel is testified to not only by the recent instances of black-white disturbance and disruption but also by the progressive discrepancy in achievement between black and white students. From differences which are not functionally significant upon entry into the school system, the educational program systematically produces greater and greater increments of learning for the white student when compared to the black student until at the high school level the black student is already several years behind the white student (who is not himself achieving at high levels relative to other areas of the country) in achievement in critical areas. The real sources of frustration which lead to the difficulties, then, are the teachers and the educational programs which contribute to this discrepancy. And yet they are not solely to blame because the colleges which produced them and the administrators who supervised them and the so-called experts who consulted with them have not provided them with a set of tangible and definable skills. Indeed, we can assume that the majority of school personnel would be motivated to have the necessary skills and competencies to give them confidence in the discharge of their responsibilities. All school department personnel need to acquire the skills in helping and human relations that will make them effective in the provision of services for which they are paid.

AN ASSESSMENT OF TYPES OF HUMAN RELATIONS TRAINING

The major types of training in human relations include (1) sensitivity or "T" groups, (2) encounter and (3) the "touch and feel" groups which have grown out of these approaches and (4) systematic human relations training.

Unfortunately, there is no evidence for a translation to human behavioral benefits for any of these first three groups.

Let us be more specific in evaluating sensitivity and encounter training (Banks and Carkhuff, 1971).

Let us be more specific without regard to interracial phenomena. Concerning the sensitivity trainer's background, the following points emerge: there is no specific description of the critical background variables for the trainer; there is no specific description of the selection procedure of trainers; there is no specific description of the trainer's training process and the resulting level of functioning; there is no answer to the basic question, "Who are the trainers and what do they have to offer?"

Concerning the training process, the following points emerge: much of the sensitivity game involves abstract intellectual exercises; the training processes do not lead to any immediate constructive behavior outcome; the actual training process is not clearly defined; there are no systematic steps to the process; the physical and nonverbal techniques employed have no established efficacy; the participants tend to be confronted without a base of understanding.

Most important, concerning the outcome measures employed, the following points emerge: the outcome measures are primarily attitudinal in nature; the outcome measures are of questionable reliability; the outcome measures bear no demonstrated validity; there is contamination in immediate outcome measures; there is contamination in long-term follow-up measures; there is no concern for translation to behavior change; there have been false claims made for the mediation of racial crises.

Briefly, then, *there is no way of telling what these orientations are doing and what they are accomplishing.*

Indeed, in the interracial area specifically there is evidence to suggest that these groups run far more risks than their potential gains warrant. Based primarily upon the encounter of whites by blacks they run the real danger of reinforcing already well-established and deeper rooted prejudices. In addition, there is increasing evidence to indicate an increasing sensitivity on the part of black people to the fact that these groups are calculated more to neutralize the translation of black attitudes to behavior than to change white behavior.

In short, *the sensitivity, encounter, and "touch and feel" orientations run a greater risk of compounding the original difficulties than they do a chance of alleviating the crises and developing constructive courses of action.*

The only remaining type of human relations training may be described as systematic human relations training.

SYSTEMATIC HUMAN RELATIONS TRAINING

The term *systematic human relations training* derives from the systematic application to selection and training of those ingredients or conditions found to be effective in all helping and human relationships. Basically, the model indicates that all human relationships, including, in particular, teaching and counseling as well as their supervision, may have constructive or retarding or even deteriorative consequences. There are certain dimensions of the human relationship which may be rated to account for effectiveness or ineffectiveness. These dimensions include responsive conditions (responding to another person's experience) such as empathic understanding, respect and specificity of expression, and initiative dimensions (initiating from one's own experience) such as genuineness, confrontation, and interpretations of immediacy. Direct translations of the scales utilized to measure these conditions in helping and human relationships are made to selection and training.

Accordingly, persons are selected on the basis of their ability to communicate at high levels of these conditions in situation-specific critical incidents. Thus, candidates may be cast in the helping role or teaching role with specific groups of helpees and rated on the basis of their functioning. The basic principle of selection is that the best index of a future criterion is a previous index of that criterion.

The same systematic extensions apply to training. Human relations training involves a systematic step-by-step succession of reinforcing experiences in which the trainee learns to communicate first the responsive dimensions, then the initiative dimensions. The model is essentially a developmental one in which the "mother" (the helper's responding, nurturing, etc.) prepares the "child" (the helpee) for "father" (the helper's initiating, directionfulness, etc.) and "mother." The trainees also learn systematic problem-solving activities in order to enable them to help their helpees to develop courses of action.

The basic principles of selection and training involve systematically exposing the trainee to alternate modes of behaving. The process is goal-directed and action-oriented. It provides a work-oriented structure within which the more traditionally therapeutic activities can take place. Perhaps most important, it emphasizes practice in the behavior which we wish to effect, thus leaving the trainee-helpee with tangible and usable skills which are retained following training. Finally, it offers a built-in means for assessing the effectiveness of the program.

With regard to assessment of both selection and training *the evidence for the efficacy of these programs in effecting constructive changes in human behavior is now voluminous.*

STRUCTURE OF TRAINING

Overview of Personnel

The key principle in the human relations program is to conduct the selection and training in such a manner as to leave the school department with its own inservice training capacity. This can be accomplished by the systematic selection and training of trainers from within the system.

From among volunteer teachers at each of the 48 schools one regular and one alternate teacher may be selected for training as trainers. Thus, a total of 96 teachers will be trained as trainers and consultants in human relations skills and will be able to conduct their own programs at the different schools. From among these trainees, the two most effective may be selected to coordinate and conduct supervision of the overall operation. In addition, these two will receive additional training to equip them with the skills necessary to serve as human relations consultants to the superintendent, with the most effective person serving ultimately as overall coordinator of the entire program.

Figure 15–2

Suggested structure for training personnel during training period.

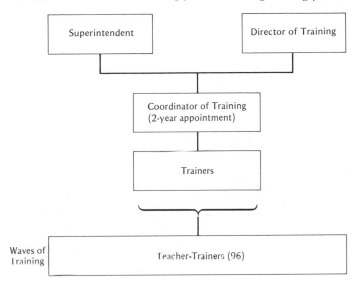

The training agency, in turn, will require several trainers: a coordinator-supervisor and the director of training. It is suggested that the coordinator-supervisor have a primary appointment in the training agency and a secondary appointment in the school department. It is further suggested that the teacher-trainers selected as consultants serve internships with the director and coordinator of training with secondary appointments in the training agency (see Figure 15–2).

Overview of Structure

The human relations training may be accomplished effectively in waves according to (1) the immediate needs of the different schools and (2) those schools where the opportunity for success is greatest. Training should take place in groups of 10–12 and should take an initial minimum of 100 hours. The total time involved will be a function of the amount of time per week that the teachers can allot to training. Supervision of the training and consultation activities of each trainer would follow. It is anticipated that the entire training program could be accomplished in the first year.

At the end of the first year, then, the teacher-trainers would replace the original training staff of trainers from the training agency. In addition, the two consultants selected from among the teacher-trainers would intern with the director and coordinator of the training agency so that at the end of the second year one could become coordinator of the entire program and one consultant to the coordinator (see Figure 15–3). The second year, then, would involve supervision, follow-up training, and assessment activities conducted by the training staff, with the consultants serving as interns.

SIMULTANEOUS PROGRAMS

Teacher training in human relations skills cannot alone accomplish the ends of educational effectiveness. A number of other programs must be carried on simultaneously in order to build in success.

Expansion of Human Relations Specialist Program

With the massive infusion of constructive black and Spanish models and helpers both desirable and necessary, the only large pool of personnel available involves lay personnel. These lay persons, it has been demonstrated, can be trained to function effectively as functional professionals in human service areas. An effective human relations program in the school department would require an expansion of the existing human relations specialist program. Expansion in waves, according to need, to two specialists per school to parallel the teacher-trainers would offer the possibility of creating integrated teams of teacher-trainers and specialists. In addition, the development of a slot for a specialist coordinator would build in the opportunity for consultation at the highest level (see Figure 15–3).

Expansion of Human Relations Training Program

The training program must be expanded to incorporate other concerned parties in the educational community. Thus, other school depart-

Figure 15–3
Suggested structure for human relations personnel following training.

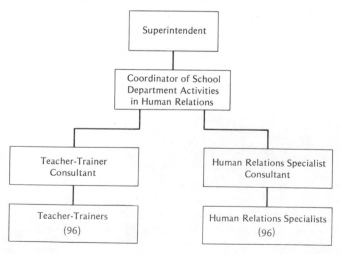

ment personnel, parents, and students as well as teachers must be involved in training. While many of these programs can be implemented later on by teacher-trainer and human relations specialist teams, it is essential that high-ranking school administrators and school board personnel be involved in training during the early phases of the program.

Expansion to Other Related Programs

Related programs must be developed and expanded in the following areas: new and creative teaching methodologies; assessments of teacher competency in subject matter; selection and orientation of new teachers on the basis of functionality; concerted and vigorous effort to raise standards of effectiveness of college education programs; programs to influence teacher expectancies; updating of test norms; development of programs to discover unique skills of minority group children; development of cross-cultural exchange programs for both teachers and students; complete re-evaluation of effective use of time spent in school; expansion of programs to include nutrition, teaching methodologies, and school management for parents as well as teachers; development of college-credited programs for master trainers and master teachers.

Reorganization of School and City Agencies

All of these positive effects cannot take place without a simultaneous reorganization both within and without the school. In effect, a human relations department has been created and it would be appropriate to formalize this designation. Pupil Personnel Services must be reorganized and integrated with the human relations department on the basis of demonstrated competencies. The activities of the human relations program must be coordinated with other city and governmental agencies and programs. The city must cooperate in the development of a centralized unit to coordinate all programs dedicated to the development of human resources, a concept which cuts across racial and ethnic boundaries. Finally, the school department must cut the Gordian knot and take an active hand in community affairs: for example, any long-term solution to educational crises must involve a creative housing plan.

OPTIONS AVAILABLE

The long-term proposal would be expensive. However, there are a number of realistic options available to the school department. First, the program can be accomplished in developmental stages, each of which makes an immediate delivery of effects.

The first option is whether or not to begin at the secondary level. While the long-term benefits for primary grade children, white as well as black and Spanish, would be most significant with a primary grade program, the distinct possibility exists that the school system may not be functional if the current difficulties at the junior high and high school levels are not attended to. Therefore, it is recommended that the program be initiated at the four high and seven junior high schools beginning first at those which have the strongest principals. Such a program would involve a first-year outlay of funds of approximately $100,000 for teacher personnel.

The second option is whether or not to expand the human relations specialist program. While this has been a controversial program in terms of local politics it has not been controversial in terms of demonstrated effectiveness. It is therefore recommended that the present 14 slots at the junior high school level be expanded to include two slots at each of the four high schools. Such an expansion would involve an additional first-year outlay of approximately $50,000. Thus, the possibility of black-white teams of specialists and teachers can be exploited for utmost effectiveness at the junior and senior high level for a personnel outlay of approximately $150,000.

Training for such a first-year program would involve several trainers and a coordinator and a training director-consultant who would also develop other related programs at a cost of approximately $100,000. Thus, the total personnel and training costs to the school department for the first year would be approximately $250,000.

SUMMARY

Human relations training would insure educational effectiveness for white as well as black and Spanish children. While the cost appears high it is low when compared with undeveloped human resources and possibly the loss of limb and life. In effect, human relations training is a very cheap insurance policy that promotes teaching effectiveness and racial harmony. Its effects will include the improvement of achievement for all students and the prevention of civil disorders and educational disruptions.

RECOMMENDATION FOR TRAINING

The Human Relations Center, American International College, declines to be considered for the human relations training program for the School Department of Springfield, Massachusetts, for the following reasons: (1) the programs which it has conducted, such as the human relations specialist program, have not been supported actively by the School Department and consequently its participants as well as promulgators have been subject to a high degree of abuse; (2) such a human relations training program cannot be conducted without the active support of certain pupil personnel service areas, which have been active in undermining innovating programs produced by the community.

SUMMARY AND OVERVIEW

Education has been the major vehicle for bringing about real social problems. Education can now be the major vehicle for bringing about real social change.

The place to intercept the cycle of social failure is at its inception. Sound, empirically based educational programs can effect this change.

Employing the criteria of functionality we must systematically utilize what we know about the development of human resources. The beauty of the concept of the development of human resources is that it treats the human being independent of his racial, sexual, or generational differences. Placing an emphasis upon the opportunity for the maximum development of human potentials surmounts all of the barriers of time and place, politics, and economics.

Urban programs must be reorganized to achieve the maximum development of human resources, for the heart of urban resources is human resources. The city has served historically as a source of opportunities for the transitional experience from lower- to middle-class status. It can continue to do so effectively by employing the internship principle: staffs of urban programs from city hall down can be systematically selected on the basis of demonstrated competencies and systematically trained to train interns from the community so that the interns can move progressively up the steps of career ladders in their chosen fields. The real challenge to the cities is not to hold their privileged middle class but to provide the opportunities for experiences that translate untapped human potential into unlimited human productivity. *In 1971 that can be the only functional justification for the existence of the city.*

A master plan for the development of human resources, then, must include a master plan for the development of urban resources. In this context the programs must be operationalized and implemented in the cities where we have the highest probability of succeeding. For the immediate future this may mean establishing middle-sized and manageable cities as models before taking on the tasks in the larger and more confused metropolises. An alternative would be to divide the great urban centers into smaller functional units built around the work-study center complex.

The work-study-satellite program offers a number of distinct possibilities for revitalizing the urban community. Besides utilizing available human resources in developing new skills that service the immediate community, such a program develops new positions for the provision of these services and at the same time prepares the community for conducting its own programs. In developing a vehicle for real opportunities for the indigenous and the indigent, it provides a true test of the capacity of the community to creatively exploit its own talents—and it does so with the structure of knowledgeability and the strength of methodology. In developing a vehicle for direct translation to human benefits, it provides a true test of the concept of "higher education"—an educational approach which is in fact *high* enough to develop both perspective and a program that can effectively deal with the most urgent needs of our time.

Finally, we must consider the possibility that our present governmental systems—city, state, and federal—are not functional for the purposes which we have attended in this volume. That they are adequate fund-collecting and fund-dispersing agencies is not contended. That they are equipped to effect programs of the magnitude which we describe is severely questioned. The personnel, both elected and appointed, have simply not been systematically selected on the basis of demonstrated competencies. Affiliations of any kind—and most of all, political party affiliations—are irrelevant to the task of developing the social and educational superstructures which we need to impose upon our urban communities.

Perhaps the only recourse is to turn to the quality control of a new kind of humanistic private industry to provide effective educational and social services. Perhaps we may look forward to the day when entire school systems, mental health systems, and social service systems like welfare and, indeed, entire communities are put in the hands of efficient and effective private industries who can deliver the benefits without the economic chaos toward which we are headed. Perhaps only such a humanistic private industry can enable this country, and perhaps the world, not just to survive—for that is the immediate issue—but to grow, to unfold, to emerge, to actualize human life.

We do not have much time. It is time to get the products of man's social conditioning—his prejudicial attitudes and behavior—out of the way—and the time is now! It is time to get on to the real issues of survival: pollution and conservation, overpopulation and annihilation. But we cannot do so until we have mastered the human problems.

Given the resources of this nation and this world, if we can conquer the enemy within, then all of us together—not privileged and deprived, but black and white and shades of brown and yellow—can conquer *any* enemy without.

REFERENCES

American Council on Education. *A declaration on campus unrest.* American Council on Education, April 1969.

Astin, A. W. Undergraduate achievement and institutional excellence. *Science,* 1968, **161,** 661–668.

Banks, G., & Carkhuff, R. R. Sensitivity training: A bibliography and review. *Professional Psychology,* 1971,**4,** in press.

Berenson, D. The effects of the employment of diverse teaching methodologies upon student achievement. Unpublished research, Fordham University, 1969.

Bolden, D. W. What can business do about Watts? *New York Times Book Review,* January 18, 1970.

Carkhuff, R. R. *Helping and human relations: A primer for lay and professional helpers.* Vol. II. *Practice and research.* New York: Holt, Rinehart and Winston, 1969.

Carkhuff, R. R., & Berenson, B. G. *Beyond counseling and therapy.* New York: Holt, Rinehart and Winston, 1967.

Carkhuff, R. R., & Reardon, J. W. Industry and the development of human resources. In *Progress in clinical psychology,* L. E. Abt & B. F. Reiss, Eds. New York: Grune & Stratton, 1971.

Coleman, J. S. *Equality of educational opportunity.* Washington, D.C.: U.S. Government Printing Office, 1966.

Eaton, W. J. Schools' overhaul urged to curb racial unrest. *Springfield Daily News,* November 6, 1969.

Educational Facilities Laboratories. *A college in the city: An alternative.* New York: Educational Facilities Laboratory, Inc., 1968.

Gardner, J. W. *What one man can do.* Presentation, Million-Dollar Round Table. Life insurance industry, 1968.

Goeke, J. R., & Weymar, C. S. Barriers to hiring the blacks. *Harvard Business Review,* September-October, 1969.

Goldfarb, R. W. Why whitey is failing in the cities. *Readers Digest,* October, 1969.

Hopkins, T. M. What is the business of business? *Public Relations Quarterly,* Winter Edition, 1968.

Letrachman, R. Business must lead the way. *Dun's Review,* April, 1968.

Lewis, R. Business leadership for urban affairs. *Management Review,* April, 1969.

McCoy, C. B. Business and the community. *Dun's Review,* May, 1968.

Moore, L. W. Whose problem is it? Commencement address, Institute for Management, August, 1967.

National Advisory Commission, *Report on civil disorders.* New York: Bantam Books, 1968.

Oates, J. F. *Business and social change.* New York: McGraw-Hill, 1969.

Reardon, J. W. *Business and social action.* Masters Thesis. American International College, 1970.

Special report, The cities. *Newsweek,* November 24, 1969.

Special report, Speak now. *Newsweek,* Special publication, 1969.

Special report, To heal a nation. *Time,* January, 1969.

Tyson, R. C. Freedom and enterprise. Address, 62nd National Savings Conference of American Bankers Association, April, 1965.

Wright, R. A. From overalls to attache case. *New York Times,* January 6, 1969.

PART SEVEN

Epilogue

PART SEVEN

CHAPTER 16
A Personal Note to Effective People

I am not so naive as to believe that even the most potent methodologies cannot be distorted and rendered impotent. If there is one central message in this volume, it is that people either make a program effective or do not. There are several principles which I have learned with regard to the attempts to neutralize otherwise effective or potentially effective programs. Those who have based their lives upon a platform of stability and permanence do not succumb easily to a platform of change. They must be convinced.

The first principle of change, profound in its simplicity, is that *if you have a problem, work on it*. There is an old principle of battle, that any action is better than no action. Too often we get caught up in the political and economic implications of action, and reprisal and retaliation dominate our experience. And yet the only real learning comes through work. It does not matter where you begin, for if you are shaped by what is effective your program, whether for yourself or your community, will become increasingly effective. Work, then, is the beginning of change. The first principle extends readily to a second.

The second principle of change is to *build success into your work*. Strange as it seems, one of the accusations most frequently flung at me has been, "You stack the cards in your favor by the way you select and train only the best to conduct programs for the rest." Of course I do! Any effective person does. The principle of functionality dominates in building in success—functionality in operationalizing final criteria, functionality in discriminating step-by-step procedures for achieving those criteria. To the first principle of work, then, we add the principle of assessment that continually improves our basic directionality and the means to implement it. The third principle incorporates the first two and directs them toward a world that opposes effective action.

The third principle of change is to *outwork the opposition*. It has been a strange experience but on the eastern college campus—and, I am sure, a lot of other campuses around the country—the doers are always seen as right-wing elements. The liberal has always made a living off his openness and opposition, but that openness has seldom involved directionful action. His days in the black revolution are numbered because he never teaches the way he got to where he is but always only accepts any attempt that the black man in his struggle may come up with. On the other hand, interestingly enough, people off campus who work with direction and, even worse, with blacks, are most assuredly seen as left-wing elements. For while the liberal professors talk about change, large segments of the community oppose it in any form. This is as it has to be, for effective workers invariably find themselves in that extreme middle position, where the depths of the right and the depths of the left can only interpret the heights of the middle to be the other extreme. The extreme middle has the advantage of a program that works effectively for all peoples. Only that stance can expose the irrationality of the extremes!

The fourth principle of change is to *make the solutions as extreme as the crisis*. In the direction and implementation of social action programs I have often been asked to put the program in terms that the people in power will find acceptable. There is an inherent contradiction here, for social action programs become necessary simply because those in power have failed to meet the needs of a segment of society. This is the crossroads for the effective person. *It is absurd for the problem solver to put his solution in the terms of the problem maker!* There is no compromise for an effective solution. It remains for the problem makers to choose between crisis and resolution. Resolution is on the terms of the effective person alone. The fifth principle flows directly from this principle.

The fifth principle of change is to *demonstrate the success of your programs and predict the failure of others less competent*. There is a point in the life of every effective person where he is done with demonstrating. That comes when he has provided the evidence for the effectiveness of his programs but, due to an intensification of resistance by the forces of ineffectuality, his base of power is no longer expanding. To go beyond this point is to function on the terms of the ineffectuals, masochistically subjecting himself and his programs to ever-intensified scrutinization, judgment, and abuse. At this point the doer can most effectively become critic. Indeed, he of all people is best equipped to become a most potent critic. For he alone understands the necessary conditions of success. He alone can generate infallible predictions concerning the failures of programs that cannot meet the necessary conditions of success. Simultaneously, he must assure himself that he has met the conditions of the sixth principle.

The sixth principle of change is that the effective person assure himself that he has *exhausted all avenues of recourse to solution of the crisis*. In this context, freedom is not something that you plead for and is granted. Freedom is something that you take. And you exercise this freedom in exploring all possible vehicles to opportunity and justice. This is a moment of truth for all parties to a conflict. For until that moment the nonexercising of freedom has provided an excuse for both sides. In the black-white conflict, it has provided a smoke-screen for those whites who continue not to provide opportunity and justice and for those blacks who continue not to take advantage of what opportunity and justice there are available. Only after exhausting all avenues of recourse will the base of power be broad enough if the grievances are not acted upon. The seventh principle, then, is a direct consequence of the powers not acting upon legitimate grievances.

The seventh principle, then, is not to intercede in the crisis. Having demonstrated the success of your programs, having exhausted all avenues of recourse, and finding yourself without the base of support necessary to effect the changes to redress the grievances, *the crisis and its effects are no longer your responsibility. You have to be willing to risk everything or you can accomplish nothing.* The great irony of the black-white conflict is that those best equipped to be warriors on opposing forces fight the hardest to prevent the crisis. And yet the others, who not being part of the solution are part of the problem, assume that preventing crises is the effective person's "thing." The effective person must break free of this predictability. His responsibility ends when he has done all that he can do. To act further means to neutralize the potent and legitimate forces of the aggrieved. He must no longer act to save the ineffectuals. For anything is worth doing right or not at all. Only if the effective person goes all the way at this point, withdrawing his supportive and preventative stance completely, is there any possibility for intercepting the spiraling cycle of social failure. The eighth principle is related.

The eighth principle, then, is to *wait*. This principle is for an effective person the most difficult of all. It requires discipline beyond work. There is little place for the truly effective person in times of only relative disturbance. And little disturbances, nurtured by programs designed for further failure, grow predictably, into big disturbances. The effective person is not a garbage man. This does not mean he does not continue to work. He simply shifts his focus to larger scenes in an attempt to develop pressures to bring to bear upon the immediate scene. But the effective person must wait until the others come to him —no sooner! He has always found himself going to them and they have known, accordingly, that he is on their schedule. Indeed, they have helped to feed him a crisis or two by precipitating them because in many instances they fear the effective person more than they do the crisis. They feel that they must keep him busy—whatever the price—for he alone is the threat to real power. Now they must come to him. And they must ask him for his terms. And he must make a decision whether he wants the prerogatives—even on his terms. He must look the ugly mess fully in the face before he decides. If he decides positively the ninth principle is operative.

The ninth principle of change is that *if the effective person takes the reins of power he does so on his terms.* He must know that the same people who cede him the power do so because they now fear the loss of things more precious than they fear his potency. He must know that the same people who brought things to the brink of disaster, to the brink of anarchy and annihilation, will do so again when there is a return to "normalcy" and "sanity." They will again make initially subtle but progressively intensified efforts to reclaim the power which they have only in fear ceded to him. He must know that only a man of great strength can maintain peace—indeed, not only maintain the peace but create the conditions for social emergence. He must know that the future of mankind in its constructive form is dependent upon the effective person's maintaining his leadership role. He must know that the only possibility for man to rise above his animal nature—indeed to rise above his own humanity—is dependent upon his maintaining his leadership role. The tenth and final principle is contingent upon how fervently he believes in this principle and guards its prerogatives.

The tenth principle of change, then, is that *the real battle is between the effective and the ineffective,* the competent and the incompetent, the worker-warriors and the politicians. The latter thrive only with the permission of the former, the weak dominate only with permission of the strong, the evil with the permission of the good. The effective person must be clear in his own mind that the system in which he functions holds nothing for him but the power and the prerogatives to make it effective. He must trust his own motives and not forget his original intentions. Just as he pits his life forces against the death forces in the life and death struggle of one of his loved ones so now does he pit himself against the destructive forces in the world. Once he has the power he must not surrender it to a lesser man, a lesser human being. He must utilize the power to extend the battleground to the territory of the real enemy, the life killers, and dictate the terms of their capitulation and surrender, the terms of a new and wholesome, healthy and growing, emerging and reaching, society of man to man.

If the effective person surrenders once again the prerogatives to the "men of peace" who perpetrated and perpetuated the atrocities in the first place, then he will find the cycle of social failure repeated to an ultimate finality.

And he will find himself once again acting out the "role" of the effective person rather than being one, straining his heart and his mind to prevent things from hitting bottom, knowing that a man who finds himself in the same situation twice is deteriorating.

Or he will find himself the rebel in the hills—without power—and destined to lose.

There are simple answers to complex problems, but the answers demand absolute integrity.

The choice is ours. The lives of our children as well as our own—the very possibility that there might not be a future generation—depends upon what we do now.

There is no world worth saving that is not built around effective people.

Index

A

F